THEOLOGICAL INVESTIGATIONS

Volume XIV

THEOLOGICAL INVESTIGATIONS

VOLUME XIV

ECCLESIOLOGY, QUESTIONS IN THE CHURCH, THE CHURCH IN THE WORLD

by

KARL RAHNER

Translated by

DAVID BOURKE

DARTON, LONGMAN & TODD

LONDON

DARTON, LONGMAN & TODD LTD
85 Gloucester Road, London, S.W.7 4SU

ISBN 0 232 51252 3

A Translation of the first part of
SCHRIFTEN ZUR THEOLOGIE, X
published by Verlagsanstalt Benziger & Co. A.G., Einsiedeln

Printed in Great Britain by Western Printing Services Ltd. Bristol.
Nihil Obstat R. J. Cuming, D.D., *Censor*
Imprimatur Mgr. David Norris, V.G.
Westminster, 5th April 1976

CONTENTS

PART ONE

Ecclesiology

I

BASIC OBSERVATIONS ON THE SUBJECT OF CHANGEABLE AND UNCHANGEABLE FACTORS IN THE CHURCH

THE essay which follows is concerned with the theme of changeable and unchangeable factors in the Church.[1] Right from the outset it must be emphasized that we shall be concerning ourselves only with certain *basic* observations. This in itself imposes certain clear limits upon our study.

For the most part it is on points of detail that internecine strife arises. Basic observations are, in fact, usually so general that they can be accepted even by groups which will subsequently find themselves vigorously fighting against one another once they come down to those concrete questions and decisions in which the general principles do indeed have to be applied, though even then in very many cases they do not, taken in isolation, yield any very precise conclusions. If, however, we were to seek here and now to draw a distinction between the changeable and unchangeable factors in concrete individual instances we would perforce be drawn into an endless study of cases, such as cannot be the subject of a single brief study.

Nevertheless we may perhaps hope that even very general principles bearing upon the distinction referred to can be of some use in finding one's way somewhat better and more confidently through the life of the Church today.

In treating of this theme we feel that we can count upon very lively interest on the part of any educated Catholic Christian. And surely we do not need to justify this feeling at any length here. As a result of the

---

[1] The subject has already long been under discussion. We may regard Y. Congar's work, *Vraie et fausse réforme dans l'Eglise* (Paris, 1950) as the first major contribution, though the question has undoubtedly acquired a fresh vitality and breadth as a result of the Second Vatican Council.

activities of John XXIII and the Second Vatican Council a great sense of unrest and great changes have been initiated in the Church whether we like it or not, whether we regard this Pope and this Council as the true cause of this process, or merely as the occasion of it and the catalyst which set it in motion. These changes have embraced all departments of the Church's thought and life: the doctrine and theology of the Church, her liturgy, her concrete constitution as affecting both the universal Church and the particular churches, her ecclesiastical law, her pastoral activities, our conception of established authority in the Church, the relationship of the Church's officials and her people to one another, the relationship of the Church to the world, our understanding of her function of service which she has to maintain and perform for the world, the states, international relationships, the various movements and parties, etc. In these and many other respects we can even now recognize that a notable transformation has already taken place. This transformation has not been concluded but is still in process. Some praise it, while others deplore it. For some it is not proceeding fast enough and is regarded merely as a starting-point for many more radical transformations. Others hope that the position will soon become stable once more. Or they are in despair, believing that the Church, no less than the world, gives the impression of an immense confusion, of contradiction, of opposed tendencies and the uncertainty arising from these as affecting the Church's officials and her people alike. When we attempt to achieve a clear picture of the background factors in terms of psychology and the history of ideas which lie behind such sharply opposed judgements on the significance of these changes, even at a quite general level, then surely we have to say that the 'progressives' greet this change and seek to accelerate it and press it on to further lengths because they regard change, becoming, transformation, and the process of breaking into a future as yet unknown as the true essence of reality and as the special characteristic of our own times, and because on this basis they regard all change in the Church as justified in itself even as applied to the Church's own life, at least to the extent that they take it for granted that that which is new is also that which is true and valuable. And in this they are often extremely naive and lacking in real thought. The 'conservatives', on the other hand, have hitherto experienced the Church precisely as the context of that which abides, of an eternal truth which does not adapt itself to intellectual fashions, of the courage to reach out to eternity, of clear unambiguous meaning and sureness. In many cases they may have become converts to Catholicism precisely on this account, because they envisaged the Catholic Church, and especially the Church since the French Revolution, precisely as the guardian and protector of that which abides and is unchangeable. These conservatives, therefore, feel a sense of shock at the current changes in the Church, and feel that they have been cast headlong by them into a cruel uncertainty. Under certain circumstances they may, as converts, ask themselves why then did we really become Catholics at all? As Catholics they miss the former clear and decisive voice of the Church in theology, morals, and canon law, and in the Church's practice as well as in the Latin liturgy. And they likewise ask themselves where that Church still survives which they once experienced as clarity, lack of ambiguity, sureness, and peace.

Before we enter into the real problems which our subject entails certain firm positions have to be defined with regard to the distinction to be drawn between changeable and unchangeable factors in the Church. These positions are correct, still continue to be valid even today, and are at the same time traditional. We must firmly and clearly define these traditional positions precisely because they remain valid, offer at least a provisional orientation, and must not be forgotten even though, as we shall have to point out at a later stage, they are incapable, of themselves, of supplying the *whole* answer. On the contrary, it is only with them that the real problems begin. We might formulate these firmly held traditional positions on our subject as follows: there is an abiding corpus of dogma in the Church, an interpretation of basic moral attitudes which has a permanent validity in Christian life (in other words an abiding Christian ethic) and a valid and permanent constitutional law of the Church. The First Vatican Council solemnly promulgated the doctrine that when the Church expresses and articulates, in the form of specific propositions, her awareness of her own faith, then, whether it be through the ordinary doctrinal channels open to her or through solemn and official doctrinal definitions on the part of the Pope or a Council, and as commanding an absolute assent of faith, these propositions are free from error, remain permanently true and binding, and must not, in any subsequent age, be interpreted in a different sense – in other words have a different interpretation placed upon them. Rather *that* sense must be firmly adhered to in faith for all future time which was intended at that point in the past when this particular proposition of faith was promulgated or defined. The Church has an abiding and permanently valid system of ethics because it has always regarded the ultimate principles of the so-called natural law and of a way of life directed by the light of the gospel as dogmatically binding, and has always taught that these principles have the same value and the same abiding validity as dogmas concerning God, the three Persons in God, the nature of Christ and his significance for salvation etc.[2] The Church also has its own basic constitution as something already predetermined for it and not subject to its own decisions. To this doubtless belong the Petrine office and an episcopal organization (which we shall have to determine in more precise detail at a later stage). The result is that in virtue of these two factors (the primacy of the Pope and the episcopal order) the Church exhibits a palpable historical continuity with the Church of the origins even at the level of visible social history.

We might go on to unfold still more precisely the material details of this unchangeable factor in the Church as just described from the three distinct aspects of creed, life, and juridical constitution. We might go on to provide a fuller exposition of the fact that so far as this immutable element is concerned the Church herself does not claim any right to introduce changes. In fact she explicitly denies that she has any such right, and recognizes herself in all this as bound by the single and definitive revelation of God in Jesus Christ. We might go on to provide a more detailed presentation of the fact that according to the Church's own understanding of her faith it is at least true that anyone who consciously and in the public life of the Church denies a dogma of this kind relating to the creed, to Christian life, or to the constitution of the Church, thereby *ipso facto* ceases to belong to the Church as a social entity. Moreover the Church herself is quite incapable of doing anything to alter this fact, though under certain circumstances she surely is obliged to ascertain that it is a fact even in those cases in which the individual concerned, despite the fact that he still continues at most partially to identify himself with the Church and does not want to separate himself from the Church or her life totally, is nevertheless denying a dogma of the Church of this kind.[3] Here, however, we must forgo the task of developing any further these traditional positions, which constitute firm principles belonging to the very existence of the Church. In what follows, therefore, we shall be applying ourselves more fully to the *problems* entailed in these firmly held positions. But in doing so we shall in no sense be casting doubt upon the

---

[2] It is primarily the well-known idea of the 'hierarchy of truths' put forward at the Second Vatican Council that enables us of today to recognize key dogmas of this kind once more as central and fundamental. Cf. 'Unitatis redintegratio' (The Decree on Ecumenism), no. 11. See also the further observations which follow in the present article.

[3] On this question cf. the author's observations in the article in the present volume entitled 'Congregation of Faith and Theological Commission'.

importance of these declarations or their practical applicability in the life of the Church. There is an unchangeable element in the Church in the three respects mentioned. This unchangeable element can be distinguished from much else which is changeable in the theology, the life, the liturgy, and the concrete constitution which we find in the Church, and which, therefore, is, under certain circumstances, capable of being reformed. The possibility of drawing this distinction gives the Christian and the official functionary in the Church the possibility of a discernment of spirits: *those* spirits, namely who call for changes in the Church. For to the extent that it is possible so to distinguish between the changeable and unchangeable factors in the Church we have a standard enabling us to decide *here* to concede that reform and change is possible, and *there* to pronounce an absolute 'no' to any such demand for change.

It is only at this point that we come to the real heart and centre of our subject: in the concrete it is not so simple to decide where the distinction is to be drawn between changeable and unchangeable factors in the Church when it is some specific doctrine, some concrete living practice, some point of the Church's juridical constitution, or some other point of law that is in question – not so simple, that is to say, as has usually been assumed to be the case whether tacitly or explicitly in the traditional theory and practice of the Church. And it is this that gives rise to the practical difficulties which disquiet us today so much within the Church. We must even go so far as to concede the following: we recognize the abiding continuity and identity of the Church in the course of her history and of the change constantly taking place afresh within that history. But however far we may be able to go in verifying this continuity and identity in empirical terms, *in the last analysis* it is an object of believing hope and of that faithfulness which dares to commit itself on the basis of hope. But it is not simply an object of which we can achieve any empirical assurance with absolute certainty. It follows from this statement that we must assign the changeable and unchangeable factors in the Church to different positions in the scale of verifiability with regard to the possibility of experiencing them in the concrete. The changeable and the unchangeable are not two entities simply existing side by side as immediately empirically apprehensible each in its own right. That which we immediately experience and make living contact with is that which is in process of change, and it is the more immediate to us and the more apprehensible of the two entities. It is precisely *in* this – for all that the unchangeable factor is relatively apprehensible to us too – that this unchangeable factor has ever afresh to be believed in, hoped in, and acted upon in a spirit of faithfulness as that which is the more hidden of the two factors. If this thesis is correct, then for the Catholic too it is the experience of change, of being on the way to a goal, of being on pilgrimage, that constitutes the primary task laid upon him and required of him, and it is in this alone that he can genuinely realize his faithfulness to the unchangeable factor. We fully recognize that the experience of the Church as that in which we find an unchangeable divine truth, a rule of life which is always the same, a juridical constitution ordained by God himself, is indeed an experience which is possible and legitimate, and in fact one which belongs to the very essence of Christian faith and life. But *precisely in that form* in which this experience has been made and evaluated in the period of a 'Pianic monolithism' in the Church, it is an experience subject to the conditions of that particular age, and not even a particularly fine one when we look more closely into the matter.

The thesis we have just formulated is very abstract, and therefore, perhaps, not readily understandable. It needs to be illustrated and given firm outlines by means of a more concrete examination of the connection which exists between the changeable and unchangeable factors. In this connection we are deliberately avoiding the process of tracing the question to a deeper level, and embarking upon the examination of a more general range of problems such as might be developed in an existential ontology or a philosophy of history and theology, with regard to the connection between essence, idea and history, truth and history etc.,[4] in other words of a range of problems which in itself should be tackled and coped with if we were seeking to answer the question here raised by tracing it to its *ultimate* roots.

UNCHANGEABLE DOGMA?

We may begin by considering the unchangeable factor in Christian *dogma*. In this we are passing over the question, in itself important, of the further and deeper distinction which might be drawn *within* this unchangeable dogma itself, that namely between an ultimate and innermost kernel, a real heart and centre of the gospel on the one hand,[5] and the manifold ways, almost beyond recounting, on the other, in which this kernel has

---

[4] More recent surveys and bibliographies are easily accessible in the volumes of *Sacramentum Mundi* under the same key terms as are mentioned here.

[5] On this cf. the author's article, 'Mitte des Glaubens' in *Hilfe zum Glauben*, A. Exeler, J. B. Metz, K. Rahner eds., Theologische Meditationen 27 (Einsiedeln, 1971), pp. 39–56.

come to be developed into a whole range of individual dogmas as formulated in the course of the history of dogma. A distinction of this kind is justified by the teaching of the Second Vatican Council on the 'hierarchy of truths'. It likewise would, in itself, be of great importance for our present question. Here, however, it must be set aside. We are examining, therefore, the individual dogmas as they have been put forward by the ordinary or extraordinary *magisterium* of the Church as unchangeable propositions in the sense of having the quality of inerrancy. Even in the case of these dogmas we recognize on closer examination that the statement that they are unchangeable is not so simple or clear as appears at first sight. To begin with, in the case of many dogmas, it is only gradually and as the outcome of a long process of reflection, that they have come to be crystallized as such in the Church's conscious faith. It is far from being the case, therefore, that all of them were as such and as dogmas formulated in this specific manner, present right from the origins of Christianity. They have *come to be* through a historical process which is inevitably bound up with changes. It would be naive to suppose that once they have actually come to *be* they are simply unchangeable in *every* respect and so absolutely withdrawn from that dimension of history in which in fact they initially emerged.

Furthermore, despite the fact that in the formulation of these dogmas there is, in the nature of things, a *mutual* influence of the original divine revelation and of human language one upon the other, they are nevertheless expressed by means of human concepts deriving from a quite specific cultural and historical situation, and which themselves had, and still continue to have, a history of their own. In this respect it would be naive to suppose that such concepts are raised to a status of absolute immutability in every respect, and so become detached from their former history merely because they have undergone a certain sacral dignity and sanction in virtue of their being used in statements of dogma, or that once used in this ecclesiastical language they justifiably achieve thereby a more durable and tenacious life with less change than they would have undergone in secular usage. But even given that they have been so used in dogmatic formulations, it is still in any case clear that such concepts, which are in origin common to all spheres of human life, or belong to philosophical contexts, continue to develop their own secular history, and that the teaching Church must take due cognizance of this further history of the concepts concerned and draw the necessary consequences from it if its teaching is not to become incomprehensible. For it is no longer in any position to appeal, without further ado, to a secular understanding of these concepts suitable to be used for its own purposes and to convey the meaning of its own teaching. Alternatively there is another possibility open to the Church. A concept of this kind, which is in origin secular, but has been used in dogmatic propositions of the Church, is simply dead, and no longer has any existence in *this* sphere either if it is totally withdrawn from secular usage. And at this stage it is also unusable or hardly usable for the Church's doctrine either. For this doctrine of the Church must necessarily work with concepts which are in themselves secular in order to become intelligible at all. Against this it might be objected that there are, after all, specifically theological concepts which have application only in a specifically ecclesiastical parlance. But to this it could equally well be rejoined that even though we may recognize the validity of this point, it still does not invalidate the point we have just made. For first such concepts which belong specifically to theology, have at most a quite modest extent of application in the real preaching of the Church to those who are not specialist theologians, and second (and this is the decisive point) such specialist theological concepts have to be explained by means of secular concepts belonging to human life in general of a kind which remain subject to the laws of history, undergo changes, and so introduce the unrest inherent in history into the dogmatic formulations as well.[6] Furthermore an individual human proposition, whether secular or theological, is in all cases only really capable of being understood in the context of human awareness *as a whole* and in a *broader* sphere of meaning. Now it inevitably follows from this that even a dogma is necessarily conceived of by means of conceptual models in contexts involving real or presumed insights of a secular kind, with correct or premature conclusions drawn from this dogma, and in combination with emotional attitudes on the part of the concrete individual which may be either justified or not by the dogma itself in a specific age. In other words it is conceived of in combination with factors affecting human awareness, not all of which are, in themselves, identical with the actual dogma formulated. If we may so express it: it is totally impossible for the individual concrete man to conceive of a dogma that is 'chemically pure'.[7] His way of conceiving of it inevitably involves an amalgamation of conceptual models. It is arrived at in contexts, and under the influence of emotional factors

---

[6] On this cf. the author's 'The Historicity of Theology', *Theological Investigations* IX (London, 1972), pp. 64–82.

[7] On this cf. the author's 'Considerations on the Development of Dogma', *Theological Investigations* IV (London and Baltimore, 1966), pp. 3–35, and also 'The Development of Dogma', *Theological Investigations* I (London, 1961), pp. 39–76.

etc., which do not really belong to the actual dogma itself at all. It is justifiable, under certain circumstances necessary, and in fact indispensable for the individual's own personal understanding of the dogma concerned, for him to attempt to purify the dogma of these concepts which are subject to the conditions of a particular age, these conceptual models and these connected factors which do not essentially belong to the matter itself, and so to arrive at the dogma 'in itself' pure and unalloyed. Under certain circumstances such an attempt may succeed. Certain ways of understanding the dogma, which are subject to the conditions of time, are overcome. Earlier misunderstandings, which inevitably influenced the individual's judgement on the dogma concerned, are eliminated, and, moreover, if this attempt *really* succeeds all this is achieved *without* any distortion of the dogma which is really intended and its true meaning as binding upon us in faith. And even then this dogma is not arrived at in a state of 'chemical purity' or 'in itself'. Rather it is presented in a new form which is likewise subject to historical conditions, and expressed in different concepts which, no less than the former ones, have a specific place in history. It is presented in contexts and by means of conceptual models which are just as subject to change as those which were formerly used. We may reflect upon those historical factors which have conditioned earlier propositions – propositions which, even though they express an abiding truth, are nevertheless subject to history. But by doing so we do not escape from history. On the contrary we draw the proposition thus reflected upon in its former historical conditions still further into *history in the true sense*. In other words we make it subject to a whole range of fresh historical conditions which we cannot reflect upon so clearly as the former ones and, moreover, in the conviction that it is *to some extent* historically and rationally demonstrable that the new proposition constitutes a formulation of what was really meant in the former one which in the present circumstances is justified and authentic as a formulation of it.

What has just been said with regard to the historical conditions to which a dogma is subject can only be rightly understood in the full range of its application if we consider that an individual man in his concrete place in history is in no sense in any position *fully and adequately* to draw a conscious distinction between the *particular* historical formulation of the truth he is expressing and that truth in itself and in its abiding validity. This is something which we do to some extent arrive at by reflecting upon *earlier* dogmatic formulations. In the case of these we can achieve a more precise theological hermeneutics and so to some extent be able to say:

'this is what is really meant by a statement of this kind, and it is this too which is binding upon us, whereas *that* is only a concrete mode of expression, the outcome of historical conditions for this truth, and as such it is no longer binding in faith upon us of today.' In drawing a distinction of this kind with regard to such a proposition we are doing something which the Christian and theologian who formulated it *in the past* could not do. Moreover we ourselves could not in any adequate sense arrive at such a distinction today with regard to *those* new propositions which we ourselves formulate as statements of our own faith. It might be asked whether the Christian and theologian of former times would himself have *drawn such a distinction* as we ourselves draw between that which he properly intended as binding in faith on the one hand and the concrete historical expression in which what was meant is formulated on the other, *supposing* he had been confronted with the possibility of drawing such a distinction. But this question, though in itself possible, is an idle one. The fact remains, however, that in many cases at least it is basically impossible to arrive at any one *unambiguous* decision on this question. In other words that there is one point on which we cannot arrive at any absolutely assured conclusion merely as the outcome of a historical investigation: the point namely that those factors in a previous dogmatic formulation which, as viewed by us of today, constitute mere concomitant effects and are subject to the conditions of time would also have been, or actually were, felt to be such by the Christian of an earlier age supposing that it had been possible to put such a question to him. It is possible to ask whether he would have recognized such factors as in this sense inessential. And the very fact that we can put this question shows, in my opinion, that the continuity and identity of dogma in the Church's awareness of her own faith cannot simply be an object merely of historical investigation. Rather it implies an element of decision at the level of faith and hope such as cannot in any adequate sense be verified merely by the investigation of historical facts as such. For a process of verification at the historical level *precisely as such*, and taken in isolation cannot draw upon the assurance of faith of the former age concerned to draw a distinction in the earlier statement of faith between that which is changeable and that which is unchangeable, both being present in that earlier formulation. The reason is that this distinction was itself precisely not present in the awareness of faith of those of former times, or at least not in full and absolute clarity.

At this point we should go on to illustrate the statement we have just made concerning dogmatic formulations by means of concrete examples drawn from the history of dogma. But this is something which we are no longer in any position really to do in the present context. Here we must precisely confine ourselves to indicating merely a few examples chosen quite at random. For instance we may ask what the term 'transubstantiation' means for us of today seeing that the 'substance of bread', regarded as the subject of transubstantiation in the Council of Trent, is something which we of today can no longer recognize as having any existence in *that* sense which this term 'substance of bread' was conceived to have in the Middle Ages.[8] Again how are we to conceive of Adam as the originator and cause of original sin, and thereby of original sin itself, nowadays, seeing that for us who accept polygenesis as an established fact this unique figure Adam, from whom all other men are allegedly descended simply did not exist precisely as an individual at the beginning of the history of the human race? Rather, as we see it, mankind was originally formed by a human population.[9] Obviously in these dogmas of transubstantiation and original sin the essential points intended by the Council of Trent remain in force for us as well. But at the same time the very fact that there is a distinction to be drawn between this essential point in its abiding validity on the one hand and a conceptual model used at that time on the other (that namely of the substance of bread or of an Adam who was numerically one) – this fact does have a modifying effect even upon these abiding dogmas. And this modification cannot be fully justified solely by the Council of Trent's own understanding of its own dogmas. For this distinction, with its modifying effects, is something which the Council of Trent neither knew nor was capable of knowing, seeing that it could not have had any knowledge of modern physics or contemporary palaeontology. We must say, therefore, that the modifications we introduce in our understanding of these dogmas do not destroy the real identity between our understanding and that of Trent – in other words that we abide by the faith of preceding generations '*in eodem dogmate eodem sensu eademque sententia*'.[10] And the identity and historical continuity we are pointing to here is, in the last analysis, itself in turn a statement of faith and hope which in fact can, to a certain extent, he historically verified, i.e. shown to carry conviction. Nevertheless it is precisely only to a

[8] On this see the author's 'The Presence of Christ in the Sacrament of the Lord's Supper', *Theological Investigations* IV (London and Baltimore, 1966), pp. 287–311, and also 'On the Duration of Christ's Presence After Communion', *ibid.*, pp. 312–320.

[9] On this see the author's 'Theological Reflexions on Monogenism', *Theological Investigations* I (London, 1961), pp. 229–296.

[10] cf. Conc. Vat. I, Const. dogmat. 'Dei Filius', DS 34 3020 (Quotation from Vinc. Lerinensis, Commonitorium primum, c. 23 (PL 50, 668 A)).

certain extent that we can achieve this, so that we cannot from the outset wholly exclude some element of anxiety and uncertainty as to whether, under certain circumstances we may not after all have lost this identity. The temptation to allow the changeable element to destroy the unchangeable in Christian dogma is to be numbered among the factors belonging intrinsically to the Christian faith in our state of pilgrimage.

AN UNCHANGEABLE ETHIC?

The same applies to the norms of the Christian ethic, and thereby to the Christian way of life. Here precisely the same points apply to these Christian norms (inasmuch as they belong to revelation) which we have already made with regard to the interrelationship between the changeable and unchangeable factors in Christian dogma. This in itself justifies us in extending what we have said to the norms of Christian morality. A further point which must straightway be added to this is the following: apart from wholly universal moral norms of an abstract kind, and apart from a radical orientation of human life towards God as the outcome of a supernatural and grace-given self-commitment, there are hardly any particular or individual norms of Christian morality which could be proclaimed by the ordinary or extraordinary teaching authorities of the Church in such a way that they could be unequivocally and certainly declared to have the force of dogmas. This fact alone justifies us in confidently arriving at the following conclusion: the sum total of the norms of Christian living, together with a specific way of life felt to be binding upon Christians, may once have been developed and held confidently and unquestioningly in a particular age. Nevertheless they contained far more changeable elements than were ever conceived of as a matter of clear and conscious reflection by those belonging to that particular age itself. This is not so very surprising if only because the moral awareness of an individual, a particular society, or a particular epoch is more or less explicitly conscious all along that what it prescribes quite in the concrete here and now applies first and foremost under the conditions of this same here and now, and that thereby there are very many cases in which in practice it can remain an open question whether a norm of this kind also remains in force under *different* conditions and in different situations, the more so since in the concrete in many cases the very possibility of these future conditions may not have been foreseen. Under these conditions universal statements of principle more or less always include elements which are highly problematical.

The element of the unchangeable in the sphere of moral norms and the

Christian way of life becomes a still more potent factor in virtue of the changes – nowadays indeed the swift changes – to which the immediate norm of natural morality is subject, this norm being man himself in his *concrete nature*. In fact we may go so far as to say that nowadays these changes are directed and controlled by man himself. It is true that we can undoubtedly speak of an enduring 'eternal nature' of man and say that from this certain abiding moral maxims, at least at the most universal level, do flow as well with the transcendental necessity of this human nature itself.[11] But this *concrete* nature of man in all its dimensions (biological, social, etc.) is itself precisely subject to a most far-reaching process of change. It is not so simple as is often supposed, therefore, to distinguish between that which is eternal and abides as a matter of transcendental necessity in human nature on the one hand, and human nature as it exists in the concrete on the other, as subject to historical conditions and capable of change. The reason is that we invariably experience this eternal nature of ours only as it exists in concrete history, and at least up to the present we have not been able to experience much change in this concrete nature 'in our own person' in so brief a space as is constituted by an individual life-span. It would have little meaning to assert that no moral maxims applicable to the here and now flow from the nature of man in the concrete and as subject to the historical conditions prevailing in each particular case as distinct from the nature of man in its metaphysical necessity. For if we were to maintain this we would be reducing the Christian morality developed in any given age, and as such fully binding, to a few universal moral principles at the metaphysical level. Now the history of Christian morality proves that this is something which we neither can nor should do, and if this is the case then human nature in the concrete, as it exists in each particular individual, but at the same time as constantly subject to change, has a moral relevance, sets up moral norms of its own which on the one hand are valid in the present, and yet on the other cannot lay claim to any absolute or permanent validity. This also of its nature involves phases which are to some extent transitional phases, that is, in which maxims which were formerly in force in practice pass through an uneasy stage in which they gradually cease to have this force, though it would be impossible to lay down the precise point in terms of days or years at which they cease to be recognized as valid. Now as we have said it is impossible by any conscious process of reflection to draw a full and adequate distinction between that which

[11] On this cf. the author's 'On the Question of a Formal Existential Ethics', *Theological Investigations* II (London and Baltimore, 1963), pp. 217–234.

belongs to human nature as of metaphysical necessity and that which belongs to human nature as it exists in concrete history. And if this is true then inevitably there emerges in concrete human morality that disquieting interaction which we have spoken of between changeable and unchangeable moral norms which cannot fully be distinguished from each other. We must not therefore, be excessively surprised when the question arises of what is really and actually changeable and what is unchangeable in Christian morality. We should in no sense expect the Church always and in every case to undertake to draw this distinction for us with absolute clarity and at the same time with absolute binding force. Indeed the Church herself must expose herself to the experience of change in human nature as it exists in the concrete, a change which cannot be foreseen with full clarity even by her. A moral requirement which she either relaxes or alternatively reiterates at a particular point in time can thereby, under certain circumstances, also be interpreted *either* as a norm which, although in process of passing away, can nevertheless *still* be claimed to be in force, or *alternatively* as an imperative designed to ensure that the individual or a society, by an act of historical decision, shall so determine and shape precisely this human nature as it exists in concrete history that this norm which is proclaimed to be such can be a norm prevailing over this human nature as thus shaped.

Even in the case of the Church, therefore, we cannot expect of her that her teaching authority either shall draw or shall be capable of drawing a fully *adequate* distinction in every case and with complete sureness between the metaphysical and unchangeable element on the one hand and that other element which, while it does indeed still remain or has already been valid, is nevertheless subject to change on the other in the moral norms which are proclaimed by that teaching authority. And it follows from this that even with regard to such norms of Christian living a process of interaction between changeable and unchangeable factors which cannot fully be distinguished continues to exist. And this is something which must be sustained and endured in patience. In relation to this concrete situations may arise in which a practical decision is demanded of us which we cannot arrive at in any adequate sense at the theoretical level. In such a case we must rely upon our individual conscience alone to draw the necessary distinctions and arrive at the necessary decision 'according to its best lights and with the utmost sincerity'. And we cannot comfortably shift the responsibility of taking this decision to the teaching authority of the Church or to a moral theology in which full agreement has already been reached on the point concerned.

HOW FAR IS THE BASIC CONSTITUTION OF THE CHURCH UNCHANGEABLE?

We encounter the same situation in the sphere of the constitution of the Church, one namely of an interaction between changeable and unchangeable factors which itself in turn is subject to historical change. Although this is a point which cannot be proved here or illustrated by examples, we are first able to observe a development taking place in this juridical constitution of the Church in the apostolic age, in other words in the primitive Church in the true sense. Yet it is precisely this juridical constitution which in a later age, and so far as we are concerned, is now claimed to be unchangeable and permanently binding upon us as of 'divine' right. Here, then, we have a juridical constitution, binding upon us now and for ever, which nevertheless has had a past history, a period of development in which it came to be what it is, even though this process of becoming did not take place as a matter of logical necessity. And this fact in itself warns us of how cautious we must be in assuming that among the principles of the Church's juridical constitution now in force we shall find it very easy to distinguish between the changeable and unchangeable factors – in other words between human and divine law. This point becomes far clearer when we reflect upon those juridical structures of the Church as a society which are declared to belong to divine and unchangeable law in theology and the official teaching of the Church on ecclesiology (e.g. that of the Second Vatican Council), and, moreover, in principle perfectly correctly so. I am referring to factors which are beyond dispute so far as Catholic ecclesiology is concerned, namely the primatial power of the Pope and the episcopal structure of the Roman Catholic Church. Since obviously the definition of the First Vatican Council concerning the plentitude of the papal power is still in force even today, and will also continue in the future to belong to the unchangeable juridical constitution of the Church despite the long dogmatic development which lies behind it, it seems at first sight that all we have here is an unchangeable factor. Yet the matter is not so simple. To begin with, the concrete forms in which this papal authority has been exercised have not only varied very greatly in the past, but in the future too can undergo such far-reaching transformations that so far as the average everyday impression of an individual Christian is concerned the directive power of the pope may be encountered in some new form in which it seems to retain only a slight connection with that authority which was once and for all defined in the First Vatican Council as permanently enduring. It is recognized that though the pope has in principle the right to intervene in the lives even of particular Churches, this does not reduce these subordinate Churches to mere administrative departments within a single unified state subject to a monarchic régime or even an authoritarian discipline from above. It is further recognized that the Roman Congregations and nunciatures are in themselves far from necessarily or certainly constituting embodiments of the primatial power of the pope as defined, and further that neither they nor the code of canon law as already embracing almost everything that takes place in the particular Churches are necessarily or certainly valid for all ages. Furthermore, the rights which in principle belong to the pope in relation to all subordinate Churches is still not such as to decide anything beforehand with regard to *how often* this authority is to be exercised in the concrete. And in view of all this even so far as this unchangeable element in the structures of the Church is concerned, the concrete form which this function assumes is capable of very wide variations. Certainly we do not need to think of a future pope in relation to the bishops as one who is powerless, or in the position of a passive Merovingian king in relation to his maior-domo or a Japanese *tenno* in the centuries before the beginning of the *Mejii* period (1868). In fact in this age of UNO, one namely of a blending and interweaving of all particular cultural spheres in the earth, we can in many respects ascribe fresh and vital tasks to the papacy, contributing to the unity and global effectiveness of the Church, such as hitherto have never needed to be ascribed to it. But all this does not for one moment alter the fact that in the future the papacy, while retaining its basic 'generic form', will be able to present a quite different 'image' (if we may so express it) from that to which we have hitherto been accustomed. Without in any sense in principle either diminishing or calling in question the *ex cathedra* teaching authority of the pope, it is conceivable that on quite other grounds (pertaining to the stage arrived at in the history of human thought or the situation prevailing in the development of faith and dogma, which precisely does not prolong itself endlessly or indefinitely etc.) the pope will hardly be in a position to define any further 'new' dogmas in the future of the kind which have been defined in the past, and which constitute something more than a mere defensive re-expressing of the ancient and basic substance of the faith which any real Christian has not doubted even before the definition was produced. The theological possibility of a change of this kind, which might take a number of conceivable forms, still does not entail any decision on the question of whether such a change is either necessary or desirable. Still less does it imply any prophecy that such a change will in fact take place.

But it does open up scope for the possibility of it and obliges us, in a spirit of obedience towards the demands of the particular age in which we live, to hold ourselves open for such changes.

A similar conclusion applies too to the episcopal structure of the Church. In its reflections upon this the Second Vatican Council showed the same one-sidedness *vis-à-vis* the people of the Church as the First Vatican Council had shown in its reflections upon the papal power of the Church *vis-à-vis* the episcopate. Here again, while recognizing the abiding validity for the future of the episcopal structure of the Church, we also recognize (though this is not something that needs to be explained at length in the present context) that many structures and institutions may be built into the Church which give the people of the Church a more active role than that which they have previously had in the life of the Church itself. In other words, if we like so to express the matter, these new structures and institutions may signify 'democratic' rights within the Church. In fact many changes in this direction have in practice already been achieved within the Church, even though we may hold the opinion that still more changes of the same kind will have to take place in the future.

But perhaps (though this must be on our responsibility and at our own peril) we may go a step further. In constitutional law we speak of a monarchic episcopate and mean by this that the regional Church is governed in each particular case by an *individual*. This structure of a monarchic episcopate has been in force everywhere throughout the Catholic Church since the beginning of the second century, though it cannot be laid down as a matter of certainty that it has existed at all times and in all places as such even before this, ever since the time of the apostles, wherever particular Churches have existed. Now on this showing, so I believe, we can at least go so far as to pose the theoretical question of whether it really does belong intrinsically to the unchangeable juridical constitution of the Church not only that there must be, within the particular Churches, an episcopal power such as a present-day bishop enjoys, but also that as a matter of divine law this can be vested in an individual person in the physical sense and not in a moral person consisting of a small central body. The question is, therefore, whether in reality not only the episcopal power but also the necessity of it being borne by an individual person is a matter of divine law, whether, in other words, the constitution of the monarchic episcopate which we have in the Catholic Church is such as to exclude a synodal or presbyteral structuring of the Church *jure divino* even if the authority of a bishop as understood in the Catholic sense were to be ascribed to a small collegiate body of this kind. Although of course my opinion is quite unauthoritative on this point, I believe that nowadays in Catholic theology we can still leave the question open as to whether the possibility of episcopal power being vested in a collegiate or presbyteral body is really irreconcilable with the principle of episcopal constitution.[12] These indications too will serve to show the extent to which changeable and unchangeable factors in the Church are interconnected.

To this a further point may now be added: an abiding divine law can never be conceived of as being in itself, or taken in isolation, such a law as can directly, and without any further additions, be capable of being put into practice. On the contrary, in order to be directly capable of being put into practice in this sense it must necessarily be rendered present in the concrete form of a human law. Just as in the secular sphere there are laws which are incapable of taking any practical effect without further practical determinations in the form either of specific legal enactments or of concrete customs, so too it is in the Church. The *jus divinum* of the Church always and wherever it exists has a concrete embodiment which is not itself *juris divini* though of course this does not mean that this *jus divinum* in the Church is not real, i.e. that it cannot be present in any effective sense. What we find ourselves directly confronted with in the constitutional law of the Church either to our joy or to our sorrow is the changeable element. And it is precisely and solely *in* this that the abiding nature of this constitutional law as given to the Church by God can be made present and effective.

The first and primary quality demanded of the Christian by this relationship between the changeable and unchangeable in the Church is that patience which in the New Testament constitutes the basic virtue of the Christian life, and so too has its application in the attitude of the Christian towards the Church. The unchangeable element in dogma in the Christian understanding of existence in the institutional Church is something which she always encounters in a form which is historically conditioned and necessarily subject to historical change. The Christian cannot simply have and enjoy this unchangeable factor in its pure intrinsic essence. He must grasp it in a form which is changing, and so, under certain circumstances, in a form which has not already been made familiar to him by lifelong custom. This is especially true since those who are contemporaries and fellows in a strictly temporal sense may still be far from contemporaries and fellows in the spirit or in terms of ecclesiastical history.

[12] On this cf. the author's article in the present volume, 'Aspects of the Episcopal Office'.

On the contrary, at one and the same period in the Church individuals belonging to the most different ages are to be found living side by side, all of them playing their part in shaping the concrete form of the Church. Hence no one individual can find in the Church simply and exclusively *his* Church, i.e. a Church of a kind which is shaped exclusively by *that particular* situation in the history of human development which belongs particularly to him. Again in relation to the unchangeable factor in the Church there is need of that patience which endures what is alien and strange in history, and so is able to recognize in this first and foremost that which is abiding in the Church. The Christian also has need of this concrete synthesis which is always present between the changeable and the unchangeable in the Church in a further respect, namely in relation to the distinction of spirits. It will be noticed that in our considerations we have laid special emphasis upon the interaction between the changeable and unchangeable elements in the Church, which is such that they can never fully or adequately be distinguished from one another. Clearly this does not imply any denial of the necessity of using our *utmost resources* to draw the necessary distinctions ever afresh between the changeable and unchangeable elements in the Church, and at all levels of its existence, because without this it would be quite impossible for there to be any responsible further historical development of the Church at all. Instead we would have to commit ourselves blindly to a process of change which unfolded at random or (in order to avoid this) we would have to adopt an attitude of false conservatism and proclaim as our ideal a state of absolute unchangeableness of the Church in all matters, even those of only relative importance.

Theology, whether in the form of dogmatics, moral theology or canon law, invariably constitutes, from this point of view, the methodically directed and conscious attempt to distinguish between the unchangeable and the changeable. The theological qualifications introduced in dogma and morals, the distinction between divine and human law, and the question of the *jus condendum* in these disciplines, are in themselves enough to illustrate this point. While theology is not a merely secular science, but is also sustained by the light of faith and by a special kind of theological charisma, still the scientific work performed in theology exhibits unmistakably a quality of 'distinction of spirits' as this term is understood in traditional religious parlance.

Finally, however, despite this distinction arrived at by scientific reflection between changeable and unchangeable factors – something which is to some extent both possible and necessary – a further factor, which neither the Christian nor the Church herself can dispense with, is never-theless the courage to experiment. For at least in very many cases it is, for all the reasons already indicated, impossible to establish by the con-scious reflection of the theoretical reason where such a distinction is to be drawn between the changeable and the unchangeable. In many cases, therefore, it is quite inevitable that tentative experiments should be made to see whether the Church can discover that which is abiding in her conscious faith, and so herself as identical with her own past, in the specific form of a theological proposition, a way of life, or a juridical institution. Experimentation in this sense is necessary. In fact every theology is the work of a theologian who does not merely confine himself to repeating monotonously the traditional formulae of faith, and thereby ultimately speaking precisely distorting them by expressing them in this form in a *new* situation. Every theology constitutes an experiment of this kind, one in which an individual with his personal awareness of faith enquires of the Church's awareness of her faith as to whether this can achieve a fresh discovery of its own nature in a new formulation of this kind. New ways of life which individuals attempt constitute modes of questioning the Church in exactly the same way in the whole breadth of her life to see whether she can recognize and accept a life-style of this kind as authentically Christian. These ways of questioning the Church in word and deed have the character of an experiment, first because they have to be expressed in words or actions by an individual on his own responsibility and by his own decision without any preliminary authori-zation on the part of the Church authorities, and second because in very many cases the favourable or unfavourable reaction of the Church as a whole, or the Church authorities is far from being achieved, or capable of being achieved, at the selfsame moment at which this process of questioning is directed to the Church. On the contrary a fairly long interval has to be endured before the reaction to it comes, whether in the form of acceptance or rejection, positive recognition, toleration, or re-jection in a form which can clearly be apprehended.

Experimental stages of this kind are also to be found in the relation between the ideas and life-styles of a particular Church and the ideas and life-style of the universal Church, and so too at the level of ecclesiastical law and pastoral practice. In the process of experimentation in this sense it is often necessary to begin by establishing whether some formulation or practice which is new in historical terms constitutes a concrete embodi-ment of that which is unchangeable in the Church, or whether it has to be rejected by this as incapable of assimilation. Such stages in the process of experimentation are not always avoidable because it is impossible to draw any full or adequate distinction between changeable and unchangeable factors solely by means of the theoretical reason. A further reason is that the process of experimentation is precisely the manner in which the distinction of spirits is achieved by the practical reason, and also that even if this were not the case a concrete embodiment which was historically speaking new as a form of expression for the unchangeable element in the Church would not *ipso facto* and unequivocally be authenticated merely by the fact that some *earlier* form was in a full and unequivocal sense shown to be distinct from this unchangeable factor and to be historically transient.

To return once more to the beginning of these considerations: the underlying purpose of the thoughts we have put forward has been first and foremost to show that we should not oversimplify the task of distinguishing between the changeable and unchangeable elements in the Church, and that for this reason a certain anxiety among the Church's members and a certain antagonism between conservatives and progressives such as cannot immediately be resolved are perfectly understandable. But while recognizing all this, a point which must not be obscured is that in the majority of cases in the practical life of the Church, in her ideas and actions, the open-minded willing and well-instructed Christian can recognize in a manner that is *sufficient* that in the Church's faith, way of life, and laws, even though this Church undergoes changes, he can still recognize and hold firm to the ancient Church in its abiding nature. In the majority of cases, therefore, the conflict that we find between Christians cannot seriously bear upon the point of whether the unchangeable in the Church has survived, even though obviously cases of such conflict can arise. The only point of real conflict can be whether the new historical form embodying the unchangeable element which does endure, and which has been present all along, is *opportune*, whether it finds acceptance with the individual and contributes to the task of the Church today and tomorrow better than the forms assumed in the past, or those which precisely it is sought to relegate to the past. Even a conflict of *this* kind may often be both strenuous and bitter. But however it is decided it does not remove the abidingly unchangeable element for the Christian, and with good will it can be conducted in such a way that the true unity of the Church, her abiding identity through history, and the love between Christians is not diminished.

2

THE FAITH OF THE CHRISTIAN AND THE
DOCTRINE OF THE CHURCH

IN view of the current unrest in the Church, no words need be wasted
in pointing out the relevance of the subject we have chosen to our
present times.[1] It will be developed in three stages. First I would like to
make a few points with regard to a traditional key thesis included in the
usual presentations of the Church's teaching concerning the relationship
between the faith of the individual who is *de facto* a Christian and the
official doctrines of the Church. It is a key thesis which we must respect,
yet which at the same time we can also regard as constituting no more than
a point of departure for the theme which we are seeking to discuss among
ourselves. We shall then go on to speak about the situation in terms of the
sociology of ideas within which this thesis, initially considered in its
traditional form, has to be understood today. Finally, in a third section,
we shall have something to say about the attitude of the Christian of
today towards the Church's official teaching on faith.

I. THE POSSIBILITY OF A HERESY THAT SEPARATES MEN
FROM THE CHURCH

As a Catholic I am convinced that the traditional doctrine of the Church is
correct, though admittedly only as subject to all the points which we
shall have to make in what follows. This traditional doctrine lays down
that if an individual Catholic Christian explicitly and publicly contradicts any dogma of the Catholic Church as upheld by her official teaching
authority, then this Christian is cut off from the Roman Catholic Church.
This basic thesis – in other words the proposition that it is possible to be
cut off from the Church by heresy – has been expressed innumerable

---

[1] This article is a written version, only lightly revised, of a lecture which the
author gave in the Union of Catholic Students at Munster on the 7 July 1971.

24

times in the Church's official documents. Even today it is both correct and necessary for the Church's essential nature, just as many explanations and interpretations which were formerly not asserted in so explicit a form may also still be necessary for this basic thesis. We cannot, while remaining within the Church, publicly uphold anything and everything in it as a proposition of which we are absolutely convinced. There are propositions which, if they are upheld in an absolute and public sense, will set the defender of such a statement outside the Church, regardless of whether he recognizes and accepts this outcome or not, or whether this outcome is or is not explicitly laid down as such by the Church's authorities. What such a thesis presupposes is that according to Catholic doctrine revelation is at basis directed, not to the individual as such or taken in isolation, but to the community of the covenant people, that is to the Church. It is the Church as single and in its totality that is the hearer of the word of the living God and (as a single collective entity) that makes the experience of revelation. And it is precisely to this revelation of God, as directed to her, the Church, as the people of God, that she responds with faith. This faith is something that she bears witness to as a community, a community which itself in turn is institutionally structured, constitutes a social and historical entity, and, moreover, does so precisely as the bearer, guardian, proclaimer, and witness to this truth which God has spoken her. On this basis it is immediately and intrinsically obvious what a dogma of the Church is and is intended to be. We are considering those cases in which the Church as one, and, furthermore, as represented by those bodies in which her institutional structures achieve their various peaks (these we do not need in the present context to analyse theologically in any greater detail), acknowledges, by an act of total commitment, a given doctrine as an element in the revelation of God in Jesus Christ. In such cases, according to Catholic teaching and Catholic understanding, the truth or the proposition concerned (for all the historical conditions or limitations to which it is subject, and for all the relative factors in the mode of its conception) cannot ultimately speaking be erroneous,[2] i.e. under the Church's laws she cannot give the individual the right to pronounce an unequivocal and definitive 'no' to the proposition concerned, amounting to a total commitment of his own personhood. This is the one point which has to be made with regard to this traditional basic thesis.

This statement needs to be made more precise in one significant respect, one which belongs to the authoritative interpretation of this statement and, moreover, needs to be added even according to the Church's

[2] cf. Vatican II, *Lumen Gentium*, no. 12.

traditional doctrine. It is this: in the case of a concrete individual contradicting the official doctrine of the Church, it is perfectly possible for the
action of the individual concerned to be objectively speaking unjustifiable
and subjectively speaking justifiable both at the same time. We may
express this in other terms. The Catholic Church does not in any sense
maintain that when an individual contradicts her doctrine (even assuming
that he knows that this is in fact her doctrine) such a contradiction necessarily means that the individual is morally disqualified from membership
of the Church. It might of course be said that nowadays this is a mere
truism, for who could seriously or honestly regard his opponent in
'questions of the philosophy of life' as stupid or ill-intentioned? But what
I mean is that we should first regard the matter from the point of view of
earlier ages, for which there are also reasons, and, perhaps, which is still
far from being completely dead, and second from the point of view of the
situation with which we ourselves now find ourselves confronted. It is in
the light of these two approaches that we should consider the doctrine
just stated, namely that it is possible for a contradiction of the Church's
official teaching to be subjectively speaking justified even though this
contradiction cannot be acknowledged as objectively justifiable by the
Church as such, since otherwise she would in fact be denying her own
truth. We must realize that this position is, after all, precisely not so self-
evident as it is sometimes presented to be by well-meaning people. A
proposition can be entirely correct and yet misunderstood or misused, if
merely from recognizing it as correct we then go on to regard it as self-
evident as well. Then it is exposed to the danger of being contested, and,
moreover, in the last analysis, more vigorously than if we had regarded
it as less self-evident and therefore as in need of more precise justification.
Only read the newspapers and other publications of the socialist countries
to see how they deal with the opponents of socialism, how they 'execrate'
them and regard hatred against them (at least as a group, but also in such
a way that ultimately it bears upon their individual opponents too) as
justified and a matter of duty. And the attitude tacitly underlying all this
is that unless the socialists adopt an aggressive attitude of this kind,
which sets their opponents morally beyond the pale, they cannot have
the energy and compulsion which they indispensably need in order to
achieve their genuine and legitimate goals. In fact they pronounce any
tolerance which involves at least a presumption of moral integrity on the
part of their opponents as a trick of the establishment, which thereby
manages to deprive its opponents from the outset of the single-minded
courage they need to promote their aims. Only read the bill-posters

which are nowadays being pasted up everywhere by student groups within our society! There you will be able to find irrefutable evidence of an attitude of aggression against their opponents according to which they qualify these in principle as men whose subjective disposition is evil. We can see, then, that such attitudes exist even today – indeed that this attitude, in which one side condemns the other as subjectively stupid or evilly disposed, seems once more to be on the increase. In the *present* context I am not attaching any *blame* for this at all. For the Church has done the same often enough in her past history, regarding every heretic who publicly and objectively contradicted the doctrines of the Church as a villain and treating him accordingly. But today at least it has obviously become a doctrine of the Church, belonging intrinsically and necessarily to the basic thesis mentioned above, that it is possible for a contradiction of the Church's official doctrine to be subjectively speaking justified. The Church recognizes that individuals stand in a specific concrete situation and have certain basic dispositions predetermined for them for which they cannot be blamed. In such a situation they can, in the development of their own individual personhood and ideas, arrive at a judgement through no fault of their own, and in fact be obliged to hold firm to their opinion, which involves a rejection of some doctrine of the Church. And this interpretation of the basic thesis referred to above, which the Church has only learnt to recognize with sufficient clarity through a long historical development, is something which she will hold firm to in the present and future even though a mentality may arise, or even come to predominate, in secular society which seeks to reject this attitude towards one's opponent in theory or in practice.

Despite this it must be said that according to the Church's understanding of her own nature, even in such a case the individual concerned ceases to belong to her. If I deny that there is a triune God, that there can be any sin or redemption at all, if I say that Jesus is at most a religious enthusiast and nothing more, then – all other considerations apart – I am no longer a Roman Catholic Christian in the sense in which the Church regards the attitude of faith of an individual as a condition for true and full membership of her (even at the level of the Church as a society). I believe that a modern man should not take offence at such an attitude on the part of a Church. There are in fact political parties too which – *mutatis mutandis* – recognize the necessity for expelling individuals from the party where necessary on these or similar grounds, and that too through a decision of an official representative body, and even though the individual thus expelled may protest against this decision and regard himself as the true upholder of the spirit of this party. If it is objected that it is inappropriate to apply this example to the Church, we must reply as follows: Why should we not, seeing that on the one hand the Church is, and must be, and always has been (and, moreover, as it exists in all confessions) a normal social entity *as well* as a spiritual one, and that on the other the basic thesis and the comparison refer precisely to the social level of the Church's life as such – in other words do not, of themselves, involve any judgement whatever as to how the individual thus expelled stands in relation to the mystery of grace of the Church as such, or as to whether or not he is excluded from *this* (something which, of course, is possible only through some grave personal fault of his own in God's sight, and through no other factor whatever)?

In all that we have been saying we do not, of course, intend in any sense to deny that in the secular sphere the question of who really represents the true spirit of a social entity in the views he upholds and who does not is ultimately speaking something which cannot be decided by any official decisions within this society, but must be decided rather through that more powerful spirit which can be seen taking effect only through the development of history. This also applies, *mutatis mutandis*, to that spirit of hope and faith of the Church in which the Church determines herself in her own nature, and rejects other interpretations as inapplicable to her. Even the officially defined faith of the Church is maintained in the hope of not being rejected by the absolute future which is God. It cannot be anything more than this. But to be this, and to draw the necessary consequences from it, is the task and duty of the Church as a social entity.

All this means that in the concrete human situation it is quite impossible to avoid a state of affairs in which a society having a body of doctrine, a party programme, or whatever name we may like to give to it, has to lay down that certain specific denials, erasures, or alterations put forward by a theologian or any other kind of Christian with regard to an official doctrine of the Church are irreconcilable with the manner in which this society understands its own nature. Hence the Church has to ask the individual involved to take due cognizance of this fact. Obviously in saying this I have still not touched upon the real problem in the concrete, the problem namely of how the foregoing remarks are to be applied in a positive and negative sense in the concrete situation of modern man at the sociological level, what further effects it has, or, under certain circumstances, does not have nowadays. There is a further question which we have not touched upon, namely which particular contradictions of official ecclesiastical doctrine have the effect of separating the individual involved from the Church in the manner described or, as the case may be, of precisely not so separating him, what form these contradictions take, which particular doctrines they relate to, and how absolute the contradiction involved is in any given case in the form in which it is asserted. Obviously there are people who pay the Church taxes and at the same time assert apodictically that the papacy should be totally abolished, or maintain similar heterodox doctrines. And there are other people in the Church who contradict points of ecclesiastical teaching which are less central. And here their contradictions are put forward more as an expression of the difficulties they feel, as a 'questioning', as a complaint about the difficulty in assimilating the doctrines concerned. Alternatively they may from the outset relate to points of doctrine which are not dogmas at all, and therefore are capable of revision in a totally different sense from the Church's dogmas in the true sense. Now the conclusions which have to be arrived at, the interpretations which have to be made in the concrete in all these cases – these are points which unhappily we cannot enlarge upon any further here, even though the concrete questions begin only at that point at which, in our present context, we are forced to break off.

II. THE MODERN PLURALISM OF IDEAS AND ITS SIGNIFICANCE FOR THE CONVICTION OF THE BELIEVER

We shall only be in a position to apply the thesis above in practice, and thereby really to understand it to some extent, when we have found an answer to the question: What form does this thesis assume in the *present* age? First and foremost the following point must be stated: In former times in a given society the truth upheld by the group as a whole was upheld and safeguarded by a few élite individual representatives and, moreover, their influence extended even to the manner in which it was effectively and really accepted by all. The responsibility for deciding and maintaining the convictions within the society concerned was in the hands of a few, and all the rest followed in the footsteps of these few. Right down to the age of the Reformation, for instance, the beliefs prevailing in a specific region were decided by its ruler, perhaps in collaboration with a few theologians or similar élite individuals, or through a few figures equipped with political power. The others unquestioningly accepted their decision, and while individual contradictions and protests did arise, they were socially speaking of no very great importance. In other words a narrowly defined group within a society, sometimes even represented by a single individual, in practice actually determined the principles which were recognized as true in a society and by which it lived. Today this is no longer the case, nor is it any longer possible. It may be true that even today there are still groups who form public opinion and set the course for the rest to follow, and which are different from other groups, though such 'formers of opinion' may make their influence felt in more anonymous ways than was formerly the case. But still this does not for one moment alter the fact that in one and the same society, in one and the same geographical region, an abiding pluralism of systems of belief is to be found such that no one specific group within the secular world can any longer succeed in bringing all the various systems of belief within society as a whole into harmony with its own ideas. We have *de facto* a pluralism in the sphere of living human thought. This pluralism is something which all of us of today can experience. Now it follows from this (and here I come to the essential point I am making) that it is no longer possible even for one who firmly and decisively accepts the official teaching of the Church to achieve a completely *positive* synthesis between that which he believes as a committed Catholic Christian and the other items of knowledge, aspirations, mental outlooks etc. by which, in the midst of which, and on the basis of which he lives his life in such a society. In this situation we do of course arrive at a point at which all those supports for the Christian's personal convictions of faith fall away which formerly, within a homogeneous Christian society, he inevitably had. He no longer finds his faith confirmed by the public opinion of society as a whole. His position is quite the opposite of this. I am not saying here that a modern man need necessarily discover an unequivocal and clearly apprehensible *contradiction* of an absolute kind between those attitudes of the modern age which are shared by the Christian too on the one hand, and that which he believes as a Catholic Christian on the other if and to the extent that he accepts the Church's doctrine. But the fact that the Catholic Christian does not assert that any such positive absolute and insoluble contradiction exists does not mean on the other hand that he can straightway achieve a positive and harmonious synthesis, such as he himself can readily understand, between his own faith as governed by the official norms of the Church on the one hand and the rest of his attitudes on the other.

This pluralism in our mental attitudes, which we can no longer completely reduce to harmony, is to be numbered among the inevitable characteristic features of the current situation in human thought. It means that faith has ceased to be a 'system of ideas' (in a sense which will have to be more precisely explained). On the contrary it is a particular element in the world of ideas to which the man of today belongs. Of course he hopes for an eschatological reconciliation of truths, and, moreover, precisely while maintaining his protest against any kind of ideological totalitarianism. A protest of this kind belongs precisely to the nature of Christianity, and is directed against any attempt at an ideological totalitarianism against a system of human thought which draws everything within its net and reduces everything to a single homogeneous whole, regardless of whether the attempt to achieve this is made by Christians or other 'systems' (examples of both are to be found). When I was young it was perfectly possible for someone who had grown up in a Catholic environment to have the impression that a man could maintain an attitude of openness towards science, could be in sympathy with the world, and at the same time could harmonize and synthesize all this with his Roman Catholic and Christian faith in an absolute and positive manner *in such a way* that what emerged was something which I would call a 'system of ideas', namely a conception of human reality as a whole in which all the individual elements were (at least approximately) reconciled in a positive sense with one another so that there was a mutual interplay and homogeneity between them. In former times we did in fact entertain a 'system of ideas' or *Weltanschauung* of this kind. For we simply did not recognize anything which was not in harmony with a mental attitude of this kind which reduced everything to a synthesis, or alternatively we suppressed it. In other words it was still possible right down to the end of the nineteenth century or the beginning of the twentieth to be an 'ideological' Christian, that is to live by a synthesis of all the data arrived at in one's own intellectual awareness, which one had, at least in one's own estimation, achieved.

I believe that such a situation no longer exists. The world we live in is one which is really pluralist even so far as our own interior and individual lives are concerned, one which does not begin only outside and beyond our own personal awareness, but constitutes an intrinsic element in the intellectual situation of each particular individual. We may of course ask what faith signifies in such a situation. I would reply: In contrast to any medieval conception, it precisely does not any longer signify that principle of synthesis which can be brought to bear even at the practical level, and which is capable of synthesizing, integrating within itself, and assigning to a quite specific place within one's intellectual life, all the non-religious data of Aristotle or of a school of medicine in Palermo. Furthermore such a unified 'outlook upon the world' (taking this in the sense described) no longer exists for the modern believer in this sense even in his own interior life, and to that extent faith constitutes one particular element in our total intellectual lives. Of course this does not mean that we fail to maintain the *hope* that precisely *this* unsynthesized pluralism in knowledge and experience will, at some eschatological point in the future completely give place to the one truth. Nor does it mean that we have to tolerate what we can recognize as a clear and certain contradiction between the individual items of knowledge within the totality of our awareness. But even with these two essential provisos, the point we are making remains valid. We no longer have any unified or fully constructed system of ideas by which to live. And for the believer it is precisely an essential task to allow this pluralism to exist, and not to seek to suppress it either from the side of 'science' or from that of faith by evolving some homogeneous and all-embracing system of ideas. Faith, which ever afresh rejects, and gives the lie to, the totalitarian claims of science, must precisely not, on its side, nowadays, seek itself to have the status of an 'all-embracing system of ideas'.

At this point I may allow myself a brief digression. Today a younger generation of theologians is arising, one which finds all that it discovers in the First Vatican Council disagreeable to it. However on a right interpretation of the First Vatican Council we can see that this Council recognizes the pluralism referred to here as true and valid. For it is precisely the First Vatican Council that finds a solution to the problem facing it of the confrontation between the Church and a world that is no longer Christian. And it solves this problem not by explaining that all human and secular knowledge is ideologically or religiously speaking indifferent and neutral in order *thereby* to be able to save the hegemony of revelation and faith. On the contrary it says that there are such secular truths, born not of the Church or of divine revelation in the narrower sense, yet which, nevertheless, affect human life in the true sense even though they do not simply or exclusively constitute data of faith. The Council precisely does not (in order to create 'peace and order') draw the kind of distinction between the various branches of human knowledge which assigns the secular ones, capable of being used for the manipulation of the world and its resources, to one side, these, therefore, having no significance for the salvation of man, for his 'existence' as one and whole, while assigning the existentially significant religious truths to the other, these then constituting by that very fact truths of pure revelation, and as such subject to the sole authority of the Church. On the contrary the Council speaks of *two* sources of knowledge which are united with one another only in their origin (God), and in no other area. Moreover (and this is the striking point), knowledge which is of fundamental significance even at the existential level is to be found in the secular source as well: the existence of God and much else besides, which is included or entailed in this. The only further point that we now need to add (and for this the First Vatican Council has at least opened some possible doors) is that these secular truths, which, nevertheless, radically affect human existence, are incapable, so far as we are concerned, of being synthesized in any positive or adequate sense with that which the Christian believes as a Catholic, because they in fact extend from another source which is made available to man in a quite different sense and given over to his history in all its unforeseeable developments. And it is here that we arrive at that which we have called the modern pluralism of ideas which is incapable of synthesis, and at the impossibility of achieving any homogeneous 'all-embracing system of ideas', regarding this as a characteristic feature of the world in which we have to live today.

To that extent, therefore, and in contrast to earlier ages, in this age faith has become in a special sense one particular element in the life of the human spirit, and so become something which historically speaking it was not in former ages. For then an order of enthusiasm prevailed, deriving from the Middle Ages, a will to achieve order, and an attitude of triumphalism which was extremely praiseworthy (conditioned as it was by the situation at that time). And this state of affairs made it possible for faith to synthesize all else within itself, and imparted a synthesizing power to it. If faith in this sense has become one particular element in our existence as intellectual beings, then the only way in which it can of itself be that which, theologically speaking, it is intended to be, is for it to recognize its own significance as constituting the hope of that eschatological unification of truth which will take place in that which we call eternal life, the consummation of history. It is here, then, that that synthesis is bestowed upon us in grace which we can neither in fact, nor to outward appearances, achieve in our present-day mode of existence.

Now an eschatological hope of this kind is, of its nature, opposed to every other ideology seeking to impose itself as absolute, and also to itself in this role, i.e. to any misunderstanding or misuse of it. It constitutes a protest against every kind of ideological totalitarianism. For such an attitude does in fact exist precisely in the claim to be able even today to have a system within which everything which can reasonably be conceived of at all, and which can claim to constitute truth, can positively be integrated. Christianity makes no such claim to an ideological totalitarianism, for it recognizes the existence of this pluralism. Obviously it recognizes it today in a conscious manner as something that cannot in any adequate sense be reduced to a synthesis, but this makes no difference whatever to what we have been saying, for thereby it recognizes precisely that it itself is subject to historical conditions, and in doing this it also constitutes a protest against the setting up of any other system as absolute when it claims this status. This is enough to indicate, at least to some extent, the situation in terms of social philosophy, within which the relationship between the faith of the individual Christian and the official teaching of the Church must be conceived of and viewed.

III. THE ATTITUDE OF THE CHRISTIAN TOWARDS THE OFFICIAL TEACHING OF FAITH

1. *Accepting the Difference Between One's Own 'Personal' Truth and the Official Teaching of the Church*

The genuine Christian, who sees and accepts the situation indicated above, recognizes and endures the difference between his own personal truth and the official teaching of the Church in that he achieves both precisely *as* open to further development (admittedly each in its own way), and understands that the difference between them is an element in that contemporary pluralism which is no longer capable of being reduced to a complete synthesis, and which is anti-ideological in character. In view of the pluralism which necessarily exists it is obvious that the individual Christian in his awareness neither is nor can be simply the mirror image, the reflection, the echo, the reproduction of the official teaching of the Church. He is far too much under the influence of historical conditions for this to be the case, far too much a concrete individual. He can recognize this difference and he must bear with it.

The Christian no longer possesses any overall awareness in which his secular knowledge, in all its departments, is brought into a *positive* synthesis with the truths of his faith. On the contrary his mode of existence is subject not only to a 'situation of moral concupiscence', but also to a 'state of intrinsic gnoseological concupiscence'. By 'an intrinsic state of gnoseological concupiscence' we mean precisely that pluralism which exists in the present-day awareness of each individual: his knowledge has various sources yielding within himself branches of knowledge which cannot from the outset be reduced to synthesis or brought into harmony with one another. His conscious capacity for reflection is only limited in scope. As a result, in very many cases the individual does not even have any clear awareness (apart, perhaps, from that which is borne in upon him by a vague general intellectual unease) that it is far from being evident how the various branches of knowledge (and the attitudes formed on the basis of them) can really be integrated with one another. Just as there is a situation of moral concupiscence which cannot adequately be resolved, and which consists in the disparity of the moral impulses to good and evil which continue to exist in their disparity even despite the understanding of himself at which an individual may freely have arrived, so too in the field of knowledge an analogous situation is to be discerned: the heterogeneous pluralism which cannot in any full or adequate sense be resolved of the various branches of knowledge which a man has. It is precisely this that we call the intrinsic state of gnoseological concupiscence in man, and can therefore apply to it (*mutatis mutandis*) all that is involved in terms of problems and answers in theology in the concept of 'concupiscence'. In response to this state of affairs, just as in response to his moral situation, the individual has the duty and the power to advance one step and to make some attempt at overcoming this situation of pluralism and of disparate forces in the direction of achieving a synthesis of all his various branches of knowledge within a single 'overall harmonized system of ideas'. But he can and must be aware at the same time that this positive process of synthesizing has still not succeeded, and will never fully succeed. This situation of concupiscence in the sphere of knowledge is something which has emerged into clear awareness only in modern times. It compels us in a quite new way to have recourse to a '*reductio in mysterium*'. In former times one's task was to pass from a well integrated, well ordered world of knowledge on to the inconceivable mystery. Today it is a disordered world of knowledge which cries out for that light which can only be that eternal light which does not yet shine upon any man here below. Today man knows too much at the level of the concrete categories of this world and its realities for him to be able to cope with it all, or for him to be in a position always and in every case to say how all this fits together. Obviously a theology works constantly and rightly to achieve a position in which it can show, by means of a realistic and bold interpretation of dogma that this must not appear positively and unequivocally irreconcilable with the secular branches of knowledge and (something which is still more important and more difficult) with the whole mentality of the current age. Certainly theology strives explicitly and unhesitatingly to rid itself of those statements, recognized as erroneous, which have been proved to be no longer tenable by the advances of secular knowledge. In this it has had some success and can also show that it is not necessary to reject the true dogma of the Church as an error merely because it must and also can manifestly be interpreted afresh in a new historical situation, though obviously without thereby being destroyed or having its meaning completely changed. Certainly these manifold efforts on the part of contemporary theologians also have their successes, successes which will be underestimated only by those who are too entrapped in an old-fashioned mentality really to feel the present-day insuperable pluralism in our awareness at all, and who therefore find it easy to be 'orthodox'. But all these theological strivings cannot (and, moreover, do not need to) invalidate the fact that the harmonization consisting in a philosophy of life in which everything is synthesized is something which is unattainable so far as we are concerned, and that we actually feel this clearly and acutely.

The official teaching of the Church viewed in itself alone is not simply reiterated in its (relative) *intrinsic* harmony in the awareness of the individual Christian who assents to this teaching in faith. For secular knowledge too is present in his mind, deriving from quite different sources. And so far as man's finite awareness is concerned this knowledge is not from the outset brought into a synthesis. Moreover nowadays it is no longer capable of being fully synthesized, within the limitations of time, with the message of revelation to us regarded as an interpretation of this same human life. The opposite view will seem to be true only to those who no longer have any real interior attitude to the modern secular understanding of existence. Such people, whether voluntarily or involuntarily, have still made the intellectual situation of Christendom which prevailed in the past and which was once justified into a present-day ghetto in which they stubbornly seek to survive and so threaten to turn the Church into a strange and old-fashioned sect (such as, for instance, that of the Adventists). In doing this they persist in regarding their entire attitude as the courage and intransigence of true Christian faith. The modern Catholic has to recognize and unreservedly to endure this pluralism in his intellectual life, painful and perilous though it may often seem. In view of the insuperable limitations in the subjectivity of his awareness it also implies a difference between his own faith and the official teaching of the Church. Difference in this context does not *ipso facto* mean a radical or total contradiction, but it does imply a distinction, e.g. in virtue of the fact that it is still far from being the case that everything which is included as dogma in the official teaching of the Church *ipso facto* also has to be appropriated and understood by the individual within his own personal existence. It also implies that order and structure as applied to the awareness of the individual and the order of the official teaching of faith are different.

There is one point which the Christian can and must recognize: his own truth, and the personal history of his own achievement of self-identity are still open to further development. We are not people who always and in every case have to uphold all that they actually state with the deep notes of ultimate interior conviction and with an 'absolute assent' (as with the dogma of the Church) as though we were convinced of the fact that we are already in absolute and total possession of the truth in its fulness. Precisely so long as we are neither willing nor able to do this, precisely so long as we are, in this sense, humble individual Christians, subject to the influence of historical conditions, there is a difference between the official teaching of the Church and that which concerns the concrete content of the personal faith of each particular individual. And this difference is not only inevitable, but perfectly justified. We do not become good, or even theologically educated Christians only at that point at which we have a precise knowledge of official seminary dogmatics, and so have a precise awareness of where the appropriate numbers in Denzinger are to be found and what they say. There is, in fact, a wholly justified attitude of indifference towards this or that particular doctrine of the Church, an indifference affecting the concrete existence of the individual which constitutes something approximating to a process of ridding oneself of a burden in one's own personal life. Under certain circumstances such an attitude is in principle justified. We do not in any sense need, so far as our own personal concrete lives are concerned (and, moreover, precisely inasmuch as they have something to do with the absolute God and his final judgement) to act absolutely as though we were in some great chemist's shop in which we had to watch over all the various doctrines of the Church, drawn off, so to say, into so many bottles.

2. Paying due heed to the hierarchy of truths

Let us attempt to translate the message we have sought to convey into practical terms. The best course for a man who calls himself a Christian would be once and for all really to understand what one thing really means: to pray. For this is anything but easy ('Lord, teach us to pray!', Luke 11:1). If he can do this, and perhaps in doing so still notice that this orientation to God has something to do with Jesus Christ and his Cross, then under certain circumstances he may remain in complete ignorance as to the number of the sacraments and still be a better Christian than if he had an exact knowledge of this, or if he could repeat every catechism answer by heart. For even so he might still have understood nothing of the real and vital point, so very simple, so very fundamental, so very radical, and precisely on this account so very difficult as it is, and therefore so easy to replace with a pious or theological verbiage. The fact that there is such a thing as indulgence is (rightly understood!) a defined truth. But this does not necessarily mean that a Catholic Christian (even an educated one) must have some knowledge of it. If Paul VI says that there is a Christian freedom to avail oneself of indulgences or not to do so, then the individual Catholic can confidently apply this Christian freedom to the question of knowing about indulgence also. We should not be too hasty in asserting that we must do one thing and not omit another. For the individual in the concrete (just the same as the pastor of souls) will notice that in view of the restrictions upon his time, his resources etc. there are many cases in which he is actually *compelled* to omit one thing if he seeks really and whole-heartedly to do another. In relation to the official teaching of the Church such a way of lightening one's burden can, under certain circumstances, be indispensable if a man is to cope with his own life (precisely as a believer). He may (as Scripture itself says) not always 'bear' everything. While 'objectively speaking' there may be no legitimate way of getting rid of a burden by a personal and resolute denial of one of the Church's dogmas, still there is manifestly, at least in the personal life of the individual Christian spirit, a way of 'getting rid of it' by failing to notice it, by 'postponing' a problematic question to a later time, just as this happens, and necessarily must happen, in other departments of life.

When the Second Vatican Council speaks of a 'hierarchy of truths'[3] it is of course clear that the real *essence* of this total structure of truth (regardless of how it should be described in more precise detail) is of greater importance and, moreover, in the sense that those truths which belong to the periphery within this total hierarchy may be such as the subject is totally unaware of without this being any ground for criticizing him. In this context we can discern not merely an objective structure in this Christian truth taken as a whole, but also (and this is just as important) a subjective 'hierarchy of truths' and, moreover, one that is perfectly justified. What we are seeking to convey is this: the various aspects and perspectives from which any Christian regards his personal life as it unfolds, or alternatively the totality of Christian doctrine from his own individual standpoint, vary very greatly. And this is quite as it should be. In this context we may do something which is also done in other depart-

---

[3] cf. Vatican II, *Unitatis redintegratio* (The Decree on Ecumenism), no. 11.

ments of human life with regard to the various areas of knowledge as they are presented to us, namely we may, with full deliberation, go out of our way to avoid this or that theological question because we instinctively feel that we cannot cope with it in the concrete circumstances of our lives. It is also possible to bring a certain subjectivity to bear in selecting certain special and preferred truths of faith to live by, and in this to allow other truths, which are just as valid and important, to recede into the background when we notice that this 'subjective attitude' is healing and liberating in its effect. A man must not in principle struggle against allowing himself to be led by God in his religious and spiritual odyssey into unforeseen depths of truth. But provided he avoids this he can, for instance, confidently live in an untroubled sureness of having been redeemed without having to endure all the darkness of anxiety about his salvation or of being lost in guilt, a state which he may perhaps already have discovered in other great Christians.

A further point which must also be taken into consideration in order to achieve a genuine understanding of this subjective hierarchy of truths is the following: the act of faith is not based upon a capacity which, being in itself neutral, is directed at will in each individual instance as it arises to one or other of the various 'objects of faith'. Rather these objects of faith are grasped in an act which in every particular instance is at basis always directed towards the single and total reality of faith which also constitutes at the same time the sustaining basis for faith as an act. *Fides quae* and *fides qua* (the content of faith and the process of the act of faith) are identical in their origins because the fundamental reality which is believed in, the self-communication of God to man, namely the Holy Spirit, is also the principle of faith itself, its sustaining force, and its active movement.[4] The act of faith is single, underived from any prior act, and in its originality always the same. It constitutes an outwards movement of the spirit towards the immediacy of God in the power of the Spirit of God moving man from within. And in the unfolding development of faith in the individual man it gradually assimilates the various 'objects of faith' and assigns them their place in this single and total movement of the spirit as it yields itself up to God in his self-disclosure. If these individual 'objects of faith' were not taken up in this single and total movement of man in God (grace) to God (eternal life), then, while it is indeed true that we might still be aware of them, that they might be either approved of or called in question etc. at the human level, still they would never constitute

[4] This identity is something in which H. de Lubac takes a special interest, primarily n his most recent work, *La foi chrétienne* (Paris, 2nd ed., 1970).

elements in faith in the true sense. This process of assimilation which faith of its very nature necessarily entails (the gradual process of being introduced to universal truth), viewed in the perspective of the particular objects in which faith as one and the single reality of faith is articulated, is in fact a process of *genuine historical development* at the collective and individual levels which never comes to an end. And this too is something of which the believer should be aware. He can experience and freely concede that the development of faith within his own personal life, regarded as a personal appropriation of the reality of faith by him as a concrete individual, is, by comparison with the development of the collective faith of the Church, less advanced. He cannot in principle deny that this personal history of his own faith has still further to go, while at the same time these further developments of it are already given to him at the collective level in the history of faith in the Church, in its theology and the history of its spirituality. If he did deny this, then this would take the form of a positive and committed rejection of the Church's dogmas. At the same time, however (*sit venia verbo*) the phylogenesis of the faith of the Church and the ontogenesis of personal faith in the individual are not simply identical. The individual believer does not need, in his primary and basic act of faith, *ipso facto* to have positively assimilated and articulated to himself everything which is objectively included in the faith of the Church. Even without this he still possesses the faith of the Church because this faith too, in and despite all its incalculably complex articulations, lives, no less than the faith of the individual, by this single basic act in which a man surrenders himself in hope and love to God as he reveals himself to him. (Here again we cannot go on to explain precisely *how*, within this basic conception of the historical process of faith, faith in *Jesus Christ*, the historical manifestation of God's triumphant turning to man, is incorporated.)

An individual form of faith of the kind we have been describing, articulating itself in a subjective hierarchy of truths, is of course present not only in each individual, but also in particular groups within the Church, in the particular Churches within the Church, at particular epochs in the Church's history, etc. But this too is something which we cannot enlarge upon any further at this point.

3. *Awareness of the Historicity of the Truth Officially Proclaimed by the Church*

A further point must be recognized: obviously the modern Christian must also have an awareness of the historical 'relativity' of the truth officially proclaimed by the Church. This is, in a true sense, relative in virtue of the conceptual models by means of which these truths are expressed. These conceptual models belong to particular epochs and are subject to change. The truth officially proclaimed by the Church has certainly a further relativity in virtue of the inevitable transformation which takes place again and again in the explosive impact of the particular truths at the individual and social levels. Not every truth has the same revolutionary force in concrete human existence or in society in every age. We are justified in recognizing a relativity in the truth officially proclaimed by the Church, and obviously this also implies an awareness of the fact that truths included in this official teaching of the Church can be obscured. A given truth is not always or necessarily assigned, or capable of being assigned, to its rightful place within the hierarchy of truths, and obviously a further factor included in this relativity which must be recognized is an awareness of the fact that this truth of the Church, even that of the Church's authorized teachers, still belongs to history, and so is itself still seeking for its own definitive consummation, and, moreover, a consummation which does not simply fall from heaven, but is obviously sustained by us ourselves in the unfolding historical development of this truth of the official teaching of the Church. It is we who may perhaps have to bring out some specific truth from the 'treasury' of the Church, dust it off, polish it, once more achieve a living understanding of it, realize it in our own concrete lives, and decide to do something more than merely to tolerate it or regard it as a matter of indifference. And to the extent that we do this, this truth of the Church, which, even while being such, never ceases to have a historical relativity, achieves its own place in history, develops, undergoes modifications, and precisely in doing so, and only in doing so, remains the same.

4. *Any absolute contradiction of dogma is false and unnecessary*

Perhaps it is only at this point that we arrive at the true and difficult outcome of our foregoing considerations. If and to the extent that a person is a Catholic Christian he cannot declare any absolute contradiction in the name of a truth which he recognizes in his own concrete personal existence to the truth officially formulated by the Church's teaching authorities. But besides this, any such absolute contradiction is quite unnecessary for him. This is, of course, the statement of a Catholic Christian. You will remember the initial point which we made, namely that precisely *as* Catholic Christians we are bound to concede that another may *subjectively* arrive at the conviction which is absolutely binding so far as we are concerned that we must declare an absolute contradiction to some doctrine of the Church. If someone is convinced that the papacy was instituted by the devil – to use a primitive example – and if this conviction is, in a true sense and so far as he is concerned, absolute within his own personal life, then obviously he has the duty and responsibility of separating himself from the Catholic Church, because otherwise, even according to Catholic teaching, he will go to hell unless he does so. This is a quite basic and obvious truth. Yet despite this, he who really believes and, moreover, is resolved to remain a believer, says that in the light of the truth and the conviction which he has grasped *for himself* in his own personal existence, he sees no necessity for declaring any absolute contradiction to a truth officially formulated as such by the Church in those cases in which it really is a dogma in the truly ecclesiastical sense that is in question. There are many people who suppose that the Church says such and such, and so gain the impression that it is simply nonsense, it is an assertion our assent to which cannot possibly be demanded, and who on this account contradict what they suppose the Church to have said. In very many cases (I do not say in every case!) such a contradiction is a contradiction not of that which the Church teaches really and in truth, but of that which we suppose to be taught by the Church. You may say: 'Jesus is God' or 'There are three persons in God'. Now among those who make such an assertion as a matter of faith and personal conviction we can assume that there are very many Christians, including even some of the Church's official representatives, who make it only at the cost of a *sacrificium intellectus*. In other words they are in reality conceiving of something which is anything but a genuinely binding doctrine of the Church, something which is simply nonsense. And when someone else then goes on to deny it, it is because he has falsely identified his own personal understanding of a dogma of this kind with the Church's official teaching, and it is this personal understanding of his that is really unacceptable.

This is something that must be taken into account when we are considering the attitude of the Catholic Christian towards the Catholic Church's official teaching of faith, and when we say that it is quite unnecessary for such a Catholic Christian to assert any absolute contradiction to the Church's official teaching. Why should he go on to make such an assertion? Ultimately speaking I do not know why so many are convinced of their own subjective opinions that they believe that they have resolutely to reject the teaching of the Church or some particular teaching of the Church. I do not know why they have so little mistrust of the capriciousness of their own subjective individualism. Nowadays even among us Westerns an attitude is already re-asserting itself which can be summed up in the axiom: the party is always right. But an attitude of this kind is certainly not identical with the attitude of the Christian towards the Church in assenting to its doctrines even when this teaching seems not immediately to be in conformity with its own subjective feelings. But this 'socialist' attitude towards life should serve to warn us of the danger of too quickly allowing our own subjective feelings and ideas to lead to a determined contradiction of a doctrine of the Church. Can we not in all honesty regard such apparent conflicts between the official teaching of the Church and our own subjectivity as provisional, as a question which does not have to be answered straightway in the present? In the eyes of a man who is self-critical and modest, must that which he fails to understand always straightway be rejected as that which is false? If he did absolutely identify himself with his own subjective feelings at any particular moment, would not such an attitude be the death of all delight in intellectual growth? Would not this be the outcome if an attitude of self-assurance of this kind became the universal law of his own thinking? At least so far as that Christian is concerned who still remains in agreement with the ultimate and basic positions of Christianity, is it not truer, and also subjectively more honest because more modest, for him from this basic position of his at least to keep himself open, despite all still unresolved conflicts, and to avoid drawing any premature conclusions? Is it not the better course for him to wait and see whether a positive solution to such conflicts is not to be found in the course of life by a maturing process applicable both to the interior man and also to his personal theology? Nowadays, however, the temptation to which we find ourselves prone is rather that of an absolute relativism in which we have a certain understanding for every possible position, regard everything as true and false at the same time, view everything as subject to a historical relativity, and therefore allow every possible position to have a certain validity. And if this is so then, after all, we should surely give the Church's teaching too at least the chance of slowly achieving intelligibility, gradually proving itself, in a genuine and true sense, capable of being assimilated. In this connection everyone should also recognize a further obligation, laid upon as a matter of truth and courage in our ordinary lives. When we find ourselves placed in a particular position by life itself we should surrender it only in favour of some better and more liberating position and never in favour of a weary scepticism, an attitude of indifference and neutrality towards all possible positions.

5. *The Ultimate Basis of Faith*

Consider further that on a radical view of the Church, however detailed may be the system of doctrines in which its faith is expressed, in reality it says very little. What it tells us is that there is an impenetrable mystery of the most real kind in our lives, namely God, and that this God is near to us; that the absolute self-communication of this God to us has been manifested in history in a manner which is irreversible and valid in Jesus and his fate. This is something that is really quite simple, yet in it we already have, fundamentally speaking, the whole of Christianity – but only provided that in addition to this you also reflect that there is, and necessarily must be, a community which confesses and lives by this truth. The community we are speaking of here is one that is sociologically constructed, an institutionalized community because that too is precisely appropriate to our human state. Once these prior assumptions are accepted, we have in a real sense already expressed the whole of Christianity. I do indeed recognize that it is still possible to set oneself up in *contradiction* to this simple basic truth and, moreover, even on the part of intelligent men. Otherwise I would have found it quite impossible to maintain the modification of my initial basic statement in the first part of this essay. But we are obliged to accept a modification of this kind as Catholic Christians, and not merely as liberal-minded men who recognize that others are no more stupid or ill-willed than ourselves. As Catholics we can, and indeed we must, whole-heartedly concede that there are men who, as a matter of their own conscience, cannot be Christians or Catholics, and therefore should not become such either. But the point that I contest is that we necessarily *must* entertain the impression that on a right understanding of the basic convictions of the Christian man, there is in them something against which we must assert an absolute contradiction. If we were compelled to assert such a contradiction, then we would no longer be Catholic Christians, and each individual would have the duty of positively deciding not to be such.

But let us try to understand the whole structure of Christianity, with all its detailed implications and explicitations, in the light of this ultimate essence of Christendom. Once we do this then, as Catholic Christians, we have no need to maintain that there is any official doctrine of the Church absolutely binding upon us against which we are compelled to assert an absolute negation as a matter of our own subjective conscience with regard to truth, and of our own intellectual honesty. For all the individual statements in the whole doctrinal structure of Catholic Christianity are capable of being read and interpreted as so many concretizations and variations of that quite simple truth which we have just pointed to as the true substance of the Christian revelation. He who posits a contradiction of *this* must of course reject the whole of Christianity and the Church. But where are the compelling grounds for such a rejection? And if we experience how freely we can live on the basis of this ultimate substance of Christianity, what reasons can we then have for allowing ourselves to be led astray by the possibility or the fact of a rejection *precisely of this kind*? To posit it would not make us more prudent, would not reduce the number of propositions which we assented to as true, would not cause us to take any less risks. On the contrary we would, in the last analysis, merely be opting for a total negation, as distinct from a total affirmation (as actually attainable in history). In order to cope with this official teaching of the Church we must precisely live by the truth which is prior to, and transcends, all verbal expression, the truth namely, of the inconceivable God, and we must live by this in participating in the fate of Jesus.

If we do this, then, it is true, we have still not achieved any full, exhaustive, or wholly comprehensible synthesis between an understanding of Catholic doctrine of this kind, and deriving from this essential attitude, and the rest of the realities by which we live in our spiritual and intellectual lives. Nevertheless, provided we accept the possibility of an existential unity of this kind with the truth which is prior to, and above, all verbal expression, that truth which, ultimately speaking, Christianity in all its propositions is seeking to express, then we can endure in hope this pluralism in our concrete personal lives which is nowadays inevitable, and can never wholly be reduced to a synthesis. Obviously in attaching ourselves to the truth of the Church we do not live in a state of utter paradisal harmony such that everything is clear, everything beautiful, and everything agreeable. Obviously this faith, in its bearing upon the personal, intellectual, and social lives of particular individuals, constitutes an element which is far from fitting immediately or smoothly into the totality of our concrete personal existence as intellectual beings. But would we be people who had achieved harmony in ourselves and in our apprehension of truth if we were not Christians, not Catholic Christians, and not individuals governed by the official teachings of our Church? We would be just as subject to pluralism, and indeed we would, to a certain extent, be men who were actually in a state of being torn asunder. Even then we would not know how really to synthesize and harmonize this pluralism within the total content of our spirit. We would still always have to advance from truth to truth through every possible kind of obscurity. We must not under-estimate our relationship to the Catholic, official, and institutionalized forms of Christianity, which also act as a standard of truth to us, in favour of some ideal state which does not exist anywhere else. And provided we avoid this, then even today we can, with complete confidence, continue to be Christians. For what has a Christian to believe? Nothing else than that the man who is a Christian precisely does *not* have the ultimate say in his own existence, but rather that all solutions, all advances in knowledge and free action, are all along already transcended by the absolute mystery, that this mystery itself wills to concern itself in some way with us, that it has addressed itself to us as the ultimate definitive word of our existence in Jesus on the Cross, the crucified and risen Lord.

If we live by this, then while the whole ideological impetus in the Church which is inevitable may still cause us pain in very many respects, we can nevertheless really entertain this hope: that our reason for grappling with this official teaching of the Church in our own personal lives and thoughts, with all the hazards it involves, is always in order that we ourselves may be liberated from our own subjective capriciousness and at the same time may make our own personal contribution to this collective awareness of faith of the Church. Even today we can be Catholics.

3

DOES THE CHURCH OFFER ANY ULTIMATE CERTAINTIES?

THE question which we are here attempting to answer within the compass of a brief article runs: Does the Church offer any ultimate certainties?

The problem is a complex and difficult one. It is in no sense a clear question, then, which we are seeking to answer. For what does the term 'Church' imply in this context? What is meant when we speak of ultimate certainties, and – assuming that any such exist at all – what can it mean to ask whether the Church can 'offer' such certainties? Questions of this kind are raised by the very meaning of the subject under investigation. And if this essential meaning is itself obscure, then obviously it is all the more difficult to find an answer to these particular questions. From this it follows that all that we can say here will remain extremely fragmentary.

One further proviso has to be made: there is a certain connection between the subject of these considerations and Hans Küng's book entitled *Unfehlbar? – eine Anfrage.*[1] Reduced to plain terms, this publication contests the defined doctrine of the First Vatican Council. In doing this, however, the book does not confine itself merely to the teaching authority of the pope, but rather refers quite in general to all propositions of faith whatsoever, whether contained in Scripture or put forward by the Councils or the teaching authority of the pope, with the intention of making an ultimately binding statement. According to the traditional doctrine such statements of the Church put forward with ultimately binding force are guaranteed to be preserved from any real error by the assistance of the Holy Spirit, even though such statements are of course historically conditioned, constantly capable of, and in need of fresh interpretation, and

[1] German publication details: Einsiedeln, 1970; English translation: *Infallible, an Inquiry* (New York, 1971).

47

always too falling short of the mystery they seek to express. Küng, however, takes up the position that while it is true that many such statements are *de facto* correct, still even statements such as these can, precisely in principle, be erroneous, and may later perhaps come to be recognized and rejected as errors.

This applies *a fortiori* to those statements which are put forward by the official doctrinal authority of the Church with a certain binding force but precisely not one that is ultimate and irrevocable. In this respect Küng clearly does not depart in his interpretation from the traditional doctrine of the Church and of the theologians. Thus it is immediately clear that our present theme for investigation has a certain connection with Küng's book, for with the publication of this book a certain question has been touched upon and has once more been rendered actual and relevant as a matter of open discussion: the question, namely, of whether there are any ultimate certainties and assurances in the Church for the believer. Nevertheless the considerations put forward in the present essay will not be concerned directly or exclusively with the positions taken up by Küng. These will be touched upon here and there as the subject-matter itself demands. But our theme for investigation is conceived of in broader terms, and intended to have a more radical meaning, for it to be regarded merely as a crossing of swords with Küng's thesis. Küng himself appears to be convinced of the fact that the Holy Spirit, by the power of his grace, constantly preserves the Church in truth even though this state of being preserved bears primarily and properly upon a truth which ultimately speaking lies behind any of those truths which are expressed in propositional form. Moreover the men of today are inclined to doubt even this ultimate assurance, which Küng himself upholds. And to the extent that this is true it is obvious that we both can and should conceive of our present theme in far broader and more fundamental terms.

In putting the question of whether the Church can offer any ultimate assurances and certainties to the believer we must begin by recognizing that the question itself has many different levels of meaning. Ultimate certainty – what does that really mean? There is a certain basic state or basic attitude (or whatever name we may choose to give to the reality referred to) that is wholly subjected to human freedom and decision: the attitude, namely of an ultimate trust in the meaningfulness of human existence, in the possibility of a full, all-embracing, and definitive salvation (as theologians are accustomed to expressing it). There are individual propositions, consisting of human concepts and words, which are put forward with the claim of being real and true – true and assured beyond any shadow of doubt, and so offering ultimate certainties. If therefore it is asked whether the Church can offer the believer any ultimate certainties this question is *ipso facto* and in itself ambiguous. For what is it that is being asked? Is it whether and how the Church can offer the believer that attitude of an ultimate calm and assured basic trust in existence and leading to the hope of salvation, or is it an enquiry into specific individual propositions as taught by the Church which as such are intended to offer ultimate certainties? The question is all the more complicated inasmuch as, obviously, that attitude of basic and ultimate trust on the one hand, and these propositional truths which can be conceived of on the other hand, are not simply two entities immediately juxtaposed to one another, but rather mutually condition one another each in its own way, even though the certainty of basic trust and the certainty of propositional truths are not identical with one another. A further distinction has to be drawn, turning the question with which we are concerned in these considerations into a twofold question. For on the one hand we may be asking whether the Church offers the believer ultimate certainties to the extent that he already is such, while on the other we may be asking whether the Church guarantees ultimate certainties to him who seeks to assent to her as the guardian of salvation and truth. For manifestly it means something different for me to ask myself what kind of certainty I can have in accepting the Church and her teaching authority from asking myself what kind of certainties the teaching authority of the Church offers me, assuming that I have already in principle accepted the validity of this teaching authority. Although it is necessary to draw this distinction it itself in turn raises special difficulties because the realities just distinguished from one another are at the same time very closely connected with one another in a way that is difficult to describe.

Assuming the validity of the distinctions we have just drawn within the basic question as such we may now go on to state the following:

First, that radical and all-embracing attitude of basic trust in the meaning of existence, the ultimate hope of salvation referred to above, is not something which can, in any strict or proper sense, be sustained by the authority of the Church or, in that sense, 'ecclesiastical'. Obviously an individual who already stands within the community of believers will find this ultimate and basic attitude of trust easier, and in this sense he does also have an ecclesiastical element, if we like to put it so, entering into the concrete circumstances of his life. But this does not alter the fact that in principle this ultimate and basic trust is both logically and psychologically prior to belief in the authority of the Church, and is rather that which sustains, than that which is sustained by, this belief in the teaching authority of the Church. Because this ultimate and basic trust, to which of course other names can be given (ultimate freedom from anxiety, ultimate readiness to believe etc.), embraces and sustains all things, and so too the specifically Christian faith, its contents, and therefore a convinced acceptance of the teaching authority of the Church as well, all assurances and certainties offered to man by this authority of the Church are from the outset incapable of being any surer or more certain than this basic attitude of trust itself. Indeed all assurances and certainties in the life of the Church actually bear within themselves the special quality of this basic attitude of trust on which, in all cases, they themselves are based. But there are two points to be made about this basic attitude of trust. First, as we shall have to explain in greater detail later, it is the most sure and most certain factor, and second that it is at the same time the factor involving the greatest exercise of freedom, that which is made subject to man's own responsibility, that which is constantly threatened, under attack by the ultimate temptation to a radical scepticism and cynicism, a temptation which can gain the upper hand even in one whose life seems to outward appearances to be very normal and governed by moral principle. It is necessary to recognize and understand this special quality of the ultimate and basic attitude of trust; to realize that it imprints its special character upon all else, and so too upon our faith in the teaching authority of the Church. And once we do recognize this it becomes obvious that even as Christians and members of the Church we should not in any sense expect her to hand down to us assurances and certainties such as would simply free us from our burdens or simply and in every respect be obvious and indubitable. No such assurances and certainties are to be found within the Church, because no such assurances and certainties can ever exist in human life at all. For even in the ultimate depths of his existence man is constantly assailed by temptations, constantly called upon to decide between light and darkness. The ultimate clarity and sureness of his own existence is bestowed upon him only in the ultimate and basic movements of his own heart, at a level at which it is no longer possible to distinguish between speculative reason and freedom. At this level, rather, either faculty conditions the other. If we understand the specifically ecclesiastical factors in the thought and action of a Christian we shall realize that it in no sense has the effect of freeing him from the task, the burden, and the secret blessedness of seizing upon the ultimate certainty only in an ultimate self-commitment in love and trust, of realizing that the first and last light that he is given is a reality indwelling the attitude of trusting freedom itself, and cannot be borrowed from any other source. In the light of this it will become clear that the ultimate surenesses and certainties even of a Christian, and, moreover, even according to Christian doctrine itself, are far from being so specifically ecclesiastical as we are all too easily prone to insinuate in an incautious apologetic on behalf of the Church and its significance for man. Augustine is quite wrong when he says that he would not believe the gospel if he had not been prompted to do so by the authority of the Church. We should understand the term 'gospel' here as signifying the liberating power of the Spirit of God, who bestows upon us this ultimate trust in existence to combat all ultimate mistrust and all despairing *angst*. And if we do take the term in this sense, then this statement of Augustine is certainly incorrect. It is the attitude of ultimate trust that sustains the authority of the Church, and not *vice versa,* even though it is easier for one who belongs to the community of believers to have this ultimate and basic attitude of trust, and even though the experience of the possibility of this ultimate and basic attitude of trust is constantly bestowed upon us Christians afresh in our encounter with all the realities which are imparted to us as Christians through the Church.

We now come to a fresh aspect of our general considerations, once we recognize that this basic attitude of trust sustaining all else, including the Church and her authority, is in fact in all cases achieved in the ultimate basis of our freedom, which is unexpressed and never fully reflected upon at the conscious level. It is only in this ultimate basis of our freedom that the ultimate and most primordial light of truth burns, though at the same time this is always imparted through the medium of an objectified knowledge expressed in propositional form. We cannot in the present context treat of the difficult problem of what the propositions are in which this objectifying knowledge of man can and must be expressed so as to give objective form to this basic attitude of trust on man's part, an attitude in which reason and freedom are one, and in which man finds his ultimate reference to God. Here we shall confine ourselves to making two points: first that such propositions do not necessarily have to have an explicitly metaphysical or religious content. On the contrary, man can achieve this basic and primordial attitude of trust and objectify it to himself in propositions which seem purely secular in character and to belong wholly to this world, provided only that he radically commits himself in his freedom through the medium of these propositions. The second point, however, is that explicitly metaphysical and religious propositions, in which the word of God etc. are expressly applied, are not an unnecessary luxury nor even a mere inevitable stage in that inescapable process by which man comes consciously to reflect upon his ultimate and basic attitudes. On the contrary, for the concrete individual in a concrete situation such specifically religious propositions constitute, under certain circumstances, the necessary medium, obligatory so far as he is concerned, for his basic decisions such that without them as medium in a given concrete situation this particular individual is quite incapable of really achieving that ultimate and basic decision of his freedom without which he would be actually denying this basic decision, thereby incurring his own damnation. To put the matter simply: there are individuals who take their decision for God in the context of their secular everyday life without this decision of their's having anything to do with the word of God explicitly or as a matter of their own conscious objectification. At the same time, however, there are men who, in the course of their personal lives, encounter personal statements about God of a kind which they can really understand. And an individual such as this cannot truly leave this word of God out of account in arriving at his ultimate basic decision. There is – to speak once more in wholly general terms – a kind of consciously objectifying human knowledge which is expressed in terms which present the reality signified as object, and which shares in the special quality of the basic decision of man. In other words it participates in his ultimate sureness and certainty and in the temptations by which these are assailed in virtue of his human freedom. Let us take, for instance, someone who says that we must accord absolute respect to our fellow men in their dignity, and who in making this statement understands what it really means, making it without reserve despite all its questionableness and lack of ultimate precision, which he himself may recognize. Such a one makes his statement with that ultimate sureness, the outcome of a freedom which is exposed to assault, which belongs intrinsically to the attitude of ultimate trust in existence. There are many such statements which share in the nature of this ultimate sureness. Obviously they differ very much among themselves, and so too have very different ways of sharing in the sureness of the free act of basic trust which is under assault – that attitude of trust in which reason and freedom and the divine grace that liberates constitute a unity. We cannot here set forth statements of this kind in all their multiplicity, their various qualities, and their varying connections with this ultimate arch-certainty. But when we say that such statements, in the sureness and certainty belonging to them, draw their life from this ultimate trust in the meaningfulness of existence, this is the most basic statement concerning the original relationship between these two entities. At the same time, however, this assertion is obviously not intended to gainsay the fact that conversely the free acceptance of this basic attitude of trust also in some respects itself draws its life from these statements which give expression to it. For one who assents to such statements and experiences their truth in those concrete ways in which they are proved capable of supporting life in the personal life of a concrete individual and within a concrete society will manifestly also find it easier to achieve that basic attitude of trust from which these statements truly draw their living force. But there is one further point of primary importance to be made about statements of this kind which derive their living certainty from this heart and centre of free human living: such statements may perfectly well have as their content elements of concrete human history. They can perfectly well relate to concrete realities in the personal life of an individual, to which in the end, at least in principle, the whole history of humanity belongs. For instance the statement that this or that man has in his own individual life a quality of absolute reliability, even though in theory we cannot absolutely rely upon any individual man, or the statement that this or that life which is of radical moral significance, and of which we have had living experience, cannot simply have been swallowed up in empty nothingness – these and similar statements have a content which is subject to the contingency of history, and yet at the same time draw their living force from that ultimate attitude of basic trust, and so share in the certainty and sureness belonging to it, and throw light upon this attitude of basic trust itself as constituting its concrete objectification.

We are speaking, then, of statements which on the one hand have an historical content, and on the other derive their living force from this ultimate and freely posited basic attitude of trust in the absolute meaning of existence, an attitude brought about by grace. At the same time these same statements give objective form to this attitude. Now for Christians statements about Jesus Christ the crucified and risen Lord as the absolute mediator of salvation are to be numbered among statements of this kind. There is no need for us here to enlarge upon these statements in respect of their content in any more precise detail. But in the message which they convey the believer, from his place in history, is enabled in the concrete to grasp that absolute and irrevocable self-utterance of God to which he assents with hope, albeit without consciously explicitating this in that attitude of ultimate and basic trust which is sustained by grace. What we encounter here in the experience of the believer is a relationship of mutual interplay and influence between the two entities, and to that extent in the last analysis a circular process – that ultimate attitude of basic trust sustained by grace and breaking in upon the freedom of God which we call the grace of faith constitutes the enabling condition for recognizing Christ with real faith as the ultimate bringer of salvation, as the manifestation and guarantee in history of God's irrevocable act in turning to man. Conversely the experience of Jesus for the believer as Christian constitutes a living experience within his own personal history in which he finds the courage to accept in freedom this ultimate basic trust through the grace that is offered him. There is, then, a relationship between the historical experience of Jesus on the one hand and the achievement of the ultimate attitude of free and basic trust on the other such that each mutually conditions the other. Nevertheless the two factors involved in this relationship differ slightly in the manner in which each sustains an element of the other. For without entering into any more profound justification of the differences involved in this relationship of mutual conditioning, a Catholic theologian must make two points: first, that an ultimate and salvific acceptance of the basic attitude of trust offered by God's grace can be present in an individual even without any explicit reference to Jesus Christ, and second that we have to hold firmly to the position that it is impossible to have any real faith in Jesus in history without this grace of faith. It is in fact nothing else than precisely this basic attitude of trust, brought about by grace, of which we have just spoken that liberates man and opens the immediacy of God to him, regardless of whether he formulates this explicitly to himself or achieves it only at an implicit level.

But abstracting from this point, we can in all confidence arrive at the following conclusion: for the Christian there is an ultimate unity, consisting in a mutually conditioning relationship, between his experience of Jesus as the crucified and risen Lord who gives him the courage freely to accept the meaning of existence on the one hand, and that ultimate and radical basic attitude of trust in the meaning of existence which, in the full development of its nature, explicates itself in faith, hope, and love. At the same time, however, in this mutually conditioning relationship between the two elements, the second element, namely the attitude of basic trust in the meaning of existence, retains an ultimate priority for the Christian over the experience of the historical Jesus. And because of this, without denying in this matter that there is such a mutually conditioning relationship, we can, even with regard to the Christian, conclude the following: the believer's experience of Jesus Christ is in its sureness and certainty upheld by that ultimate basic attitude of trust in its sureness and certainty, even though, because it is free, it is also liable to the assaults of temptation. One who despairs in an ultimate manner, denying any absolute meaning of existence and failing freely to maintain hope for himself, cannot recognize Jesus either as him who by dying entered into the life of God and so as the final and definitive self-utterance of God to man in history. From this it obviously follows *ipso facto* that from the basic statements of Christianity about Jesus Christ we cannot truly expect any other certainty or sureness than that which is inherent in that ultimate basic attitude of trust: in other words a certainty that is always liable to the assaults of temptation, always to be achieved afresh in freedom and responsibility, one which is not simply given to us beforehand as an achieved reality, but is always too the free act of our own lives, which we ourselves sustain and only so are sustained by it. Indeed, from the points we have already indicated above we can as Christians and Catholics even go so far as to concede freely and confidently that the sureness and certainty relating to Jesus is in a certain respect a sureness that is more derived, more threatened, more fragile than the sureness of this basic attitude of trust in itself. While this is, as we have said, correct only in a certain respect, still it is something which we should freely recognize because ultimately speaking it imparts to belief in Jesus Christ a greater sureness and a greater facility than if we were falsely to claim for this faith that it possessed this certainty as an ultimate and intrinsic factor within itself such as no historically contingent fact can ever have. There are in fact countless individuals who find their salvation through Christ, and thereby in a true sense, through his grace and the hope arising from it, have arrived at the historical manifestation of salvation, even though at the level of their conscious and verbal objectification they know nothing of him or even suppose, at this level, that they have to reject him because even this situation can prevail without any fault on their part. But after all that has been said the fact still remains that there is an historical experience in faith of the historical Jesus as the absolute bringer of salvation, and this experience of faith is – at least *sensu positivo* – upheld and defined by the sureness and certainty attending upon this ultimate and grace-given basic attitude of trus t.

We can now proceed a step further in our approach to the question of whether the Church itself can offer the Christian any ultimate certainties. First we must recognize that faith in Jesus Christ as the absolute bringer of salvation, as the ultimate messenger of God's self-utterance to the world from within the world is something which henceforward can never disappear. And this quality of indestructibility in such faith is itself an element in the content of this faith. If the believer failed to understand the content of his faith as enduring finally and definitively in the world in this sense he could not recognize Jesus as the final and definitive Word of God's self-utterance to the world. Alternatively he would have to reckon with the fact that God has once more radically turned away from the world. Faith asserts its own indestructibility as faith in Christ and in the world and mankind in general, even though obviously the individual believer cannot assert that his own personal faith as entertained in the openness of his own life of personal freedom possesses the same quality of indestructibility. Faith as faith in Christ, in the manifestation of the grace of God imposing itself victoriously, involves faith in its own indestructibility in the world as a whole, not as the autonomous achievement of man but as the deed of God's grace which can impose itself within the freedom of man without suppressing it. Christ himself has promised that it will do this, so that faith in Jesus itself participates in the victoriousness of God's grace, which has been addressed to the world in Jesus.

If this is the case, then faith in Jesus Christ also implies faith in the survival of a community of faith gathered about Jesus Christ, which exercises, sustains, and bears witness to this indestructible faith in Jesus Christ. It is true that we cannot say that this community of faith called the Church always has a membership which is increasing in relation to the total number of mankind within the world, that it always has among the nations and within the world that social status which we experience it as having. All this and much else of a similar kind we cannot know, because the Church in history has, and necessarily must have, a future that opens upon the unknown. But that the community of faith gathered about Jesus will not cease throughout history, that Jesus, therefore, will always be acknowledged – these are points that belong to the very content of Christian faith, and which have, even though in a sense that is derived and exposed to danger, that sureness, certainty and liability to assault which shares in the ultimate and basic attitude of trust, a sureness and certainty which belong to Christian faith in general. To the extent that the individual believer shares in the faith of the Church as such, and draws his life force from this community of faith, albeit only as sustained by that basic attitude of trust brought about by grace, we can by all means go on to say also that the sureness and certainty of his Christian faith in general and in the indestructibility of the faith of the Church and therefore of the Church herself, receives a supplementary element from the Church herself even though this does not gainsay the fact that this faith too is ultimately sustained in this part of its content by that basic attitude of trust, the innermost certainty of which we are accustomed to call the grace of faith.

Let us go a step further: faith in the indestructibility of the Church's faith, in the fact that she will abide in the truth of Christ, implies a faith in the fact that there are propositions in which, taken individually, this faith of the Church is articulated, and which at the same time share in the indestructibility of this faith. Christian faith means faith in Jesus Christ expressed in a historical mode and having a historical reference to Jesus Christ over and above the reference to him achieved through grace. Now it is quite impossible for this faith to exist otherwise than as expressed in propositions. For while it may be true that a historical connection with an earlier historical event need not be expressed solely and exclusively through propositions expressing historical tradition, still a connection of this kind can never in any case be established without such propositions. The indestructibility, the historical permanence of faith in Jesus Christ implies that certain propositions about him will endure permanently too, and of course this applies to true propositions, for erroneous ones as such cannot cause faith in him to endure permanently in any true sense. The certain and sure faith in the abidingness of Jesus Christ, of faith in him, and so too in the community of faith belonging to him, implies the abidingness of true propositions about him, and of course also about those realities (such as God etc.) without which Jesus himself cannot in any sense be understood and expressed. Faith in the indestructible permanence of faith and of the community of faith necessarily constitutes faith in the fact that the truth as expressed in propositions about Jesus Christ in the community of faith, the Church, is not destroyed. In this connection it is obvious that the Church must at least recognize certain propositions as belonging to the true and indestructible propositions constitutive of her own faith – that in other words it is impossible for the Church, while having such propositions, to be herself totally incapable of recognizing them as such in the individual concrete case. A point on which there cannot in fact be any doubt is that the Church is convinced that she actually knows of such true and indestructible propositions as such. At least it can be said that the most fundamental assertions about Jesus Christ as the Lord, the bringer of salvation, the unsurpassable presence of God with us, are propositions of this kind, which the Church recognizes as constitutive of her faith and declares to be true and ever-abiding propositions. These assertions are in ecclesiastical parlance called infallible and inerrant propositions. Propositions of this kind the Church expresses as objectifications of her own ultimate Christian basic understanding, and of her basic attitude of trust as brought about in her by the Spirit. She expresses them as belonging to her faith, as sharing in the certainty and sureness with which she asserts her faith in general and as a whole, and she therefore assents to them with an irrevocable commitment of faith. To the extent that the Church believes in and proclaims such propositions as, in the sense described, infallible, she extends to those Christians who have united themselves with, and inserted themselves into the Church's understanding of faith as one and whole, ultimate certainties and surenesses with regard to these propositions in the sense previously ascribed to these terms, 'certainty' and 'sureness'. In this connection, however, two points, arising from the very nature of what has been said, have to be noticed: first, as applied to a specific proposition, this sureness deriving from the authority of the Church's own explicit faith taken as a whole can obviously be applied only to one who has in principle accepted in faith the abidingness of the Church in the truth of Christ, and that abidingness too which is communicated in propositional form. As we have already previously pointed out, this certainty which belongs to the acceptance of the Church herself as a whole comes to the individual believer in the Church primarily and in principle not properly speaking from the Church but from the experience of the Spirit and the encounter with Christ in the basic attitude of trust as brought about by the Spirit. This pre-Christian (if we may so express it) certainty upholds the certainty with regard to the Church in general, and thereby *a fortiori* that which relates to the individual propositions taught by the Church and not *e converso*. At the same time, however, the point we have previously made remains true, that namely concerning the mutually conditioning relationship which exists between the basic attitude of trust as brought about by the Spirit on the one hand, and the individual's membership of the Church on the other. There is now a second and further point to be noticed: the formal sureness belonging to a specific proposition taught by the Church (when the Church believes and teaches it with an absolute commitment), and from this communicated to the believer within the Church, does not simply replace that interior and, to a certain extent, material sureness which an individual Christian can have with regard to a particular proposition of this kind when he succeeds in arriving at and realizing for himself the intrinsic connection which exists between his basic attitude of trust as brought about by the Spirit, his grace-given basic Christianity, the ultimate basic statements of the Christian faith on the one hand, and on the other the specific individual proposition at the more derived level which the Church herself teaches. If an individual Christian in the concrete given case does not succeed in arriving at this intrinsic connection, then he will generally be permitted to leave an individual derived proposition of this kind respectfully alone, or to some extent to regard it as a remote goal to be attained in the development of his own personal history of faith, which is still in process of achievement. At the same time, however, he must obviously not on this account *ipso facto* deny or reject the proposition concerned on the grounds that he himself cannot, or cannot as yet, arrive at it or recognize how it is derived from the original wellsprings of faith which he has attained to.

Before we go on to what is, properly speaking, a fresh and further step in our considerations, one further supplementary explanation remains to be added for a right understanding of what has just been said. An individual man lives not only by ultimate basic convictions which he recognizes as absolutely and permanently binding with an ultimate certainty so far as he is concerned. An individual man, rather, has at the same time many recognized points, convictions, opinions, norms of behaviour, which he regards as right and valid for him here and now. No one can live solely on the basis of ultimate basic convictions assented to as final and definitive. In the concrete decisions taken in human life it is impossible to eliminate from the outset opinions which are merely provisional, conditional, and capable of being revised. It is not only the absolute truths, but also provisional opinions that sustain life and personal development. The former give history its continuity, while the latter give it its movement and its openness to a future still unknown. Indeed the situation is far from being such that we can, in the concrete, press our conscious reflections upon these two kinds of propositions and the difference between them so far that we can in all cases and in concrete detail draw the precise line of distinction between the two kinds of propositions. It can even be the case within an individual man that in the course of the personal development of his own individual recognition of truth a specific proposition which formerly appeared to him as a mere provisional opinion now comes to be recognized and accepted by this same individual as a statement of absolute validity. Now what applies to the individual's life with regard to his quest for truth inevitably applies in a similar sense too to the Church in her conscious awareness of her own faith. She does not live out her Christian faith solely by those propositions which she herself has already recognized at the fully conscious level as belonging absolutely and irreformably to her awareness of her faith. In her life of faith in the concrete she also inevitably and necessarily has propositions which are merely provisional, which, under certain circumstances will later come to be recognized as erroneous. She does not even have any explicit, sure, and unequivocal awareness right from the outset in every case as to whether a specific proposition which she firmly holds and teaches belongs to the class of infallible propositions or to the class of theological opinions and provisional interpretations of her faith. Theology, therefore, draws an obvious distinction between propositions of the Church which are 'dogmas' and others which, while under certain circumstances they are indeed taught with a certain authority and binding force so far as the individual is concerned by the Church, for the protection of dogma in the true sense and for its application in practical life, are not claimed by the Church on this account to be adhered to by the individual with an absolute commitment of faith such as is appropriate to dogma properly so called. A certain respect is due even to propositions of this kind, which are taught by the Church yet which are, in principle, reformable and possibly erroneous. The situation is similar to that of a man who follows the advice of a learned and conscientious doctor acting according to his best lights. This too, under certain circumstances, must be considered a matter of duty, even while recognizing that such medical advice is not infallible and may be rendered out of date by advances in medical knowledge or by a still more detailed examination. The Church has *de facto* very often made mistakes in the past in propositions of this kind. And obviously even though with the best will in the world it is quite unavoidable, this makes a Christian's life of faith difficult to the extent that such individual erroneous propositions may have very notable consequences for his practical life, while at the same time erroneous sentences of this kind may come so to be amalgamated with dogmas in the true sense that they can cause considerable difficulty too in giving the assent of faith to such dogmas. (Unfortunately it is not possible here actually to adduce examples of this.)

We can now advance yet a further step. We have made a number of points with regard to the truth and sureness of specific propositions included in the Church's awareness of her faith and as such imparting sureness and certainty to the faith of the individual Christian in the Church. These points must now be given further precision by a process of reflecting upon the structure of the Church herself. The Church is not solely and exclusively the sum total of those who, by their faith in Jesus Christ, are *de facto* gathered about him. It has actively to bear witness to this faith, and is in this respect a social entity capable of acting positively. In the present context there is one question which we do not need to decide: whether this social unity, organized structure, and constitution of the Church as witness to the truth of Christ flows solely and necessarily from the very nature of Christian faith itself, or whether it constitutes a supplementary property of this community of faith called the Church. In any case it belongs to the conviction of faith, at least of the Catholic Church, that she constitutes a socially structured unity and, moreover, precisely to the extent that she remains abidingly in the truth of Christ and cannot depart from it. Furthermore she remains in that truth as expressed in propositional form. In other words (viewing the matter from the opposite side) she achieves her state of abiding in the truth and also standing by true propositions through her socially structured constitution and so, to put it in more concrete terms, through her established officials. That social constitution which is inevitable for any community – in other words its established officialdom – is, according to Catholic faith, related as an element in the Church not merely to the external social factors in the life of such a believing society but also to its true and proper nature, to its faith as such. The authority vested in officials in the Church, therefore, is also a teaching authority or *magisterium*, through which the Church's conscious faith realizes its own true nature more and more explicitly and clearly and becomes active in bearing witness to its faith within and without. This teaching authority of the officials in the Church is, it is true, itself upheld by the Spirit and through the activity of God, which preserves not merely those vested with official authority but also and primarily the believers, whether authorized officials or not, in faith in Jesus Christ. This teaching authority of the established officials of the Church can take effect in the lives of the individual believers, and give rise to specific doctrinal propositions in support of this certainty and sureness only if and to the extent that the Church and the teaching authority of the Church make affirmation to these individuals in a decision the sureness and certainty of which derive not from the Church as such but from the sureness and certainty of that ultimate attitude of basic trust, of the Spirit, of the experience of Jesus Christ of which we have already spoken. But assuming this affirmation to have been made, and also unreservedly accepted and applied in concrete Christian practical living, it must be said that according to Catholic faith in the Church there is a genuine teaching authority of the Church's officialdom as concretized in the pope and the college of bishops considered as a unity. Under certain circumstances which we cannot develop in any greater detail here this officialdom can actually teach a specific proposition as infallible, as dogma to be held and maintained by the Church with an absolute commitment of faith. When such a dogma is defined or is capable of being defined (whether it be by the ordinary or extraordinary *magisterium* of the Church) the individual Christian has a duty to give his assent of faith as already defined in greater detail above. Thereby he also acquires the sureness and certainty that by assenting to such a proposition he is not departing from the truth of Christ. To this extent and in this sense the Church can also offer ultimate surenesses and certainties in virtue of her teaching authority even though on a precise view such certainties are not primary but rather derived, and even though these certainties are obviously liable to those assaults, that state of subordination to the free decision of the conscience which we ourselves must have recognized in our very first and most primary human surenesses and certainties. With these provisos (and a few others which still have to be explained in greater detail at a later stage) we can say that there are ultimate certainties with regard to the dogmatic propositions of the Church and that too as proceeding from her official teaching authority.

We have stated that in her propositions of faith promulgated by her official teaching authority the Church offers the believer an ultimate sureness and certainty. To this statement certain further essential precisions must now be added. We must reiterate once more what we have already said: the sureness of the Church, to the extent that it is intended to be a sureness for the conscience of the individual, is sustained by that sureness with which the Church and her teaching authority are assented to by the believing conscience of the individual without reliance upon the teaching authority of the Church itself; that the assimilation of an individual dogmatic proposition by an individual believer, while involving an acknowledgement of the Church's teaching authority, can take place in very different ways (ways which obviously are continually liable to converge, blend, or pass into one another); these ways of assimilating a specific dogmatic proposition may range from an attitude of leaving the proposition concerned unexplored and accepting it merely on the authority of the Church to an innermost understanding of it proceeding from the heart and centre of the individual's own Christianity as a personal living force; that even the understanding of such dogmatic propositions can be obscured and rendered more difficult in the individual and even for the Church as a whole at a specific point in time by unconsciously amalgamating the dogmatic proposition concerned with other theological opinions which are reformable, capable of error, and far from belonging intrinsically to the dogma itself. So far from this being the case, in fact, there is still more to be said, over and above this, on these dogmatic propositions and the sureness and certainty guaranteed for them by the Church's official teaching authority. Even propositions such as these, ultimately binding and valid as they are, and having an ultimate sureness in them, are always expressed in terms which are conditioned by history from the standpoint of ideas which are historically conditioned and subject to change. The mode of their formulation is embedded in human awareness, which is itself subject to historical change and does not share in the special force of these propositions themselves. Even dogmatic propositions are analogous in character, i.e. they never give full or adequate expression to the reality signified. They view that which is signified from certain quite specific points of view, selecting these, whether consciously or, more often, unconsciously, from a whole range of other aspects which are in themselves also possible but *de facto* neglected. Such expressions are always, or almost always, bound up with a special parlance or style which is preferred, whether consciously or unconsciously, for the purpose of achieving a common agreement in the Church and a common language to be used by the teaching authorities of the Church even though one and the same dogma might be expressed in a different parlance. In view of the special qualities we have mentioned as belonging to a dogmatic proposition, we may even go so far as freely to concede that it is far from easy for the individual Christian and theologian to recognize clearly and unambiguously where he should draw the line between a proposition which though true is subject to these special limitations and historical conditions, and an erroneous proposition which, however, may depart from the truth only very slightly. And a further point which may also freely be conceded bears upon the awareness of an individual as influenced by his own subjective conditions and the way he comes to recognize the element of untruth (from a Christian point of view) underlying a given mode of expression, and constituting the *fons et origo* of it. He may find it easier to grasp this in a proposition which the teaching authority of the Church declares to be erroneous, or at least as unacceptable by the standards of its own mode of parlance, than in a proposition which is guaranteed to be true by the Church's doctrinal authority. The infallibility of a proposition promulgated by the teaching authority of the Church does not imply that this may not be replaced at some point in the future within the total development of the Church's awareness of her faith by another and better formulation, more easily assimilable to the men of the epoch concerned. Such a thing has often taken place in the past history of dogma, and obviously this history has not yet come to an end even today. Advances in it will be achieved only if Christians and theologians, when confronted with such particular dogmatic propositions, make known their conclusions or their feelings as to how a particular dogmatic proposition has proved inadequate or is capable of revision once it is viewed from the intellectual standpoints proper to these Christians and theologians. Dogma, even in its most ultimate and binding form, is open to the future. That which is truly signified in a given dogmatic proposition is open to a further course of development in terms of truth in the Church's awareness of her faith, even after it has been defined. And this course of development extends outwards into a future which it is quite impossible to calculate. In the light of this let us consider, then, a situation in which one man holds that, with the reservations and due distinctions mentioned above, a dogmatic proposition is certainly true and incapable of retrospective revision, and another who regards such a proposition as possibly erroneous while still acknowledging that the Church herself abides in the truth. It would almost be possible to say that judged in the light of our foregoing observations the disagreement between these two amounts to little more than an argument over words, because neither side can define precisely enough where the boundary is to be drawn in such propositions between one that is erroneous and one which all Catholic theologians would concede to be inadequate and capable of subsequent reform. But the very raising of such a question necessarily leads to the raising of a counter-question which will be found difficult to answer. It springs from the fact that some theologians who are, and who intend to remain, Christians, and so who give their absolute assent to the basic substance of Christianity, nevertheless run counter to the teaching of the Church, or at least to her authorized mode of parlance (for after all this too has its importance) in regarding it as possible for her dogmatic propositions to be erroneous. Now in the light of what has been said why should this be so? For after all what they are seeking to assert amounts to no more than what is in fact and in material substance already said by the Church's own theology, even when translated into normal terminology. Those who believe that a formulation such as that propagated by Küng is clearer and more honest must allow a further question to be put to them: when they feel that they must disavow as erroneous propositions which are genuinely dogmatic and not merely theological and subject to revision, is not this a way of avoiding the necessity of having to interpret earlier dogmatic formulations, constantly having to translate them into fresh terms, except on condition of being allowed totally to disregard any continuity in the process of expressing the faith in propositional form, as though the substance of Christianity in its concrete historical mode was something totally outside the statements contained in the New Testament and in the official proclamations of the Church? Unless we took this as our prior assumption we would be able to achieve all that Küng is concerned with in real terms without adopting his thesis of the possibility of error in each and every statement of Scripture, of the Councils, or of the ordinary and extraordinary *magisterium* of the bishops and the pope.

4

ON THE CONCEPT OF INFALLIBILITY IN CATHOLIC THEOLOGY

THE title of this essay is deliberately, and without any false modesty, intended to cover *some* aspects bearing upon the concept of infallibility in Catholic ecclesiology.[1] Some aspects only will be treated of, if only because, for lack of competence, it is no part of my purpose to bring the concept of infallibility in Catholic ecclesiology into confrontation with similar concepts to be found in the history of religion, in philosophy, or in other disciplines. Equally it is no part of my purpose here to give an exposition of the traditional Catholic official teaching on the infallibility of the Church's teaching office. This doctrine taken as a whole can be assumed to be already known. So far as *our* consideration is concerned, therefore, the fact that the pope *and* the whole episcopate are to be accounted the subject of this doctrinal infallibility represents a secondary element in the content of this doctrine. It is taken as given that these two entities possess this charisma of infallibility only under quite specific conditions; that the charisma itself bears only upon the content of Christian revelation in the interpreting and upholding of it, and does not conduce to any increase of it. On the other hand what we mean is the dogma of infallibility in its traditional sense, in which it actually refers to the truth of the *individual* defined proposition as such, and so not *merely* in that sense in which, for instance, H. Küng and W. Kasper seem to interpret it, namely that the indestructibility and infallibility of the Church's faith bears ultimately speaking merely upon the abiding union

---

[1] This paper was composed for the conference held at Rome from the 5th to the 10th January 1970 on the occasion of the centenary of the dogma of infallibility, and for inclusion in the Symposium, 'L'Infaillibilité. Son Aspect philosophique et théologique'. On the same subject cf. W. Kasper, *Dogma unter dem Wort Gottes* (Mainz, 1965); *idem, Glaube und Geschichte* (Mainz, 1970); Y. Congar, 'Infaillibilité et indéfectibilité', *Ministères et communion ecclésiale* (Paris, 1971), pp. 141–165.

of the Church with her Lord taken as a single whole, so that even in 'definitions' errors in individual cases can occur again and again, and can exist temporarily. Here, therefore, only a few observations remain to be made, in which a Catholic theologian makes a tentative attempt, without any claims to a systematic treatment, at putting forward ideas concerning that which he has received, believes, presents, and defends as the doctrine of his Church, and of which he now seeks to achieve a better understanding. In this connection it must be recognized that the doctrine itself has a special function of its own, and we must begin by gaining some initial insight into this, realizing that such an approach constitutes a stage in the process of achieving our goal and arriving at a deeper understanding of this doctrine.

At this stage, however, there is only one point to be made by way of introduction. If we take the dogma of infallibility or the claim to doctrinal authority which it entails in isolation, then obviously it appears as though by it a process of arriving at new knowledge were being arbitrarily cut short at a certain point by the intervention of an authority external to itself, and as though thereby specific areas of the believer's convictions were being unlawfully immunized against that critique which belongs to the very essence of human knowledge, especially as achieved through an historical development. It seems too as though this privileged knowledge likewise implied according a social pre-eminence to an individual (because infallibility is subjected in a person), and as though the Church were in consequence ultimately speaking a totalitarian system, on the grounds that the Church (from being initially a system based on faith, and from this becoming a reality at the sociological level) is capable of being definitively fixed and frozen at any time by an individual element within this system. Now let us, with all brevity, indicate a few points bearing on this.

First, a point that must not be overlooked is that, as distinct from the state, the Church is a *free* believing community, which we belong to only as a matter of our own free decision. Even if it were in fact an authoritarian or totalitarian structure, it would still only affect him who freely accepts it. But from the very outset it is surely difficult to describe any such system as 'totalitarian'.

On any existential-ontological approach it could be shown as a matter of *general principle* that an *absolute* assent to a proposition and an abiding attitude of criticism with regard to it are not mutually exclusive. This also applies to a dogmatic declaration arrived at on the basis of infallibility, the more so since every defined dogma is objectively open to further development, and even the law of infallibility is (as we shall have to discuss further at a later stage) not self-authenticating, and so is incapable of being immunized by its own nature against critical enquiry.

With regard to a Church endowed with an official doctrinal *magisterium* of this kind it is obvious that the only kind of conviction which a believer in such a Church can have without viewing it as an authoritarian and totalitarian system is *that particular* conviction which involves belief in the assistance of the Spirit precisely at *this particular* point. Once we view the doctrinal laws involved in the constitution of the Church in isolation from *this particular* belief, it does indeed become in fact totalitarian, because within the dimension of her juridical and constitutional life as such she does not possess any absolute guard against the *possibility* of misusing her teaching authority in a totalitarian way. Yet the situation here is analogous to that of Christ Jesus the Lord. The Christian believes in him as the absolute mediator of salvation despite the historical dimension belonging to him. In the same way too, in an attitude of hope which is essentially eschatological, and which springs from his faith, he believes that the Church will *de facto* never fall victim to that danger which is really immanent in her very constitution. For this hope the sole final and definitive ground is simply Jesus Christ. Obviously in appealing in this way to Jesus Christ as the true and ultimate ground of faith, we are not in any sense pretending that the problems of speculative epistemology and sociological epistemology are *ipso facto* to be regarded as disposed of. On the contrary, even with this appeal to Jesus Christ they still remain. This applies, for instance, to the obvious question of whether this basis of faith does not merely lead us to assent to the content of faith as a whole as infallible, that is precisely to Jesus Christ, but also guarantees the infallibility of the individual defined proposition as such. And it also applies to the further question arising from this of how, in what sense, and in what manner this takes place. But these are questions which cannot be treated of at present. Yet motives can be pointed to which make it easier for the believer to have this hope nowadays, because the dogma of infallibility itself has a history of development of its own, which renders it in a certain sense less endangered and less 'dangerous' than formerly. And it is upon this history that we must concentrate here.

I. THE HISTORICITY OF THE DOGMA OF INFALLIBILITY

What does it mean for our understanding of the Catholic dogma of infallibility – this is the first question which we must pose – if we recognize that element of historicity present in every human recognition of truth as applicable to this dogma too? In posing this question and attempting to find an answer to it we cannot develop the whole range of problems involved, and the whole meaning of, the *general* proposition of the historicity inherent in all human truth. We are therefore indeed aware of the lack of clarity in the prior assumptions involved in our own question. But we believe that even so we can gain from it certain useful insights into the dogma of infallibility. This is not to dispute the fact that in so far as our particular question is concerned we could achieve far better insights if we could presuppose a more detailed general theory of the historicity of truth.

The Dogma of Infallibility as an Historical Proposition

The Catholic theologian must begin by frankly and explicitly taking cognizance of the fact that the declaration of infallibility is a proposition which has a history and will have a further one, a history which bears both upon the existence of the explicit proposition itself and also upon its content, though this is not *ipso facto* or necessarily to deny the abiding identity of these within that history.

First and foremost the *dogma* of infallibility, as applied to the *pope*, is, regarded as an explicit proposition of faith, a datum of relatively late date. And even if we say that the infallibility of the Church as a whole in her faith, in scripture, in the councils, has been a conviction of the Church right from the first, this still does not make any difference to the point we have just made. This is not only because this *later* conviction in turn has an historical beginning, but also because of a further point over and above this: the *earlier* understanding of the infallibility of the Church related less strongly, less explicitly than today, to the infallible correctness of a *new* decision to be arrived at afresh on a question of truth under dispute. In earlier times it related rather to the possession of the reality of salvation in the Church as handed down and possessed in faith, and in this sense 'ancient', as something already given and abiding within her. And even if we say that the ancient councils too did, after all, arrive at certain decisions and formulated fresh propositions in fresh terms, we must still point out that they did this not with an awareness of having achieved anything fresh or creative within history, but rather with the awareness of merely formulating the ancient content of faith in different terms, and almost while denying that through this fresh formulation anything new had taken place with regard to the recognition of truth itself. So clearly was this taken for granted as a self-evident fact that almost down to the *present* day the officially authorized theology denied that there was any '*objective*' development in the history of dogma.

This official position, into which we cannot enter in any greater detail at this point, does in any case show that one position is far from self-evident, namely an understanding of the fact that a doctrinal decision by council or pope is an *event* of truth or itself involves a history of truth. It shows that when the Vatican definition of infallibility was arrived at it did not entail any conscious awareness of the fact that this involved an acknowledgement of the historicity of truth; that the only way in which we can come to recognize the possibility of an infallible new decision about the ancient truth is if we ascribe an historical dimension to this (ancient) truth itself. For a fresh definition of this kind is precisely more than merely a formulation in different terms of an unchangeable proposition which remains quite unaltered by the new formulation itself.

There is a further point to be made about the two possible ways o understanding the infallibility of the Church in faith and doctrine. There may indeed be a necessary connection between them, and, moreover, precisely when we consider two points: first we should realize that the inalienable possession of the reality of salvation as a truth that is believed in precisely demands, in view of the historicity of man and his knowledge, a constant fresh appropriation of this reality of salvation in the form of a decision. Second we must not forget that even the modern, juridical, and actualizing interpretation of infallibility does not imply any absolutely assured knowledge of some kind of reality and truth which is quite new to us, but rather has guaranteed nothing else than that we shall abide in the ancient truth.

The two interpretations mentioned above are, nevertheless, still different from one another, and the development of the second from the first itself in turn demonstrates the historicity of the dogma of infallibility, even if we regard it as bearing upon the Church as a whole and not merely upon the pope in particular. This history, however, is not merely a history inasmuch as the explicit declaration on infallibility has not always existed with the character of a *juridical* obligation of faith. What we are speaking of, rather, is a history of the actual *meaningful content* of this proposition in itself. This meaning which it has has itself not always been in existence because it was not conceived of. The meaning which it has could not formerly take effect as it has taken effect, and continues to do so, *since* its formulation. This meaning appears again and again from ever fresh standpoints and under fresh aspects. The elements of meaning inherent in it are themselves incapable of being fully or adequately defined once and for all. And so that which is consciously apprehended in these elements undergoes a constant and unending process of change. In a word: the *meaning* of a dogma of this kind has itself a history, and one that is obviously never concluded.

This historicity of the dogma of infallibility appears for instance in the fact that in its definition a hundred years ago no one consciously adverted to the fact that the exercise of an infallible teaching authority is determined not merely by the *subject* in whom that authority is vested and the *content* which the declaration is designed to convey, but also by the 'situation' in which the addressee of the declaration is involved, the modes of expression available to those promulgating it which are always restricted, the more immediate historical context (rejection of a heresy etc.), the predominant interests of the time (which can never fully be brought under control) with their special outlooks and limitations etc. These and much else besides are factors which do not appear explicitly in the declaration promulgated at a given point in time, and so serve to demonstrate the historicity of the declaration itself. In fact this proposition has, since 1870 (the point in history at which it appeared), *already undergone* a further history, though this is something into which we shall enter only in a second section and from a different point of view. But before this there is yet another question to be raised.

Is it Possible to Have 'New' Dogmas in the Future?

Can an *approaching* section of this history of the declaration of infallibility (together with the reality to which it points) already be indicated or estimated here and now to some extent by 'futurological' methods? It may *perhaps* be possible to supply a small part of the answer to this question: In the foreseeable future there will be no further really new definitions.[2]

[2] I am conscious of the fact that in drawing a distinction (applying to some extent to the content too) between 'new' dogmas and those which merely repeat a former dogma, a distinction, that is to say, which will be repeatedly used in what follows, we are properly speaking being too hasty in assuming that a solution to a fairly difficult problem has been found, and our arguments in support of this are too sketchy. This is not only because there cannot be any absolutely new dogmas, since even those which are 'new' must have been present from the outset in some sense in the background of faith which has existed all along from apostolic times. A further reason is that any precise classification of dogmas from this questionable point of view is a problem in itself, and one which cannot be solved here. But for all this the distinction we have in mind does have its validity. If the pope were to define that Mary is the

The situation lying before us in the future makes it impossible for the Church's teaching authority to produce any further infallible definitions in the manner in which it was conceived to do so *formerly*. At the time of the First Vatican Council the anti-infallibilists waged an utterly distorted polemic, in which they supposed that a fresh papal definition would be recorded every day in the 'Times'. Not only these, however, but Catholic theologians too entertained the idea that the infallible teaching authority of the pope is (a) a kind of habitual power *of such a kind* that this power would be meaningless if it were not exercised from time to time and so actually gave demonstrations of its necessity, and (b) that this teaching authority, in the decisions it arrived at, led to a continual process of the formation of constant *new* individual propositions distinct from one another, so that the original revelation would be progressively unfolded and explicitated in these in a continuous 'process of development' resulting in a quantitative increase in the number of defined, and yet in some sense new, propositions.

Now the idea that the teaching authority will remain active in the (conceivable) future in producing definitions in *this* sense is one that we can hardly accept. For instance after the dogma of the assumption of Mary into heaven (1950) many theologians supposed that the exercise of the definitorial power of the Church's teaching authority would develop further in the same direction. They were already looking forward to new conceivable statements in Mariology which might be defined. Today no one any longer thinks of such a thing. Nothing was defined at the Second Vatican Council. Today a pluralism exists in regional cultures, philosophies, terminologies, outlooks, theologies, and so on which can no longer be fully reduced to any one synthesis, and so vividly has the Church become aware of this that I can no longer imagine that any specific, and

---

'Queen of the world' (or even merely 'the Mother of the Church') then such a dogma would certainly be 'more new' (even though pious people may already have entertained some such ideas) than if the pope were to define that the resurrection of Jesus is not *only* an event which takes place within the individual subjectivity of the believer. Here we shall not be prolonging the discussion of how this distinction might be defined in more precise terms at the speculative level. It is possible to say for our present purposes that when we speak of dogma as 'new' in this sense we mean one that will surprise even the Christian believer in its newness, though he has entertained a lively belief in the substance of the faith as hitherto believed in (it would surprise him at least as a dogma). But dogma of the other kind would not surprise him at all. We might also say that 'new' dogma will be felt as in some sense additional, whereas the other kind will be regarded merely as defensive in character and not as 'increasing' the former stock of faith.

at the same time genuinely *new* proposition can so be expressed that it can be felt throughout to be an expression of the conscious faith of the whole Church, and so be capable of definition.[3]

To this a further point might be added. Every genuinely new definition, which does not merely repeat or defend an earlier one, requires for its formulation *one and the same* theology (with the stock of ideas, lines of reasoning etc., belonging to this), and moreover a theology accepted as that of the *whole* Church herself. This uniformity in theology, which was formerly to be found underlying all the differences between the schools, no longer exists today, and moreover can no longer fully be restored (at least in the foreseeable future). New definitions ('new' in the sense not only of a new approach but also of a new, i.e. expanded, meaning such as is conveyed by 'new' definitions) would have as their prior condition that lack of sophistication which fails to advert to the conditioning factors in history affecting any given language or standpoint, and the indeterminacy of the particular concepts employed etc., without actually denying that such factors are present. Properly speaking we should make use of con-

---

[3] When we say that despite the unity of the creed there is a pluralism of theologies in the Church which can no longer be eliminated in any adequate sense this statement is of course of fundamental importance in the present context, and should therefore be developed and justified in greater detail. This is not possible here. I may therefore refer to my article, 'Pluralism in Theology and the Unity of the Creed in the Church', *Concilium* 5 (1969). But in order to realise the consequences following from this pluralism for our present question we have only to consider that dogma too is always formulated by means of and in terms of a theology, yet that for this purpose it is impossible to choose one theology among many which are in principle equally justified, seeing that a pluralism in theology is now in force. It might be said that in a new definition all that we do is simply and precisely to achieve a fresh grasp of the common and universally acknowledged stock of ideas etc. present in the previous proclamation of faith and the previously formulated dogma, which must in fact be respected by all theologies. But in saying this we are merely expressing in somewhat more veiled form the fact that we do not formulate any 'new' dogmas, but simply repeat the old ones (chiefly to guard against distortions of them). These distinctions are of course fluid and tend to pass into one another, so that no detailed prophecies can be entered into with regard to the more precise boundaries between old and reiterated dogmas and 'new' dogmas. It is of course also conceivable that one particular major individual Church within the universal Church gains control over a general theology which is understood and used chiefly in the subordinate Church in such a way that this subordinate Church could express a point that was binding in faith in terms of this common theology. On this basis it would be conceivable to regard the teaching office of a 'bishops' conference' as of more 'value' than we have been accustomed to think in the last thousand years. On pluralism in theology cf. also K. Rahner,"Pluralism in Theology and the Unity of the Creed in the Church", Theological Investigations, XI, (London & New York 1974) pp. 3–23

crete examples such as can easily be found in contemporary theology in order to clarify our meaning. But unfortunately this is not possible here, although in the second section we shall be approaching the same material factors from the other side, and in somewhat more concrete terms.

We have arrived at a state, then, in which the possibility of any really *new* definitions being produced by the Church's teaching authority is at an 'end'. And it is now that the historicity of the dogma of infallibility is manifested at its most acute. But this means neither that from now on the dogma hitherto defined will retrospectively dissolve, nor that the infallible teaching office in the future will no longer have any function of its own.

The reason that past dogma does not retrospectively disappear is that it no longer has the *same* history in the future as it has had in the past. In order to understand this two points must be borne in mind:

(a) Man remains, even today, the historical being *par excellence*. In his faculty of memory, that is to say (regarding this as providing him with a critical standpoint[4] from which to judge his present in order to create his future) he emerges from his own past.

(b) This Christian *memoria*, which also embraces and expresses the totality of this past as pregnant of the future and as providing a critique of the future (although not as dominating the future) and of the content of it, is something very simple, which is *prior* to all future pluralism in conscious thought, namely this: that the ineffable mystery of our existence which we call God has victoriously addressed itself to us in Jesus, the dead and definitively delivered Lord, so as to communicate itself to us and to be our absolute future. Because all previous Christian dogma merely expresses this, it will be able to abide, and will abide, even though it no longer develops in its former manner in the 'development' of further distinctions within it.[5] This does not mean that it will become frozen or petrified, because the process of reducing the dogma handed down, and still abidingly valid, to this true and indissoluble reality of Jesus as the

[4] On this cf. J. B. Metz, ' "Politische Theologie" in der Diskussion', *StdZ* 184 (1969), pp. 289–308, and esp. 296ff.

[5] This is only to apply to the history of dogma the objections which J. B. Metz has formulated in more general terms against an 'evolutive' and ultimately speaking uncreative conceptual model for history (partly against Teilhard de Chardin). The difference between this and the more general objection against a false understanding of history consists in our case, however, in the fact that here we have to consider that in any eschatologically correct understanding of the 'once and for all-ness' of the event of Christ the rejection of a process of explicitation and evolution which continues endlessly into the future achieves concrete form in the manner which we have attempted to indicate. The fact that this does not mean that dogma is cut off from history as that which is dead or frozen has been (or will be), it is hoped, clear enough.

historical and irrevocable self-utterance of God is something that has to be achieved ever anew, and it is this that renders this dogma living and implies an ever-fresh and unforeseeable history for it.

Furthermore the function of the infallible teaching office of the Church does not cease with the end of its history as understood in the sense of producing definitions which are in a true sense 'new'. The solemn delimitation of the ancient body of dogma to protect it against interpretations which would eliminate it is still even today an abiding task of the infallible teaching office of the Church. On the contrary in this connection it will still be able to appeal directly, and in a more enlightening way than in any possible 'new' definitions, to the conscious faith of the Church as a whole. Its function, certainly in itself distinct and autonomous, will thus in a certain sense become a more modest one than was envisaged in earlier times, since it will be brought into alignment with the totality of the Church's conscious faith.

II. THE DEVELOPMENT OF THE DOGMA OF INFALLIBILITY SINCE 1870

We can view the historicity of the dogma of infallibility and the reality signified in it from yet another point of view. During the First Vatican Council the opponents of this dogma had the impression – as non- Catholic opponents still have to this day – that with this dogma the Church, and above all the pope, were being given a sort of blank cheque such as no critical conscience in relation to truth could ever give, seeing that it has a responsibility either to give or to withhold its assent in any given case according to the content of the particular proposition involved. Here we have no intention of repeating the reply which the traditional school theology is accustomed to give to this serious consideration: the reply, namely, that this infallibility constitutes merely the gnoseological aspect of the indestructibility of the believing Church, which itself in turn is the outcome of the unique and eschatologically victorious event of Christ; that in their decisions Church and pope are bound by scripture and tradition, and by the previous decisions of the Church; and that we must not overlook that factor which we call the assistance of the Spirit. Our intention, rather, is to draw attention to an historical process which *has already* had its effect upon this dogma of infallibility in the developing history of the concrete situation in which it stands, a historical process which also, in a very empirical way, rules out (or at least reduces to a notable extent) the danger of that 'blank cheque', so that it is possible to say, to a certain extent that this dogma has, in the last hundred years, already passed through its danger zone, in which, according to human estimation, that danger signified by the term 'blank cheque' has been at its most acute. In order to understand what is meant several factors have to be weighed in the balance. We must probe somewhat deeper and also not shrink from developing further incipient points which have already been mentioned in the course of our arguments in Section I. For it is obvious that the history of the dogma of infallibility which we have to foresee for the future, and that history which has already run its course since 1870, are intrinsically connected with one another, and ultimately either have emerged or are emerging from the same basis.

The Dogma of Infallibility Within the Totality of the Truths of Faith

So far as logic is concerned as a factor in Catholic theology, the declaration of infallibility is a strange one. Abstracting from the fact that as a consciously explicated proposition it has not always been in existence, we can arrive at the following conclusion: it is a proposition which, if it is assumed to be and accepted as valid, renders the *other* dogmatic propositions infallibly sure. It itself, however, can in itself not be sure in *that* manner which applies to those propositions which are guaranteed by it to be infallibly true. We say that a decision taken by the teaching authority of the pope in defining a specific dogma is, under certain specific conditions, infallibly correct. And this is something which it can guarantee, given the necessary subjective and objective conditions, with regard to all other propositions. The only proposition to which this does not apply is that concerning the infallibility of this doctrinal authority itself. The dogma of the First Vatican Council is different from all other dogmatic propositions in that it cannot itself in turn be based upon the infallibility of the pope. And if we say that it invokes the infallibility of a council, or that of the Church, then we are merely shifting the problem a stage further back, for even this proposition can be arrived at only on the basis of other propositions which we already believe in. And our belief in these is not itself in turn based on the validity of the proposition of infallibility. The dogma of infallibility is one individual proposition immanent within a system, and not the foundation of the system itself. The system of the Christian and Catholic truths of faith taken as a whole, and the subjective acceptance of this, are not based upon the statement of infallibility. On the contrary this is objectively and subjectively sustained by the system. From this basis its function is confined to that of a relatively secondary checking-point within the system applicable to secondary cases of conflict, and in this it depends upon the system itself as its prior condition and does not itself call this in question in any direct sense. From this point of view it would be possible to say that this dogma is not itself infallible (i.e. not sustained by the infallible authority of the Church *quoad nos*), but merely renders other propositions infallible.

We shall not pursue the logical peculiarities of this state of affairs taken in itself any further at this point. But from what we have just said, namely that this proposition can render all other propositions infallible so far as we are concerned, itself only being excluded, we can conclude the following: this proposition is an application of the purely formal principle that that which provides a basis cannot be the basis of itself. Now taking this principle as correct, we must go on to give further precision and clearer lines of demarcation to the proposition as such. The declaration of infallibility can be accepted only if the 'system' (i.e. the real factors and the revealed truths which provide the basis of Christianity) is itself grasped and accepted without any *logical* appeal properly so called to the declaration of infallibility as such. (The question of whether, as a matter of concrete human *psychology* a certain mutually conditioning relationship can nevertheless prevail does not affect the point we are making here.) This means that logically speaking one has to be a believing Christian even before, and 'without' *ipso facto* having to believe in the infallibility of the pope (or the Church, or a council). It means further that the sureness entailed in the expectation that the pope or a council will not produce any false definitions cannot be greater, and subjectively speaking must not be greater, than the sureness with which the dogma of infallibility, without being based on itself, has come to be recognized. (Admittedly this is a statement about the sureness in terms of fundamental theology, and not about that of faith as such. But this latter sureness neither suppresses nor increases the former one.)

This secondary function of the dogma of infallibility, taken as a proposition which is rather sustained than sustaining itself, also makes it possible to ascribe a greater degree of historicity to it than applies to the basic dogmas of Christianity. This appears not merely from the circumstance already mentioned, that this dogma is far from having always been present in the explicit conscious faith of the Church, but chiefly from that history which it has already undergone since its initial proclamation, a historicity which we must gradually proceed to make still clearer. But even before this: if the dogma of infallibility is a proposition which is ultimately sustained by something outside itself rather than one which

sustains the system as a whole, then it immediately acquires another subjective 'value' in its significance for a specific subject in that this subject
achieves a relationship to the 'system' as a whole which is in some respects different. Formerly the situation could be, and generally was, such
(and this is something which is shown by the internal controversies
between the Christian confessions) that the system itself, the (general)
basic substance of Christianity, did not represent any special problem for
human life in the concrete. Then, rather, the question was simply whether,
for instance, a specific individual dogma such as that of infallibility did in
fact belong to that system. Today the situation, differing in this from that
of the First Vatican Council, is quite otherwise. Even for Catholics it is a
question of the single whole directly and explicitly as such demanding the
ultimate decision of the subject.

From this point of view alone the dogma of infallibility has a different
value to the subject from that which it formerly had. It is by no means so
'vital' as in the times of a Pius IX simply because the radical question of
whether and how we can be Christians at all nowadays absorbs the (always finite) attention and concentration involved in a radical decision of
conscience. Admittedly anyone who has been able positively to arrive at
this decision, *and at the same time* in doing so understands it from the
point of view of the modern mentality (as contrasted with an individualistic liberalism of an earlier stamp) will once more return to a position in
which he finds it easier to accept the ecclesiastical factor in faith – and that
too as applied to the concrete Church – than it might perhaps have
appeared to an individual of the nineteenth century. Admittedly precisely
an individual of this modern type has a right to achieve an understanding
of why and how he must not betray the heritage bequeathed to him from
the earlier liberalism, a freedom of faith and a spirit of critical enquiry, a
heritage which he too will defend in a 'socialistic' society, and which also
raises a question for the Church with regard to the dogma of infallibility.

Teaching Authority as Having an Authorized Language

Every exercise of an infallible teaching authority involves, whether consciously or unconsciously, the use of an authorized language as one of its
intrinsic elements. One reason for this is that this authority is addressed
to a believing community and is intended to formulate the common
creed of that community, indeed derives from and is upheld by the common faith of the Church as a whole. In other words it has, right from the
outset and of its very nature, a sociological side; here at any rate truth and

society are involved with one another. But there is a further reason apart from this. An element of authorized terminology is involved in the exercise of teaching authority, because the very nature of the reality being taught is such that it is *incapable* of being expressed otherwise than in inadequate and analogous concepts. Now in relation to the truth being expressed in a proposition analogous concepts differ from univocal ones, which can be strictly defined and verified by directly empirical methods, in that substitute concepts are available which do not necessarily do violence to the truth of propositions capable of being expressed in several different ways, but remain unexpressed, or at any rate are not expressed in *that particular* way in which the defined proposition is – indeed perhaps even *should not* be expressed precisely in *that* way. Concepts such as person, nature, sin, and original sin, transubstantiation, eternity, glorification of the body, infallibility itself and so on are, as analogous, themselves necessarily not fully determined as concepts, so that a proposition in the opposite sense is not necessarily false provided that it is not intended merely as a formal contradiction or negation of the alternative proposition, but rather is taken as a proposition which itself is intended to make a positive statement.

The proposition, for instance, that there is such a thing as original sin, and the proposition that there is not any such thing as original sin can of course not both be true at the same time so long as the one is taken merely as a denial of the other. But it can be the case that each is understood as having a positive content of its own through which one expresses that which the other leaves open, must leave open, yet itself fails to express because of the analogous nature of the concepts used in it. And if this is the situation, then both propositions can be correct. The meaning of the statement 'There is no such thing as original sin' would then be: 'There is no state of guilt in God's sight of that kind which is incurred solely through man's inalienable personal decision taken in freedom.' From the point of view of dogmatics this statement is perfectly correct. It could just as well be the subject of a definition as the statement: 'There is such a thing as original sin.' In this *latter* case it would still remain a constant task and duty for theology to explain the fact that despite the non-existence of an 'original sin' (in the sense just mentioned) there is nevertheless an 'inherited guilt' (inherited deficiency, a collective situation conditioned by guilt). But this theological explanation would not be expressed in the form of a definition.

In this case, as properly speaking in all others in which concepts are used analogously, the reality signified is expressed in such a way that one aspect is brought into the forefront as a matter of conscious faith and doctrine, while the other, which would have explicated the merely 'analogous' aspects of the concept, remains in the background. And the fact that the reality is expressed in this way, and that there is a positive directive that it should be so expressed, brings out one factor which is purely the outcome of historical conditions: a particular authorized language or mode of parlance. On a precise view it must be recognized that one inevitable and essential element in the infallible teaching authority of the Church is the right to prefer one mode of parlance, which in itself might have taken a different form, to others in a believing community and a community bound together by a common doctrine. But this does not mean that the question of truth is *ipso facto* being unequivocally affected.[6] In the last few decades a clearer awareness of this fact has been achieved (as a result of a more explicit recognition of the analogous nature of dogmatic concepts, this in turn being due to the work of historians of dogma on the history of such concepts and the recognition of the inevitable pluralism in theology which prevails today etc.). And this in itself has the force of ushering in a new epoch in the history of the dogma of infallibility since the First Vatican Council.

On the Character of New Dogmatic Formulae

But this is not all. Within the last hundred years we have arrived at a situation in which a new definition can no longer be false because in any such new definition the *legitimate* range of interpretation is so wide that it no longer leaves any room for error outside it. A question which we may leave open at this point is whether the impossibility we have declared to exist is capable of absolute proof at the theoretical level, or merely a

---

[6] An authorized mode of parlance of this kind does not of course imply that theology should merely repeat propositions as thus regulated (in the style of leading arguments in the journals of totalitarian systems). Theology must in fact explain such propositions, enquire critically into their meaning, and make men explicitly aware of the merely analogous and historically conditioned elements in these propositions. Theology must even, under certain circumstances, offer formulations to the Church's conscious faith which are designed to replace the former authorized modes of parlance and gradually eliminate them from the linguistic usage of the Church (whether tacitly or as a matter of official declaration). (We may think of the way which leads from the Council of Ephesus to that of Chalcedon or of that leading from Augustine to the condemnation of Baianism and Jansenism). But on this account such authorized modes of parlance do nevertheless remain officially in force and run counter to such fresh formulations, amounting at least to a theoretical schism (which is then sometimes too hastily regarded as 'heresy'.)

practical one. But in order not to misunderstand from the outset the possibility of holding the thesis we have set forth two points have to be noticed:

(1) Any fresh dogmas which might possibly be conceived of would still in any case continue to relate to the former ones as remaining in force. A pope who altogether failed to recognize this fact in his new definition, and ran counter in it to earlier definitions, would show himself to be a heretic who had lost his doctrinal authority. This in itself is enough to show that the range of any possible dogmas has become very restricted in certain essential respects precisely *because* hitherto we have had a relatively great 'development of dogma'. This factor, therefore, so far from being an argument in favour of a further prolongation of the same kind of development actually points to the contrary. Any new definitions that are put forward (whether at the practical or the theoretical level) can only be put forward as interpretations and as upholding 'earlier' dogmas in which we already believe, which themselves in turn are and remain the norm of interpretation. If it is maintained that any conceivable 'new' dogma nowadays inevitably entails so wide a range of possible interpretations that it is no longer in any sense possible for it to be false, this still does not mean that on this showing it will necessarily be devoid of content or tautological, or that it must be in every respect and manner no longer capable of verification. For it remains, or would remain, related to those basic facts of the Christian faith which constitute the content and (on a right understanding) the verifiability of such theologically formulated propositions of faith. But must they then seek to say more than these basic facts? Can they draw upon the basic understanding of the teaching authority of the Church to say anything more at all, seeing that all that this contains is the revelation that has been 'closed'? In this abiding reference to the basic facts of the faith they have a content which is capable of being clarified by a 'fresh' dogma of this kind, and which perhaps *needs* to be expressed more clearly in the specific situation, even though the new dogmatic formula in itself cannot be counterbalanced by any compelling alternative to the contrary (unless one that amounts to a sheer denial of the basic facts of the faith) in comparison with which it must necessarily be either false or true, even though, in other words, the range of possible interpretations to be placed upon it is in itself so great that it is no longer possible for any proposition to be formulated which can be put forward with the claim of being correct, *and at the same time* such that it necessarily eliminates the 'new' dogmatic formulae absolutely (abstracting from the question of an authorized mode of parlance).

(2) This situation, in which a 'new' dogmatic formula is no longer

capable of being false, is not simply a mere abiding quality present all along in any declaration on the part of the teaching authority of the Church, but is rather a circumstance which has *come to prevail* in history. Let us take one example. It concerns the relationship between God and the world and the concrete possibilities of understanding this and interpreting it in the Church's conscious awareness of her faith in the concrete. Formerly the only way in which it was possible to define this *basic* relationship was in terms of 'difference'. It was necessary to entertain the conviction that in this the decisive point, and in fact one which was straightway comprehensible, had been stated (as in a definition, for instance, such as that found in DS 3023). This statement remains true, but *nowadays* it is inevitably made in the awareness that a process of interpretation is needed which can never be brought to an end. And if today it were to be defined (as a statement with a positive content of its own, and not as the mere empty negation of the definition given above) that God had taken to himself an identity with the world, then this would not necessarily imply (over and above the introduction of a new authorized mode of parlance) any elimination of that other definition, because this too would be arrived at in the awareness that in this case 'identity' is an analogous concept which is subject to the same process of interpretation which is never concluded as the concept of 'difference'. And it is precisely this that would apply if a definition such as that in DS 3023 were arrived at today in its turn as 'new'. The awareness that a process of interpretation is in principle incapable of conclusion, the awareness that all metaphysical and theological statements are limited, is, at least so far as a sociologically *effective* awareness of faith in the Church is concerned, an event which has only manifested itself, or even is only gradually doing so, within the last hundred years. This awareness makes any 'new' ecclesiastical definition, if it were to be arrived at, *ipso facto* 'old' from the outset. In other words even as it is formulated it is confronted with such a number of possible or conceivable interpretations that it does not signify any real 'advance' in clarification as compared with former statements of faith (except for introducing a certain perfectly reasonable and respectable authorized parlance and a new reference to the basic historical experiences and basic historical realities of Christianity). And, as we have already pointed out, this does not mean that the function of the teaching office of the Church or the meaning of the earlier dogmas are eliminated or destroyed.

(3) Now it might be objected that what we have said does indeed apply to that particular 'category' of dogmas in which it is sought to express a 'transcendent' (in the popular sense) or 'metaphysical' reality (e.g. the

Trinity, the hypostatic union etc.), in which the analogous character of the concepts employed is particularly clear. But there is a quite different 'category' of propositions of faith, to which all that we have said does not apply. And here we may refer above all to propositions of moral theology. Why, for instance, could the pope not define his moral theological teaching, such as that contained in '*Humanae Vitae*', without thereby so broadening the range of possible variations and interpretations open to us that it would no longer be possible to find any contrary proposition to it which could be regarded as an error? For our present purposes we must set aside the question of the (logical) 'categories' of propositions of faith even though it is in itself important and has nowhere been radically thought out. But in any such investigation it would emerge that the difference between propositions in moral theology which were apparently signed and sealed and concretely verifiable in their meaning on the one hand, and other 'metaphysical' propositions of faith on the other, is not so great or so clear as we might at first be inclined to suppose. For even propositions in moral theology of the kind we are thinking of must be, and are intended to be, propositions of faith. They imply a relation to God, and only achieve their true nature when our acceptance of them is accompanied by a realization of the relationship they bear to the absolute mystery. They are never *merely* norms of the natural law. Even as such they themselves in turn have their place in the unfolding history of truth. The concrete reality which they are designed to embody in the form of concrete imperatives is a dynamic one. It is in process of change, and leaves the question open of whether these propositions in their concrete formulation do not themselves presuppose a concrete dimension of reality which is no longer present, or is in process of disappearing, or the further question of whether as norms defining the *goal* to be aimed at they do not presuppose a reality which has still to emerge in the future. For these and many other reasons they are, at least today, never of such a nature that they cannot be interpreted in many different ways. And since in the case of many of the reasons for such a pluralism of interpretations (above all those belonging to the spheres of sociology, psychology etc.) it is impossible to achieve any full or adequate awareness of them, such a pluralism is not altogether to be excluded even in the case of formulations belonging to moral theology.

Furthermore the following three points about the teaching office of the church cannot be merely accidental:

(a) There are many questions of moral theology which are important for human living in the concrete, yet on which the Church has never taken up any firm position, and so one which would materially speaking be of the highest importance and would serve to clear away controversies.

(b) In cases in which it has taught (though not defined) doctrine, it has often used concepts which, without the fact being noticed by it itself, never signified any unambiguously concrete reality at all (e.g. civic freedom, private property, revolution etc.), though as a matter of moral practice it has absolutely arrived at these realities.

(c) That the teaching office of the Church has hardly ever produced definitions on such questions (not even at the Second Vatican Council or in '*Humanae Vitae*').

With regard to the objection with which we are here concerned, therefore, we can confidently reply with the counter-question of where concrete examples are to be found for propositions belonging to the sphere of moral theology in which a definition is conceivable precisely as *new* which creates a lack of ambiguity such as had not been present formerly.

At the conclusion of these few remarks one anecdote may be added. About eighteen months ago I met a young Catholic priest in Scandinavia, and together with other Christians (the rest being Protestants) I fell into a theological discussion with him. My impression was that the priest had a fairly broad theological conscience. When I put the question to him in a certain context of how this fitted in with the dogma of the First Vatican Council he replied: 'Oh, that is something which we in the Catholic Church must gradually forget.' We neither will nor should forget it! But it has a history of its own. It has already been having it throughout the last hundred years, and will continue to have it in the future. And why not? Identity survives through change. The reality that exists in personal life and in the Church is as mysterious as this. We can in fact not even express the dogma of the Incarnation of the eternal Logos without doing justice to this paradox if we want to avoid distorting one or another aspect of this christological dogma.[7]

[7] cf. K. Rahner, 'On the Theology of the Incarnation', *Theological Investigations* IV (London and Baltimore, 1966), pp. 105–120.

5

THE DISPUTE CONCERNING THE CHURCH'S TEACHING OFFICE

On the Problem of Non-Infallible Doctrinal Decisions on the Part of the Church

In 1967, in the course of what may be accounted an initial period following upon the Second Vatican Council, the German bishops undertook to produce a document in which they attempted to apply the claims of the Council to the special circumstances of the German Church. It is not our intention here to examine this document in its entirety. We shall confine ourselves rather to a few observations on a single brief passage in the document, and, moreover, from the standpoint of a particular episode of which we shall shortly have to speak in more detail.

The Document of the German Bishops

In order to avoid imposing upon the reader the wearisome task of having to search out the text referred to for himself,[1] let us repeat the relevant section of the document here:

'17. At this point a difficult problem arises, calling for realistic discussion. It is one which today more than formerly threatens either the faith of many Catholics or their attitude of free and unreserved trust towards the teaching authorities of the Church. We refer to the fact that in the exercise of its official function this teaching authority of the Church can, and on occasion actually does, fall into errors. The fact that such a thing is possible is something of which the Church has always been aware and which she has actually expressed in her theology. Moreover she has

---

[1] The text was published by the Secretariat of the Conference of German Bishops in the autumn of 1967 as a semi-private document and disseminated at diocesan level. Hence it is relatively difficult to achieve access to it. cf. *Herder-Korrespondenz* 21 (1967), col. 549.

evolved rules of conduct to cater for the kind of situations which arise from this. This possibility of error refers not to those statements of doctrine which are proclaimed as propositions to be embraced with the absolute assent of faith, whether by a solemn definition on the part of the Pope, a general council, or by the exercise of the ordinary *magisterium*. Historically speaking it is also incorrect to maintain that any error has subsequently arisen in such dogmas as proclaimed by the Church. This is of course not to dispute the fact that even in the case of such a dogma, while we must uphold its original meaning, it is always possible and always necessary for a development in our understanding of it to take place, involving a progressive elimination of any misinterpretations which may perhaps have been attached to it hitherto. Nor should we confuse the question which we have raised here with the manifest fact that side by side with the immutable divine law there is also a human law in the Church which is subject to change. Changes in this latter have from the outset nothing to do with error. At most they raise the question of how far some juridical decision in the remote or recent past was opportune.

'18. Now let us consider the possibility or the fact of error in non-defined statements of doctrine on the part of the Church, recognizing that these themselves in turn may differ very widely among themselves in their degree of binding force. The first point to be recognized resolutely and realistically is that human life, even at a wholly general level, must always be lived "by doing one's best according to one's lights" and by recognized principles which, while at the theoretical level they cannot be recognized as absolutely certain, nevertheless command our respect in the "here and now" as valid norms of thinking and acting because in the existing circumstances they are the best that can be found. This is something that everyone recognizes from the concrete experience of his own life. Every doctor in his diagnoses, every statesman in the political judgements he arrives at on particular situations and the decisions he bases on these, is aware of this fact. The Church too in her doctrine and practice cannot always and in every case allow herself to be caught in the dilemma of either arriving at a doctrinal decision which is ultimately binding or simply being silent and leaving everything to the free opinion of the individual. In order to maintain the true and ultimate substance of faith she must, even at the risk of error in points of detail, give expression to doctrinal directives which have a certain degree of binding force and yet, since they are not *de fide* definitions, involve a certain element of the provisional even to the point of being capable of including error. Otherwise it would be quite impossible for her to preach or interpret her faith as a decisive force in real life or to apply it to each new situation in human life as it arises. In such a case the position of the individual Christian in regard to the Church is analogous to that of a man who knows that he is bound to accept the decision of a specialist even while recognizing that it is not infallible.

'19. At any rate any opinion which runs contrary to a current statement of doctrine on the part of the Church has no place in preaching or cate-chesis, even though the faithful may, under certain circumstances, have to be instructed as to the nature of, and the limited weight to be attached to, a current doctrinal decision of this kind. This is a point which has already been discussed. Anyone who believes that he is justified in holding, as a matter of his own private opinion, that he has already even now arrived at some better insight which the Church will come to in the future must ask himself in all sober self-criticism before God and his conscience whether he has the necessary breadth and depth of specialized theological knowledge to permit himself in his private theory and practice to depart from the current teaching of the official Church. Such a case is conceivable in principle, but subjective presumptuousness and an un-warranted attitude of knowing better will be called to account before the judgement-seat of God.

'20. It belongs intrinsically to the right attitude of faith of any Catholic seriously to strive to attach a positive value to even a provisional state-ment of doctrine on the part of the Church, and to make it his own. In secular life too far-reaching decisions have to be taken on the basis of fallible findings on the part of others, which have been arrived at according to their best lights. And it is no less true in Church matters that the indi-vidual need not feel any shame or diminishment of his own personality if in his findings he relies upon the Church's teaching even in cases in which it cannot be accounted as definitive from the outset. It is possible that in specific cases the development of the Church's doctrine proceeds too slowly. But even in arriving at a judgement of this kind we must be prudent and humble. For in any such development of doctrine within a Church made up of men subject to historical conditions time is needed. For it cannot proceed any faster than the task permits of preserving the substance of the faith without loss.

'21. We do not need to fear that in adopting the positions of the Church in the manner described we are failing to respond to the claims of our own age. Often enough the serious questions raised for us by our own age, and which we are called upon to answer on the basis of our faith, make it necessary for us to think out the truths of our faith afresh. It is perfectly possible that in this process fresh points will come to be emphasized. But this is not to call the faith itself in question. Rather it contributes to a deeper grasp of the truths of divine revelation and of the Church's teaching. For we are firmly convinced, and we see that experience confirms us in this, that we need neither deny any truth for the Catholic faith, nor deny the Catholic faith for the sake of any truth, provided only that we understand this faith in the spirit of the Church and seek always to achieve a deeper grasp of it.'[2]

At a later stage we shall have a few brief remarks to make on the theological importance of this document in general and of the passage quoted in particular. The only observation to be made at this point is that an Italian version of the document appeared in the *Osservatore Romano* of the 15 December 1967 (in a translation commissioned, so it is reported, by the Secretariat of State). Incidentally I know that the document was read in the refectory in the presence of the learned professors of the Gregorianum and was received most favourably there. (It can hardly be as bad, therefore, as it is judged to be in the text which we are about to quote.) This text is particularly remarkable to the extent that so far as I know this is the first occasion on which this problem has been explicitly tackled at all in a (relatively) offical document. Previously it had been left solely to the theologians to discuss.

Critique of the Document

At the current time (and probably for some time previously) a mimeographed paper has been circulating among higher ecclesiastical circles which amounts to a critique of this document. The passage in this text which is of special interest to us here is that which is concerned with the passage in the document of the German bishops cited above. On this it has the following to say:

'The "Document of the German Bishops Addressed to All Members of the Church who are Commissioned to Preach the Faith" of the 22nd September 1967 has made a very favourable impression here. Nevertheless the document is in error in the distinction it draws between the concept of a "provisional" statement of doctrine and an infallible doctrinal decision and when it says on this: "In such a case the position of the individual Christian in regard to the Church is first and foremost analogous to that of a man who knows that he is bound to accept the decision of a specialist

[2] cf. pp. 12–14 of the official text.

even while recognizing that it is not infallible" (p. 13).[3] A statement of doctrine on the part of the Church which does not claim to be infallible can *per accidens* prove erroneous, but this does not mean that it can be characterized as provisional. Whoever speaks in the name of the Church's teaching authority can speak and should speak only if he is convinced of the fact that the doctrine to be put forward is *true*. This means that he never meets the individual Christian in the role of a specialist, either "first and foremost" or at all. A specialist is subject to the basic principle: "*Tantum valet quantum probat*". In any statement of doctrine on the part of the Church the arguments adduced in support of it have in all cases merely the character of aids to the free and voluntary acceptance of the decision concerned, and it is in this again that the radical difference is to be found between the Church's teaching authority and theological science. The wrong estimation of the force of a non-infallible decision of doctrine has led, not least in the question of the acceptance of "*Humanae Vitae*", to the following journalistic formula appearing even in the Church's own press: "No infallible decision – conscience decides". This represents a complete distortion of the real function of conscience. A point that is overlooked is that in *any and every* human act the conscience is called upon to play its part, even in the case of accepting an infallible decision of doctrine. And a further point no longer recognized here is that the conscience of the Christian needs to be guided and directed by Christ, and so by her whom the Lord has entrusted with his mission.'

What is to be said of this paper? In a single word I maintain that this critique of the bishop's document is theologically and practically speaking radically mistaken.

Interior Contradictions Within the Critique

First and primarily: the reader of this critique may ask himself with some amazement how in all logic the writer manages to make the accusation that the document concerned undervalues that very teaching office of the Church which derives exactly and precisely from the bishops and their teaching. After all we cannot, as a matter of sound logic, uphold an authority for the bishops which they themselves authoritatively reject. Of course it is possible to say that an episcopal document is not necessarily either infallible or correct in all its points, and so that one is justified in disagreeing with a document of this kind or with individual points in

[3] We should notice the word 'analogous', which the critic reads as though it were equivalent to 'absolutely the same'.

it provided one has good reasons for doing so and has given full and mature consideration to it. That is perfectly correct. But the critic quoted above is in fact disputing the very conditions which make it possible for a critique to exist, and prescribes a more or less unconditional obedience to such doctrinal declarations even though they themselves make no explicit claim to be infallible, and even though *in this particular case* the author of the critique we have quoted is in fact contradicting his own general principle in regarding doctrinal pronouncements of this kind as not being beyond dispute. The real situation, however, is in fact this: our present-day Catholic authoritarians are only too ready to uphold pope and bishop so long as they teach what they themselves regard as right. Otherwise they dispense themselves from that very attitude of unconditional obedience to doctrine which they defend indiscriminately against the 'modernists' of today as a sacred principle. One of the points which, so the critique asserts, has been overlooked in the bishops' document is that the doctrinal authority of the bishops and the pope (even in cases in which no definitions are arrived at) is a distinct entity in its own right such that on the one hand we are obliged to assent to it and on the other it has to be distinguished from the material arguments adduced in support of the official doctrinal declaration and has a value of its own independent of these. Now in the authoritative doctrinal statement of the bishops there is no attempt whatever to identify in any sense these two factors: the material theological arguments and the teaching authority of the Church. The *comparison* which has led the critic to this totally false imputation is precisely one which, in common with all comparisons, has to be taken with a grain of salt. It is actually a sound and intelligible comparison. For when someone finds himself in certain circumstances obliged to submit himself to the (non-infallible) diagnosis of a doctor, then in this situation too he is acting not on the basis of the arguments put to him by the doctor, and which he is quite incapable of understanding, but on the basis of the doctor's authority, albeit this is ultimately speaking different in kind from the teaching authority of the Church. Are we unable to understand a comparison of this kind? After all the true *tertium comparationis* consists simply in the fact that one individual is presenting another with a decision which is clearly recognized by both parties to be non-infallible and capable of error. Hence while there are indeed solid grounds to support the decision (including, amongst other factors, that of 'authority' of the most varied kinds), still, since it is not infallible, the party addressed retains the right, under certain circumstances (notice we say 'circumstances', not mere capriciousness), to reject the proposal that he shall come to this decision (in doctrinal matters etc.) so long as he believes that his reasons for doing so are good or better than those of the person proposing the decision to him.

Now it might be said that while it is true that formally speaking all this is quite correct it is not applicable to our present case because an individual Catholic theologian, or even a layman, is never in a position here and now (unless the decision concerned is revised by the teaching authorities themselves) to be *capable* of having good or better reasons to depart from the decision of the teaching authorities even though in principle it is conceded by both sides that this official doctrinal decision on the part of the Church is in itself and at basis capable of being revised. In such cases the position may be compared to that of a stone-breaker who declares that he regards the most recent theory of Professor XY on plasma physics as erroneous, for this professor does in fact admit that his theory is not absolutely certain. It is not for one moment to be denied that there can be, and often are, *cases of this kind* of dissent from the non-infallible doctrinal decisions of the Church, a dissent which is theoretically false and morally unjustified. Those who wish can confidently and reasonably go beyond this in maintaining that in cases of such dissent it is to be presumed that they are of this kind (whereas the opposite presumption is invalid). The bishops' doctrinal document too leaves no room for doubt that there are such cases and that any Christian who presumptuously or without grave reasons departs from the Church's teaching even when it does not contain any definition will have to answer for it before God.

But the alternative case is precisely possible too, and this is a point which is boldly and honestly expressed in the bishops' document. Cases may perfectly well arise in which a Catholic Christian has a right and, under certain circumstances, a moral duty, to depart from some official doctrine of the Church of this kind. This is something which the critic refuses to recognize yet which is true. This is not the place to give a more detailed exposition of the question of whether a distinction is to be drawn in this principle between the rights and duties of specialist theologians on the one hand and laymen on the other (any such distinction would be strongly dependent upon the nature of the individual case). Nor do we intend here to adopt a casuistic approach in enlarging upon the question of *what precise form* the attitude of the dissenter should take in such cases according to the traditional principles of fundamental theology and morals. Nor shall we attempt to establish, on the grounds of wholly traditional theology, the point that the principle expressed in the bishops' document is itself traditional. All this would take us too far afield.

Examples of Erroneous Decisions

I will adopt another approach by putting a simple question, arising from the practice of theologians, to the critic and giving some explanation of this. A brief but true anecdote may serve by way of introduction. During the modernist period the great Dominican exegete Lagrange had to listen to the following reproach from a friend in the course of a private conversation: 'In fact on this point (an anti-modernist declaration on the part of the doctrinal authorities of the Church of that time on a question of exegesis) the only response you can manage is a *"silentium obsequiosum"* (meaning that while you do indeed hold your tongue, you in fact interiorly reject this declaration).' To this Lagrange replied: 'That is true. But I would actually be committing a mortal sin (against my own conscience with regard to truth) if I were to act in any other way.'

Now let us consider the question itself in fuller detail. I have no time to search through Denzinger for official doctrinal decisions belonging to the last few decades which have proved false, and which virtually no Catholic theologian any longer accepts nowadays. Accordingly I will merely rummage a little through my own memory. For my purpose the fact that my examples are primarily of an exegetical kind makes no very great difference. Not all of them are of this kind however. For it has been explicitly stated at an earlier stage that the same weight is to be attached to such exegetical decisions as to the doctrinal decisions of other Roman authorities. Again we must ask to be excused if our approach is very unsystematic, and I shall not extend my researches further back than our own century. If these doctrinal decisions were all true or still valid for me today (they are never officially taken back with the same degree of explicitness and weight with which they were promulgated) then I would still today have to give my assent to propositions such as the following: Most of the psalms are by David himself; there are no post-exilic psalms; there are no Deutero-Pauline epistles; the discourses of Jesus in John are not theological compositions; the gospels were written in the same sequence in which we enumerate them today; there is no 'Q' Source; there is no Deutero-Isaiah; the Epistle to the Hebrews was written by Paul; the Pentateuch is 'a Mosaic text' (written virtually in its entirety by Moses himself), and not (as a French exegete once maliciously put it) 'une mosaïque de textes'. I must maintain it as certain that the baptismal formula in Mt. 28 was laid down by Jesus himself. I must be convinced that the Lucan gospel was written prior to the destruction of Jerusalem; I should be convinced that it is *ipso facto* modernism for me to call for any alteration to the Holy Office or to support the abolition of the Index; I would not be allowed to give even a modest support to the idea that so-called polygenism is reconcilable with a right interpretation of the doctrine of original sin; I should regard any participation of clergy and laity in the government of the Church, whatever form it took, as *ipso facto* modernist. As I have said, I am quoting from memory. But the reader too, even without having to look up any of the numbers in Denzinger, can rely on the fact that these points are valid. Every specialist theologian is aware of them. And over and above these and similar examples we might quote many other propositions in which the condemnation of one implies, in practice, the acceptance of its alternative even though this is far from being much of an improvement upon the condemned proposition, and even though under certain circumstances condemnation may have been just.

In referring to these propositions I have no intention of writing a *chronique scandaleuse* of the life of the Church during the first half of the twentieth century. Anyone who takes the references I have given in this sense is being foolish, knows nothing of the burden of history upon the Church, is failing to take due cognizance of the context in which such erroneous decisions were taken, a context which also exists even though it cannot be included in our presentation here, is failing to understand how inevitable it is that even in the Church the developing awareness of faith and doctrine must proceed slowly (even though I hold the opinion that sometimes it has proceeded more slowly than was necessary).

Provisional Decisions and the Advance of Doctrine

My intention in this section is to put the following question to the critic of the bishops' document: What is my lord the critic's view, working from *his own* principles, of the advance which the Church has made in overcoming these erroneous decisions, the advance which has been achieved, at least tacitly on many points, since the decisions were initially promulgated? In terms of his principles I cannot find any place for it at all within my purview. But I certainly can find one according to the principles underlying the bishops' document. For whence can we achieve the insight we need into the erroneousness of such wrong decisions if, at least in practice (if not in theory as well), theologians and layfolk have nothing else to do than to regard these wrong official decisions in matters of doctrine as *absolutely* binding norms in virtue of the authority of the Church's official teachers as the critic recommends. Anyone at all – and this includes any member of the Catholic Church itself – must, after all, take the initiative in saying that this or that point is simply not true and showing the reasons why. He must take this initiative even though according to Denzinger 2007 an 'interior assent' (*'assensus internus'*) is required of him, and Denzinger 2113 threatens that the exegete incurs 'grave guilt' (*'culpa gravis'*) if he does not submit to the decisions of the Biblical Commission. And all this even though no trouble is taken to draw even a few of the necessary distinctions, and even though it would have been possible even at that time to find from 'approved authors' that on this point those very distinctions have to be drawn which the German bishops have drawn in our own times.

Formerly anyone entertaining such doubts on a doctrinal decision of this kind was advised to keep silent about them even though they were, in the nature of the case, authorized. He was advised simply to be patient, and in the meantime to observe a *silentium obsequiosum*. One point to be made about this is that in contemporary society the constantly increasing communication of everyone with everyone else, reaching down into the most private spheres of human life, makes any such *silentium obsequiosum* quite impossible to maintain any longer. But quite apart from this the situation today is such that time is running out too quickly for us to be able to wait patiently in every case until the mental attitudes of the official teachers who set the standards has changed spontaneously and without conscious thought in such a way that they themselves, without noticing it, have, of their own volition, undertaken to bring about this change of views or feel that such a change as put forward by others no longer in any sense constitutes a deviation from earlier doctrines. (I recall an episode from the period of the Council in which a Roman cardinal assured me in all seriousness that in Rome there had *never* been any objection to the theory that on his physical side man is descended from animals.) Such cases of a gradual and unconscious change in theological views within the Church may still be going on even today. (One such instance can be found in the attitude of optimism of the Second Vatican Council with regard to the possibility of salvation for all men.)

But in general it is no longer possible to proceed by these methods alone. We have become too consciously aware of the factors involved and time is running out too quickly for this. Hence the question to the critic: How in your view is such a change to take place in the Church's awareness (not in the true and ultimate substance of its faith but in opinions which are put forward as matters of official doctrine yet are nevertheless erroneous) if there is never any case in which a Christian has the right to disagree with a doctrine of the Church on well-considered grounds and, moreover, not merely some decades after this doctrine has been promulgated? The fact that the principle relevant to this question and expressed in the bishops' document can be misused does not make any difference to its correctness. Any example of such misuse in relation to such a principle has just as little to do with the question of its truth as if I (with perfect justice and adducing historical proofs which are ready to hand) were to say that the principle of the critic leads to heresy hunting, stagnation in Catholic theology, and the falling away of many from the faith.

Nor is it any argument against this to say that the principle expressed in the bishops' document is not in fact the sole principle, so that the application of it to a particular concrete case leads to delicate situations of conscience for the individual in which each one remains fairly isolated in his relationship with God and with his own conscience. The same might also be said of innumerable other cases in Christian life. For instance my eternal salvation may perhaps to a large extent depend on my choosing the right vocation. Here too I find myself thrown on my own resources by the official Church (apart from very general principles in matters the details of which involve life-and-death decisions) and rightly so. For this is how God has willed it to be. Now according to Catholic doctrine there is in fact no authority in this world constituting an absolute norm for the individual without the personal decision of his own conscience. The existence and justification of the Church's teaching office is something which each individual must in fact recognize and accept as such *without* being able to base himself on the authority of this teaching office. In other words he must act solely 'at his own risk'. And if this is the case, then why should it be so particularly surprising to concede that even *after* acknowledging the validity of this teaching office in principle, situations of personal risk of this kind still continue constantly to be present, *analogous* to those which existed and still exist prior to the individual accepting the validity of the teaching office (for this acceptance in fact constitutes a decision requiring constantly to be renewed)?

Obviously we should not overlook the point that 'the conscience of the Christian needs to be guided by Christ and so by that which the Lord has entrusted with his mission'. But is not this point constantly being reiterated throughout the whole of the bishops' document itself? And is this statement of the necessity of this guidance gainsaid when the document draws the distinction it does, and points out that in particular cases this guidance is, after all, precisely a provisional one and *therefore* gives the one so guided, under certain circumstances a right and a duty, as a matter of concrete practice and not merely of abstract theory, to take such guidance for what it is and for what it is intended to be and nothing more, namely as provisional? And if the critic maintains that we should not describe a declaration of this kind of the teaching office as provisional on the grounds that in such a doctrine those entrusted with the teaching office are convinced that this doctrine is true, then his position becomes totally incomprehensible to me. Obviously the only doctrines they can teach are those which they are convinced are correct. But can they not be convinced in this way and yet, even in being so, be aware that they are *capable* of error? Or are they in that case no longer to teach at all? Yet even this course would in fact in its turn fail to measure up to the critic's statement that such a doctrine can be erroneous *per accidens*. After all a doctor may be convinced that his diagnosis is correct yet at the same time be aware that in this he can be mistaken. And he then has the right to express this diagnosis of his as correct and as something to be followed.

When, therefore, the critic quite explicitly condemns the term 'provisional' as used in the document and as applied to non-infallible doctrines of the Church's teaching office of this kind, then I must once more raise the question: How then are we ever to be in a position to reject doctrines of this kind seeing that they are never at any stage claimed to be irreformable, and have often in the past been shown to be erroneous? Supposing I had been alive when Leo X declared, against Luther, that the practice of burning heretics is fully in accordance with the will of the Holy Spirit, could I not even then have been in a position to think to myself: 'Thank God, this is only a provisional doctrine!'?

By way of conclusion I may be permitted one more earnest observation, even though to many it may sound somewhat pathetic. A few days ago I received the copy of a letter (I accept its genuineness because I myself have often heard similar things from behind the 'iron curtain'). The writer declares that he has spent twelve years in prison and suffered terrible things for his Catholic faith and his loyalty to the pope. He then came to the West only to receive the impression that in the Church here everything which he had suffered for was being squandered in unbelief. He would rather return once more to live in such a prison, for he was happier in it. I can understand this, for I myself have friends of the same kind in the East. It may be that many of the factors included in this condemnation of the West are to be explained on historical and sociological grounds, and that his condemnation of them does not *merely* reflect the mentality of the saint. It may be true that a Christian of the West views this martyr for Christianity with a holy envy. But if anyone supposes that the problems of the Church of the West are to be solved by an attitude of stubborn conservatism and that the Church is thereby to be confirmed in her faith and unity he is deceiving himself.

Under God's disposing power history has presented us with these present-day problems, and only courage, truthfulness, resolution in the faith *and at the same time* in positive thinking, can solve them by God's grace. Remembering the theology of the Cross, our attitude to martyrs can be very favourable, whereas our attitude to mere reactionaries who are just as well off as the rest of us prosperous citizens is less so. But if we intend to fulfil the tasks of the future for the Church of the West, then there are elements from the Church's past which must be overcome, and among the methods for overcoming them is to be numbered that principle which the German bishops have expressed in the document we have been discussing. It is to be hoped that they will not let themselves be held back from recognizing it and acting upon it as well. It may be said that the unity of the faith (which does not mean union with the opinion of Mr XY), acknowledgement of Jesus Christ as our Lord and Saviour, loyalty to the Church, and much else besides, are factors which are *still more* important than the principle we are defending here. But this is something that we neo-modernists (the name which our opponents like to reproach us with) are aware of too. We would be happy not to be put in the position nowadays of having to conduct a special defence of this principle which the German bishops have taught us.

6

THE CONGREGATION OF THE FAITH AND THE COMMISSION OF THEOLOGIANS

STRICTLY speaking all I have set myself as a task is to mention a few points calling for treatment by this commission[1] as a matter of priority and with special urgency. But in order to do justice to this task and to choose the sort of themes to which this description would apply certain prior considerations are necessary, for without them the task will not be discharged at all. For if we were to concentrate immediately upon those questions which everyone regards as 'actual and relevant' then nobody could know for sure whether he was pursuing a topic that was of real urgency or a subject which is today on everyone's lips, yet tomorrow will straightway be forgotten.

The Commission of Theologians has close connections with the Congregation of the Faith. These connections are altogether essential to it for without them it would constitute merely some random group of theologians concerning themselves with controversial questions in theology. It would be on the same level as innumerable other groups of the same kind, and would not possess any exclusive function belonging to it of its very nature. It is true that these close connections do not imply that the Commission of Theologians should not develop any special approaches of its own, or have its own spontaneity. It does not imply that it should be merely a subordinate instrument, so that any initiative it took would

[1] This paper is based on a report by the author to the first session of the International Papal Commission of Theologians of the 6 October 1969. Because of an indiscretion the article was published in a distorted and partly falsified form in *IDOC international*, no. 13 (of the 1 December 1969), pp. 46–62, and excerpts from it in *Informations Catholiques Internationales*, no. 350 (of the 15 December 1969), pp. 33–35. The author arranged for the German version to be translated from the Latin original by his colleague, Dr E. Klinger, so as to present an authentic text of the arguments put forward at Rome. cf. also K. Rahner, 'Die Freiheit theologischer Forschung in der Kirche', *StdZ* 184 (1969), pp. 73–82.

depend solely on the appropriate directive of the papal Congregation. On the contrary, it is only by having its own spontaneity and responsibility that the Commission can act as an aid to the Roman Congregation. Yet its responsible and active collaboration must be *totally* ordered to the activity precisely of this Congregation. In itself this is obvious. The Commission is restricted in the number of its members and the choice of them is reserved to the Pope alone. For these reasons alone the group of theologians has neither the capacity nor the intention of being representative of all Catholic theologians throughout the world. Whether a collegiate body of this kind, representative of all theologians and distinct from those representing the bishops, is regarded as legitimate in itself is a different question and one not to be decided upon here. But at any rate there can be no doubt that this group does not constitute such a representative body, and it would be acting in contradiction to its own nature if it did not regard itself as an instrument of the papal Congregation and hence restricted its functions to those matters which really fall within the purview of this Congregation.

But this only makes the question all the more pressing of what the task of this commission is in itself, and in particular what it is in the contemporary scene. A reply might be attempted merely in the sense indicated above, namely that it has to serve the Roman Congregation. But this would merely shift the question onto a different ground, for straightway the counter-question would have to be put of what this means and what the task is of the Roman Congregation itself. This is a question to which hardly anyone nowadays has a correct and practical answer to give. It is indeed clear, absolutely speaking, that the Congregation, as an organ of the pope, has the right and the duty to guard and defend the Christian and Catholic faith against all errors and dangers to which it is exposed whether from within or from without. But it would be gravely erroneous of us to suppose that we could solve this question as applied to our contemporary world merely by an abstract answer of this kind and thereby imagine that in all other respects we could proceed in the future in the same accustomed manner as formerly. The abstract formulae applied to the Congregation hitherto and the practical activities in which it itself has engaged no longer correspond to the present-day situation with which it finds itself confronted in the concrete and in terms of which its concrete functions should be defined in their greater detail. The basic question concerning this commission, therefore, which has to be solved first and foremost, is the question of the nature and function of the Congregation of the Faith itself. Our answer to this will determine too the special choice of themes to be treated of by the commission. Yet as I see it no full or adequate answer has yet been found to this basic question itself of the function of the Congregation of the Faith in the contemporary world. Hence I cannot refrain from mentioning a few of the obstacles which manifestly bar the way to such an answer.

I. THE NATURE AND FUNCTION OF THE ROMAN CONGREGATION OF THE FAITH

The Situation

Permit me, by way of preliminary, to give a brief outline of the procedures of the Congregation of the Faith as followed hitherto. I readily concede that such an outline can only be very sketchy. If in addition to this deficiency it strikes this or that individual as insufficiently 'respectful', I must crave indulgence for this. Up to the present the Congregation has proceeded on the assumption that new ideas and theological theses which have been freshly developed, and do not seem at first sight to be in agreement with the traditions of the faith, derive from one and the same milieu as that of the Congregation itself, and that there are direct contacts between them and theology as handed down and as formulated elsewhere. The result of this would be that the same terminology, the same philosophical assumptions, the same cultural outlooks, could be assumed to exist and could be used on both sides, and that it would be easy enough to establish and discover any fresh differences of opinion that emerged. It was formerly considered that when faced with a new proposition which struck one as suspicious it was easy enough to adduce a definition from Denzinger so that it could be readily seen that this ran counter to the doctrine under attack.

In cases in which it was believed that some fresh doctrinal propositions had been rejected, they were regarded either as already familiar or as readily accessible to the average intelligence, or else were quickly translated into the kind of statements which were in direct contradiction to traditional doctrine. No attention was paid to the fresh outlooks, tacit assumptions, and experiences not yet worked out in terms of conscious theory forming the background from which the new doctrinal opinions emerged. The Roman censors working in the Roman Congregations were in fact undoubtedly acute and learned men in every way. But even they regarded their own mentality and their own intellectual and social milieu as the only one existing, and as accessible from the outset to all others. The historical factors influencing their own mentality and the conditions affecting their own cultural, scientific, or even human milieux were things which they neither consciously recognized nor were able to take into account in the decisions they arrived at.

It is in the light of this that we must explain the fact that while in the Roman condemnations of the last century the true faith was indeed effectively defended, it was so, nevertheless, only in an extremely sterile and almost wholly repressive manner. No positive integration of the new problems was achieved by any such action on the part of Rome, and these problems were solved in other ways, whole decades too late, and generally speaking only by the kind of people who were regarded with particular suspicion by the Roman authorities. Undoubtedly the Catholic truth was defended even though its defence was often combined far too long with obsolete opinions drawn from the theological manuals. Thereby many were lost who would have agreed with this truth and who in themselves were actually ready to do so; yet they were lost to the faith. The reason was first that they lived in an intellectual and social environment far removed from that of the Roman doctors, and second that this doctrine was presented to them in a manner which was quite inappropriate to them. On any honest appraisal of the history of this Congregation over the last century it appears as an *historia calamitatum* and a history of lost opportunities, a history fashioned by people who, without prejudice to their legitimate authority and their task of defending the Catholic truth, were all too ready to present themselves as the *beati possidentes*.

Unquestionably the Church cannot escape from the burdens and the cramping effects imposed upon her by history. Unquestionably it is better to defend the Catholic truth in less agreeable ways than simply to surrender this even in its smallest detail. But even taking all this into account it would have been possible to avoid in this history much that is regrettable, many errors, and very many decisions which were objectively false. Let us not suppose that there have not been errors of this kind. Almost all the statements on biblical questions put forward by the Roman bodies in the last century prior to the Second Vatican Council are obsolete, and are no longer heeded by anyone. Modernism, it is true, is rightly evaluated as an amalgam of heresies, but even so it has to be said that the concrete condemnation under Pius X is full of over-hasty assertions which fail to do justice either to the importance of the problems involved or to the mentality of those against whom they are directed. Many of the statements of the popes in our own time on social and economic matters undoubtedly deserve the highest praise. Nevertheless the manner in which they are presented is often such as to suggest that support can be found for all of them in the gospel or the eternal law of nature even though in many cases they were applicable only to a particular period or culture. Let us take, for example, the modern theory of evolution and the attitude of the Church to the modern sciences, psychology and sociology: for whole decades (for almost a whole century) the idea of a development of man from the universal sphere of life was suppressed. Even today the official rejection of polygenism has not been withdrawn. The reaction of the Church to depth psychology and all scientific progress has almost invariably, so far as the Roman authorities are concerned, been inspired by a spirit of conservative mistrust.

Once we consider all these factors honestly and in the light of history we find that nowadays there is a further point to be added: that prescribed attitudes of mind of this kind have become ineffective even within the Church itself. What we are nowadays observing is an immense upheaval in human ideas and society, the nature and consequences of which have been, up to now, to a large extent unknown. In earlier decades, when a decision was issued by the Congregation of the Faith or some other Roman body, any Christian or theologian affected by it had two courses open to him: either he submitted to a decree of this kind or he left the Church. Nowadays, however, cases are proliferating in which the Christian affected takes neither the one nor the other course. He neither accepts the teaching of such a body nor leaves the Church. Instead he continues to take part in the life of the Church, contenting himself with a so-called mere 'partial identification'.[2] To the objection that such a course is dishonest and perhaps even dishonourable he replies that it only seems so from the point of view of the authorities, whose pronouncements on doctrine he precisely rejects. From this it is clear that the procedures and policies customary in the Roman curias hitherto have to a large extent become ineffective. Nevertheless it must be insisted that the Roman Congregations have not only the right and the duty to defend the traditions of the faith, but that over and above this they are also obliged in the same way to seek for the most effective possible policies and procedures to make this defence of theirs really successful.

Now what we have said above is far from amounting in itself to a full or adequate description of the situation in its entirety in which the Congregation of the Faith has to discharge its office nowadays. It seems to me that a radical shift has taken place as compared with former times in our entire conscious attitudes even with regard to the relationship between

---

[2] On the subject of partial identification in its wider aspects cf. the observations of Fr. Roustang, 'Le troisième homme', *Christus* 13 (1966), pp. 561–567.

the theoretical and the practical reason. In the light of this it becomes easy to understand why it should be that, at least according to my modest experience, it is no longer possible to say that the majority of the younger members of the clergy in Germany regard all dogmas promulgated in the Church as absolutely true in every particular. But this does not seem to cause excessive disquiet to the younger generation because as a rule they do not trouble themselves very much about theoretical truth as such once one abstracts from the practical claims it makes upon us in our concrete human lives. In brief: the present-day climate in terms of human ideas and human society is totally different from what it formerly was, and that too in such a way that we cannot expect that the mere formal authority of a Roman Congregation will *de facto*, or in any effective sense, influence those to whom such decrees are directed. It is not enough to insist against this attitude that the individual involved must either agree to the papal pronouncements concerned or cease to be a Catholic. For first there is a *de facto* refusal to recognize this principle on the part of the people concerned, and second there is a lack of the concrete means to carry through such an axiom effectively under present-day conditions.

In addition a third reason, distinct from the above, must be explicitly adduced at this point, and one which calls in question the approaches and policies customarily adopted by this Congregation hitherto. Formerly we proceeded from the assumption that the Congregation is in a position to watch over everything affecting the faith within the Catholic Church. It was assumed that we could assign to the Index of Prohibited Books at least all those writings which are of Catholic authorship and represent a threat to the Catholic faith. Hence a watch was kept over all teachers of theology or at least there was a belief that this was being done. It was the custom to send out documents – in a fairly arbitrary manner – with regard to the choice of subject-matter. But the content of these documents seldom touched upon the really basic problems of the time or, when they aimed at doing this, the exclusively negative character of the decisions taken had the effect of leaving these basic problems more or less unresolved. Everything was worked out by a small group of theologians living almost exclusively in Rome, and their specialized knowledge and competence in the relevant fields was not such as to be beyond all question. For the purpose of such decrees the bishops functioned in practice as mere executive instruments or as the sort of officials who denounced to the Roman curias those whose teaching they suspected of being heretical. For many reasons an approach of this kind, after the manner of a 'doctrinal police', is unrealistic nowadays.

One reason for this ineffectiveness must be specially emphasized. It is the task of the Congregation of the Faith to defend the Catholic faith and the acknowledgement of it by all. But the ways and methods formerly used for this purpose presuppose a quite specific unity between theology and faith such as *de facto* no longer exists today, and, moreover, is no longer capable of existing. Certainly there is an essential connection between theology and faith. Not merely has theology, as the scientific interpretation of faith, constantly to keep faith in view, but conversely every statement of faith inevitably and of its very nature contains right from the outset an element of reflection and hence of theology. Despite this this close relationship between the two does not imply an identity. For if theology always consists in a scientific interpretation of the faith, and this interpretation must presuppose much in the way of the philosophy, culture, and scientific experience of the age in which it is promulgated – thus the factors presupposed are subject to change and are not the same for all – then it follows not merely that there is a difference between theology and faith, but also that different theologies are possible, even though all of them refer to the same faith.

This difference is something that we are far more conscious of nowadays than was the case in the past. It is already felt to be insuperable nowadays because the prior assumptions underlying these different theologies of today are such that no one can any longer have a comprehensive view of them all at the same time, and use them to constitute a single theology reducing all the rest to a synthesis. In earlier times the Congregation of the Faith was able to assume and invoke for its work a theology that was common to all and which, moreover, everyone was perfectly well able to view as a comprehensive whole. Today, however, without prejudice to the unity of the faith, that theology which formerly all held in common is more and more being split up into the numerous different theologies which no one can any longer reduce simultaneously to one and the same common denominator.

Hitherto it has been extremely difficult to see how this Congregation, in view of the paucity of its members, can be familiar with, and distinguish, these different theologies or can couch its own doctrinal pronouncements in a language which will be effectively intelligible to all and recognized as appropriate for solving the particular questions arising within the single theology prevailing in any given age. Even today we observe disputes arising from this situation of theological pluralism. Some seek to reject a given proposition as heretical while others declare that this demand arises from a false interpretation of the statement objected to on the grounds that this interpretation is not in conformity with the under-lying assumptions in terms of terminology, philosophy, etc. on which such a proposition is based, and without which no true judgement of it can be arrived at. Formerly controversies arose as to the truth of a doctrine when no one had any doubt that the meaning of it was understood in the same sense by both sides. Nowadays each of the two parties to such a dispute argues that his opponent has failed to grasp the true meaning of the doctrine he is putting forward. Hence it comes about that the judgement we arrive at upon such a condemned proposition is often regarded not as a condemnation of the proposition itself, but of the false interpretation placed upon it.

Consequences

What consequences are to be drawn from the situation briefly delineated here for the work of the Roman Congregation and the Commission of Theologians? Above all what conclusions are to be drawn for the choice of themes which are particularly pressing?

Before we can proceed with our special theme it seems necessary to make yet a few further remarks at a general level. If we have described the situation aright, then the first conclusion which we can draw from it is a recognition that we do not know what our precise attitude should be. The first mistake we usually commit consists in the conviction that we have a sound grasp of the situation in which we live and already possess the principles and norms which we need to master the situation, so that all that we have to do is rightly to apply them to it. We often suppose that the only oversight we can commit is to neglect the practical applications of principles the nature and value of which are beyond question. *De facto,* however, there are no cases in which we really penetrate to the roots of the situation in which the Church and her official doctrinal authorities find themselves. We interpret the situation of today and tomorrow in terms of the situation of the yesterday to which we have been accustomed. Yet ultimately speaking we are in no sense achieving any effective or radical view of what the real reasons are for so profound a change in the situation in terms of sociology and human ideas. We take for granted certain norms of behaviour which *de facto* men no longer observe nowadays. We lay down principles and maxims which may in themselves be very sound, yet which unfortunately have the defect that modern man is precisely refusing to recognize them as applying to him. We suppose that the modes and attitudes of thought, of feeling, and of living customary in a clerical milieu also apply outside this milieu. We invoke in support of our position the universal authority of the Church and her teaching office in order to give assurance that a specific principle has been proclaimed by this authority, whereas in reality this principle might far better – as authenticated by its own content – provide the basis for acknowledging the authority in general.

The first step to be taken is the recognition in all honesty that we do not know the situation in which we ourselves stand in terms of sociology and human ideas. It is true that among ourselves we often say that fresh theological investigations are necessary. In fact, however, we often entertain the tacit conviction that everything that is in any way important for Christian life is undoubtedly already to hand, and only still needs to be defended and translated into practical terms, whereas those things which we do not know affect not merely the manner of presentation and preaching of the Christian truth but the actual content itself which, under present-day conditions, we have to preach. This is, it is true, the faith as revealed once and for all and to be preached in every age. But to the extent that it is precisely today that it has to be preached it is, without prejudice to its ultimate and basic identity with faith in the absolute, itself subject to a far-reaching historical change. The recognition of one's own ignorance undoubtedly signifies the first step towards an effective recognition of the true position and of what has to be done in it.

This point should also be emphasized in its application to recognizing the faith. For with regard to the object of knowledge here we are easily led into the erroneous supposition that we must either already know everything or are absolutely incapable of deciding anything for sure. In the past a developing process of maturity of this kind in our knowledge of matters of faith, i.e. the 'development of dogma', was achieved gradually, so that the individual steps were often hardly perceptible. And as a result of the gradual process of maturity in knowledge of this kind within the Church later generations hardly retained any awareness of the uncertainties of earlier ones. The earlier pronouncements of the official teaching authorities, though they may have run counter to some specific conviction held in more recent times, did not constitute any difficulties for the generation coming after them, if only because there was often a complete lack of awareness of them. Today, however, everything is developing more swiftly, so that the same peaceful maturing process of a doctrinal decision can hardly be expected. Hence the people of the Church, and even the members of the Roman bodies, must accustom themselves to the explicit withdrawing of past decisions. In individual cases these must frankly and

honestly be declared no longer to be in force, or even explicitly acknowledged to be mistaken. Unless we have the courage explicitly to withdraw
past errors the teaching authorities of the Church of today will retain
neither their credibility nor the trust reposed in them.

In all these questions, which need to be tackled afresh, there is much in
terms of methodology which should be thought out and applied anew.
In former times, when faced with questions calling for decision, it was
more or less universal practice to have recourse to the doctrine and practice of the Church in the immediate past. Biblical and historical studies,
which might have cast serious doubts upon this tradition of the practice
and teaching of the immediate past, were *de facto* not adduced or applied.
The more remote theological past was in practice always regarded as an
evolutionary stage already left behind, and as the age of an obscurity
which had already given way to something altogether better, clearer, and
surer as a result of the efforts of more recent schools of thought. History
was not really taken as providing a critical standpoint from which to
judge present-day positions, but merely as the description of a way which
had already attained its goal and could no longer be called in question.

The Congregation or Commission cannot continue to employ such
methods in the future. The methods used must really be open, seeing that
they will be used to seek that which is as yet unknown, however true it
may be that that which we seek has not merely a theoretical interest but
great practical importance as well. Other methods, e.g. the approach of
higher criticism in exegesis, must be accorded their due value and given
genuine scope to take effect even though the findings thereby arrived at
may contradict the ideas of the traditional schools of thought. (In this
respect even the exegetical methods of the Second Vatican Council still
do not provide a good example for a future methodology. They quote
scripture only as a storehouse of *dicta probantia* in order to give substance
to theses already recognized and assured on other grounds.) A methodological 'legalism', devoid of any real regard for the milieu in which a given
text emerged or the assumptions tacitly underlying it etc., and interpreting
texts as positive juridical norms, is something that we must resolutely
overcome. We must never forget that agreement with tradition on a
particular question is still far from constituting any proof that the doctrine concerned belongs to divine revelation unless it has been established
beyond dispute that such a doctrine has been unanimously accepted as
revealed by God and that at the same time the 'more original' revelation
necessarily contains all that the text appears to express.[3]

[3] The author is drawing a distinction between the 'original' revelation and the

This and many other points in methodology need to be tested afresh and translated into practice if the work of the Congregation and Commission is really to serve the interests of those who live in this situation of ours as it affects human knowledge.

II. TASKS FOR THE COMMISSION OF THEOLOGIANS

From the preliminary remarks which it has been necessary to make here we can now go on to treat of a few special themes which take priority and claim our special attention. We are not proceeding from the assumption that such themes should necessarily be the subject of a public and authoritative declaration addressed to the Church by the Congregation of the Faith. On the contrary it will be assumed that there can be themes which require to be considered and, as it were, pondered upon by the Congregation without such consideration having to lead immediately and *ipso facto* to a decree needing to be promulgated. All this taken as given, I shall draw a distinction between more general and more particular themes. Under the heading of more general themes I am grouping those which, without being the subject of public official doctrinal declaration, bear particularly upon the Congregation's own interpretation of itself, even though such more general considerations may have secondary consequences for the doctrine and practice of the Church.

General Themes

The *first* theme touches upon the possibility, the limitations, and the methods which today, as distinct from the past, are used by the Church and her official teachers in the *defence and proclamation of the faith*. From what has already been said the range and complexity of such a consideration will be clear. What is to be done, for instance, in view of the fact that the attitude of modern man to theoretical truth is manifestly completely different from that of his predecessors so long as this theoretical truth is incapable of direct practical verification? How can the unity of the faith be defended – indeed even assured – in any sense if it cannot now be presented as it formerly was, directly in terms of a single theology using one and the same terminology and based on the same philosophical assumptions etc.? In these circumstances how can we still regard holy

concepts in which it is objectified. On this cf. K. Rahner, 'Theology in the New Testament', *Theological Investigations* V (London and Baltimore, 1966), pp. 23–41.

Scripture nowadays as *norma non normata et omnia normans*, seeing that it itself is nowadays recognized as an entity which is in manifold ways conditioned by historical factors, one which depends upon many factors which have either ceased to exist nowadays, or at least seem to us not to be binding? How can the teaching authorities with their doctrines concerning specific subjects aim at making these doctrines effective, seeing that their formal authority itself is called in question and such questioning can with some justice adduce in its support many authentic instances in which these official teaching authorities have in fact erred? What is it which, regarded as the ultimate substance and innermost kernel of the faith, can be preached in such a way first that this basic preaching convinces the hearer of its living truth as a vital force in human living in virtue of the mystery and simplicity combined in it and of its affinity with the innermost will of man, and second that the authority which a truth of this kind carries evokes trust in its hearers? Are we in a position nowadays to distinguish between various fundamental kinds of preaching suitable to proclaim the one truth of faith? When an error against the faith is promulgated by a Catholic how can the official rejection of such an error be rendered effective straightway? Which are the cases in which such rejection is opportune, and which are the ones in which it is not so? Seeing that nowadays men require of even formal authority that it shall give the intrinsic reasons supporting its decision, the question must be raised of whether and how such a demand can be satisfied in the case of the decisions of this Congregation. A distinction which we have often adumbrated is that between the unity of faith and creed on the one hand and the pluralism among the theologies on the other. This is something which requires to be worked out with still greater precision. For first this distinction is far greater than formerly, and second, speaking about faith and creed in a so-called scientific age cannot be allowed to lead to a vague pietism.

In order to formulate such a theory as to the right methods to be used in the teaching of the faith we must also nowadays raise the question of what approach to adopt to the very great number of individuals who, as a consequence of their intellectual formation, in itself very advanced, are psychologically speaking hardly ready to accept the pronouncements of the doctrinal authorities merely in virtue of their formal authority as such so long as they are unable to integrate those pronouncements in a really positive sense with the rest of their ideas. On the other hand, however, in the intellectual and psychological situation in which they stand they themselves are in no position to achieve such a positive integration by their own powers. Such dilemmas as this were less frequent in earlier days because men were either still so uneducated that on the subtler questions they simply left the doctrines of the Church's official teachers to their implicit faith or else were able to cope with the situation with that single common language of the educated classes in which the pronouncements on the faith were themselves couched. So far as we are concerned we have no particular theory to offer on this sociological question of cognition.

A *second* general theme concerns the question of *Church membership*. This question seems to a large extent already to have been clarified. For many centuries it has been familiar enough to theologians and seems to have been brought for the most part to a conclusion by the Second Vatican Council. Yet this is true only from certain specific standpoints. There are many other aspects of this question which still remain wholly obscure even today, although in themselves they have been of the utmost importance for the practice of the Church. Formerly every answer to this question was more or less based upon the assumption that it was easy to establish whether belief or unbelief was present in an individual in relation to the doctrines of the Church. Such an assumption, however, is no longer justified. We have already spoken of that peculiar state of merely partial identification with the Church and her faith, of that strange psychological and sociological attitude of mind in which two seemingly incompatible resolves co-exist: on the one hand the resolve to remain in the Church and to take part in her life, and yet on the other to maintain a fairly clear attitude of dissent from her authority and her teaching on many questions. How are we to judge an attitude of this kind in the individual's conscious awareness from the psychological and theological points of view? What attitude should the Church adopt towards such individuals?

It is easy to recognize that this question has consequences for ecumenism. For often we look more askance at many men as non-Catholics on the grounds that as a matter of Church sociology they live beyond the bounds of the Roman Church although so far as faith itself is concerned they are Catholics, than at many others who sociologically speaking do belong to the Catholic Church and call themselves Catholics. We are pointing, then, to a distinction between membership of the Church at the sociological level on the one hand and at a truly theological level (to be estimated on the basis of faith) on the other in the contemporary scene. We are suggesting that it is a distinction which in practice cannot be overcome. And even the question of whom we can regard as a believer is far more difficult than was formerly supposed. Now given that such a distinction does to a large extent exist nowadays, what course should the Church and her official teachers pursue in such a situation? Whom is she to recognize as belonging to her? Whom is she to admit to the sacraments? To whom does she extend *communio in sacris*? Why does she extend this to one individual and not to another when there is no theological difference between them whatever?

The *third* general theme seems to me to be that concerning the distinction between *morality and justice in the Church*. One of the schemes projected for the Council was explicitly concerned with the duty of moralists to preserve a strictly defined distinction between the juridical and moral orders within the Church, and this for good reasons. But the basic question of where to draw the line of this distinction in itself and of the practical consequences following from it seems to me to remain unresolved. For we are accustomed tacitly to assume as obvious the view that the moral and juridical standing of a Christian within the Church is such that, at least so long as there is good will on both sides, both departments can so be brought into harmony that there cannot be any opposition between them. And yet such an opposition is possible. There is a kind of failure in morality which does not *ipso facto* involve a transgression of the law and is in this sense to be pronounced 'illegitimate' (i.e. contrary to a law to the extent that this is enforced by the Church under penalty of juridical or more general sociological consequences). There can be a kind of illegitimate behaviour, or behaviour deviating from the Church's law, which cannot *ipso facto* be said to constitute any real immorality in God's sight.

To regard the two factors as distinct and to some extent opposed in this way does not create any very great difficulties in secular society. But because the Church as such always has to guard and defend human morality in God's sight as well, the distinction and opposition which we have discerned do of their very nature entail notable difficulties so far as she is concerned. For at times, without any sufficiently exact thought on the principles involved, the juridical and legal claims for a particular course of action are urged without sufficient regard to its morality. There is a failure to admit that this latter factor has any concrete effects in the life of the Church. (For instance we allow a man to contract a Church marriage with one woman even though as a matter of deep personal involvement and for a long period he has united himself with another, albeit without concluding a juridically valid marriage with her.) Conversely we tend to refuse this juridical status to another even though from the standpoint of his *moral* situation such a status could have been accorded to him merely on the grounds that the legitimacy of this status cannot be established in the *forum externum* (for instance marriage is denied to a man when he cannot supply juridical proof of his freedom from the marriage bond even though he is in fact free in this sense). There are many instances in canon law in which we can discern confusion and entanglements of this kind between the juridical and moral orders. For instance the idea of a punishment *latae sententiae*, a fairly strange conception, derives from confusing the two in this way. The effect of allowing the two orders to interact upon each other in this way is that we are all too ready to attach forthwith to any kind of irregularity in the juridical sphere a moral significance in God's sight which does not belong to it in itself at all except in those cases in which such irregularity really endangers the public order in the Church. If this danger were solved in principle and unambiguously then we could establish more easily and more precisely the borderline between the exercise of official authority in the Church and the conscience of the individual. Moreover the whole question is connected, as we can readily perceive, with that other question of whether and to what extent the individual may be pressed by his own conscience publicly to declare his opposition to a doctrine of the teaching authorities which, while it is indeed authoritative and authentic, has nevertheless not been defined. All the theologians regard an internal dissent as possible. The question would be, however, what degree of public, and perhaps even juridical value could be attached to such a withholding of assent without the attitude of the individual expressing it doing damage to the Church herself.

The *fourth* general theme seems to me to touch upon the concrete *constitution of the Church* and of the local and regional Churches. It is clear that the Church has of her very nature a constitution which is *juris divini* (even though it is not so easy as it appears to many to say in what this 'divine right' precisely consists). But many of the factors in the concrete organization and constitution of the Church do not belong to it as of divine right. Many factors may perhaps seem to have this status but in reality do not do so. The concrete constitution of human right or human law, however, which derives from the historical circumstances and the demands of a particular age, can nowadays not be left to the paternalistic discretion of the Church authorities. On the contrary there is need of prior reflection from the aspects of history, psychology, futurology, and sociology, and this is something which it is precisely for theology to achieve. It is true that here again the juridical changes require that the level of concrete organization belong to the sphere of administration of the Church's authorities, but it in no sense follows from this that these authorities can nowadays shape their course solely in accordance with their own 'well-informed' personal 'conscience' and fatherly benevolence

Nowadays all these decisions call for a prior information which has to be acquired in new ways and by scientific methods, information as to tendencies and concerns which are *de facto* present in the Church. And while it is true that the Church authorities are not mere passive instruments dependent upon these tendencies and existing merely to give effect to them, still they cannot remain totally independent of them either, acting as though they were the overlords and nothing more.

I have deliberately avoided including among these more general themes the most basic questions of Christianity, the questions concerning God, the Incarnation, and similar truths. For while these questions are indeed of fundamental importance, it is not a Congregation or Commission of this kind which can give the answer to them in terms which are really appropriate to our particular age. On the contrary the giving of this answer is a task for the whole of Christian theology. It may indeed be true that in the future too there will be occasions on which the teaching authorities cannot avoid pronouncing an anathema through this Congregation in order to defend the faith. Nevertheless such merely negative decisions generally have a fairly limited effectiveness. And again no official Church institution nowadays can in practice achieve anything more than these purely negative decisions. It might be asked, however, whether and in what way an institution such as the Congregation of the Faith might indirectly call for positive and effective answers to these fundamental questions. This would be quite a different question. Undoubtedly it would militate against any such goal if the Congregation, from an untimely zeal to weed out the tares, were to destroy the good seed as well, as has often happened in the past.

Particular Themes

At this point a few more *particular* themes must briefly be indicated which primarily call for the attention of the Congregation of the Faith and the Commission of Theologians. These themes will be adduced only briefly, and we shall make no attempt to explain the importance of their subject-matter and the methods of enquiry to be followed in them any further.

(a) The *question of mixed marriages* still remains to a large extent unsolved today at both the theoretical and the practical level. Many questions bearing upon this theme have still not received sufficient attention. In practice there is often a complete failure to draw the necessary distinction between that which pertains to genuinely divine law and that which pertains merely to ecclesiastical law. Over and above this, it is often wrongly assumed that everything in this sphere depends on the free consent of the Church's authorities, and there is a failure to recognize that the matter itself and the concrete circumstances prevailing today impose their own norms and limitations upon the Church's authorities. It is vital that in this sphere effective, imaginative, and practical laws should be devised, and that the preliminary deliberations leading to this should be embarked upon. These should be exact and detailed indeed, but also brisk and swiftly set in motion, and the laws they lead to should apply to all. Moreover these laws should be effective without innumerable special measures and legalistic procedures. Unless this is done then the only alternative will be that most of the members of the Church, and even the younger clergy, will cease to trouble themselves any longer about these laws.

(b) One question which is recognized to be very urgent is that of *communicatio in sacris*. There is a danger that in practice people will soon cease to pay any further heed to the prescriptions of both the Catholic and the non-Catholic Church authorities. The rules which have hitherto been in force in this sphere are not simple and imaginative enough and, on the contrary, give the impression of a somewhat illogical compromise. The basic question of what our attitude should be to unity in the sphere of ritual observance seems to me to remain unsolved, the more so since the prior question of what unity of faith can really be achieved, demanded, or looked for in the future still remains obscure.

(c) *Infant baptism* is also a question which seems likely soon to give rise to great difficulties among us. I believe that here too we must guard against the view, all too easy to fall into, that this question has already been solved in all its aspects.

(d) Another particular question of great practical urgency is concerned with the *indissolubility of a Christian marriage* which has been sealed and consummated. Even if we assume the basic principle of indissolubility – an assumption which is certainly not altogether free from historical and theoretical difficulties – many concrete and practical questions still always remain, calling for full and adequate answers. At what point, for instance, is that degree of intellectual and moral maturity present really and not merely presumptively, without which that consent which provides the basis for an indissoluble marriage is quite impossible? Can maturity of this kind be the same under any and every sociological and cultural conditions? Even if we accept the objective indissolubility of a Christian marriage, the question still remains open of whether all men can effectively 'realize' the duty of an objective indissolubility of this kind at the subjective level and in terms of their own concrete human lives. And at least in the light of this the extremely obscure question then arises of what the attitude of the Church should be towards those who are subjectively convinced that it is permissible for them to enter upon a new marriage after civil divorce, and whose attitude on this point cannot easily be contested. This and much else besides seems obscure and still unsolved in relation to the indissolubility of marriage.

(e) I must confess my personal view that many of the factors connected with the *law of celibacy* call for fresh consideration even at the theoretical level. For not infrequently principles are invoked and urged upon us in defence of celibacy which, while they are indeed asserted as beyond question, can in fact perfectly well be challenged by others as unproved. In this question too, so it seems to me, we have not sufficiently reflected upon the bounds which the Church authorities too must observe. Here again in the eyes of many the legality of a prescription issued with the force of official authority is all too readily regarded as proof of the effectiveness of this prescription also, whereas in reality the converse is equally true. Those issuing the prescription must also have due regard to the question of its effectiveness if it is to be legitimate in *every* respect.

7

ON THE THEOLOGY OF
A 'PASTORAL SYNOD'

I F the science of theology, as understood by Catholics, is to contribute to the preaching of the gospel and the life of the Church, then it has the right and the duty to make its message known in the concrete everyday life of the Church as well, and to play its part in throwing light upon the questions of the moment. It is in this sense that we should listen in particular to the message of theology in the preliminary considerations on the nature and task of a pastoral synod.[1]

It may be that the idea of a twofold teaching office in the Church approximately as maintained by Y. Congar or H. Küng,[2] is somewhat problematical. But at least this much is correct in it, that in an age of science and of growing intellectual and social differences in the Church the theologians have a task calling for their serious attention, and one which – viewed in concrete terms – only they can fulfil, regardless of how their more precise relationship to the official doctrinal authority of the bishops should be conceived of according to Catholic doctrine. In this undertaking the work of the theologians is related, of course, to the concrete

---

[1] The original context of the ideas here expressed was the group lectures of the faculty of Catholic theology at the university of Munster/Westphalia on Problems in Preparing for the German Pastoral Synod held during the winter semester of 1969/70. The observations there put forward have been lightly revised for purposes of publication.

[2] On this cf. Y. Congar, 'Dogmatische Tatsachen und "Kirchliche Glaube" ', *Heilige Kirche* (Stuttgart, 1966), pp. 371–388; also 'Die Grenzen der kirchlichen Autorität und ihre Ausübung', *Die Tradition und die Traditionen* I (Mainz, 1965), pp. 274–280 (Hist. Material) as well as various articles in the more recent symposium, *Ministères et communion ecclésiale* (Paris, 1971).

Likewise see H. Küng, 'What Does Infallibility Mean?' *Structures of the Church* (New York, 1965), pp. 305–351 and *Theologe und Kirche*, Theol. Meditationen 3 (Einsiedeln, 1964) as well as *Unfehlbar? – Eine Anfrage* (Einsiedeln, 1970) and the controversies included in the appendix to this work.

practice and decisions of the Church. But while fully recognizing this, we must also recognize that in this task of theirs the theologians have to perform the function of critical reflection, and thereby discharge their special task in the Church in relation alike to the bishops and to the people of God as a whole. Now all this makes the significance of this task for the theologian, as applied to a synod of the kind we are thinking of, not less but on the contrary even greater. For critical theological reflection – even abstracting from the creative freedom required for new charismatic discoveries and decisions – is the sole factor which makes it possible for the Church to avoid becoming entangled in the encumbrances of mere tradition and custom and so clears the ground from which she can develop her future. Indeed it can actually be said that nowadays that factor of the original and the charismatic which abides right from the Church's origins should to a large extent appear in the everyday garb of sober realistic reflection.

There is a further question which cannot be entered into here, that namely of the order in which the representatives of the individual theological disciplines should express themselves on the subject under consideration in view of the way in which these particular disciplines are related to one another as established by a preliminary consideration at the level of scientific theory. It is obvious that a dogmatic theologian, from the very nature of his particular science, can make only very general statements on a synod of the kind we are thinking of in the awareness that it is the concrete particular details which are of really vital importance here.

I would like *first* to attempt to make a few points on the theology of a *particular* synod. With regard to the relationship between the individual regional Churches and the one Church the Church now finds itself in a quite new situation, so that it is not really so very surprising that it has so far not really been able to cope with this new situation. Ever since the Middle Ages there have always been Churches which were in some respect particular, each having special characteristics of its own, a special history, and a special way of life, and this is of course true, though obviously in a lesser degree even of the Latin Church. There have always been patriarchates, different rites, different theological traditions, particular synods, national synods, gatherings of the clergy of a particular nation, tendencies on the part of national states to absorb and appropriate to themselves in territorial and juridical terms the Churches existing within their dominions. There have been national protests against the claims and practices of the Roman see. In brief, the Church has never constituted an unity of the kind which is constructed from parts which are absolutely homogeneous. But first and foremost it must be recognized that these internal differences have, after all, to a large extent been the outcome of a mere pragmatic and unconscious development. It is something which has rather been accepted as an inescapable *fait accompli* than positively affirmed. The difficulties and struggles which these differences between the particular Churches have of course entailed throughout the entire history of the Church have been sustained by an attitude which has always been taken for granted yet which is, basically speaking, nevertheless naive. For those living in earlier times have always held that that which is 'given' by their own tradition is also that which must be taken as the standard for everything else. The differences within the Church have been in this sense a rendering present of the past, but not a rendering present of, and a task for, the future. A further point is that for all the respect accorded to the Churches of the East, it has been felt by almost all Catholics that 'Church' is identical with the Latin Church of the West. Now this Latin Church of the West has been, and still is, in all dimensions of Church life, homogenized to such an extent that it can hardly be seen how the process can continue any further. The result is that tendencies arise from time to time at the national level, or within particular Churches, which are hostile to this process of homogenization which has been continuously growing and extending ever since the early Middle Ages. And every time they do arise they have invariably ended in heresies and schisms, and thereby merely served to strengthen this tendency to unification within the Catholic Church. Hence this homogenized Church of the Latin West has in practice extended itself everywhere in the world by its missions ever since the beginning of the modern age, and despite the resolve which has repeatedly manifested itself to accommodate itself to the practices of other cultures. Furthermore virtually no attempt has been made in ecclesiology to achieve a serious theological reflection upon internal differences within the Church that are justified. The single overall uniformity within the Church was felt as something to be taken for granted and lived by, even though it involved the danger which is entailed by all those factors which are merely taken for granted whereas in truth they are merely the outcome of historical conditions. In fact men's attitudes have gone beyond even this, and they have come to regard the uniformity which exists in liturgy, law, Church practice, and the organization of the Church after the pattern of a modern state with a single centralized government as to a large extent an inevitable consequence of the dogma of the papal primacy. Again it is quite impossible to deny that right down to the present day any tendencies which run counter to this uniformity are all too easily regarded by Rome as an opposition to the primatial function of the pope and are resisted as such. Now this situation has gradually begun to change. At the Second Vatican Council conciliar ecclesiology has for the first time entered upon a process of theological reflection as to the justification for having a pluralism of Churches within the one Church. The importance of the bishops in dogmatic developments, and thereby too the autonomy of dioceses, are becoming clearer. The latter are something more than mere administrative departments within a single centralized state. The *de facto* abolition (apart from minor remnants) of Latin as the language of worship in place of living languages, the growing importance of the national conferences of bishops which the Council has recognized, the higher regard paid to the Eastern Churches, the autonomy of many Churches which has inevitably developed here and there through external political circumstances – these and many similar symptoms show that the age in which the uniformity prevailing within the Latin Church was taken for granted is over. Admittedly on an honest appraisal this is still no very great gain. For it has to be recognized first and foremost that at the dogmatic level and as a matter of ecclesiology no more precise and generally recognized interpretation has really been arrived at yet which can provide the basis for a more concrete relationship between the unity of the Church as represented by her primate on the one hand, and the justified, and indeed necessary, pluralism of the Churches within the one Church on the other. In this matter the Second Vatican Council has, after all, advanced only to the extent of asserting the possibility and justification in principle of such a pluralism without thereby *ipso facto* making it clear precisely *how*, in practical and concrete terms, this is to be reconciled with the authority of the pope and the unity of the Church. Juridically speaking we still do not know whether the new code of canon law which must come will give sufficient scope to the autonomy and self-responsibility of the national Churches. The 'schema' of the extraordinary synod of bishops of 1969 put forward by the Roman curia as a working paper hardly goes beyond a vague and uncommitted statement on the kind of pluralism within the Church that is justified. The schema either cannot or will not say anything whatsoever which brings this question any nearer to a solution conceived of at the *juridical* level. But the decisive point is, after all, surely this: that apart from a few hostile reactions to Rome, which seem to be the outcome of 'allergies' to it, the individual Churches have still not in any sense come to recognize that in which their concrete character and function consists or should consist as particular Churches within the one Church. It is certainly true that the ultimate individuality of an historical reality achieving its fulness through the exercise of freedom does not emerge in the test-tube of speculative theory and critique. But it is equally true that the individuality of a social entity of our time cannot take shape and live without decisions being arrived at at the conscious and reflective level and being institutionalized at the collective level. The individuality of a social reality of today is not a flower which blooms in a dreamlike and unconscious manner. But what the distinctive character of a given particular Church could and should be in fact and in the concrete is something which we do not know even so far as our own German Church is concerned. For this it is not sufficient to have the dogmatic thesis as expressed in 'Lumen Gentium', the thesis namely that a distinction between the Churches of this kind is both justified and necessary, or that it does not run counter to the unity of the Church but rather represents a blessing for the whole Church. All that this achieves is to give expression to an abstract principle which does little to advance our enquiry. There is a lack of certainty, then, in recognizing the distinctive identity of any given particular Church on the basis of abstract theory or by pointing to a past in which greater uniformity prevailed. But there is an additional circumstance making the question still more difficult. It is this: today, in the age of a world civilization which is one at the rational and technical level, the age of UNO and the age in which the destinies of all peoples are becoming ever more closely interwoven, there is certainly no lack of factors and influences at work which from many points of view must necessarily cause the unity of the Church, and inevitably thereby a certain uniformity within her as well, to increase. There can be no escaping this tendency if the Church is to be able effectively to fulfil its task for the *world*, quite abstracting from the question and the problem entailed in the fact that today too a unity of the Church which is necessary on the basis of faith is being threatened, and that the Church has to ward off such threats and has to allow this basic unity of hers to take form in the concrete at the historical and social level as well. It would be terrible – and after all this is no mere imaginary danger – if the Church were now to do something which she omitted to do in earlier times even though then it was reasonable and necessary, yet which would nowadays signify nothing else than an anachronism if we were at this stage to make it a 'compensatory requirement'.

The assertion of the principle of autonomy for the regional Churches should not be put forward nowadays within the universal Church in such a way as to sound somewhat like the programme of a Bavarian Nationalist

Party. Once we recognize this the following point becomes clearer: what the concrete individuality of our German Church should really be, and how it should differ from, and at the same time be united with, the Church as a whole, is something which, if we are completely honest, we basically speaking precisely do not know. But what we are saying is that the theoretical principle, at the level of dogmatic theology, that there is a plurality of Churches within the one Church, represents something more than a mere attitude of tolerance towards something that *de facto* exists. It also implies a positive task of achieving that which has still to be brought into being. And if this is true then the German Church cannot stick fast in an attitude of naive ignorance as to its own individual character. Can a regional or national synod recognize that there is a task for it here? I believe that we must answer this question in the affirmative. Obviously not in the sense that a pastoral synod of this kind constitutes a sort of mirror image of such a Church at the speculative level, indulging in idle disquisitions concerning the special character of this Church. But this task of the synod might be approached in such a way that the synod recognizes on quite concrete questions the right and the duty of this Church to a specific solution, even though this solution is not that of any other particular Church. This would have the effect that the synod would be championing the right of the German Church to arrive at a particular solution of this kind while remaining within the one Church. Why must the mixed marriage law, assuming perhaps that it may be appropriate to Spaniards, take exactly the same form in Germany? Why must a parish community among us be constructed on more or less exactly the same lines as in Sicily? Why must the relationship between bishop and clergy even at the purely juridical level be organized in exactly the same way as in a Latin country or in Indonesia. In taking action on behalf of the Third World, has not a country which is economically rich quite different tasks and duties from the Church in Portugal or Jugoslavia? If practical theology includes that element which it has been found possible with a certain justification to call 'political theology', without thereby falling into a clerical exercise of power in relation to the secular world, then a political theology in Germany must assume a different form from that which it takes in any other country, and can contribute towards a concrete process of self-discovery on the part of the German Church. The synod of a particular region has of its very nature precisely as belonging to *that particular* region a task which is proper to it alone, and which cannot be taken over from the regional Church which it represents by any other authority in the Church. Despite the current tendency towards uniformity in the world, it is neither necessary nor desirable that the distinctive character of the individual nations in terms of civilization and even of institutions should simply disappear. On the contrary among the peoples of the world each must discover its own individuality, and this represents a fresh task for the future (regardless of whether it is taken seriously or merely played at). And if all this is true, then the discovery of the special character of a particular regional Church is a task for the Church concerned, and so for the synod which represents it as particular and regional. The most pressing and spectacular part of this task may be the justifiable defence of this character against attack from Rome. But it does not constitute the decisive factor or the most difficult one. The living concrete form which Christianity assumes in the future situation and conditions in which a given concrete nation has to live, and the special character which it thereby acquires as a national Church, is, from the formal point of view, the task of a particular synod at the national level.

Secondly I would like to make a few quite brief observations on the theology of a *pastoral* synod. The synod envisaged and planned for is called a pastoral synod. Hence we should also devote some theological consideration to the true meaning of the term 'pastoral' in all its ramifications. We might take this term as applying merely to the task of the clergy and other official functionaries of the Church. Or we might suppose that this term implies from the outset and in principle either a prohibition or a dispensation bearing upon the process of reflecting upon the gospel to be preached as to its content and the manner in which it should be preached, factors which mutually condition one another. But this would be to misunderstand the term 'pastoral'. A pastoral theology which is pursued with a view to arriving at practical decisions as to the nature of a pastoral synod is 'practical theology', which has to consider the concrete modes in which the Church *as a whole* has to achieve its own fulness in *all* of its members and in all its dimensions, and, moreover, in the light of the situation of the Church in the world as reflected upon theologically. Hence the theme and the task of the coming synod, if it is really to deserve the name of a *pastoral* synod, is this: to discover how the entire Catholic Church of Germany in all its members and in all its dimensions can achieve the fulness of its own nature by reflecting theologically on the situation of the Church and the world with a view to the future. This is of course not to deny that a synod of this kind must in practice, in its initial session, actually choose its themes for investigation. But if we take what has been said with all due seriousness, then we shall conclude that even the discovery of the concrete themes for discussion is an extremely difficult task, that there is a danger that those taking part will be too self-assured and too self-willed, and so that they will overlook the most important and the most crucial themes because these will have remained quite undiscovered throughout their considerations. Certainly a further point is that a pastoral synod should not seek to present itself in any direct sense as having doctrinal authority. Certainly it should not seek officially and authoritatively to promulgate any new doctrinal decisions or declarations. But it might concern itself, for instance, with the necessities of preaching in the pulpit and in schools. It might seek to define the task of the priest for today and tomorrow and to cater for this in special juridical enactments and pastoral directives. It might seek to formulate practical directives for the task of the people as a whole in the Church. Such directives and enactments would, moreover, be concrete, at least to some little extent while being at the same time taken in a spirit of responsibility for maintaining the Church's faith. But in the very process of undertaking all such tasks as these – and after all they certainly are the tasks of a pastoral synod – the synod will find itself inescapably confronted by theological questions which are anything but simple or already long since fully explained. This means that the synod will have to engage in theology. Why, for instance, should a pastoral synod, precisely as the synod of a particular region, in principle avoid the question of whether an age-limit should not be laid down from the outset for every bishop in the German Church, or whether a part-time priesthood is conceivable or desirable in our case? But such questions presuppose considerations of a theological kind, which still need to be clarified first, and in order to answer such questions and arrive at concrete decisions upon them we may perhaps first have to fight for the individual Church to have a place within the Church as a whole. Questions such as these must be considered in their theological aspects at a synod which is intended both to represent a particular region and to be pastoral in character.

A *third* theme on which certain observations have to be made is constituted by the question of what resolutions the synod as such should have legal powers to make. It is a known fact that in the projected plan for a statute for synods, despite many alterations and objections even at the development stages, the legal powers of decision ascribed to the synod have no higher status than that of mere recommendations to the conference of bishops or to individual bishops, according to whether, in any given case, the material under consideration is such as to be subject to a decision binding upon all the bishops of the bishops' conference or to the decision of an individual bishop. In the nature of the case, therefore, although the bishops are included in the synod to help in advising it and in arriving at its decisions, the synod itself is merely an advisory organ of the bishops, at least so far as the juridical aspects of the synod as such are concerned. This small degree of competence ascribed to the synod as such obviously raises many questions: the question of whether another synodal constitution could have found any favour at all with Rome on this point; the question of whether, given sufficient boldness and sufficiently skilful tactics, such acceptance could not after all have been achieved; the question of how the public in the Church and in secular society would react to the synodal constitution on this point; the question of whether the expansion of the legal powers of decision of the synod in any essential respects would not lead inescapably to changes in many other prescriptions contained in the statute; the first and fundamental question of what is desirable at all in this matter; the question of what, on this assumption, the attitude of the members of the synod should be towards the synod; the question of whether the position of the synod will not be, to a certain extent, paracanonical, and whether it cannot in practice achieve a greater significance than that juridically accorded to it in virtue of the importance of the personalities taking part in it, the publicity attached to it, the power of its arguments, and the pressure of public opinion; the question of whether a different juridical status cannot and should not be striven for for later synods which must in fact come than is envisaged for this first one. To these and similar questions many more might be added concerning those prescriptions in the statute which, next to the paragraphs on the actual composition of the synod in itself, are surely the most important in the entire statute. In this present consideration on the part of a dogmatic theologian only one from among all such questions will be considered, yet one which is, after all, surely basic: the question of whether in view of the primatial and episcopal constitution of the Church regarded as *juris divini* such a synod can in principle have any greater juridical power of decision at all than that ascribed to it here by the proposed statute.[3] For it might be considered that the powers and authorities of the pope, the episcopate, and the individual bishop which, according to Catholic ecclesiology, belong to them inalienably and *jure divino*, cannot admit of

---

[3] We find a *prise de position* representing the viewpoints of the specialist in Church law and the historian in the following articles: J. G. Gerhartz, 'Keine Mitentscheidung von Laien auf der Synode? Erwägungen zum Beschlussrechts der Gemeinsamen Synode der deutschen Bistümer', *StdZ* 184 (1969), pp. 145–159, and R. Kottje, 'Probleme der deutschen Synode in historischer Sicht', *StdZ* 185 (1970), pp. 27–33.

other authoritative institutions, and so for example a synod, to have any further rights whatever than those of recommending and advising, especially when the members of the synod consist principally of priests and laymen. It is this dogmatic question of whether this really is the case that will occupy our exclusive attention here. What we are concerned with at the moment, therefore, is not whether a greater participation of all members of the Church in her authentic decisions is desirable – in other words a greater 'democratization' in view of our contemporary social situation, nor the question of how such a thing can be achieved in the concrete without thereby endangering the true substance of the Church and her unity. All that we are concerned with here is the simple preliminary question of whether and in what sense any such thing is possible at all from the point of view of dogmatic theology.

We believe that it is possible from the dogmatic point of view for the synod as such to have a true right of decision which would in principle also be binding upon the conference of bishops and upon the individual bishop. In saying this, however, we are not taking any prior decision at this stage as to whether it is opportune to accord such rights to the synod or as to the concrete forms in which such rights might be granted to it. Furthermore certain important points still have to be made with regard to the intrinsic limitations of such rights.

In order to make the thesis we have put forward intelligible and to justify it we must enlarge a little on what we have said. We are assuming as recognized the distinction between divine and merely human right in the Church. We are passing over the difficult question of what *jus divinum* really means if we are not to fall into an unjustified simplification of this concept. We are setting on one side the questions of whether this so-called *jus divinum* has itself undergone a process of development in the Church, at least in the apostolic age, and so at least down to the first decades of the second century; whether it is not conveivable that a further development of the *jus divinum*, still within its own true bounds, may not have taken place, extending beyond this point in history, precisely because the ultimately abiding nature of the Church demands urgently a change in the definition of right in accordance with a new historical situation, and this new conception of right can perhaps then with justice be called *jus divinum*. Let us set all these questions aside here. But surely one point can be laid down: once we recognize precisely and accurately the true nature of human right in the Church, we will see that it is not merely a supplementary right simply added on *ab externo* to the immutable principles of the *jus divinum* enclosed upon themselves; rather this human right constitutes – at least in many cases – the concretization of the *jus divinum* such that without it this would have no reality at all. This means that on a right understanding this *jus divinum*, so far from constituting a concrete law capable of being put into practice solely in its own right, properly speaking serves merely to bring out the aspect of *continuity of law* in the Church's law, which according to a Catholic understanding of the Church must be ascribed to it as a society in its abiding identity and indestructibility. In order to throw some further light on what we mean by this let us begin by introducing a large-scale example. The First Vatican Council produced a dogma concerning the primacy of the pope, and the Second Vatican Council has reiterated this binding doctrine. Now at least at first sight it may strike us as surprising that a dogmatic ecclesiology, and even 'Lumen Gentium' at the Second Vatican Council, should be totally silent concerning the legally valid modes for instituting a pope or concerning the election of a pope, as we are accustomed to express it, already even here indulging in a naive concretization. And yet the real existence of the primatial power belonging to a pope depends totally on this mode of institution. Every theologian and every canonist will say that the law governing the choice of a pope as in force in the concrete is merely human law in the Church, if only because it has undergone certain very vital changes in the course of history. There is a further question, still totally unconsidered, of how we can say that everything in the way of juridical powers in the Church depends upon the agreement or tolerance of the pope, when the Church manages the appointment of her supreme juridical head – in other words a most crucial act of decision – without the collaboration of a pope. But abstracting from this question, the point which we have come to recognize from what has been said still always retains its force, namely that so-called human Church law constitutes the concretization of a *jus divinum* such that without it this cannot have any reality at all. It is totally untenable to object to this recognition on the grounds that the human law for the election of a pope is laid down by the pope using his executive power and promulgating these prescriptions as binding on the basis of the primatial power which he holds *juris divini*. For we have only to envisage the case (which is absurd but not impossible) of the college of cardinals being totally destroyed by physical power after the death of the pope and before it has chosen a new pope. In such a case the Church could certainly choose itself a pope, for instance through its united episcopate, and the mode of selection would fall under human 'law' and, moreover, law of such a kind that according to the positive law actually in force it would not exist at all. Such a law, since it would not be laid down by any human juridical authority, would properly speaking constitute divine law or a homogeneous consequence flowing from it. Alternatively, if someone finds that too much to say, it would be a new concretization of the *jus divinum* of the primatial power such as had not existed previously. After all a simple example of this kind surely shows that divine and human law in the Church are one and continuous and interwoven with one another to an extent which is far greater and more complex than is generally recognized. If we were to analyse such an example in still closer detail it would become even clearer that divine law in the Church always and necessarily has a mode of concretization in so-called human law which is conditioned by history and subject to change, and that that which we customarily call *jus divinum* is not of itself, or taken in isolation, a law that can straightway be applied in practice. What the term stands for, rather, is the expression of an indestructible continuity of law in the Church. Yet at the unreflecting level of concrete practice and, it may be, even at that of explicitated theory, we proceed from the tacit assumption that the norms of divine law are, even taken in isolation, the kind of norms which can immediately be applied in practice. Every modification ('narrower application', if we like to put it so) *ipso facto* constitutes a violation of these sacrosanct norms.

Now let us apply our findings on this point as indicated above to our present question. The law of the bishops in the Church is not simply a law which can be formulated in abstract terms once and for all, and as such *ipso facto* a law that can straightway be applied in practice. It has always and inevitably a mode of concretization which is historically conditioned and subject to change. This mode of concretization as it *de facto* exists today has certainly a validity of its own such that it cannot be altered simply at will. But it is not immutable, and it is in principle perfectly possible for situations to arise in history which demand such change as a matter of moral principle and in the light of the gospel. If due heed is paid to such a demand of the particular moment in history, then in the concrete this means that, for instance, the bishops extend to others, their clergy and the people of God, the right to share in the process of decision-making as a human right within the Church and one which they will then recognize as binding upon themselves too in the concrete individual case. The fact that it is necessary *juridically speaking* for the pope and the bishops to give their assent to such new human law does not rule out a duty which may, under certain circumstances, exist at the *moral* level for the pope and the bishops to give such agreement. In the same way the fact that under certain circumstances such assent may be revoked does not derogate from the binding character of such a right. There are innumerable legal decisions in the Church which are capable of being radically changed, for instance by the pope, and yet by which he is juridically or at least morally bound in the concrete. If we want to explain what we have just sought to convey in a different way, one that is less dependent upon the assumptions expressed above, we can also put it in this way: an arrangement which is immediately intelligible, for instance in the case of concordats, could also perfectly well be applied to the rights and powers of the pope and the episcopate. These rights and powers are partly *juris divini* and partly, as they *de facto* exist, *juris humani*. And it is perfectly possible for those vested with them so to restrict their application by human law that others can in concrete fact share in the exercise of them in arriving at binding decisions. It might of course be said that a right which was conceded in this sense would always and constantly be kept alive merely by the grace of those vested with official authority *jure divino*. And an abiding suspicion might remain that, to the extent that such human law within the Church would necessarily be devised by those vested with official authority *jure divino*, it would after all remain subject to the arbitrary decisions of the official authorities so that the people of the Church would have no abidingly stable role in the process of decision-making on the part of the bishops. It is, of course, true that in such an arrangement a certain element of uncertainty is constantly present. But *in practice* a law of this kind in the Church, even a merely human one, has, despite its dependence on those who are officials *jure divino*, an immense stability deriving from the historical situation, public opinion, and the power of custom, factors which still have their influence even upon the minds of popes. For centuries at a time the law of the Spanish kings relating to the nomination of bishops was less threatened – even though it was human law and as such capable of revision – than many of the norms of divine law within the Church. And over and above this, even *in principle* this attitude of mistrust towards such human law in the Church is unjustified. In a specific historical situation affecting mankind and the Church merely 'human' law of this kind within the Church can have the force of an absolute moral requirement or even be authenticated as a demand of the *jus divinum* of the Church. It can have the force of an absolute moral demand, arising from the very nature of the Church, that the abiding character of the Church as the community of free faith, hope, and love shall assume a form appropriate to a particular age precisely *in* this age and *for* it. In fact there are innumerable possibilities of juridical pronouncements and decisions by the official authorities of the Church which, though conceivable in terms of the abstract nature of the authority ascribed to the Church's officials, have in fact never been realized because they were not justified even from the moral point of view by the concrete situation and the basic attitudes of the individuals within the Church. Conversely many structures and institutions have imposed themselves even despite any arbitrary decisions – in themselves conceivable – which might have been taken by individuals vested with official authority, even though in themselves such intsitutions did or do belong merely to the sphere of human law. If, therefore, we conceive of the clergy and the people of the Church being accorded a more active role and one which is more strongly rooted in law in collaborating with the bishops in arriving at binding decisions, we should not seek to discredit efforts made towards this end from the outset by considering that such collaboration ultimately remains at the mercy of the free arbitrary decision of those in the Church vested with official authority *jure divino*. Conversely we should not maintain that such collaboration is irreconcilable with the concept of an official authority which is *juris divini*. This is just as incorrect as it is false to maintain that the choice of a bishop by the people of the Church is necessarily in contradiction to that constitution which belongs to the Church *jure divino*.

The resistance to such ideas which is fairly clearly being shown by Rome and by the bishops surely stems not so much from an undeclared and ultimately unchristian desire for power, or from some naive attitude of self-assertion, but rather from the fear that the result of such 'democratization' in the Church will be that among the people of the Church as they *de facto* exist the purity of faith, the truth of the gospel, and the abiding nature of the Church would be exposed to danger. In rejoinder we might of course recall the simple faith and hope that God's grace can ultimately speaking just as well preserve the people of God in the truth of the gospel as popes or bishops, and in fact that it will so preserve them because the people of God belong to the true Church just as vitally as those who hold official positions in it. But even apart from this we still must, on any showing, maintain this: the thesis we have formulated is that from the point of view of dogmatic theology it is perfectly possible for the people of God to have an active part to play, which belongs to them *jure humano* and as of right, in the decision-making of the bishops (just as in the actual choosing of these). This thesis does not exclude the fact that the bishops ultimately speaking continue to have a right recognized as binding to object to such decisions arrived at in common when they are outvoted *in those cases in which* the dictates of their consciences warn them that such a decision would damage the purity and integrity of the Christian truth, that unity of the Church which is necessary even at the institutional level, and the union of particular and regional Churches with the pope. A conscience clause of this kind does not from the outset reduce such a decision once more to the level of a mere recommendation. For first there will be many cases of such decisions which in themselves will not be acceptable to a particular bishop or even to the majority of the conference of bishops, yet which nevertheless cannot be rejected by a conscience clause of this kind and so are binding in human law even for the bishops. And a further point which we will be able to make is that even in the secular sphere such cases of conflict can take the form of 'constitutional conflicts', cases of conscience, or emergencies, and can be subject to an ultimate right of veto. And this does not mean that such decisions, arrived at democratically and through parliamentary procedures etc., would from the outset or in all cases, cease to be binding in law. If for instance a law were passed in the parliament of the Federal Republic of Germany and by its government, and, moreover, without any objection on the part of the national constitutional courts, such that this law represented an encroachment on the basic rights of man in some essential respect, then unless we choose to adopt an attitude of absolute juridical positivism, we shall have to say that the individual nevertheless has the moral duty to resist, that such a law would be invalid, and that the true Germany would continue to exist among those participating in this protest. A protest of conscience of this kind on the part of the bishops (at least in those cases in which the entire episcopate came forward in union with the pope) would, on our assumptions, certainly not *ipso facto* constitute positive law solely in virtue of the decisions of these authorities since in fact *ex supposito* such law should be enacted by the episcopate and the people of the Church together, and the collaboration of the people of God belongs or can belong to the concrete modes in which the *jus divinum* of the Church's official authority is realized. But in the eyes of a Catholic ecclesiology a protest of conscience of this kind on the part of the episcopate would constitute an unambiguous sign of the fact that in the concrete case the authoritative body empowered to take the decision, and *ex supposito* made up of the episcopate and people together, no longer had in any sense that institutional and juridical continuity and identity with the Church which is necessary in order that such a decision may be the legal decision of the Church itself and as such binding in conscience. Thus with the above-mentioned provisos we can surely unreservedly commit ourselves to the following position: with regard to the arrangement whereby all members of a synod are given an active voice in the taking of decisions, these decisions being themselves of their nature decisions of the German Church and not mere recommendations to the episcopate, this arrangement is perfectly reconcilable with the rights which belong to the episcopate *jure divino*, and might constitute the mode which does most justice to the contemporary situation for realizing in the concrete the rights attached to the episcopal office. We are declaring then without reserve at the level of dogmatic theology that the statute should be formulated in such a way as to give the synod as such the right to take part in the decision-making, and not merely to have an advisory function. But obviously even when we have said this we have still not answered the questions of whether such a formulation is opportune, whether really practicable ways can be found of carrying it out, and of whether it will not possibly turn out to be desirable to describe in more precise detail the subject-matter to be covered by juridical decisions of this kind. Likewise a further question would become still more pressing, that namely of what forms should be used in the election of members of the synod such that they would be chosen 'from below', and in order that these forms clearly would correspond to the nature of the Church, and would not contribute to the synod being composed in a way which would represent a threat to the nature of the Church or the purity of the gospel over and above that threat which all that is human constantly represents for the gospel. If we had really radically Christian and 'integrated' communities which knew who belonged to them, then the question of the forms of election to the synod would probably raise no particular problem. As matters stand today, however, such a problem does exist.

All these questions belong, however, not to the department of the dogmatic theologian but rather to that of the individual man and Christian of today as such, to that of the pastoral theologian and the canonist, to that presided over by those who have drawn their wisdom from scripture and the history of the Church and yet still remain bold and courageous in outlook. This contribution could only serve as a green light, ensuring that the Church is neither dispensed from nor hindered in the task of creatively shaping its future anew by dogmatic theology and the law actually in force.

PART TWO

Questions in the Church

8

WHAT IS A SACRAMENT?

THE attempt to answer the question 'What is a sacrament?' within
the compass of a brief article will inevitably occasion us some
embarrassment. This question has almost two thousand years of
history behind it in which fresh answers have constantly been put forward. It has been the subject of controversy among the Christian confessions for many centuries. In view of this, then, what new points shall we
have to make about it? We need not go beyond the pages of *A. Skowronek*'s book on the Protestant theology of the sacraments today in order
to realize how many different points of view have to be allowed for in
treating of this question.[1] *E. Schillebeeckx*'s major work on the sacramental theology of Thomas Aquinas shows clearly that on the Catholic
side too we have anything but an official theology of the sacraments which
is uniform and accepted on all hands.[2] This means that if we are to
attempt in any sense to make a useful contribution to the discussion on
the question we have posed it can in the nature of things only take the
form of a few observations, chosen somewhat at random. There can never
be any question of a comprehensive reply according due weight to all
aspects of it.

When we compare the age of the Reformation and the controversial

---

[1] A. Skowronek, *Sakrament in der evangelische Theologie der Gegenwart* (Munich,
1971). But cf. also the discussion initiated from the Protestant side, with the Catholic
viewpoint being put, in M. Köhnlein, *Was bringt das Sakrament? Disputation mit
Karl Rahner* (Göttingen, 1971).

[2] cf. E. Schillebeeckx, *De sacramentele heilseconomie. Theologische bezinning op S.
Thomas' sacramentenleer in het licht van de traditie en van de hedendaagse sacraments
problematiek* (Antwerp, 1952). But see also the numerous suggestions by the author,
especially *The Church and the Sacraments*, Quaestiones Disputatae 9 (Edinburgh/
London, 1963) and also, in the present volume, 'Considerations on the Active Role
of the Person in the Sacramental Event' and 'Introductory Observations on Thomas
Aquinas' Theology of the Sacraments in General'.

theology ensuing from it with the age of the Fathers and of the Medieval theologians we notice that in the former greater weight was attached to the question of the institution of the sacraments by Christ. One of the arguments used to support the rejection of several sacraments of the Catholic Church was that it could not be established from Scripture that they were instituted by Jesus Christ. The Council of Trent, on the other hand, laid down that all seven sacraments were instituted by Jesus Christ in this sense, and according to established and orthodox ideas in post-Tridentine theology each of the seven sacraments was regarded as having been instituted by the explicit words of Jesus. The situation today, as I see it, so far as the historical question of the institution of the sacraments is concerned, is that both confessions have drawn together to the extent that even the Protestant exegete and theologian will no longer assert with such boldness and apodictic certainty that the institution of baptism and the eucharist in the New Testament goes back to explicit words of institution on the part of the historical Jesus. For the Protestant exegete and theologian, therefore, the situation with regard to the sacraments recognized in the Protestant Churches seems to be in principle no longer so radically different from the situation at which the Catholic exegete and systematic theologian had previously arrived from his own standpoint with regard to the institution of the other sacraments.[3] My only reason for referring to the new common ground which has thus been gained is in order to make it clear that the theologians of both confessions can and must seek afresh for a common point of departure in investigating the question of the institution and the existence of sacraments in the Christian Church. I believe that this point of departure is the distinctive theological character of the word uttered in the Church as the eschatological presence of God.

[3] G. Ebeling, 'Erwägungen zum evangelischen Sakramentenverständnis', *Wort Gottes und Tradition* (Göttingen, 1964), p. 225, where we find: 'It is peculiar to the sacraments that they draw attention with absolutely penetrating insistence to the basic situation from which the gospel emerged. To suppose that the sacraments necessarily must have had their origins in some explicit act of institution on Christ's part is to interpret the fact that they are rooted in Christ in a sense that is short-sighted and over-rigid. For instance in order to maintain that Jesus is the foundation of the Church it is not absolutely necessary to say that Jesus founded the Church by some explicit act. . . . It is the same with the sacraments too. They derive from Jesus in the sense that they bear witness to himself as the *summa et compendium evangelii*'. cf. also E. Jüngel and K. Rahner, *Was ist ein Sakrament?*, Kleine ökumenische Schriften 6 (Freiburg, 1971); *Das Sakrament – Was ist das?* by E. Jüngel, pp. 9–61.

WORD OF GOD AND SACRAMENT

It is in fact correct to say that in Catholic theology, if we abstract from a few attempts in recent years, there has been hardly any developed theology of the word at all. The usual and officially accepted theology does, it is true, include among the various ramifications of fundamental theology, a doctrine of the word of divine revelation. Right down to the Second Vatican Council the approach of fundamental theologians, as upheld in the official and established theology, was to regard this word as the bearer of truths which were 'objective' and correct. Properly speaking it was taken into consideration only to the extent that this word proceeds from the original bearer of revelation. On this showing, then, this fundamental theology of the word can certainly not be regarded as that theology of the word in the absolute which is both necessary and possible today. This is not to deny that the *membra disjecta* of such a theology are not to be discovered at the most varied points within Catholic theology where they have been latent all along.[4]

A theology of the word in this sense could perfectly well become the basis for a theology of the sacraments in which the sacrament figures as the supreme human and ecclesiastical stage of the word in all its dimensions which has been uttered in the Church as such. One has the impression that in the past word and sacrament have been regarded as two different entities right from the origins, so that the only task for theology is to work out the difference between sacrament and word as clearly as possible.[5] This view has prevailed presumably since Augustine. It then appears chiefly in the controversies between Catholic and Reformation theologians, and even figures not infrequently in Protestant theology. The real position, however, seems to me to be this: we must first recognize clearly what happens to words between men as a result of factors in history and in concrete human living. They are liable to great variations. Furthermore we must work out the essential character of the word uttered in the Church and through the Church as event of grace – in other words as the word which is in principle exhibitive, and, moreover,

---

[4] cf. for instance the author's article, 'Priest and Poet', *Theological Investigations* III (London and Baltimore, 1967), pp. 294–317; 'The Word and the Eucharist', *ibid.* IV (London and Baltimore, 1966), pp. 253–286; 'Poetry and the Christian', *ibid.*, pp. 357–367; 'Gottes Wort, den Menschen aufgetragen', *Knechte Christi* (Freiburg, 1967), pp. 45–56, and also the summarizing presentation on the proclamation of the word in *Handbuch der Pastoraltheologie* I (Freiburg, 2nd ed. 1970), pp. 237–317.

[5] cf. in this connection H. Fries, *Wort und Sakrament* (Munich, 1966).

exists in the Church as the eschatological presence of God's salvation in the world. We must also recognize that the variability of the human word in general, as due to factors in history and in concrete human living, also applies to this word of the Church and in the Church. Now if we recognize all these factors then we can arrive at a concept of the sacraments in which the sacrament is understood as one quite specific word-event within a theology of the word. Nevertheless such a concept does not reduce the sacrament in its own specific character to the level of any other kind of words, the uttering of which has a justified place within the Church.

It is precisely the Catholic theology of the sacraments which should least of all dispute the fact that the word constitutes the basic essence of the sacrament and that by comparison with the word the 'matter', the *elementum* has at basis the merely secondary function of providing an illustration of the significance of the word. For the Catholic theology of the sacraments recognizes seven sacraments such that, however strongly we may have to emphasize the intrinsic differences between them, they have a common nature at least in an analogous sense. And yet in the case of matrimony and penance this theology of the sacraments recognizes two sacraments which consist merely in the word. All the speculations of medieval or modern times aimed at preserving a sacramental hylomorphism of matter and form, element and word, even in these two instances fail to escape from a needless splitting of hairs. According to Catholic teaching there are sacraments which are enacted in words alone, and it follows that the true nature of sacrament as such must consist in the word. In no sense, however, does this imply anything against the binding prescriptions governing the use of the element, the matter, in the case of other sacraments for the very reason that as a matter of quite general principle the validity and effectiveness of a word in a social dimension can be dependent upon conditions which are positively laid down to accompany or to be combined with the pronouncing of this word.[6]

A Protestant theology of the sacraments should on a true view really have the fewest objections of all to raise to taking the theology of the word as a point of departure in this sense for the theology of the sacraments. The most recent Catholic theology is actually orientated towards such a point of departure from several different points of view.

From among all such factors prompting us to take the theology of the word as a starting-point in this sense for our theology of the sacraments

[6] The thesis that the material element of the sacrament is not the decisive factor is treated of and established at length by the author in 'The Word and the Eucharist', *Theological Investigations* IV (London and Baltimore, 1966), pp. 253–286.

we may confine ourselves to mentioning three in particular: the question already mentioned in our opening remarks of how we can give an intelligible account of the institution of the sacraments, and above all of those sacraments which are matters of dispute in theology, without coming into conflict with the findings of modern exegesis;[7] the doctrine made explicit in Catholic theology during and since the Second Vatican Council that already in the word itself the proclamation of a genuine presence of the Lord as bringing about salvation is achieved,[8] in other words the word pronounced at the behest of the Church always and in principle has an event character, an exhibitive character; the doctrine of the Church as the basic sacrament of salvation. I would like to enlarge a little on the two last-named ideas in order thereby to indicate at least the source from which we could probably arrive at a description of the nature of sacrament as such at the level of abstract theory.

THE SAVING CHARACTER OF THE WORD

I believe that it is a conviction common to all Christians, and in the last analysis transcending the differences between the confessions, that the word pronounced in the Church in the name and at the behest of God and Christ has in principle an exhibitive character, that it effects what it signifies, to express it straightway in the formula which is classic to the theology of the sacraments.[9] Obviously this character which the word has in the Church as event and as exhibitive can and must have been instituted at some specific point, and it would be possible to insist that what is involved in this act of institution, in which the character referred

---

[7] On this cf. the author's *The Church and the Sacraments*, Quaestiones Disputatae 9 (Edinburgh/London, 1963).

[8] cf. *Conc. Vat.* II 'Sacrosanctum Concilium' (Constitution on the Liturgy) no. 7, where we find: '. . . Christ is always present in his Church. . . . In the sacrifice of the Mass . . . under the Eucharistic species . . . in the sacraments . . . in his word'; and 'Dei Verbum' (The Dogmatic Constitution on Divine Revelation) no. 2: 'This plan of revelation is realized by deeds and words having an inner unity: the deeds wrought by God in the history of salvation manifest and confirm the teaching and realities signified by the words, while the words proclaim the deeds and clarify the mystery contained in them.' Finally 'Lumen Gentium' (The Dogmatic Constitution on the Church) no. 19, 23 etc., where the proclamation of the gospel assumes pride of place throughout in the teaching of the Church's officials.

[9] On this cf. the author's *The Church and the Sacraments*, Quaestiones Disputae 9 (Edinburgh/London, 1963), the explanations on the *opus operatum*. See also O. Semmelroth, 'Opus operatum – opus operantis', *LTK* VII (Freiburg, 1962), cols. 1184–1186.

to was imparted to the sacrament, is not merely some purely gradual process by which the distinctive qualities were introduced into it. But this would not contradict the thesis enunciated above. On the contrary, the overall 'event' character of the word in the Church regarded as word of God fully admits of further essential distinctions existing between different words which have this status.

This is in fact the case even at the level of secular terminology. Words conveying mere information, words properly belonging to the sphere of human intercommunication, words expressing personal and ultimate decision and imparting it to others etc., share in the single common nature of the human word and yet at the same time differ essentially from one another. But the difference involved here is after all one of degree. The words used have a greater or lesser depth in terms of concrete human living and of radical importance in their implications for society, and so in the various levels of significance which speaker and hearer alike are called upon to enter into when such a word is used. Hence the same can unreservedly be said of that word which the Church utters. The word conveying catechetical information has certainly not the same character as word as that which proclaims the death of the Lord or that which assures the individual in his concrete situation of the forgiveness of his sins. But in any case, so I believe, a point on which Catholic and Protestant theology could agree is that the truly kerygmatic and ecclesiastical word achieves the full realization of its own nature in those cases in which it has an exhibitive character, in which that which it expresses is actually brought about *through it,* or in which it is addressed to the hearer in ways that bring salvation to him. But what of those cases in which the word used does not have this true character of the Christian word? In such cases, while we can and should speak of a truly Christian word, what is in fact involved is a form of the Christian word which, while it is perfectly legitimate, is nevertheless of a deficient mode. And all such words have the function of preparing for, surrounding, or following from this true word, the exhibitive word of grace, and are orientated to it.[10]

The following point may be noticed in passing: If and to the extent that

[10] The word of God in its full and original sense is not to be conceived of as belonging to the level of instruction in propositional form 'about something', nor merely as pointing in an intentional sense to a state of affairs which for its part is totally independent of this instructional reference. Rather it is to be conceived of as an exhibitive word, a word that renders present. It is in it and through it that the reality designated is first and foremost given, and, moreover, in a relationship of mutual conditioning of such a kind that the word is constituted by the reality which thereby comes to be, and the reality comes to be in that, and because, it reveals itself

the Christian community is something more than the mere sum total of the individual Christians who hearken in a spirit of grace and respond to the justifying grace of God, then it must be conceivable at least in principle that a word of God which is, in the strictest sense, exhibitive, and has an 'event' character in this way, is addressed to this single community as such. This consideration could open the way for, and actually lead to, an understanding of the fact that the eucharist can and must be called a sacramental 'word' event not merely or exclusively to the extent that the individual receives the body of the Lord for his own personal salvation, but also to the extent that the proclamation of the presence of the Lord's death as bringing about salvation takes place within the community as such and for it as such. But this is merely in parenthesis.

Evidently it cannot be our task here to establish this 'event' character – in other words this character which the Christian word in the strict sense has as being at basis and essentially sacramental from the theological sources. All that we need say in order to define in the most general terms the general area within Catholic theology where such a proof might be given is this: that apart from grace (at least as offered, albeit perhaps continuing to exist in conditions in which it has been rejected) the word of God as revelation would not really be, or continue to be, the word of *God* in any true sense at all. Rather it would be degraded to the level of a human word about God, albeit one which might perhaps have been caused *by* God.[11] The word of God in the strictest and truest sense, therefore, can exist at all only as an event of grace. Hence it must have an exhibitive character. It must be a saving event. For that grace in which alone it can be hearkened to is at the same time itself the reality of salvation. As we have said, this is not to exclude the fact that there are specific degrees of sharing in the power of this word according to the way in which it is hearkened to in the concrete conditions of human living. To that extent too there are varying ways and varying degrees in which this word itself achieves its own true nature. In the light of this we can understand and take seriously what we are told in the theology of Paul VI too when he speaks boldly and uncompromisingly of a true presence of Christ in the word of preaching.

---

in this way. All these are points which are established by the author in his article, 'The Word and the Eucharist', *Theological Investigations* IV (London and Baltimore, 1966), pp. 253–286; but see also *Conc. Vat.* II 'Dei Verbum' (The Dogmatic Constitution on Divine Revelation), no. 2.

[11] On this cf. the author's article, 'Wort Gottes', *LTK* X (Freiburg, 1965), cols. 1235–1238.

THE FUNCTION OF THE CHURCH AS SIGN

We have been speaking of a theology of the word which includes as intrinsic to itself and as its own proper supreme point a theology of the sacraments. A second approach to a theology of this kind is the doctrine of the Church as the basic sacrament of the salvation of the world.[12] For the moment we are not concerned with the relationship in terms of connection, distinction, and subordination in which the Church as basic sacrament stands to Christ as the historical arch-sacrament in whom God's self-utterance as forgiveness and divinization comes to its historical manifestation and its irrevocable fulness. It is in any case an explicit word of the Second Vatican Council, which itself in turn is connected with the patristic theology with its more comprehensive concept of the *mysterion* and *sacramentum*, the 'sacrament of unity', the 'sacrament, i.e. sign and instrument of intimate union with God and of the unity of all mankind' (*Lumen Gentium* no. 1). The Second Vatican Council never developed in any truly systematic or explicit way the concept of the sacrament of the salvation of the world which is the Church. For this reason it is not very easy to say what precisely is being expressed by this term in the mind of the Council. At best we will have to take as our starting-point the fact that ultimately speaking it is in virtue of her entire reality, and so above all through those factors which belong to her very nature as determinative and constitutive, that the Church constitutes this basic sacrament, and at the same time we shall have to apply to the Church precisely those basic properties which are familiar to us from the official and established theology of the individual sacraments. This latter approach is justifiable if only because the Church is in fact intended to be the sacrament of the salvation of the world and of the unity of mankind as a unity in God which brings about salvation – in other words between the Church on the one hand and salvation and unity on the other a distinction is drawn and at the same time a connection is established which is characterized as 'sacramental', signifying that in the concrete it can consist only in the fact that the Church is the sign in history which brings to manifestation at the

---

[12] On this cf. O. Semmelroth, *Die Kirche als Ursakrament* (Frankfurt, 1953); P, Smulders, 'Die Kirche als Sakrament des Heils', *De Ecclesia* I, G. Baraúna ed. (Freiburg, 1966), pp. 289–321; J. L. Witte, 'Die Kirche "Sacramentum unitatis" für die ganze Welt', *ibid.*, pp. 420–452; E. Schillebeeckx, 'Die Kirche als Dialogsakrament', *Gott – Die Zukunft des Menschen* (Mainz, 1969), pp. 100–118; *idem*, 'Die Kirche "Sakrament der Welt" ', *Gott – Kirche – Welt* (Mainz, 1970), pp. 263–269; J. Groot, "The Church as Sacrament of the World" *Concilium* I/u, (January 1968), pp. 27–34.

historical level, and thereby also 'effects', that will of God towards the world which creates salvation and unity.

This becomes still clearer when we take as our basis the nature of the Church and regard her as fulfilling two roles in *one*. She is both the proclaiming bearer of the revealing word of God as his utterance of salvation to the world, *and at the same time* she is the subject, hearkening and believing, to whom that word of salvation of God in Christ is addressed. Thus we regard the Church as the believing one who preaches and as the proclaiming one who believes both in one. In this view of the Church two aspects must be borne in mind. This word of revelation from God sustained by the Church both as proclaimer and as hearer is that which imposes itself as eschatologically irrevocable, unsurpassable and victorious. For it is the word which has not gone forth provisionally and in a manner which can be surpassed on the lips of some prophet, but is rather the ultimate and definitive word which God has pronounced in his own Son as his victorious self-utterance. At an earlier stage we said that for a Catholic theology of the word this word should be understood simply as that which is sustained in grace as the self-communication of God. To this we must now add a further point (to express it in the same scholastic terminology): the word of the gospel is always sustained by a grace which is *de facto* effective by the power of God and not merely by good will on man's part, at least so far as the world as a whole is concerned, a world to which in Christ not merely an offering of the grace of God is given so as to be simply subject to and made over to the capricious exercise of freedom in this world; rather a grace is bestowed which, however unconscious the individual may be of salvation, predestines the world as a whole to salvation and not to perdition. Finally this word of salvation in the mouth of the believing and proclaiming Church, regarded as a word that is eschatologically victorious, is directed not to the Church but to the world. In the documents of the Second Vatican Council the Church is in fact called the sacrament of the salvation of the world and of the unity of mankind as brought about by grace. The Church neither is nor needs to be conceived of as the holy remnant, consisting exclusively of those predestined to salvation. Rather she is the bearer of that eschatologically victorious word that creates salvation, of the self-utterance of God to the world. And with the Second Vatican Council we can at least say that this eschatological word of grace addressed to the world and sustained by the Church can still be victorious in ways known to God even in those cases in which the individual becomes a believer through this grace of God as proclaimed in this way, despite the fact that throughout his lifetime at the conscious and empirical level this faith of his has not brought him through baptism into union with the Christian Church or Churches as constituting a visible society.

Our findings, therefore, can be stated as follows: in virtue of her faith, which she herself hearkens to in faith and proclaims in the grace of God as eschatologically victorious in Christ, the Church is the sacrament of salvation for the world because she points to and renders present that grace in the world as eschatologically victorious which will never more disappear from the world, and which is insuperable in impelling this world towards the consummation of the kingdom of God, whatever the pitfalls which may lie in its path. This sacramental sign of grace is an effective sign not inasmuch as it would call forth a resolve of God to bestow grace which would not exist without it, but inasmuch as through it precisely this will of God to bestow grace manifests itself at the historical level, and thereby at the same time also renders itself historically irreversible. The general effectiveness of the Church as sacrament, therefore, can be conceived of in the same way as we can reasonably conceive of the effectiveness of the individual sacraments precisely as signs of this kind (though obviously even in officially accepted Catholic theology there are many other theories with regard to the effectiveness of the individual sacraments than that which I have just indicated above, and which, if we want to have a term in which to express it, we might call the real and symbolic effectiveness of the individual sacraments). This means that we can attain to a theology of the exhibitive character of the Christian word from a theology of the Church as sacrament as well, just as, of course, a corresponding line of thought can be developed in the opposite direction.

CONCERNING THE NATURE OF THE SACRAMENTS

On the basis of the considerations put forward above concerning the theology of the word and the Church as sacrament of the salvation of the world we can now surely go on to achieve an understanding of the special quality of the sacraments themselves. They constitute the highest stages in the word of grace in the Church in its character as exhibitive and as event. A word of this kind (this is in fact a point which we have already adumbrated in our foregoing remarks) can be pronounced as the word of grace to the community as such, in other words as that proclamation of the death and resurrection of the Lord which renders present in the community the reality of salvation. It is then called eucharist or Last Supper.

This word can be uttered to the individual by the Church and in the Church in situations which are, in the existing conditions, of radical importance in concrete human living. Then – though this is a point which we do not have to develop in detail here – we have the rest of the sacraments which are recognized by the Catholic Church and, moreover, in a sense which we must now go on to say something more about under the heading of the institution of the sacraments by Christ. Such a word has an exhibitive character. It is that word which, from God's point of view, he does not repent of, that word which is effective in itself, which is the manifestation of that effective grace which, from God's standpoint, predestines men to salvation, which is bestowed victoriously upon the world and in principle transcends its resistance. It should therefore be characterized as capable of being refused only to the extent that its nature as eschatologically victorious from God's point of view should not simply or undialectically be thought of as a denial of the possibility of a spirit of lovelessness and unbelief in the *individual*. In saying this we have *ipso facto* also expressed that which, in the theology of the sacraments, is signified by the Catholic doctrine of the sacrament as *opus operatum*. Basically speaking this doctrine expresses nothing else whatever than the victorious power which belongs, from the standpoint of God, to the exhibitive word of faith, which in fact achieves the true fulness of its own nature precisely in the word[13] of the sacrament.

The impression is borne in upon me that by taking the starting-point for a theology of the sacraments indicated above we could also arrive at a solution of the old problem of the *institution of the sacraments by Christ* in a manner which avoids any great speculative subtleties or any historical improbabilities.[14] With regard to the theory that specific sacraments have

[13] The Mystery of the word (*sacramentum*) consists, indeed, precisely in the fact that it is effective. The Church as *creatura Verbi* is based upon its *opus operatum*. On this cf. the author's article, 'Ekklesiologische Grundlegung', *Handbuch der Pastoraltheologie* I (Freiburg, 2nd ed. 1970), pp. 121–157, and also *ibid.*, 'Die Sakramente als Grundfunktionen der Kirche', pp. 356–366. A further work which may be found helpful in this connection is A. Winklhofer, *Kirche in den Sakramenten* (Frankfurt, 1968).

[14] Right down to the present day theology has failed to come to any unequivocal conclusion as to the precise significance of the expression 'institution by Jesus Christ'. On this cf. H. Lennerz, *De Sacramentis Novae Legis in genere* (Rome, 3rd ed. 1950); A. Vanneste, 'De instelling van de sacramenten door Christus', *Collationes Brugensis et Gandavensis* I (1950), pp. 433–448; K. Rahner, *The Church and the Sacraments*, Quaestiones Disputatae 9 (Edinburgh and London, 1963), pp. 41–74; M. Schmaus, *Der Glaube der Kirche* II (Munich, 1970), pp. 279–280. It may be noticed that both the Council of Trent and the medieval theologians who are the standard

a direct historical connection with the pre-Easter Jesus and his words, this is a theory which, for our present purposes, we must neither accept nor deny prematurely. But we can adopt the following simple conclusion: the sacraments in general have been instituted by Christ because and to the extent that the Church as such derives from him.

In my opinion this statement can and must be taken as applying also to those sacraments which, as for instance in the case of the eucharist or even perhaps baptism, have a palpable historical connection with Jesus himself and his explicit words or deeds. For even in the case of sacraments such as these their ultimate nature as *opus operatum*, as effective, exhibitive word, can be rendered intelligible only in the light of the more general theological considerations indicated above concerning the nature of the Christian word and the Church. Only in a Church of the eschatological

---

witnesses for this are thinking, when they use this term, not of the history but of the effectiveness of the sacraments, and this in itself is enough to show that an historicizing interpretation of the term is unnecessary. On this cf., amongst others, F. Scholz, *Die Lehre von der Einsetzung der Sakramente nach Alexander von Hales* (Breslau, 1940). There we find on p. 125, with reference to the Council of Trent: 'On the basis of the records which were kept there can be no room for doubt that the Council was confining its attention within the framework of the declarations provoked by the Protestants, and that what it sought to define, and in fact did define, when it spoke of the sacraments being instituted by Christ was intended in the sense of the sacraments being given their force by Christ.' The support of Lugo is invoked in the following further considerations on the subject on p. 126: 'The institution attributed to Christ by the Council, therefore, consists in an interior decree of the Lord whereby the statement of the conditions expressing the causal connection between the enacting of the rite and the imparting of grace achieves its validity. This connection established by the act of institution is valid in itself independently of whether it is in fact posited or recognized at all, if only Christ has effectively caused it. We would therefore actually be justified in saying that the sacraments were instituted by Christ even supposing that the fact that Christ actually had brought them into a conditional mode of existence (*causatio in esse condicionato*) had never been known to anyone, and supposing no individual sacrament had been conferred, i.e. caused actually to come into concrete existence. We find a similar view in Thomas Aquinas, namely that the sacraments, in virtue of their institution, have the power of conferring grace: 'It seems, therefore, that a sacrament is instituted at that point at which it receives the power to bring about its effect', *Summa Theologica* III, Q.66 a.2. On the question of the 'historical' institution of matter and form there were different interpretations both before and after Trent. The school of Löwen explicitly invoked the authority of the Council in steadfastly maintaining the thesis of an *institutio immediata sed generalis*. Word and spirit are ordered to one another to the extent that both have their same historical point of departure in Jesus. Where this can be discerned from our view of the basic living situations actually mentioned in Scripture, there we speak of a sacrament.

word of Christ can the sacraments, which also held a special promise of grace for early Protestantism, be rendered intelligible in a genuinely theological sense precisely in this character which they have as promise. But if we then go on to the further consideration of what great difficulties present-day exegesis, whether from the Catholic or the Protestant side, meets with even with regard to these sacraments, then I cannot really see why we should deny this sacramental and exhibitive character to the rest of the sacraments acknowledged by the Catholic Church so long as there are sacraments in the Church at all. But this is, after all, a conviction common to all Christians.

If I were permitted to formulate one further hypothesis in this connection it would be this one: despite all the numerous difficulties and obscurities in the fields of dogma and the history of theology which go right back to the High Middle Ages and affect the Catholic Church's awareness of her faith, she has at the Council of Trent defined that there are precisely seven sacraments and no more.[15] It is true that the two sacraments which for Catholics are the sacraments of initiation, namely baptism and confirmation, are, even for the most orthodox Catholic theology, more closely interconnected than the rest of the sacraments. In other words even from this point of view there is a certain lack of precision intrinsic to the doctrine that there are seven sacraments. But let us abstract from this particular difficulty. A further point concerns the sacrament of order. This subsumes within itself a multiplicity of sacramental conferments of office, and it has not even clearly been laid down about these that the Church has not the power to decide what their number and content should be. In other words from this point of view too considerable problems arise in the average officially accepted theology with regard to the number seven. But again let us abstract from this. But apart from all these points we can perhaps even go so far as to say this: without denying that the sacraments derive from Christ the fact that there are seven such radical and exhibitive words of grace in the Church is not simply laid down as given by the authority of the Church alone, but implies an historical decision on the part of the Church herself (albeit one that was arrived at at a very unreflecting level), a decision in which the Church ascribed to these

---

[15] How in more precise detail we conceive of the number of the sacraments is always dependent on the point of how we define the concept itself. On the various possibilities cf. J. Finkenzeller, 'Die Zählung und die Zahl der Sakramente', *Wahrheit und Verkündigung* II, *Festschrift M. Schmaus* (Munich, 1967), pp. 1005–1033. On the symbolic interpretation of the number seven cf. J. Dournes, 'Why Are There Seven Sacraments?', *Concilium* I/4 (January 1968), pp. 35–44.

words and to no others that absolute commitment of the Church which is necessary from the very nature of the case for a radical and exhibitive word of grace of this kind called a sacrament. Such a conception does not necessarily imply that the Church either now, later, or from some specific point in the past, could actually have created either more or less such words of grace called sacraments, in which she could actualize her own nature as basic sacrament, applying it to situations in the concrete life of the individual which were crucially important. For it is perfectly conceivable, as I have attempted to explain elsewhere, that the Church, in the linear advance of her history, arrives at irreversible decisions such that she can no longer turn back to her former state prior to taking them.[16]

If we assume that what has been merely sketched out above is theologically speaking at least possible, then, I believe, we might achieve a juster and more impartial view of the *de facto* historical development both of the sacraments and also of the theology of the sacraments than is the case in Catholic theology and history of dogma, which hitherto has had to regard the sacraments as deriving from Christ in a manner which (except in the case of baptism and the eucharist) involves very great historical difficulties. It might perhaps be possible on this basis gradually to resolve and to bury the controversy between the confessions as to the number of the sacraments. A Catholic theology of the sacraments not merely does not need to – it actually must not – deny, as a result of the Council of Trent's decision, that the sacraments when compared with one another differ very essentially in importance among themselves.[17] And a modern Protestant theology which respects its own exegesis and is convinced of the exhibitive character of the word of God in the Church, and of the fact that humanly speaking it is necessarily subject to variations, does not need after all in principle to oppose the idea that in the Church there can be words of the Church to the individual which vary very greatly among themselves and yet have an exhibitive and 'event' character. The existence, meaning, and range of these are naturally to a large extent dependent on the will of the Church which utters them. All these points are, of course, merely indications by which we are attempting to show that in the discussion between the theologies it is by no means so necessary to remain stuck fast in those controversial blind alleys in which we nowadays seem at first sight to find ourselves trapped.

[16] cf. the author's article, 'Reflection on the Concept of "Jus Divinum" in Catholic Thought', *Theological Investigations* V (London and Baltimore, 1966), pp. 219–243.

[17] cf. Y. Congar, 'The Idea of "Major" or "Principal" Sacraments', *Concilium* I/4 (January 1968), pp. 12–17.

9

INTRODUCTORY OBSERVATIONS ON THOMAS AQUINAS' THEOLOGY OF THE SACRAMENTS IN GENERAL

Thomas Aquinas has devoted five questions of his *Summa Theologica* to the doctrine of the sacraments in general.[1] Even from a purely formal point of view the structure of this small treatise appears extremely simple and clear. It opens with the question of the nature of a sacrament. From this it goes on to treat of the reality and necessity of the sacraments in the various sections of saving history. Only then does he come to consider the New Testament sacraments proper, above all under the aspect of the relationship they bear to the grace imparted by them. Thomas speaks here of the instrumental causality of the sacraments in imparting grace, and of the manner in which this instrumental causality is related to God and Christ. In addition to the grace which they cause some of the sacraments also confer a further special effect, that namely of sacramental character, a question to which Aquinas devotes a special exposition at this point. Finally there are certain further causes and conditions to be discussed which are necessary for a sacramental sign to be brought about, whether in its initial institution or in the specific act of conferring it in the concrete. In conclusion one more question has to be investigated, that concerning the number of the New Testament sacraments, as also the way in which they are interconnected. Since Thomas regards the effectiveness of the sacraments as a distinct question in its own right, the doctrine of the sacraments in general, as he approaches it, gives rise to five main themes. Following upon this he then presents his

[1] cf. *Summa Theologica* III, Qq. 60–65. But see also St Thomas Aquinas, *Opusculum* 5 (*De articulis fidei et Ecclesiae sacramentis*). [It subsequently served as a model for the 'Decretum pro Armeniis' at the Council of Florence; cf. DS[34] 1310–1328.] We should notice A. Ferland's work, *Commentarius in Summam D. Thomae –* 'De Gratia. De sacramentis in communi' (Montreal, 1938).

considerations of the individual sacraments in the sequence which he himself has established.[2]

After this general view of Aquinas's presentation of the doctrine of the sacraments in general, and bearing in mind the difficulty of the subject-matter involved, it cannot be regarded as any criticism of Thomas if we feel bound to conclude first and foremost that this initial impression of simplicity and clarity in the structure of the treatise is after all not altogether correct. Indeed the order in which the individual themes are developed, and above all the internal arrangement of them into a series of articles, turns out to be problematical. Nor does it make any difference to this fact to find that the beginning of the treatise, represented by the first two questions, is wholly convincing. For here the sacraments are presented in a context of general anthropology (as we might call it). Yet the first point that is spoken of is the character of the sacraments as signs and, as a concomitant of this, their setting in saving history (we might almost speak of a general perspective of history of religion). For in fact such signs, in their nature and existence, are not confined to the New Testament age of salvation.

Admittedly as the exposition continues from this point onwards the development of ideas in it becomes less clear. For one thing the place assigned to many of the articles is far from convincing. And again the overall context within which this or that individual subject is treated of seems disproportionately broad. Moreover ideas which are quite disparate are set side by side.[3] But surely the ultimate reason for this lack of clarity, over and above all these others, is the fact that the relationship between the 'sign' function[4] and the instrumental causality[5] of the sacraments as Thomas presents them is not fully thought out in its ultimate significance. Yet it is emphasized that both aspects belong to the sacrament. The first represents a further extension of the ancient theological tradition of Augustine, and the second – probably developed more by Aquinas himself – is designed to overcome a danger which – it is evident – Thomas himself clearly recognized, the danger, namely, that the sacraments themselves might be regarded merely as sheer external manifestations of an event of grace which in itself is totally independent of these signs.

[2] cf. *Summa Theologica* III, Q. 65, art. 2.

[3] We might, for instance, conceive of art. 4 of Q. 65 equally well as an article of Q. 61. For instance the fact that the treatment of sacramental character occupies six articles seems disproportionate. We may also compare the very disparate themes discussed in Q. 64 etc.

[4] On this above all Q. 60.

[5] On this above all Q. 62.

These, then, according to Aquinas, are the two basic aspects under which we have to view the sacraments. Yet in his own treatment the precise connection between them has still not been conveyed in an adequate manner. Hence his presentation of the duality of these two aspects has subsequently led to the most varied interpretations of his doctrine as to the nature and effectiveness of the sacraments. These variations in interpreting Thomas' doctrine have followed almost perforce according to whether the one aspect or the other has been regarded as the predominant one. But this is a point which cannot be entered into in any greater detail here.[6]

It is true that even on this doctrine of the sacraments in general a modern theologian will derive great profit from the work of Thomas Aquinas.[7] But there is no need for him to refuse to recognize that in this work much remains unsaid which nowadays calls for explicit and extensive consideration in the doctrine of the sacraments. In the present context we must take up some of these points and throw them into stronger relief.

It must be remembered that the *Summa Theologica* of Thomas Aquinas does not include any developed ecclesiology, and that the treatise on the sacraments follows immediately upon that of christology, which is itself included only at relatively late stage. In view of these facts it is of course impossible for there to be any really effective treatment of the Church as

[6] On this cf. E. Schillebeeckx, *De sacramentele heilseconomie. Theologische bezinning op S. Thomas' sacramentenleer in het licht van de traditie en van de hedendaagse sacramentsproblematiek* (Antwerp, 1952); *idem, De Christusontmoeting als sacrament van de Godsmoeting* (Antwerp, 1957); E. Fritsaert, 'La définition du sacrement dans S. Thomas', *Nouv.Rev.Th.* 55 (1928), pp. 401–409; J. Menessier, 'Les réalités sacrées dans le culte chrétien d'après S. Thomas', *Rev. Sc.Ph. Th.* 20 (1931), pp. 276–286, 453–471; M. Gierens, 'Zur Lehre des hl. Thomas über die Kausalität der Sakramente', *Scholastik* 9 (134), pp. 321–345; A. M. Hoffmann, 'Der Begriff des Mysteriums bei Thomas von Aquin', *Div.Th.* (Fribourg, Switzerland) 17 (1939), pp. 30–60; B. Brazzarola, *La natura della grazia sacramentale nella dottrina di S. Tommaso* (Grottaferrata, 1941); H. Dondaine, 'La définition des sacrements dans la Somme théologique', *Rev.Sc.Ph.Th.* 31 (1947), pp. 213–218; P. B. Garland, *The Definition of Sacrament According to St Thomas* (Ottawa, 1959); O. Semmelroth, *Vom Sinn der Sakramente* (Frankfurt, 1960); J. M. R. Tillard, 'La triple dimension du signe sacramentel. A propos de Summ. Theol. III, 60, 3', *Nouv.Rev.Th.* 83 (1961), pp. 225–254. But see also the various studies by the author, especially in the present volume, 'What is a Sacrament?' and 'Considerations on the Active Role of the Person in the Sacramental Event'.

[7] On this cf. merely the studies of the author in Vol. XIII of this series, 'Homage to Thomas Aquinas' and the attempt at a dialogue on material points in 'The Truth in Thomas Aquinas'.

'basic sacrament'[8] as a distinct theme. This inevitably has a damaging effect on the doctrine of the sacraments in general too, for the connecting member, so to say, is missing. Or to put it in other terms: the truly ecclesiological dimension of the sacraments is not taken into consideration. Even at those points at which Thomas interprets sacramental character as deputing the subject concerned to the Christian cult,[9] and at which, as a result, there is a suggestion of an ecclesiological view of the sacraments, the Church is still not clearly included as a vital factor. For as Aquinas presents it this Christian cult is precisely viewed too much as a task of the individual functionary officially appointed in each case.

Obviously the theological tradition of the Church has right from the outset included many statements about the word of God as proclaimed by the Church and its effectiveness in imparting grace. But this is still far from saying that there is any explicit or systematic theology on the subject. Hence in the theology of the sacraments too the unity and the distinction between word and sacrament remain ultimately obscure.[10] It would do no harm if we were to regard the doctrine of the sacraments in general as one quite specific section of the theology of the word of God and its exhibitive force.[11] For then we would understand the sacraments as those words in which that which is expressed by them is rendered present by this expression itself when these words are addressed by the Church as basic sacrament to the individual man with a radical commitment as the irreversible and historical presence of the grace of God to him. But so far as Thomas Aquinas is concerned this connection between a theology of the word and a theology of the sacraments still remains wholly in the background. In drawing attention in this way to the limitations of a great theologian such as Thomas we are not in any sense detracting from his greatness or his relevance for today.[12] All we are doing, rather, is to point out that there is something further, extending beyond the works of Aquinas, which should not simply be forgotten: the still greater riches of the whole theological tradition as well as the tasks which confront the

[8] On this cf. *Conc. Vat.* II, 'Sacrosanctum concilium' (The Constitution on the Liturgy), nos. 5 and 26.

[9] cf. Q. 63.

[10] This remains valid despite some isolated indications to the contrary in Thomas. cf. e.g. Q. 60, art. 6.

[11] On this cf. the author's study in the present volume, 'What is a Sacrament?' and also 'Considerations on the Active Role of the Person in the Sacramental Event'.

[12] On this cf. the author's study in *Theological Investigations* XIII, 'Homage to Thomas Aquinas'.

theology of today, and which could not possibly have emerged into relevance in the thirteenth century.

Introductory observations such as these cannot have the function of providing a direct commentary on the text of Aquinas. Such a commentary would have to present first and foremost in the form of explanations everything which can be gleaned from the text itself. As we have already said above, the purpose of these observations is quite different. They are intended to draw attention to certain points, aspects, and dimensions in Thomas Aquinas' teaching on the sacraments in general which would not be recognized clearly enough on a simple reading, but which must not be overlooked by any modern theologian in the use he makes of the teachings of Aquinas. In this connection what we are concerned with is not so much to provide a full or comprehensive treatment as to present a few random examples and starting-points, and so to afford fresh insights and to habituate our readers to an approach which is indispensable if we are to take due account of the work both of Thomas Aquinas and of tradition in general in a way which is necessary and fruitful even today.

Right at the beginning of these observations[13] Aquinas makes it clear that according to his convictions the primary and most radical point of departure for our understanding of the sacraments is to be found in the concept of 'sign' and so of 'symbol'. This is a point which must not be forgotten precisely when in his subsequent treatment of the New Testament sacraments Thomas goes on to emphasize their instrumental causality.[14] This causality, which is described only in very formal terms, is not to be interpreted as a causality *added on ab externo* to the (eschatological) signs of the New Testament, but rather as a power of originating which belongs to these *signs* as radical acts of self-realization on the part of the Church as being of her very nature (as sign) the eschatological basic sacrament.

It is noteworthy that right from the outset St Thomas presents the seven sacraments (in the proper sense) within a broader context of religiously symbolic realities, and thereby from the outset prevents them from being isolated in a sense which would be unjustified both from the point of view of Christian religious practice and from that of the history of religion. Man is in principle always he who achieves his innermost relationship with God in and through the religious symbol.

---

[13] cf. Q. 60, art. 1. From this point onwards we shall normally be following the development of ideas as presented by Thomas Aquinas in the five questions. From time to time we shall include notes to contribute to a wider orientation for those interested.   [14] On this cf. Q. 62.

A further point which is of basic theological importance is the threefold orientation of the sacramental sign. The sacrament of the New Covenant is *signum rememorativum, demonstrativum,* and *prognosticum.* Here the modern theology of the future, of promise, of hope, might find a starting-point in Thomas Aquinas in its aim to integrate within itself the idea of the sacraments precisely as *signs* of eschatological promise and hope.

But this would also serve to bring to light the task of evaluating the sacraments still more effectively in their special quality from the point of view of the unity of man's nature as composed of body and spirit.[15] Yet at the same time we would have to pay due heed too to the human word as *res sensibilis,* if only so as to achieve a true appreciation of specific sacraments, such as those of penance and matrimony, within the general framework of this conception. These sacraments are in fact conferred through words alone without any 'element' distinct from and supplementary to the words themselves.

A further point which might be re-expressed in terms of present-day problems,[16] and which would call for consideration here, would be the historical contingency of the concrete sacramental signs, which despite the fact that they are mere representations, are nevertheless binding for each individual according to the particular stage of development in the history of mankind to which he belongs.

Following the development of Aquinas' ideas, we should then emphasize the intrinsic mutual interrelationship which exists between the ritual actions and the *word,* for it is in virtue of this that the factor of ritual is from the outset inserted into the dimension of history as well, and does not merely belong to that of nature.

The unity of word and sacramental 'element' (including gestures) is made particularly plain in Thomas by means of a sacramental 'hylomorphism'. Yet this conception also has all the disadvantages which have arisen in the course of time and which are entailed in an excessively physical understanding of such a hylomorphism. In the light of this a certain reserve is advisable for the modern theologian, though in the same connection he will certainly gladly take cognizance of certain points of departure for an approach through linguistic philosophy.[17]

The following considerations of Thomas might be taken as a starting-

[15] On this cf. the author's study in *Theological Investigations* XIII, 'The Truth in Thomas Aquinas', where he treats explicitly of the body-spirit constitution of man and its significance for knowledge.

[16] On this cf. Q. 60, art. 5.

[17] On this cf. Q. 60, art. 7 ad 2 and ad 3.

point for a theology of the history of the Church which might serve to enable us to understand the factors of continuity and distinction in the history of the sacraments. As a matter of historical fact the sacraments have in the past undergone an extraordinary number of changes in their rites, the place they occupy in Christian life, and the theological interpretations placed upon them, so that precisely today there are many who feel themselves disquieted and deprived of their security when they discover this fact.

The anthropological arguments for the necessity of the sacraments as seen by Thomas should serve to warn us not to be too one-sided in regarding these as depending *solely* on a positive act of institution by Christ. Such an act of institution itself in turn presupposes those grounds which Thomas sets forth in their own right.[18]

The force of the arguments in the ensuing development of ideas[19] is somewhat questionable when compared with the first *ratio* which Thomas had previously presented. But in any case a more significant effect of Aquinas' presentation is to suggest that we should view the sacraments within the totality of the history of religion in general as well as within the universal history of salvation, the central point of which is Christ himself. This naturally suggests the idea that in other places too and at other periods within the history of religion, i.e. outside the New Testament revelation, analogates to the Christian sacraments may be discovered. But to return to the Christian sacraments proper. They are interpreted as *signa protestantia fidem*, i.e. a unity becomes discernible within the duality such that – as early as the writings of St Paul – justification is attributed sometimes to faith and sometimes to baptism. Faith is the deciding factor. The sacrament is the proclamation (obviously in an exhibitive sense) of this faith.

The article which now follows is, in Aquinas' conception, one of the most important ones.[20] Thomas is right when on the one hand he presents the sacraments as being 'in a certain manner' a cause of grace and on the other simultaneously qualifies this causality, which he cautiously accepts as affirmed by tradition, as merely instrumental in character. But this instrumental causality is not interpreted on the basis of the sign itself, and the instrumental causality as such also remains at a very formal level. As the subsequent history of theology shows, it is still open to the most varied interpretations. The axiom that Thomas formulates in this

[18] On this and on what follows cf. Q. 61, art. 1ff.
[19] Here we are treating of Q. 61, art. 2.
[20] On this cf. Q. 62, art. 1ff.

connection, *efficiunt quod figurant*, is a fine one, but one which surely calls for considerable further thinking out.

In this connection in Thomas' presentation[21] a good point of departure is offered from which we could cease to regard the individual sacraments merely as designed to meet particular situations in Christian living, but would also interpret them precisely *as* manifestations ('signs') of basic acts in which the fulness of Christian existence is achieved in the visible and manifest life of the Church. For the grace which they signify is no abstract grace, but rather the human radicality and the divine depths of those acts in which the fulness of human existence itself is achieved.

What follows basically speaking represents merely a translation of the ideas of Hugo of St Victor according to which the sacraments contain grace as in a 'vessel' into the demythologizing language, so to say, of Aquinas.

In this connection the concept of instrumental causality is still further developed, though on a true reading there is still a failure to reach beyond the formal abstraction of the concept of instrumental causality. We must guard against an excessively 'physical' interpretation of the *'virtus'* together with its *'esse transiens'* which is conferred in the sacrament by God as the true cause of grace. But the question now arises of how the Christian sacraments impart 'objective redemption', i.e. render it present in the achievement of the fulness of existence on man's part as sustained by grace. The key word here is the *humanitas Christi* as the instrument of redemption which is united with the Godhead. Yet this should not be interpreted as though it were merely the 'glorified Lord' who was referred to, or as though we did not also at the same moment have to think of the crucified and risen Lord in his place in concrete history. Only so long as we keep clearly in mind the identity between the historical and the glorified Lord can the instrumental causality of the humanity of Christ be conceived of as an effective element for communicating grace through the mediation of the sacraments, and only so can we avoid falling into an incomprehensible 'ideology'.

But this in itself indicates an expansion leading to a whole theology of the history of salvation with its unity, with the essential difference between its various sections, with the special eschatological quality of the 'new and eternal covenant' in which alone, in virtue of this special quality which it has, the sacraments can constitute an *opus operatum* (i.e. a promise of his grace on God's part which from his point of view is eschatological, and of which he will not 'repent').

[21] cf. Q. 62, art. 2.

Sacramental character was subsequently defined at the Council of Trent, and the interpretation of it as a *deputatio ad cultum* is reasonable and has, moreover, come to a large extent to win general acceptance in the theology subsequent to Thomas. But we should still avoid any excessive separation of this sign in the '*soul*' from the *sensibile sacramentum*. For unless we do this, according to Thomas Aquinas too it would in fact no longer have any 'sign' character. In the same way, in order to do justice to the earliest theological tradition concerning sacramental character we should not overlook the ecclesiological dimension of this sign. Character in fact imparts a quite specific place and function to its subject in the *visible* Church as worshipping community. Properly speaking, character is 'invisible' only in the sense in which other social relationships too are not simply visible in a direct sense and capable of being verified by our eyes.

If sacramental character is interpreted as a commissioning to divine worship according to the rites of Christianity, then obviously it also implies a 'spiritual power'. Admittedly it is noteworthy that Thomas uncompromisingly regards this divine cult itself in turn as consisting either in the *reception* of a gift from God or as the further transmission of such gifts to other men – in other words as itself in turn an act of *God* in relation to us.

The development of ideas which follows can be interpreted as a doctrine of the universal priesthood of all Christians as consisting in a participation in the eternal priesthood of Jesus Christ. In this way the universal priesthood of the Lord will not have to be interpreted as something that is derived in a weakened form from the priesthood of the official ministry of the clergy.

This will lead to emphasis being laid on the dynamic, 'operative', and functional characteristics of the sacraments, as well as on the grace bestowed in them, and upon the sacramental character in relation to these characteristics. As a general approach for our understanding of the further arguments developed by St Thomas we may recommend the recognition that the freedom of man as an historical factor still in process of achievement in time is already comprehended by the eschatologically definitive decree of God for man. This will lead on to a further and connected idea concerning the more recent theology of marriage. It regards the indissolubility of the marriage bond as an abiding promise of divine grace, and recognizes in this that marriage bears a certain resemblance to those sacraments which imprint a character.

After these very particular developments the next line of argument returns once more to the central point. Here Thomas throws into relief the absolute sovereignty of God's grace even in the sacraments, and rejects in unmistakable terms any kind of magical interpretation of this sign as misconceived, as well as any kind of clericalism such as might represent a threat to the immediacy of man to God. Thomas does in fact again and again pose questions to himself even though his answers frequently – and in this case too – remain at a very formal level. So far as the historical question is concerned of the institution of the sacraments by Jesus Christ (as the Council of Trent has defined it for all the sacraments), and of the precise form and manner in which this would have taken place, obviously no such answer can be adduced even in broad outline. If we come to speak, in connection with this question, of the rejection of Donatism, then we should avoid any ill-considered transition from the dispenser of the sacrament to its recipient. For the true effect of the sacraments as conferring grace is achieved in the case of the adult only in a genuine personal belief and in an actual disposition of love on the recipient's part. The doctrine that the personal dispositions of the conferrer of a sacrament too should be in conformity with his sacramental act does in fact ultimately show too that the Church taken as a whole, in which, under certain circumstances, sacraments can be conferred even by sinners, not only should be, but actually *is* holy, i.e. taken as a whole it never lacks that grace, the basic sacrament of which is the Church itself in the world.

St Thomas then goes on to remind us of a principle[22] which it is all too easy to overlook again and again, and which may remain unheeded both in theory and practice: God has not attached his power to the sacraments in such a way that he could not also impart the effects of sacramental grace even without the sacraments themselves. Now taking this as our starting-point we can adopt an approach to the entire theology of the sacraments which is the opposite of that usually envisaged. According to this, what is brought to effective manifestation in the dimension of the Church in the sacraments is precisely *that* grace which, in virtue of God's universal will to save, is effective everywhere in the world where man does not react to it with an absolute denial.[23] Thomas is further concerned to reconcile the objectivity of the sacrament as *opus operatum* with the recognition that if ever the sacrament ceased to constitute a personal

[22] cf. Q. 64, art. 7.

[23] cf. on this the various studies by the author including in their titles the key term 'anonymous christian', and in the present volume, 'Observations on the Problem of the "Anonymous Christian" ' and the literature there adduced.

act and at the same time (which does not imply any opposition) an act of the Church as society, and, moreover, in relation to its conferrer as well, it would be reduced to mere magic. He then takes up once more his anti-Donatist defence of the objective validity of the sacrament, and it is here that we find the statement that the conferrer of a sacrament 'acts in the person of the Church as a whole'. In this it is the nature of the sacraments precisely as factors in the life of the Church as a society that achieves clear and forcible expression, still more clearly than if Thomas was speaking only of the fact that the conferrer acts as an instrument of Jesus Christ. It is noteworthy too that Thomas envisages only the case of heretical baptism in which the sacrament is valid indeed but does not impart any grace. Today we would surely regard the other case as the normal one.

In his considerations Thomas Aquinas can assume as already given the development, in the history of dogma within the Church, which had led to the conscious distinguishing of the true sacraments as contrasted precisely with other ecclesiastical rites, and thereby too to the fact that they are seven in number. Against this background he finds ready to hand a speculative argument *ex convenientia* in support of this idea. Yet it cannot be denied that the place thereby assigned to the Eucharist among the other sacraments is such as to reduce it too much to the same level as they, and that an unbalanced view of the importance of marriage is arrived at whereby it is regarded merely as a means to counter concupiscence and to promote human reproduction. But even of Thomas it must be said on the one hand that he cannot really transcend his age or his environment, while on the other that he cannot say everything whatsoever that deserves mention.

For the rest the further points to be found in the text of Aquinas are wholly convincing only if we have already taken as established beyond question the traditional sequence of the sacraments. In any case Thomas is fully aware of the problems arising from the fact that we subsume, and reduce to a single uniform level, under the concept of 'sacrament' ways in which the Church achieves the fulness of her own nature which essentially differ from one another.[24] It may be observed that in the case of

---

[24] Obviously the only case in which the concept of 'sacrament' can justifiably be described as reducing all to the same level is if it is regarded and used in an explicitly univocal and horizontal sense and reduced to a few purely formal characteristics. But if we include in our view of it a reference to its origins and its history, then we arrive at the idea that the manifestation of Jesus Christ was itself a sacrament, that the Church as a whole is a sacrament in the sense of a sign effecting salvation. Since the

baptism Thomas says that it is necessary for salvation only in a conditional sense when he is treating of the baptism of adults, even though he holds the opinion (which is nowadays disputed) that for the immature it is necessary for their salvation in an absolute sense.

These brief and almost catalogue-like observations arising from a reading of Thomas Aquinas' arguments on the doctrine of the sacraments in general provide, it is true, no more than indications, and do little to complete the picture. Yet we can perhaps precisely on this account offer a useful key and a line of approach which promises to be fruitful – not merely for the text of Aquinas but also for the questions which have been mentioned.

Second Vatican Council an explanation seems to have been arrived at even in conceptual terms which it is helpful to keep firmly before our eyes in order to retain a more comprehensive and more appropriate view of the sacrament as such and of the concrete sacraments in particular. According to this Jesus Christ is to be appealed to as the 'arch-sacrament' while the Church is to be characterized as the 'basic sacrament', so that its derived character is made clear. But the idea of the Church as sacrament is of basic importance in its turn for the individual sacraments conferred within the Church, which hitherto have constituted the almost exclusive, and in many ways isolated, subject-matter of the doctrine of the sacraments in dogmatic theology. For the indications provided by the Second Vatican Council see n. 8.

I O

CONSIDERATIONS ON THE ACTIVE ROLE OF THE PERSON IN THE SACRAMENTAL EVENT

I N the considerations which follow we shall be examining the active role of the person in the conferring of the sacraments. We shall, of course, be including within our purview all those sacraments in which the full consciousness and living faith of the subject is engaged in his act of receiving them. In practice, therefore, only infant baptism will remain outside the scope of our present considerations. However, since the theme is so broad in scope, we shall concentrate chiefly on the Eucharist. Here the distinction between the sacrificial act and the reception of the sacrament will be left in the background. Yet for our present purposes the Eucharist is taken as representative of all the sacraments. One who is theologically educated can easily apply our statements about the Eucharist and the points which apply first and foremost to it to the other sacraments, each according to its special character, and there is no necessity to provide a special exposition of this in each particular case. While, therefore, we are treating explicitly of the Eucharist, our remarks are intended to apply to all the sacraments.

We have set ourselves to state, to justify, and to elucidate certain principles, and to show them to be orthodox in terms of dogmatic theology. This implies something like an application of a Copernican approach[1] to the general conception of the sacraments, consisting in an

[1] This special approach has to be applied within the context of a distinction which is fundamental for any sacramental theology, the distinction namely between the sacrament itself and the effectiveness of grace in personal life. To clarify this cf. also, therefore, the following articles by the author: 'Personal and Sacramental Piety', *Theological Investigations* II (London and Baltimore, 1963), pp. 109–133; 'The Eucharist and Suffering', *ibid.* III (London and Baltimore, 1967), pp. 161–170; 'Formale Grundstrukturen der Heilsvermittlung', *Handbuch der Pastoraltheologie* II/1 (Freiburg im Breisgau, 1966), pp. 55–79. Similarly E. Schillebeeckx, *De*

intellectual and spiritual movement of the sacramental event outwards to take effect in the 'world', and backwards in a spiritual movement leading from the world to the sacrament. This way of putting it may sound some-what grandiose, and is presumably still not wholly comprehensible. The whole of the considerations which follow are intended to contribute towards an elucidation of this initial statement. Only so can the religious significance of this 'Copernican application' effectively be rendered intelli-gible. In this connection we are of course aware that in order to clarify our special concern we must in some respects simplify, and must separate and draw contrasts between realities which in concrete life always exist in unison, albeit in varying proportions and with some more apparent than others.

THE OLD MODEL: SACRAMENT AS ISOLATED ENCOUNTER WITH GOD

How does the average Catholic Christian feel about a sacrament as he customarily receives it? We might describe this act of receiving (though of course with the provisos already mentioned) as follows: the Christian feels that he lives in a secular world. He is aware that his life in this world is subject to commandments of God which are difficult to fulfil. He is aware of being summoned by God and set upon a course which leads him out of this present life through the gates of death and beyond into the eternity of God. He has to maintain union with God, his true future and the law-giver presiding over his life even in the present. He passes to and fro from this secular world into a sacral sphere a 'fanum' or 'temple'. It is only here (and in a true sense exclusively here, so far as his personal feelings are concerned, whatever his head may tell him from its stock of theological knowledge) that it is possible to achieve any real encounter with God in which this God meets him not merely as making moral demands upon him but as sanctifying him and bestowing grace and strength upon him. This is achieved precisely in the sacraments and above all by holy Mass in the Eucharist. In these sacraments God's actions upon humanity touch the individual as it were from without, penetrate him, sanctify him, and transform him (at least carrying these processes a stage further, although for the most part the effects are experienced as very transitory and in a sense peripheral). Here man encounters God and Jesus the Lord so that afterwards he can (ideally speaking) be sent by him to go forth once more into a secular world, there to pursue his monotonous everyday duties in a certain sense remote from God. Here in the sacrament (as in no other circumstances) man achieves closeness and union with God. Here he has left the secular world behind him. Here, and in a true sense here alone, that takes place which renders life meaningful and 'religious' (i.e. united to God).

In the achievement of Christian living is such a viewpoint really the only possible one in the light of our understanding of the Christian faith – a viewpoint in which the sacramental event constitutes the true apogee of Christian living? This can be doubted and indeed denied. But in denying it we are not rejecting the legitimacy of this common conceptual model of the place which the Eucharist and the sacraments have in general in our lives. What we are rejecting, rather, is the idea that we are compelled to accept this viewpoint as the only possible one. We can also 'experience' the sacraments in a quite different way.

We may begin by stating quite freely that the earlier conceptual model we have described is nowadays much under attack. Modern man's awareness of reality is such (it makes no difference whether this in itself should be subjected to critical questioning or whether it is anything but an absolute norm) that the sacraments as taken in this sense are all too easily thought of as religious rites which bypass the dimension of 'real reality' or 'real life'. The sacraments fall under the suspicion of being empty ritualism, so that it is only in terms of an ideology which is nowadays difficult to achieve or to maintain that they can be felt as important or as an effective force in human life. In this conceptual model we all too easily receive the impression that the sacraments, the Mass, are 'useless', that they are incapable of bringing about any real effects in human life, that after Mass everything goes on as before and as it would go on even without Mass. If the 'religious man' attributes 'consolation' and strengthening to his religious experiences, which after all he undergoes in receiving the sacraments, then the less 'religious' man will reflect that the other is fleeing from the harsh realities of life into an ideological world of unreality, albeit one of a psychic unburdening, and that this world of unreality on the one hand does nothing to alter the 'realities' of life while on the other it endures only so long as we fail to see through the psychic mechanisms and techniques involved in such 'consolation'. And if we are then called upon to 'take out with us into our everyday life' the sacrifice of Christ, to let the sacraments take effect in our lives, then this is merely to set up a moral norm and obligation the powerlessness of which is something from which it is sought to flee precisely through the sacraments. For (on this view) it is not the sacraments which carry the individual out into life by their power, but rather the individual himself who must carry them out into life by his own new moral strivings to meet and so to fulfil the claims of morality which they make upon him. That which we experience as their power is in reality the special new moral striving which we regard as required of us in order to fulfil their ideals. More acutely than in former times we have the feeling that the numerical frequency of our reception of the sacraments does not *ipso facto* have any true religious significance (even when it is undertaken with good will) unless we regard the reception of the sacraments as being itself in turn a 'good work', the value of which increases *ipso facto* according to the number of times it is repeated, in which case we are running counter to the intrinsic meaning of the sacraments themselves.[2] The present-day tendencies, even within the Catholic sphere, towards a 'desacralization' of Christianity and of Christian living may in many respects be false or questionable. But in any case they do produce unease with regard to sacral and sacramental activities. With regard to the statement of the Second Vatican Council that the Mass constitutes the supreme point of Christian living it may be doubted whether, even if we confine ourselves to serious Christians only, this *ipso facto* expresses their real attitude of mind.[3]

It is not only fashionable tendencies towards 'secularization' of one kind or another that nowadays represent a threat to the free use of the sacraments. A far more basic danger is represented by that recognition, which is nowadays becoming clearer, of the difference between a genuine and authentic achievement of human living on the one hand and our conceptual models of, and reflections upon it at a secondary level on the other. What do we mean by this? If, for instance, someone prays: 'O God I will love you with my whole heart. This is my conscious, free, and unconditional decision', then surely everyone will admit that even in any genuine and well-intentioned declaration (in prayer etc.) of this kind the individual concerned is still far from really loving God 'with his whole heart'. By a process of objectification he has, in his own conscious reflections, constructed a conceptual or verbal model of a whole-hearted love

---

[2] The author has already discussed this question at length elsewhere. Cf. *Die vielen Messen und das eine Opfer*, Quaestiones Disputatae 31 (Freiburg im Breisgau, 2nd ed., 1966); 'Messopfer und Jugendaskese', *Sendung und Gnade* (Innsbruck, 4th ed., 1966), pp. 148–183; 'The Meaning of Frequent Confession of Devotion', *Theological Investigations* III (London and Baltimore, 1967), pp. 177–189.

[3] On this cf. the author's article, 'Das Gebet des Einzelnen und die Liturgie der Kirche' in *Gnade als Freiheit* (Freiburg im Breisgau, 1968), pp. 101–112.

of this kind, and has also in some sense affirmed it. But this replica of whole-hearted love is not the whole-hearted love itself. For this latter (if it is present at all) is achieved at a more basic level seeing that freedom is more basic than the reflective concept of it by which we name it (even when we may be seeking to achieve it). A further point is that even at its more basic level freedom is far from being empowered at every moment of the individual's personal history to achieve that towards which it is of its very nature orientated: radically to control the total and ultimate reality of the person in all dimensions in such a way as to determine its final and irrevocable state. Now of their very nature the acts in which we receive the sacraments are attempts, as a matter of the radical decision of our freedom, in a spirit of love and from our whole hearts to orientate ourselves irrevocably to God. Yet precisely in the light of his experience of the nature of freedom, which always remains ultimately beyond the scope of any conscious manipulation on the part of the subject, modern man feels himself beset by problems in his reception of the sacraments precisely when this takes place very frequently and without any special reference to the unfolding process of freedom in the true sense and the *kairos* it contains, which it is not given to the subject to decide upon at will. Modern man all too easily has the impression of acting ungenuinely and even dishonestly, and precisely in those cases in which this reception of the sacraments is related excessively and exclusively from the outset to the individual's own personal saving history taken in isolation. For in this act of receiving the sacraments it is not always possible for something particularly decisive to take place such as can be readily brought to fruition through the ritual celebration of a sacrament. Evidently such problems are not fully disposed of by that factor which we are seeking to treat of here, namely the broadening of the awareness of the recipient of the sacraments so as to view saving history within world history as a whole or by relating them in faith to that grace which constitutes the dynamic force and the *entelecheia* of this whole saving history, drawing the individual man into this history and shaping its own manifestation in the sacramental sign within the individual life. Nevertheless these problems are diminished and made easier to solve if the recipient of the sacrament is conscious from the outset of being drawn into this 'cosmic' history of grace.

A NEW MODEL: USING THE WHOLE OF LIFE TO BRING THE SACRAMENT TO ITS FULNESS

But is there another view of the Eucharist and of the sacraments? Yes there is. It is based upon the simple fact of dogmatics that that which we call sanctifying grace and divine life is present *everywhere* where the individual does not close himself to God who creates salvation by a real and culpable denial, and further on the fact that in a real sense, albeit to some extent unconsciously, this grace is brought about and made manifest in the concrete conditions of history and of human life wherever men live and die so long as this life of theirs has not come to imply mortal guilt. We have no intention here of developing, justifying, or defending this fact of dogmatics in any greater detail here.[4] All that we shall do is to elucidate it in its further implications for an understanding of the sacraments that either has been, or is to be transformed, and that too as concretely as possible.

GOD'S GRACE AS CREATING SALVATION AT THE ROOTS OF HUMAN EXISTENCE

The world is permeated by the grace of God. The sacraments are specific events of God's grace as forgiving, sanctifying, and imparting the divine nature. But while they have this significance this does not mean that it is solely in the moment of the sacramental act that the grace of God impinges upon a world that is secular and devoid of grace as from without, as though it sought to penetrate this world and, in the very act of so seeking, gradually lost its pristine force and receded until a fresh act of the same kind renewed it once more. The world is constantly and ceaselessly possessed by grace from its innermost roots, from the innermost personal centre of the spiritual subject. It is constantly and ceaselessly sustained and moved by God's self-bestowal even prior to the question (admittedly always crucial) of how creaturely freedom reacts to this 'engracing' of the world and of the spiritual creature as already given and 'offered', the question, in other words, of whether this creaturely freedom accepts the grace to its salvation or closes itself to it to its perdition. Whether the world gives the impression, so far as our superficial everyday experience is concerned, of being imbued with grace in this way, or whether it constantly seems to give the lie to this state of being permeated by God's

---

[4] On this cf. the author's article in the present volume, 'Observations on the Problem of the "Anonymous Christian" ', and the further literature there adduced.

grace which it has, this in no sense alters the fact that it is so. And without this belief and hope that the world has been endowed with grace in precisely *this* sense, the appeal to the sacraments as almost intermittent moments when such 'engracing' takes place would seem to modern man unworthy of belief. He would be unable to avoid the impression that what is involved in the doctrine of the sacraments is an ideological elevation of a world that is hideously secular, and one which conceals the truth without really changing the world itself.

At the present moment the time is not ripe to enquire what meaning the sacraments can then have, if they are not to be thought of as the particular moments in which God 'intervenes' in his world from without. If we say that grace has all along possessed reality from the innermost heart and centre of the world and of persons as spiritual, then this too is still to express the matter in terms which are far too abstract. It is true that we can speak of God as the nameless and incomprehensible mystery only in very abstract terms. And for this reason too the reference of man to God, the fact that his existence is open to and orientated towards the mystery of God has of its very nature something unnameable in it. How could it be so easy to describe the path, seeing that it leads into the pathlessness of the inconceivable God? How could we find it easy to describe in words the ultimate act of man in which, surrendering himself, hoping, loving, adoring – in a word believing, he allows himself to fall into this ineffable mystery which constitutes the innermost basis, *and at the same time* the infinite remoteness of his existence that draws him out of himself? And if grace constitutes precisely that power which enabled him to achieve this making over of himself to the absolute mystery and that most special quality given by God enabling him to achieve this, how then can it be easy to speak about it in 'intelligible' terms?

But one point must be emphasized about this grace precisely to the extent that it proceeds from the innermost heart and centre of the world and of man: it takes place not as a special phenomenon, as one particular process *apart from* the rest of human life. Rather it is quite simply the ultimate depths and the radical dimension of all that which the spiritual creature experiences, achieves and suffers in all those areas in which it achieves its own fulness, and so in its laughter and its tears, in its taking of responsibility, in its loving, living, and dying, whenever man keeps faith with the truth, breaks through his own egoism in his relationships with his fellows, whenever he hopes against all hope, whenever he smiles and refuses to be disquieted or embittered by the folly of everyday pursuits, whenever he is able to be silent, and whenever within this silence of the heart that evil which a man has engendered against another in his heart does not develop any further into external action, but rather dies within this heart as its grave – whenever, in a word, life is lived as man would seek to live it, in such a way as to overcome his own egoism and the despair of the heart which constantly assails him. *There* grace has the force of an event, because all this of its very nature (i.e. precisely through God's grace which has all along broken open mere 'nature', leading it beyond itself and into the infinitude of God) no longer has any limits or any end but (as willingly accepted) loses itself in the silent infinitude of God, is hidden in his absolute unconditionality in the future of the fulness of victory which in turn is God himself.

And precisely here one further point must be made concerning this grace which constitutes the innermost depths and the mystery of human life at its average and everyday level: this innermost dynamism of the normal 'secular' life of man as it exists always and everywhere has found in Jesus of Nazareth its clearest manifestation, and in him has proved itself as real, victorious and attaining to God. And it has done this precisely in a life of this kind, in which he has become like us in all things, in other words in a life which is completely everyday in character, a life bound up with birth, toil, courage, hope, failure and death. Something which cannot be set forth *here* (though in itself it is perfectly possible to do so) is this: anyone who believes in the fact that in the human life of Jesus (and so in his death and in his resurrection as the radical dimension of *his own* everyday life) the victory of his personal life has irrevocably and definitively been promised him, and that in this (not in any other fact) the ultimate and definitive, the unsurpassable word of God has been promised him, this man also *ipso facto* (with greater or lesser degree of explicitness or implicitness) affirms in faith that which is stated about Jesus in the classic and traditional christology. A further factor *ipso facto* given in this is that anyone who seizes upon the grace of God as the radical dimension of his own personal life, as its ultimate and definitive hope, has *ipso facto* posited an assent to the historical manifestation of the definitive nature of this grace in Jesus Christ, whether or not he explicitly recognizes this definitive assent as having been posited in the dimension of his own personal history.

And finally: this grace unites us to one another in love and participation in the common lot of all. Abstracting from all more profound considerations, this is something that we recognize once we recognize that grace constitutes the innermost meaning and the holiness of the secular dimension, and this in virtue of the fact that this life, provided only that our acceptance of it is genuine, true, and loving, itself mysteriously unites us in that each one in his own personal destiny experiences and accepts that of all the rest, and conversely each one recognizes and discovers himself once he directs his gaze into the life and death of the rest.

SACRAMENT AS A SYMBOLIC MANIFESTATION OF THE LITURGY OF THE WORLD

On the basis we have defined above the sacraments constitute the manifestation of the holiness and the redeemed state of the secular dimension of human life and of the world. Man does not enter a temple, a fane which encloses the holy and cuts it off from a godless and secular world which remains outside. Rather in the free breadth of a divine world he erects a landmark, a sign of the fact that this entire world belongs to God, a sign precisely of the fact that God is adored, experienced and accepted everywhere as he who, through his 'grace', has himself set all things free to attain to himself, and a sign that this adoration of him takes place not in Jerusalem alone but everywhere in spirit and in truth. The sacrament constitutes a small sign, necessary, reasonable and indispensable, within the infinitude of the world as permeated by God. It is the sign which reminds *us* of this limitlessness of the presence of divine grace, and *in this sense* and in no other, precisely in *this particular* kind of anamnesis, is intended to be an event of grace. Now it is a lasting and tragic misunderstanding for us to turn these sacramental signs once more into a circumscribed enclave, such that it is in this alone that God is present, and that the event of his grace takes place.

Let us attempt to clarify what has been expressed in abstract terms by re-stating it in somewhat more concrete ones, and moreover concentrating especially upon the Eucharist. The world and its history are the terrible and sublime liturgy, breathing of death and sacrifice,[5] which God celebrates and causes to be celebrated in and through human history in its freedom, this being something which he in turn sustains in grace by his sovereign disposition. In the entire length and breadth of this immense history of birth and death, complete superficiality, folly, inadequacy and hatred (all of which 'crucify') on the one hand, and silent submission, responsibility even to death in dying and in joyfulness, in attaining the heights and plumbing the depths, on the other, the true liturgy of the world is present — present in such a way that the liturgy which the Son

---

[5] On this subject cf. chiefly the world of ideas of Teilhard de Chardin, e.g. *Hymn of the Universe* (London and Glasgow, 1965).

has brought to its absolute fulness on his Cross belongs intrinsically to it, emerges from it, i.e. from the ultimate source of the grace of the world, and constitutes the supreme point of *this* liturgy from which all else draws its life, because everything else is always dependent upon the supreme point as upon its goal and at the same time sustained by it. This liturgy of the world is as it were veiled to the darkened eyes and the dulled heart of man which fails to understand its own true nature. This liturgy, therefore must, if the individual is really to share in the celebration of it in all freedom and self-commitment even to death, be interpreted, 'reflected upon' in its ultimate depths in the celebration of that which we are accustomed to call liturgy in the more usual sense. This 'must' primarily expresses simply that necessity in virtue of which man must accept such manifestations *when* they are present and *when* they confront him, otherwise he himself is denying and giving the lie to those existential modalities which thereby manifest themselves to his own perdition (unless he eliminates these too).

But there is a further point, just as valid and indeed still more radical: we are understanding this liturgy only in the usual sense of the term. We can only achieve a genuine enactment of it, without causing it to degenerate into an empty ritual attitudinizing, full of unbelief (so far as our participation in it is concerned) if we draw our strength from this liturgy of the world, from the liturgy of faith as expressed in concrete 'this worldly' terms, which is identical with the history of the world as rightly enacted.

THE EUCHARISTIC MEAL

It is in this spirit, then, that the individual goes to Mass. He is filled with the knowledge of that drama into which his life is constantly being drawn: the drama of the world, the divine tragedy and comedy. He thinks of the dying who face death with the death rattle in their throats and with glazed eyes, and he knows that even now this fate has its roots within his own being. He senses within himself the sighing of creaturehood, of the world, as it yearns for a brighter future. He entertains a feeling for the responsibility of statesmen with their decisions, which call for all their courage, and yet have to be launched into an unknown future, something of the laughter of children in their unclouded joy in the future, of the tears of hungry children, of the pains of the sick, of the disappointment of love betrayed, of the dedicated realism of scientists in their laboratories, of the dedicated austerities of those who struggle for a liberated humanity – something of all these is in him. He is also aware; even though he may be living day after day with a heart full of withered superficiality, that he *cannot* give pride of place here and now to this entire history of mankind, that even this primitive and uncultivated crudity of a dried-up heart still demands in its turn, and with anguish, to be filled with all that which moves the world. And he is not surprised when the secret essence of world history, something as it were numbing and stimulating at the same time, rises up from the depths of his own inner life and floods over the dry land of his heart. He is not surprised to find that all this too is the experience of the grace of the world, which permeates the whole of history as judgement when it is denied, as a blessed future when it is accepted, and that precisely in the Cross of Jesus it has achieved its supreme point, the point at which it is no longer possible for victory to be lost to it. In his faith the Mass attender experiences the fact that this Cross still constantly is and remains a present fact right to the end of all history. He knows that those who mourn weep the tears of Jesus, those in prison sit in the cell of the Lord, those who rejoice share in the joy of Jesus, those who are lonely share his lonely nights, and so on. He knows that it is only in this indissoluble polarity between man and the Son of man that mankind and he can be understood, because it is only in him that the mystery of mankind can be grasped in its inconceivability and the hope for the future which it contains, and because it is only in the light of the meaning of humanity and in sharing in its lot that we can avoid degrading the presence of Jesus in us to the level of a mere abstract ideology. The attender at Mass, even before he has arrived at it, has already been drawn into the drama of Golgotha that was, that is, and that shall be, the drama that is world-wide, the drama that has all along taken him up in its unfolding process even before he explicitly adverts to it, that embraces 'head and members' alike, Jesus and all men in the same measure and in a relationship of mutual conditioning (albeit one that is special to each individual). For the Son of man too is willed by God 'for our salvation' because God wills a humanity consisting of 'divine beings', because a firstborn among many brethren is conceivable only among these many, so that the Spirit of Jesus is from the outset the Spirit of the world as it has been willed by God.

And so the individual goes to Mass. What is initiated there is not something which does not exist anywhere else in the world, but something which is there brought to manifestation at a conscious level and celebrated in a cultic enactment, something which really takes place in the world as God's deed of salvation and pertains to the redeemed freedom of mankind. The Cross of Jesus is not, properly speaking, set up afresh, but rather its mysterious presence in the world is proclaimed. This individual allows something which is already alive in his heart to come to the fore, to proclaim itself. For this he himself posits his explicit assent (even if he knows that the most real assent – something that God and life decide and not he through his liturgical calendar – may perhaps be posited outside the context of cultic celebration in the compassion he shows in his average everyday life or in those hours in which life reaches its ultimate extremity). Under the forms of bread and wine he offers the world in that he knows that it itself is already ceaselessly offering itself up into the inconceivability of God in rejoicing, tears and blood. He looks with praise at the ineffable light of God for he knows that this looking of his only really takes place at that point at which man's eyes see death drawing near. He knows that he is proclaiming the death of the Lord because and in that this death, as that which was died once and for all, is constantly present in the world and has already been inserted into the innermost centre of the world and in a true sense continues to be died in everyone who, whether he explicitly recognizes it or not, 'dies in the Lord'. He knows that in the Mass he is proclaiming the coming of the Lord because the Lord actually *is* in the process of coming in the world in everything which impels the world forwards towards its goal. In the holy sign he receives the true body of the Lord in that he knows that this would be useless if he were not in communion with *that* body of God which is the world itself with its destiny, that he is receiving the former body so that in the reality of his own life he may stand in an abiding communion with the latter body. He hears and utters the word of God who reveals himself in the Mass in the awareness that this word constitutes the verbal expression of that word which God himself utters in that he utters the world as his word and eternally utters himself to this world itself in his Word. He hears this word in the 'liturgy of the word' in order that it, together with the world, may become that other word, may utter it, hearken to it and accept it, that word which, though it is uttered everywhere (as nature and grace) so often falls only upon deaf ears, and 'strengthened' and in turn reflected upon in this word, seeks to make its impact in this way too at the human level.

A man goes to Mass. In doing so he is not necessarily called upon always or exclusively to fulfil in an explicit sense the claims of his oneness in destiny with the world and history as a whole. It can also be enough that in his conscious mind he opens himself to the depths of grace contained in that life which is his in a narrower sense. For this life too is in itself, and as part of the great drama of the world, broken into by the grace of God and orientated towards the inconceivability and absoluteness of God. In fact provided this man seizes upon this seemingly everyday life in a spirit of faith (that is in a willing and unreserved acceptance of the movement of this everyday life in itself) he experiences every day in it that this everyday life is sustained by the movement towards God. This is what takes place when someone loves unconditionally and even in situations in which his love is exploited and not returned, in which some-one really forgives without 'gaining anything' from it (not even the feeling of being the better man) when someone experiences the miracle of love which is bestowed upon him, he does not know why, when a man is suddenly struck with fear by some insight into the majestic inexorability of truth, when someone remains faithful to the claims of his conscience even though this faithfulness of his is exploited and used against him, and so on. In innumerable occurrences of this kind in everyday life there is always something more mysteriously present than the data yielded by direct experience. There is always a sum which defies all reckoning, an account which cannot be brought into balance by the addition of any one specific assignable item. Always in this there is a tacit reference to God who by his grace frees us in our everyday life, admitting us to his own freedom, assuming that we recognize and acknowledge this claim in our everyday life, and do so through that death which egoism can die un-noticed in our everyday lives, and assuming too that we allow ourselves to be set free for the life of God.

The individual concerned need not fear that his basic conviction of faith is under assault if he suddenly finds himself tempted to regard the sacramental rites as 'empty ceremonies', if he experiences that which takes place at the altar as a 'game' which, while it may be touching, ini-tially makes the same impression upon him as the sacrificial ceremony of a Vedic priest who feeds the gods and believes that by his actions he is keeping the world in harmony with them. Faced with such temptations a Christian of this kind does not need merely to formulate an additional ideological postulate by which, so to say, he *adds on* to these rites which he seeks to keep a divine event which would not take place apart from such ritual (though in that case, surely, the divine event would not freely and personally be appropriated!). But there is something which he has to 'add on in his mind', something in the light of which he must view these rites. Yet it is something which he does not have to create from his own ideology. In other words he does not, in any true sense, have to add it on in his mind at all (though he certainly can and should consciously reflect upon it). This extra 'something' is the divine depths inherent in real life, which are constituted always and everywhere through the grace of God with Christ as its focal point and in the self-bestowal of God upon the world. It is from this that these rites derive, to this that they point back, and without this 'something' whence they derive and towards which they tend they would truly be empty, and any other content would indeed merely be added on in the mind. He who is assailed by the fear of engaging in a ritualism which is at basis empty, which is merely filled out with ideological notions conjured up at will, must have recourse to the experience of God and of grace in his seemingly secular life, and so must say: 'This experience and the "subject matter" precisely of *it* are made apprehensible at the cultic and ritual level.' Obviously this presupposes that we have actually made an experience of this kind in our everyday life of the divine depths inherent precisely in this 'secularity' and of the grace they bring. Anyone who says that he fails to find any such experience in his life (an experience which always comes through faith, but a faith which really is 'experienced') should be answered as follows: So long as he *really* has experienced nothing of this, the sacraments must inevitably seem to him to be mere magical ritual, and according to Christian doctrine he should not even receive them, because this doctrine unequivocally forbids anyone to receive the sacraments without faith (that is without a believing experience). It would be necessary to provide such an one with instruction *and* mystagogy in the religious experience of grace in this sense, such as cannot of course be provided *in the present context*. (In this connection a point which should admittedly be taken into account is that such an individual is all along making this experience in itself, but is incapable of reflecting upon it and objectifying it in sufficient measure, and it is at *this* process of reflection and objectification that all instruction and mystagogy is aimed, and not at a process of indoctrination *ab initio*.)

THE EUCHARIST AND THE LITURGY OF THE WORLD

If this individual sees the Mass simply as a sign in miniature of the Mass of the world, to which obviously Christ himself belongs, then it follows that the Mass is after all not so unimportant to this individual. Only in a very conditional sense can he regard it as the 'supreme moment' of his life and the source of his life. It is a 'supreme moment' only to the extent that he allows God to determine *which particular* moment of his life, and under which particular 'forms', whether sacred or profane, he will encounter in his life that decisive moment, that sidereal hour, in which his ultimate self-surrender to God is really achieved for him – that self-surrender which definitively determines what is to be for him for all eternity. It is a 'source' only to the extent that he is aware in all this that this source is only derived from the real source of God who creates salvation in his supra-worldly and absolute primacy, and of the unique and definitive event of the death of the Lord that creates salvation. Furthermore it is a source only to the extent that in all this he knows that provided only he opens his heart in faith, hope, and love, the whole of his existence will be permeated throughout as a land from the depths of which flow the waters of eternal life. And if the objection were put to him that after all it is only at Mass that he receives the Body of the Lord really and substantially, then he would rejoin that while he gratefully acknowledges this unique gift of grace of Christ within his Church, still in responding to this substantial presence of Christ the only way in which he can avoid occupying the seat of a Judas next to the physical presence of Christ at the Last Supper is for this Lord to rise up, together with the whole yearning of the entire world and together with its destiny from the midst of his own personal life, and to bestow his grace from this (a grace that is called love for God and for mankind). This is what must take place before he can say that he is physically near to him and *also* bears witness to him in *such a way that* he loves him to the end.

But all this does not make the sacrament superfluous or meaningless. It bears witness to a truth which is otherwise so much hidden in the darkness of the world and the depths of one's conscience. It gives a better opportunity to look outwards from the harmonious recollection of a cultic event into the world, and there to recognize what threatens again and again to disappear from the flagging spirit and the despondent heart within its midst. The sacrament does not dispense us from striving in the night of the world as Jacob strove by night with the angel until he had blessed him. Rather it brings home to us *the fact that* this struggle of life is a striving like Jacob's. It paves the way for, and is the promise of, the same victorious outcome. If the sacrament is the sign of the *res sacramenti*, the reality designated, which is identical with the whole unfolding history of the world (because it is a *signum commemorativum, exhibitivum* and *prognosticum*, as we may express it in the terms of Aquinas, for everything which takes place in saving history from the beginning to the end which has still to come), does it follow from this that the significance of the sacrament becomes smaller and less important than if it were a procedure of a bare individualistic pastoral care in which it was no longer possible really to believe that anything was taking place there that could really and seriously be believed in as significant for salvation? In other words could such a thing really be believed in as something which is in God's sight the definitive and irrevocable outcome of freedom, abiding and never more able to be overthrown?

Let it not be said that to celebrate the sacrament in this sense implies any denial or obscuring of its sacramental 'causality'. It is no denial or obscuring of the significance of the baptism of an adult either if we say that even as he enters upon it he is acting in accordance with the just claims of faith and love, and so is already justified as he comes to receive the baptism of water. Nor are we denying or obscuring the significance of the sacrament of penance when in accordance with the whole of traditional theology we say that in the normal instance the Christian approaches this sacrament of reconciliation as one who has already been justified through charity – indeed that, as Thomas Aquinas held, he must approach it in this state. Obviously Peter in no sense underestimated baptism when he conferred baptism upon Cornelius precisely *because* he had already received the Holy Spirit and not because he had not yet experienced it. In accordance with traditional theology we hold firm to the position that it is far from being necessarily the case that the recipient of the sacraments does not yet have that which the sacrament confers upon him and declares to have been conferred upon him. In this traditional formulation of the question we also really understand what is properly meant by this grace which the recipient of the sacraments already possesses, namely a state of having been drawn into the dynamic process which holds the world together, impelling it towards its goal, the inconceivability of God, uniting all earthly realities and spirits and blending them into a single history of the world as the coming of God through his self-bestowal. And it cannot be said that the approach to the sacraments suggested here in any sense tells against their significance or necessity. It may be that it is not easy or even possible to explain down to the last detail the harmony between these two truths: that of the grace which is always already present and effective from within, and that of the sacramental sign as posited from without at a particular point in time. But any theology in any case is faced with the task of showing that such a harmony exists. It is not a special difficulty arising only from the approach to the reception of the sacraments suggested here.

THE EFFECTIVENESS OF THE SACRAMENT IN THE SIGN

But in still more precise terms: What, in terms of this basic conception, is to be made of the 'effectiveness' of the sacraments?[6] If we emphasize the 'sign' character of the sacraments, then we are straightway in line with the best and earliest theological traditions. If we are to speak of an effectiveness belonging to the sacramental sign, then it is in accordance with this tradition that the effectiveness referred to is not to be conceived of as something added on to its 'sign' function from without, but rather is to be envisaged as an effectiveness inherent in the sign precisely *as* such. The development of the modern theology of the sacraments likewise tends in this direction even in those areas in which it is in no sense concerned with the special points which are of interest to us here.[7]

This effectiveness of the sign as such (the sign of that grace of God which is already taking effect always and everywhere throughout the world right from its very roots!) can be explained in several stages. First the concrete process by which man in his physical exteriority brings himself to his fulness in his own personal history always has from the first the character of a sign, a physical expression of that which is already present in the basic attitude of a man, *and at the same time* of the fact that there is a counter influence proceeding from the sign and affecting the basic attitude. Thus this concrete process of self-fulfilment is itself all along and in all cases a 'real symbol' under which the individual brings to fruition this basic attitude of his, his *option fondamentale*. Precisely *in the fact that* he expresses himself man posits that which is expressed. In the gesture that he makes the interior disposition of the individual asserts itself. This is not simply (at least not in all cases) the *mere* subsequent promulgation such that in itself it would be unimportant for the existence of the reality promulgated. The real symbol[8] is the sign which

---

[6] cf. the author's article 'Sakrament' V in *LTK* IX (Freiburg im Breisgau, 1964), cols. 227–230, and also in the present volume, 'What is a Sacrament?'

[7] cf. R. Schulte's summarizing article 'Sacrament', *Sacramentum Mundi* V (London and New York, 1970), pp. 378–384; also A. Winkelhofer, *Kirche in den Sakramenten* (Frankfurt, 1968). The relevant enactments, to which the Eucharist belongs, nowadays also have a decisive bearing on our understanding of the Eucharistic presence of the Lord. On this cf. the relevant studies by B. Welte, E. Schillebeeckx and J. Ratzinger. The Constitution on the Liturgy of the Second Vatican Council likewise points in this direction. Cf. the author's article, 'The Presence of the Lord in the Christian Community at Worship', *Theological Investigations* X (London and New York, 1973), pp. 71–83.

[8] cf. the author's 'The Theology of the Symbol', *Theological Investigations* IV

promulgates in the unity of the body-spirit *compositum* which is man, and *at the same time* is the 'cause' of that which is promulgated. It is not a cause which acts *ab externo* to posit something subsequent to and quite different from itself. Rather it is a cause to the extent that the true cause, the interior decision of freedom, can posit itself only in that it brings itself to its fulness by issuing in this its promulgation.

From this basic standpoint it is now easy to advance a step further: first all what has just been said also applies to the act of the free individual as brought to its fulness in grace. This *free individual* brings himself to his fulness as an event of grace in this sense *in that* he expresses himself, and this expression is, in the sense explained, the cause of the act imbued with grace and of the grace itself. (In the light of this the point made by the traditional established teaching of the Church is perfectly reasonable, namely that in the case of one who has already been justified receiving the sacraments, this grace – which produces a fruitful reception of the sacraments! – is always still further 'increased'.)

And finally: this grace is bestowed upon the world as such from its heart and centre. It is constantly offered as the innermost finality of the world's history. It unfolds itself in the history of salvation and revelation, and brings to manifestation, and precisely in virtue of this, that which we call the sacraments when it brings to fruition this decision, taken in its power at decisive moments in the individual human life, and, moreover, in a manifestation which is posited by the Church as the basic sacrament of grace, her own nature being fully engaged in this.[9] On this showing, then, a manifestation of this kind is not merely a subsequent promulgation of something which is in any case present even without such promulgation. Rather it is something *in which* the reality promulgated brings its own individual history to its fulness and so extends its own real nature in that it integrates within its own individual history more 'material'. In this sense, then, the manifestation is the 'cause' of that which is manifesting. Now it follows from all this that in terms of our basic conception too a true causality, precisely a causality in signifying (that of the 'real symbol') can be ascribed to the sacramental sign.

(London and Baltimore, 1966), pp. 221–252, and P. de Jong, *Die Eucharistie als Symbolwirklichkeit* (Regensburg, 1969).

[9] Apart from the well-known studies by O. Semmelroth, E. Schillebeeckx and others, cf. also the author's *The Church and the Sacraments*, Quaestiones Disputatae 9 (Edinburgh and London, 1963), as well as 'Ekklesiologische Grundlegung der Pastoraltheologie als praktischer Theologie', *Handbuch der Pastoraltheologie* I (Freiburg im Breisgau, 2nd ed., 1970).

THE CHURCH AS THE BASIC SACRAMENT OF THE SALVATION OF THE WORLD

We shall understand this whole approach still better if we reflect upon the relationship between the world and the Church. According to what probably is both the most relevant and the most original statement in the ecclesiology of the Second Vatican Council the Church is the 'sacrament of salvation' for the *world*.[10] What does this mean? The earlier view was that the Church is the sign of salvation for those who already positively belong to her, the sheltering ark in the Flood of the world the sheepfold which protects the flock of Christ and that which points the way of salvation to those who are gathered in this ark or in this fold. On this view the world constituted the sphere of perdition which was set over against the Church as the realm of the evil one. Now this view is certainly not regarded as simply false. There is a world which is in an evil state, a world dominated over by those principalities and powers which are hostile to God, a world made up of spirits and of men.[11] But today it is recognized more clearly that as an historical and social entity the Church is precisely not in any possible sense simply or primarily the promise of salvation for those who are 'within' her. Rather she is this for those who are 'still' without, and those who are perhaps destined never to belong to her in this present age in a sociological or empirical sense. For there are men who have been sanctified and redeemed by grace who have never belonged to the Church in an empirical sense, and the reason is that God never denies salvation in his grace to anyone who follows his own conscience, not even when he has not yet explicitly come to recognize the existence of God. For these men who have been sanctified and saved at an anonymous level, for these redeemed ones (there is no need whatever to use the term 'anonymous Christians' if it is found unsatisfactory) the Church is the social and historical sign of salvation, the basic sacrament of that promise which applies to such as these, because she constitutes the visible community of those who acknowledge that in the deed of God salvation is victoriously present for the whole world through the death and resurrection of his Christ. Those who explicitly belong to the visible

[10] On this cf., amongst others, E. Schillebeeckx, 'De ecclesia ut sacramentum mundi', *Acta congressus internationalis de theologia Concilii Vaticani* II, E. Dhanis, A. Schönmetzer edd. (Rome, 1968), pp. 48–53.

[11] Of course this 'world' is also constantly present within the sphere which we call in an empirical and social sense, the Church. This in itself should make us cautious in drawing this traditional distinction between the realm of God and that of sin.

Church are not so much those who are called and predestined to salvation, as though there could not be any others similarly called and predestined. Rather they are those who, through their life, their confessing, their membership of the Church, have to make salvation manifest sacramentally to those *others* within the solidarity which embraces all men within a human race which has been redeemed by Christ. The members of the Church in the true sense work out their salvation precisely *in that* they fulfil to the full this function which they have to the rest. This does not exclude the fact that in principle all men are called to such a function, i.e. that it cannot in principle, or from the outset, be said of anyone that this particular concrete individual certainly does not enter a situation in which he develops his own individual saving history to the point at which he cannot only receive salvation, but also, precisely *in order to* receive it and to maintain it, must proclaim it too as an element in this basic sacrament called the Church.

In the light of this the relationship between world and Church is not one between the sphere of the godless and the sphere of the holy, between the Flood and the ark, but resembles rather a relationship between a hidden reality on the one hand, which is still seeking to express itself to the full in history, and on the other the full historical manifestation of this, in which that reality which, though hidden, was already present in the world achieves its own fulness in history, expresses itself, and so enters upon that mode of existence towards which it has been orientated from the outset.

The true *entelecheia* of the Church is present in the world at its innermost heart and centre, but in a manner which is already recognizable to her believers in the light of her own nature. This is not to contest the fact that this hidden *entelecheia* of the Church within the world is not the 'natural' dynamism of the world or of history, but rather is constituted by the grace of God – indeed ultimately by God himself in his self-bestowal upon the world. Nor is it contested that the Church is an extremely imperfect manifestation of this ultimate and victorious *entelecheia* of world history such that it is still guilty of selfishness, still precisely of such a nature that it is only gradually that it can fulfil its task of integrating within itself the particular elements in this manifestation which are constituted 'outside' the Church by this grace-given *entelecheia* present within the history of the world and the history of salvation.[12]

[12] The 'adaptation' of the Church to the world is at basis the recognition of the factor of 'anonymous Christianity' and of the Church as a factor in the world and in its history, not the condescension of the divine power stooping to a godless world.

SACRAMENT AS SELF-FULFILMENT OF THE CHURCH

It is on this basis that we now have to view the individual sacraments: they are nothing else than acts in a process of concrete self-fulfilment on the part of the Church as the basic sacrament of salvation for the world as applicable to the individual and to the specific situation of his own personal life.[13] The abiding union of the Church with Christ, which cannot be destroyed, achieves a further projection in the individual sacraments as positive concretizations of the basic sacrament. At this level it is called *opus operatum*, which properly speaking does not imply any opposition to the *opus operantis*, but is rather a quality inherent in a specific *opus operantis* (which is in fact posited both in the conferrer and the recipient of the sacraments), the fact namely that this *opus operantis ecclesiae* (and of her minister) is posited with the full involvement of the Church as such, and so of its very nature cannot fall outside the sphere of Christ's grace.[14] If therefore the sacraments are projections and actualizations of the 'sign' function of the Church as the basic sacrament, then it follows from this that the sacraments designate and promulgate at the level of society and history that grace which is designated and borne witness to by the basic sacrament of the Church. In other words they constitute signs of the grace of the *world*, that grace which is present and effective within the world constantly and from the first. That grace of God which is implanted in the world also sustains the Church and her sacraments. In the reception of the sacraments this too is precisely something which must be 'realized'. If that is realized or made real, then the sacraments are no 'extrinsic' processes touching upon an unhallowed world from 'without', but rather the pro-cesses (in the etymological sense!) of the grace of the world which even within the world is perceived by him who, through word and sacrament, has experienced the fact that the life of himself and of the world has all along been sanctified and opened up to the inconceivability of God as no longer concealed.

[13] The utterance of salvation is the concretization of the basic sacrament in the life of the individual. A point constantly to be borne in mind in this connection is that this individual, even within the Church in which he is an element in the constitution of the basic sacrament, always remains at once a recipient of salvation and a seeker for salvation just as much as he who is still 'outside' it.

[14] cf. O. Semmelroth, 'Opus operatum – Opus operantis', *LTK* VII (Freiburg im Breisgau, 1962), cols. 1184–1186.

THE APPLICATION OF THE SACRAMENT IN THE CONCRETE
CIRCUMSTANCES OF HUMAN LIFE (THE FREQUENCY OF THE
SACRAMENTS)

This conception, though not strictly speaking new, is intended to bring out more clearly a point which is of special importance today. Against the entire conception, however, it might be objected that it lays excessive demands upon the average recipient of the sacraments. In rejoinder it must first be said that every conception of the sacraments demands too much of the recipient. For each individual has, in the concrete circumstances of his personal life, to achieve a personal encounter with God. Yet in attempting such a thing how can he escape from having too much demanded of him on any conceivable interpretation of the sacraments? The fact that this is perhaps less clearly borne in upon us in our usual way of receiving the sacraments comes from sheer custom, which causes us to suppose that we understand and fully go through with the realities expressed by terms such as grace, means of grace, causality of the sign of grace etc. We can freely assert that the way of approaching the sacraments put forward and recommended here demands nothing more than what is always demanded in any such approach: to realize in concrete personal terms what is meant by the grace of God, and to realize it *in such a way* that the idea of receiving such grace is also really credible. Properly speaking all that we are attempting in this interpretation is to convey a concept of grace which modern man can feel to be verifiable because it proceeds from everyday experience and regards an individualistic narrowing down of the idea of grace as something to be avoided. Of course it may be asked whether in the concrete practice of life it is possible to achieve a reception of the sacraments such as we are attempting to describe here so frequently as has been regarded as genuinely possible and worth striving for by traditional piety over many centuries (especially in the case of the Eucharist and penance). But what we are concerned with is the question of a genuine reception of the sacraments in their fulness in the concrete personal circumstances of our lives, without which any mere numerical accumulation of such receptions of the sacraments becomes meaningless. In no conceivable sense does it really increase grace, and it leads merely to a legalistic and mechanical approach to the sacramental event. But whatever interpretation we may put upon the sacrament in the concrete, this question has to be posed, and no one will find it very easy to answer. It does no harm whatever if in our devotion we avoid deciding how frequently we ought to receive the sacraments simply on the basis of the almost magical idea that the more often we receive them the better provided only that a right intention and a certain amount of good will is present, to increase the 'treasury of grace' through the sacraments. Moreover, according to the way of receiving the sacraments which we are suggesting here, it is manifestly far from desirable to receive them so often as to demand too much of the recipient in the sense of over-straining his capacity to realize the significance of his act in the concrete circumstances of his personal life. But this tells against receiving the sacraments too often for us fully to realize their significance, and not against the conception we are putting forward here.[15] Each of the two factors involved must be taken as a criterion for determining the other: frequency of reception on the one hand, and genuine realization of what is involved on the other. But obviously a further factor constantly to be taken into account is the due claims of everyday life. Again the supreme point which, when it is fully achieved, can and will enable us to orientate our lives as a whole towards their final consummation is first of all exceptional and at the same time needs to be fitted into the claims of our everyday life in such a way that it acts upon us as though it were actually being achieved in the here and now. Our everyday living must very broadly approximate to that which constitutes its true significance, the supremely decisive factor in our lives, in such a way as in a certain measure creatively to anticipate such moments of radical fulness. Only in this way shall we really achieve them aright and avoid wasting the *kairos* for them, the crucial moment at which it is possible really to receive them. The phrase 'I love you' can also be uttered in our everyday lives and moreover should be, even though it is a phrase which properly speaking applies to the fulness of those crucial moments in life. And this can also be said of the sacraments, even though when we do so we have not once more any intention of denying what has just been said with regard to adopting a critical attitude towards an indiscrete frequency in receiving them. Presumably there are 'styles' conditioned by the particular epochs to which they belong, and determining where we strike the balance between the supreme demand which the sacraments in their fulness represent and so which they make upon man on the one hand, and the tribute which the individual can freely and willingly pay to his everyday conditions, which also still plays its part in characterizing that which is supreme in his own life. In fact we have no objection to make either to the individual intercessions which we formulate in the liturgy: on behalf of the hungry, the dying, those subjected to political persecution etc., even though such intercessions often seem to

[15] On this see n. 2.

come 'from the heart' only to a small extent so far as we are concerned. Should we on this account omit them, or should we not rather allow ourselves to be warned by them ever afresh to make sure that our hearts do not stick fast in a primitive form of egoism (albeit perhaps a religious one)?

RELIGIOUS AND SECULAR

Now that we have put forward our theory on the basis of the usual data of traditional theology, with all the circumstantial details inevitably entailed in this, we should now once more develop this theory quite simply and independently of this our starting-point. In this way it should be possible to make it clear far more effectively how possible it is to 'realize' it and to verify it in religious terms. Man is not in any explicit sense endowed with religious instincts of his very nature. He easily feels all that is explicitly religious as almost impudent, and in any case excessively burdensome. Yet once we have so made clear our thesis we should be in a position to say: What is here being achieved is simply a plainer and more explicit awareness of what takes place in my life, and what precisely need not after all be suppressed or denied expression, that to which I must give my explicit adherence, however much I may be tempted to venerate all this merely silently, and however much I may be justified in claiming that there is a limit to the saving efficacy in certain forms of religious expression of this sort or in the frequency with which they are repeated. And he who is already 'devout' would notice that his 'spiritual life' does not constitute any dispensation from the responsibilities of his secular life, or even, properly and ultimately speaking, a point of transcendence in relation to this. Rather it is precisely the explicit taking over of this life which only seems to be secular. But it is no longer possible to set forth the conception of the sacraments we have in mind here without 'taking the long way round' with the traditional form as our starting-point for the kerygmatic statement itself. This is no longer possible however desirable it may be, however true it may be that only thus would it become effective in our religious lives. In theology proper it is something else. For this always has to answer precisely for its doctrine to the earlier history of faith.

I I

ASPECTS OF THE EPISCOPAL OFFICE

IN the ideas which follow we shall be assuming as accepted the Catholic doctrine concerning the episcopal office, on a balanced view of it in which all elements in it are taken into account. In this approach it is admittedly no part of our intention to put forward objections from the point of view of pastoral theology,[1] for instance as to what kind of image the bishop of today ought to present, which are the crucial points for our present age within the total scope of a bishop's task, what form ought nowadays to be given to those institutions on which he has to rely for the fulfilment of his task, etc. As against this a point we shall seek to demonstrate in this study is how broad a scope is still left, from the point of view of pastoral theology, for considerations and decisions with regard to the concrete form which the episcopal office ought to assume in our own times, even while we recognize the doctrine of the Catholic Church on this point which is effectively and dogmatically binding. The scope still left by this is far greater than is commonly assumed, and hence offers the pastoral theologian, provided he understands his task and includes within it the *jus condendum*, great opportunities but at the same time corresponding responsibilities too, which are likewise greater than is supposed on the common view.

For when we speak of office, of a bishop, of episcopal authority, a monarchical episcopate etc. in doctrinal statements, we are unconsciously filling these formal and very broad concepts with a concrete content which is *de facto* bound up with these concepts in our own experience of the Church. We do this even though we should have learnt from the history of the Church from the New Testament onwards how wide the variations

---

[1] The considerations put forward in this study were prepared for a conference of pastoral theologians. It is from this that the ideas it contains acquire their theological bearing and their special character, something which belongs essentially to the present considerations.

can be in the concrete forms in which these concepts are realized, and so too possible from the point of view of dogmatic theology. This should be enough to tell us that for the future too we are offered a broad scope for creatively re-shaping this office, and that this is a task which we must tackle genuinely and seriously. The study which follows is intended to help in laying bare still more the further and unexplored areas for the re-shaping of these ideas. What we are concerned with here is not the task of presenting possible models for the office, the different content of which has already been determined by historical factors or at the theoretical level. For this would precisely be the task of the historian who may perhaps discover such different concrete forms of the office already present at earlier stages in history – forms which, even though now forgotten and having fallen into desuetude, could nowadays perhaps once more be revived and renovated.

The pastoral theologian and canonist, on the other hand, has the special task of creatively filling out with new concrete ideas those formal and, to some extent, empty concepts which the dogmatic theologian supplies him with when he shows on dogmatic grounds that this factor of the empty and the unexplored in his concepts is dogmatically justified, and by doing so also makes it right for the Church to provide scope for creative freedom for her pastoral theologians, canonists, and also those vested with her offices. In this negative task of the dogmatic theologian (one, that is, which creates scope in theory and practice for the pastoral theologians), we have a longer path to tread, for there are many factors and circumstances to be considered, so that a considerable degree of patience is called for. For in such considerations there is much that must remain problematical and uncertain. The ultimate certainty that a future measure is legitimate can be achieved only in the free decision to embark upon this future measure, and not in the preliminary considerations leading up to it. If we sought to achieve a certainty of this kind, assuring us that these unexplored areas for further development were present and doctrinally justified even prior to any such decision on the part of the Church, then it would be clear from the outset that we had totally failed to discover any such areas for a true and effective future, and that we were only projecting forwards into the future in an innocuous manner the already justified present as modified for that future. The considerations are prior only in the sense that on the basis of the different approaches, which are in no sense all brought under a single overall system, we feel our way towards the existence of the free scope for further development of the kind we are speaking of for the future concrete realization of the episcopal office.

Hence it is also superfluous to enumerate these different approaches by way of preliminary. After these introductory remarks, let us now proceed directly to tackle the question itself.

It is of immediate and primary importance for our entire question to be clear upon one point: the sense in which, on the basis of the exegesis and biblical theology of the New Testament, and of the earlier history of the Church, we can nowadays assert that the historical Jesus did found a Church. The fact that this question is of radical importance for our entire theme hardly calls for any special explanation. It is also obvious that all that need be stated here is a quite simple and summary answer, without any special justifying arguments. While it is true that 'Lumen Gentium', the document of the Second Vatican Council, has said nothing in this context that is false concerning the hierarchical structure of the Church, provided that we interpret its doctrines in broad outline (which is perfectly justifiable from the point of view of dogmatics), still even this doctrine of the Council does not provide a really positive picture of the present position on the question of the founding of the Church by Jesus with all the problems this entails and the possibility of their solution.[2] When we ask 'Did Jesus found the Church?' it may be that this is a somewhat inappropriate way of framing the question in view of the matters to be found here, and which we now have in mind. Alternatively we must achieve a clear recognition of what is meant by 'founding' here, and the special kind of variability involved in it, and we need not presume that the only way of applying this idea in practice in the case we are considering is precisely that way which we ourselves quite arbitrarily associate with it. For it is possible to conceive of the founding of a society as signifying that way of bringing it into being that necessarily involves a conscious and clear idea of the constitution of that society, together with the will to bring it to reality in the human awareness of the 'founder'. Now it cannot be established as a matter of historical fact that the historical Jesus either willed or carried through the founding of the Church as understood here. Even at this early stage we may draw attention to something which we shall have to enlarge upon later in these considerations of ours, namely that something like a revealed constitutional law of the Church – in other words a *jus divinum* of a juridical and constitutional kind – is conceivable. Later we shall have to show how this can be.

---

[2] On the subject of the institution or founding of the Church by Jesus cf. the author's study, *Inspiration in the Bible* (Edinburgh and London, 1961), pp. 39–42, and also, in the present volume, 'Considerations on the Role of the Person in the Sacramental Event'.

Obviously Jesus did have a group of disciples about him. It is perfectly possible that this group also had, in the broadest sense, a juridical structure in conformity with Jesus' own will, one which accorded a special place within this group of disciples to Peter. As a matter of their experience the disciples of Jesus knew him as the crucified and risen Lord, and so recognized him and his message (or his new message, and in this himself also) as the unsurpassable word of the living God, of the ultimate freedom. And to the extent that they did so experience him it was obviously also the case that this group of disciples, which as a society of persons necessarily must have had a social and juridical constitution, must also remain, right to the end of history, as a community of faith in Jesus and as the upholder of his message. In the light of this it is absolutely possible and necessary to assert that the Church derives from Jesus, is in this sense founded by him, even though he himself in his genuinely human awareness presumably never formulated any clear or conscious idea of what kind of social constitution the community of his message would have, how it would achieve it, or under what forms it would continue to exist, that community made up of those who believe in the liberating proximity of God and of those who lay hold of this message as something eternally inseparable from himself and his fate. On these grounds alone it is evident that it is only in a very limited and indirect way if at all that the office of the bishops in the Church can be traced back to any decision to found this office on the part of Jesus himself. In any case the episcopal office is not to be authenticated by claiming that Jesus founded it in the sense of explicitly and consciously adverting to it in itself, for this is something which cannot be established as a matter of historical fact. The existence of this office is justified, rather, on the grounds that in the concrete it constitutes the legitimate and, in the long run historically speaking, indispensable way of ensuring the necessary continuity of the community of Jesus with its origins. It is in the light of this that we have to allow for the wide range of possible variations we have spoken of, in which such a factor as the episcopal office can be given concrete embodiment.

If we assume that the foregoing points are correct, can we then still speak of a *jus divinum* for the basic constitutional structures of the Catholic Church?[3] This question arises directly from what we have said above, and is also of vital importance for any interpretation of the episcopal

[3] On what follows cf. the author's article, 'Reflection on the Concept of the "Jus Divinum" in Catholic Thought', *Theological Investigations* V (London and Baltimore, 1966), pp. 219–243.

office with a view to finding concrete models for its embodiment in concrete reality. I believe that this question can be answered along the following lines: the episcopal office derives from the will of Jesus to found the Church as interpreted above in a process which, while in the eyes of modern theologians it seems to be conditioned by historical factors, is nevertheless in terms of its meaning perfectly reasonable and irreversible. Now to the extent that this is true there is a perfectly sound and valid sense in which we can speak of a *jus divinum* of the episcopal office. In this statement we are assuming two principles: First according to the witness of history it seems that at one time the monarchic episcopate existed side by side with other community structures in the apostolic age, and that at the time these were not regarded either as illegitimate or as embryonic or provisional. The monarchical episcopate, then, seems to have imposed itself and to have rendered these other structures obsolete, though of course this took place at a very early stage. A further factor to be taken into account, of course, in all this is that the concept of a monarchic episcopate is abstract in the extreme and was given concrete embodiment in early times in the most varied forms. The result is that in the constitution of any given local Church it is after all only particular elements which are brought to the fore by means of such a concept. Other elements of very great importance were *de facto* implicit in it side by side with these, and these other elements modify this absolute concept very greatly when compared with the form which the present-day monarchic episcopate assumes.[4] The second point which our statement about the *jus divinum* inherent in the monarchical episcopate asserts is this: without prejudice to the historical contingency of this episcopate which we have just established, this *jus divinum* can and indeed must nevertheless be regarded as an abiding element in the constitution of the Church. The reason is that the concept of a reality that is contingent and brought about in historical freedom is far from necessarily implying that that reality can once more be withdrawn from the stage of history. On the contrary, under certain circumstances it is in principle perfectly consistent with a contingency of origin of this kind for such a contingent reality to be permanent and irreversible. This is not the place to demonstrate how or why a reality emerging from the free course of history in this sense, the history of human decision, may in principle have this character of being

[4] The doctrine of the monarchic episcopate is accounted as fully worked out by the beginning of the second century in the Letters of Ignatius of Antioch. Nevertheless it is disputed how far the general situation of the contemporary Church is reflected in these.

permanent and irreversible. This would lead us too far afield. Yet it would be naive and ultimately less than human to suppose that we have to deny the true nature of historical freedom by saying that it is impossible for the Church to recognize in her faith that a given decision can have an eternal validity in this sense once that decision has been freely posited. For even though it cannot be perceived that that decision follows necessarily from the very nature of the case, still it is in harmony with the nature of the case. The historical decision of the Church that her own constitution should include a monarchic episcopate was arrived at towards the end of the apostolic age, albeit as the outcome of a long process of development, and in the Church's conscious faith this decision can perfectly well be irreversible and, because in conformity with her own nature, albeit not in any demonstrable way following necessarily from that nature, can still justifiably be regarded as a *jus divinum* and as intrinsically involving the factors of authentic derivation from a Church that has been willed by God and of the irreversibility and permanence that belong to the institution of this. A further point that is of course likewise clear from all this is that the dogmatic concept of the episcopate can have a wide range of variations in the forms in which it is realized in practice. For the criterion by which its concrete form can and must be measured is whether it actually and effectively has fulfilled and is capable of fulfilling those dispositions and functions which are entailed by the origin of the episcopate as thus determined. In any case it is clear that we cannot use the concept of the *jus divinum* to justify and defend any and every factor which is present in the concrete in the present-day form of the episcopate. On the other hand there is no need to cast doubt upon the monarchic episcopate as an abiding factor in the Church by reason of its having emerged as a free and contingent phenomenon. Two points must be borne in mind here: first, regardless of whatever forms the concrete juridical constitution of a given society may assume, the powers vested in that society must be borne by individuals; second, even a monarchic episcopate, as it exists within a community, must be, and *de facto* in the Catholic Church actually is – surrounded by collegiate organs. Now in the light of these two points there is properly speaking no valid meaning any longer in casting doubt on the monarchic form of episcopate. In terms of its actual meaning the only question which still remains open – though in practice it is not an unimportant one – is how we should devise rules in greater detail to ensure the necessary collaboration between the primary holder of the office within a community, who is quite indispensable, and the collegiate bodies which are also inevitably present within it. We have to devise rules for this collaboration in such a way that taken together as a single whole the bearers of the office in the Church are really capable of discharging the functions pertaining to that office. At most the question might be posed of whether it might not be possible to recognize such collegiate ('presbyteral') elements in the constitution of a community as covered by the *jus divinum* when, in a given concrete situation, they are felt to be here and now indispensable, even though this indispensability which is binding upon us is clearly present only at a later epoch of the Church's history and not already at the end of the apostolic age, and even though it emerged from the concrete historical and social situation of the community.[5]

As I see it, we could in principle and as a matter of abstract speculation even go a step further and put the hypothesis that it would not be un-equivocally contrary to the Catholic doctrine of the episcopal office to say that this episcopal authority could be borne by a *collegium*. What is asserted in the doctrinal declarations of the Church with regard to the episcopal office refers to the nature, the origin and the scope of this office. In these declarations it is indeed tacitly assumed as self-evident, in view of the *de facto* conditions prevailing in the Church, that at times this office is vested in an individual person. But whether this fact of history, that the office is vested in individuals, is necessarily identical with the episcopal office as such and of its very nature – this is a point on which, so it seems to me, no ultimately binding statement has been made. Surely too it is at least conceivable that it is possible from the point of view of dogmatic theology for the episcopal office to be vested in a collegiate body. The difference between the presbyteral constitution of some non-Catholic Churches of the Reformation on the one hand, and the monarchic consti-tution of the Catholic Church on the other points (if we abstract from the question of the papacy) not so much to a difference in the conception of the office holder, but rather to a difference as to the nature of this office itself. (Merely in passing it may be remarked that at the Council of Trent many factors which were legitimately present in the Church, but which had emerged as a result of free decisions on the Church's part, are pre-sented as though they had been directly posited *jure divino* by divine revelation itself. This is a point that must also be borne in mind in our case by anyone who seeks to invoke the authority of Trent.) The fact

[5] On the basis of historical researches Y. Congar concerns himself with various aspects of the relationship of the episcopal office to the pope, Church, and com-munities in several studies in his most recent work, *Ministères et communion ecclésiale* (Paris, 1971).

that we should not be too hasty in assuming that it would be contrary to the very nature of the Church according to a Catholic understanding for the episcopal office to be vested in a collegiate body in this way becomes apparent once we recognize the fact that a collegiate entity, namely the college of bishops in union with the pope as the head of this college, is as such the bearer of the powers of the Church in their fulness.[6] Now this consideration should not give the impression that we are seeking to imply that it is opportune for individual Churches to have a presbyteral constitution of this kind, one in which the bearer of the episcopal office as Catholics understand it should be a *collegium* (which in the nature of things would be small). All that we are seeking to make clear by this consideration is that at least at first sight the relationship of a bishop to the directive bodies subordinate to him and collaborating with him within a local Church can be conceived of in very varied ways, seeing that it is not simply or certainly contrary to Catholic doctrine to conceive of a local Church having a truly collegiate form of leadership at its head. The importance of directive bodies which are collegiate in character working with and under the bishop can certainly be greater than it *de facto* is nowadays according to the valid juridical norms without the dogmatically valid juridical constitution of the Church necessarily being threatened thereby.

This brings us to a further consideration. The relationship of the bishop to those other bodies who share in the direction of a local Church could juridically speaking assume more precise and more intelligible forms without the prerogatives certainly or probably belonging to the bishop as a matter of dogmatic theology being threatened or diminished thereby. In order to throw light upon this statement let us begin by pointing to an analogous case in which the example intended to throw light upon the question actually constitutes the higher analogate. In 1970 the International Commission of Theologians at Rome unanimously declared that it was desirable for the pope himself juridically and as a matter of principle, though obviously *jure humano*, to devise rules for the way in which he might collaborate with the college of bishops rather than for him to decide the forms which this collaboration should take intermittently and according to the particular case involved. They declared that so far from

[6] On the subject of the relationship between the episcopate and the primate cf. the volume published by the author in collaboration with J. Ratzinger: *Episkopat und Primat*, Quaestiones Disputatae II (Freiburg, 2nd ed., 1963), and the article, 'On the Relationship between the Pope and the College of Bishops', *Theological Investigations* X (London and New York, 1973), pp. 50–70.

being in contradiction to the prerogatives certainly belonging to the pope as a matter of doctrine, this would actually be opportune nowadays, and would conduce to the efficiency and credibility of his office. Just as a pope can draw up rules in collaboration with a secular sovereign for the nomination of a bishop by means of a general concordat (and not a fresh concordat for each individual case), and just as these rules are in principle binding upon him, so too he can *a fortiori* arrive at a juridically speaking more precise set of rules governing his collaboration with the episcopate, and of course such rules would also be binding upon him (as in the case of a concordat with secular powers) even when in particular cases he found this less agreeable, or when it led to consequences in which he did not find himself involved when such general rules did not exist. As we have said, the International Commission of Theologians declared that such a course was not only doctrinally possible but was actually opportune for present-day conditions because through it the rule of the pope would achieve a higher intelligibility and effectiveness, and thereby too this office would acquire a greater credibility. Now *a fortiori* the same applies to the bishop in his office in relation to those other directive bodies and the rest of the institutions within his diocese. And this remains true even if we assume that the episcopal office is monarchic in character. The decisions which a bishop arrives at in virtue of those powers attributed to him alone within his Church are bound by the nature of the matters involved. It is true that according to the Church's laws as at present in force, apart from the pope there is no higher authority to test whether a given decision on the part of a bishop is in conformity with the nature of the matter involved so far as the practical validity of such a decision is concerned. At the same time when we say this we have no intention of disputing the fact that it is possible for bishops to take decisions which a Christian can and must refuse to obey as a matter of his conscience. But since in any case the decisions of a bishop are objectively bound by the nature of the matter involved and cannot be arrived at arbitrarily, it is necessary for the bishop to arrive at a preliminary judgement before taking any such decision. Now it is certain that included among the factors which a bishop must first take into consideration before arriving at such a decision are those various bodies which exist within a diocese and which can contribute their specialist knowledge and counsel in the process of arriving at the prior judgement. Obviously such counsels are, and always have been, available to him. But the point we are concerned with here is the recognition of the fact that it is perfectly consistent with the nature of the monarchic episcopate, and actually opportune for the effectiveness, intelligibility and credibility of the bishop's office, for the collaboration between these consultative bodies and the bishop to be juridically regulated, and moreover in general terms, not in a way that is always dependent from case to case upon the prudent estimate of the bishop alone. To put the matter in blunter and more general terms: it is not contrary to the nature of the episcopal office for the bishop, in specific cases governed by general rules, to be dependent in his decisions upon a *votum deliberativum* over and above a *votum consultativum*. In such a case the right of recourse to the Holy See would still always remain open to him, and even, in extreme cases, the right of reserving his conscience in virtue of which he could refuse his consent to a decision by which he would otherwise be juridically bound, thereby rendering the decision invalid. But these two possibilities, which leave intact the power of decision belonging to a monarchic episcopate, still do not rule out the possibility of formulating juridical rules of a general kind governing that collaboration between a bishop and his official bodies which he needs in order to arrive at decisions which do due justice to the matters involved. The precise form which such regulations should assume in terms of diocesan laws or general laws applicable to all dioceses cannot be set forth here by a dogmatic theologian. Diocesan synods should apply themselves to such questions, and should not be too hasty in allowing themselves to be frustrated in decisions on this question by assertions (such for instance as that put forward against the Synod of Meissen) that such rules derogate from the inalienable rights of the bishop. Rules of this kind could for instance perfectly well include the setting up of a court of appeal such that even a bishop, at least in normal cases, would be bound by its decisions.

By means of such rules it would be possible gradually to eliminate from the Church and her officials a certain paternalism which certainly does not belong to the *jus divinum* in the Church, yet which is nevertheless very often present and, moreover, still present even in the Church of today and in her official ministers. I believe that instances of such paternalism are to be found when the official concerned is too hasty in having recourse merely to his formal authority, and in which he makes it impossible to achieve any insight into the reasons justifying his decision or feels that his formal authority is being attacked and is unwilling to submit his judgement to a critical examination by some other authoritative body (whether in a theoretical or a juridical sense). Paternalism arises in those cases in which the chief shepherd of the flock feels himself to be in the position of a 'father' who, in virtue of his own 'experience' or of the Holy Spirit, knows better in all matters than his immature children, even though in the case we are supposing we are concerned neither with children nor with those who certainly do not recognize the Holy Spirit. Paternalism arises in those cases in which the decision and the formulation of it lack that intelligibility which they might have. To counteract paternalism of this kind the framing of positive juridical rules governing the relationship and collaboration between bishop and other authoritative bodies in the diocese would be very valuable, though of course only provided that these juridical rules did not make the opinion and judgement of these other authoritative bodies once more answerable merely to the prudent estimation of the bishop alone. In this connection what we have in mind is obviously not the kind of rules which merely generate a sort of bureaucracy by some kind of Parkinson's law, frustrating the freedom and personal initiative of all, or even merely the personal charism of a bishop. Rightly framed rules can perfectly well be means of setting freedom itself free, and act precisely as a guard against any regimentation of it.

Many further dogmatic considerations could certainly be put forward, which would still further promote a creative re-shaping of the episcopal office for today. For instance a point which might be considered in greater detail is that the election of the pope at least emerges from a collegiate body which arrives at a juridical decision of supreme importance. Again in this connection we may consider that not all the problems entailed are solved merely by saying that it is the designation of the person that is in question and not the handing over of an authority possessed by the elective body itself. And if we bear these points in mind then we shall at any rate recognize that an election from below need not necessarily be in principle inconsistent with the nature of the Church seeing that the creation of the supreme official in the Church takes place in no other way whatever than by election from below.[7] Furthermore there are very many dogmatic questions which still remain completely open and which need to be thought out concerning the precise relationship between the episcopal office and the priesthood. And the answers to these questions would also be important for our present-day understanding of the episcopal office. Thus for instance the usual distinction between *potestas ordinis* and *potestas jurisdictionis* is far from being unambiguously clear and fully able to be applied, and the problems involved in it were to some extent recognized even at the Second Vatican Council. For instance the power of the priest to celebrate the Eucharist, which, according to the traditional theory can never wholly be withdrawn from him, *eo ipso,* on a

[7] cf. the author's observations on the principles involved in 'The Episcopal Office', *Theological Investigations* VI (London and Baltimore, 1969), pp. 313–360.

right understanding of the Eucharist constitutes the power of presiding over the supreme celebration of a community. And if this is the case how can the usual theological teaching deny to a priest any kind of fundamental *potestas jurisdictionis* unless he holds it as a power that is totally distinct from the *potestas ordinis* as a result of a special act on the part of the bishop? On this showing the question would then arise, for instance, of whether the formation of a Christian community under the direction of a priest can be conceived of altogether in these terms as the formation of a further extension of the sphere of authority by an act of the bishop from above, as after all it is commonly conceived of. These and similar questions which the dogmatic theologian poses to himself could be pursued further, and the answers we find to them could presumably also bring us a more enlightened understanding of that doctrine which really is dogmatically binding of the episcopate and of the scope which remains open to us for a future re-shaping of it. But we cannot enter in any greater detail into such questions at this point.

The problem can also be used from a quite different theological aspect. The question can be posed of whence we can really adduce a valid criterion for the concrete shaping of ecclesiastical office. Here we are proceeding from an assumption which, it is true, is not universally accepted by all theologians, yet which is perfectly sustainable, the assumption, namely, that the Church herself has been given the power to articulate the Church's own official ministry, which is ultimately *one*, and to break it down into specific offices of various kinds and degrees according to the demands of the time. The triad which is current among us of bishop, priest and deacon, therefore, is regarded as *jus divinum* to the extent that the one office in the Church which she must have of her very nature has such a hierarchical structure, but it is not assumed that the dividing up of this one office into these three offices is the only possible way in which it could be divided. If we take this assumption as our starting-point – and in itself it does not imply any prejudice against this triad as inopportune for today – then the theological question arises of what the criterion is for dividing up this office in a way that is appropriate to the particular conditions. Of course it is possible to reply to this question that it is the fulfilling of the function of the Church that constitutes this criterion; that the official ministry must be divided up and formulated in positive terms among the particular officials in such a way that this function of the Church can be fulfilled in the most effective way possible. And we might add to this reply that the function of the Church is rightly to preach the gospel and to dispense the sacraments throughout the ages, that faith, hope and charity may be present in as many individuals as possible and in the most radical forms possible, and that this may be manifested even at the social level and in the constitution of the Church herself. This statement, together with the further precisions which can be made within it, is certainly correct. Yet we must after all be conscious of how formal and abstract, and of how ineffectual this reply is, factors which are still present even if we assume that we know in quite precise terms what is meant by preaching the gospel and administering the sacraments. We should ask ourselves whether it is clear that the present-day forms in which the official ministry of the Church is structured as they *de facto* exist at a quite concrete level, together with all the offices and institutions they entail, are really capable of being traced back to so formal a principle as this. And we have only to put this question to ourselves for it to become clear to us that we must reply to it in the negative, that this principle is inadequate to determine the concrete forms which the episcopal office should assume, even if we take into account that in such matters there is much that is matter for human estimation and which in no sense needs to be based on profound arguments. Perhaps, therefore, without seeking to provide any more precise justification for the point we are making, we might formulate the 'principle' we are seeking in the following terms: the principle and criterion for arriving at the concrete forms in which the Church's official ministry is to be articulated, and so too for the episcopal office, are to be deduced from the encounter at the empirical level which this official ministry makes with the concrete general social conditions, and, on this basis, the ecclesiastical conditions too affecting the preaching of the gospel.[8]

All that can still be attempted here is to give some little explanation of the meaning and possible effectiveness of this principle, without claiming to provide any precise justification for it in theological terms, or to pursue it in its concrete consequences, the more so since this latter course is precisely the concern of the pastoral rather than the dogmatic theologian. In the principle we have formulated we have spoken of an empirical encounter. Here we are proceeding from the conviction that the practical application (and so too the ways in which we institutionalize the official ministry in practice) is not the mere application of prior general principles, but is rather an event of freedom, and thereby of a future which is unique in each particular case and as such has an autonomy of its own, being something more than merely the handmaid of theory. If this is correct,

---

[8] cf. the author's 'Pastoral-Theological Observations on Episcopacy in the Teaching of Vatican II', *Theological Investigations* VI (London and Baltimore, 1969), pp. 361–368.

then in order for the concrete forms in which the Church's office is institutionalized to be right the discovery of them can be arrived at only at the level of concrete experience and by experimentation. In this process we are of course right from the outset working from an enlightening awareness of what the Church is and what the preaching of the gospel is. But even this knowledge, which guides us in our experimentation, is merely present to us in its special historical concretion, which is constituted by the concrete situation of the present, yet constantly open to the future; a situation which, as the situation of the Church herself, of a society, is obviously in a primary sense a social situation. In consequence of this, in its concrete modalities and in the conceptual models and models for action which it contains this knowledge too is constantly subject to change in its encounter with the concrete social situation of the Church. And precisely on this account the discovery of the principles for the concrete forms in which the official ministry of the Church is institutionalized, forms which have to be continuously arrived at afresh, consists not merely in the application of an *a priori* theological knowledge of ecclesiology which we already have, but is matter for a process of experimentation in which theological ecclesiology itself, without being deprived of its own nature, is subjected ever afresh to the pressures of the social situation in which the gospel has to be preached. This situation, therefore, is not one which exists over against the Church's awareness of her own nature as a concrete exterior reality upon which the Church acts from within itself. Rather it constitutes an intrinsic element in the Church's own concrete understanding of its own nature as it continuously discovers this afresh in a process of experimentation, an understanding which is discovered afresh only in a living process of experimentation of this kind, the outcome of which cannot be established beforehand.

We may now in a quite incidental way provide a few indications intended to show what is entailed in the principle we have just developed, which inevitably always remains at a still very abstract level. The exterior and interior situation of the Church is a situation which no longer needs to be monocultural, European or Western, one which albeit in varying degrees, survives in a diaspora situation in the midst of a pluralist environment or one which is in principle and in its institutions hostile to the Church itself. For the Church itself has either lost or not yet gained for itself not merely individuals but broad social groups. Everywhere it encounters a secular society which tolerates large marginal elements, i.e. groups with a notable range of variation which are not integrated into the society. Here we should surely discover and give an intelligible account of an intrinsic connection which exists between those groups which are peripheral in a social sense and those which are so in an ecclesiastical sense. (It would be possible and important for the preaching strategy of the Church if those groups which have become alienated from the Church or have never really had any connections with her were also shown to be the groups which are socially disintegrated, if it could be established that the Church can only seriously come close to these groups and render itself credible to them for the preaching of the gospel if it seriously and effectively achieves solidarity with their social situation and their struggle, albeit in a manner appropriate to the Church as such.)

If any clear analysis of the social situation of the Church were arrived at with a view to its preaching and as an intrinsic element in its own understanding of itself, then surely it would become clear that the Church as it exists in its communities can only live in solidarity with those groups which are marginal in an ecclesiastical and social sense, and can only make its mission effective as a missionary Church. From being a national Church the Church either is or is of necessity becoming in the situation of today and tomorrow a Church of free believers in the midst of a diaspora situation. (Obviously this does not mean that the Church should not strive to awaken the greatest possible number of individuals to the faith in order to avoid becoming a sect in a defeatist sense.) The focal point for the Church to discharge its function, to achieve credibility and to perform its task of preaching the gospel, therefore, is now to be found in the local community at the roots of society, for it is here that its encounter with the special social situation is achieved, here that faith must emerge ever afresh, that faith which is no longer sustained by a homogeneous Christian public opinion or a socially homogeneous society. Here is achieved that solidarity with the struggle of the socially marginal groups. In the light of this it cannot be the case that the normal parish, i.e. the living community of the faith as based upon society and the Church, can continue to remain an extension of the administrative authority of a bishop as organized from above. If this way of putting it had not already been applied to a quite specific concrete attempt at forming such a community, and hence were not capable of provoking misunderstandings, we could say in all confidence: the life of the Church today is primarily lived in an 'integrated community'. At this point we may permit ourselves a digression. The relationship between the bishop and the kind of priest, generally called a parish priest, who presides over a genuine, living, and fraternal community of the faith in fact remains theologically and historically speaking unexplained right down to the present day. This much can confidently be asserted: in the old days the leader of such a community would have been called a bishop. And the question may be raised whether present-day bishops, by the standards of the patristic theology of the episcopate, are not somewhat in the position of supreme bishops or metropolitans or similar higher officials. This is no idle question of terminology. For behind this terminology a crucial fact might under certain circumstances lie concealed, the fact, namely, that by our use of this term 'bishop' we have deprived the leader of the concrete community, who, for the theology of the early Church is a bishop, of those tasks, powers and liberties which should really belong to him. The further question might then arise of whether what is asserted in theology of the college of bishops should not properly speaking apply, from a theological point of view to the college of parish priests, and whether that which we nowadays call the college of bishops is not after all at basis simply the inevitable organizational body representing the college of the parish priests = bishops. This question should not be regarded from the outset as heretical. We may for instance remember the many hundreds of Italian bishops who, by our standards, are after all simply parish priests of so many larger parishes. This digression acquires a practical significance the moment the basic community in the Church achieves a new importance, the moment that such a community, for all its union with the universal Church, forms itself from below by charismatic forces. For it has to be a 'parish of persons'. It must be the kind of community in which it is a far more crucial question whether it has the power to win over afresh an individual from the secularized world than to preserve ten individuals from the remnants of the traditionally Christian society which still remain. Once a community of this kind has come to be the normal type of parish (and presumably it must so become), then the concrete reality of a diocese and of the episcopal office must alter too. In the case supposed the diocese is made up of such communities of free believers in a secularized world, of communities, that is to say which acquire very varied structures in the way in which they find themselves socially committed as the concretizations of the fraternal love of Christians, communities which differ very notably from one another in their relationship to the ordained leader of the Eucharistic celebration, and so too to the leader of their community (assuming that these two personages are and are intended to remain identical). As a result the institution of them by the bishop, to the extent that any such institution is demanded by the unity of the Church, is in any case achieved in quite different forms of collaboration with the community itself than has formerly been the case. A diocese composed of such communities of its very nature implies a different kind of bishop than that to which we have hitherto been accustomed. He will be one who has proved himself through the power of his charismatic personality, in virtue of which he has won fresh ground in the missionary field and has not merely presided over traditional territories inherited from the past. Presumably in the future the individual community will have a greater autonomy, and on this showing it would actually be conceivable that the bishop, as representing the unity of such communities, would be one of the (episcopal) parish priests presiding over one such community. And this in itself would be enough to ensure a fraternal union with his fellow parish priests. Perhaps – this is something which appears to follow from what has been said – we should conduct real experiments among ourselves as well and not for instance merely in Latin America or in the missionary countries in the usual sense of the term. Perhaps the attempt should be made to found new communities existing in genuine solidarity with those groups which are marginal in a social and ecclesiastical sense even though these might initially cut across the normal territorial boundaries of the local parishes. We should in all confidence put up with the resulting mixture between the two. Such communities, which we would be attempting to integrate in a quite new way in an ecclesiastical and social sense with the groups which are socially and ecclesiastically marginal should in this respect develop their structures from within themselves in a manner appropriate to this task. It would then *ipso facto* emerge at the empirical level (obviously in combination with a theological process of reflection, which is indispensable) what structures, what offices a community of this kind needs, how it can live in a vital and fraternal union with other communities both of the new and the old kind, and what supra-communal juridical structures are necessary for such a union to be achieved. A form of diocese and a form of episcopal office of a new kind would gradually be developed without the historical continuity with the earlier form of diocese and episcopal office having to be lost. It would surely appear that the true theological nature of the episcopal office continues to be maintained by the ultimate identity of the Church through all ages, though this does not mean that the concrete form of the episcopal office, in which this true nature is concretized, simply has to maintain itself in petrified form with the result that the fulfilment of the functions which a bishop of today and tomorrow has would be frustrated. But, as we recognize, the dogmatic theologian is already going beyond his brief and entering upon an area in which it is the task of the practical theologian to operate.

12

HOW THE PRIEST SHOULD VIEW
HIS OFFICIAL MINISTRY

WHAT we are concerned with here is the dogmatic principles in the light of which a priest of the Catholic Church should view his official ministry. Obviously within the limited setting of an article these will not be expounded as systematically or as fully as would be necessary in a treatise on the sacramental theology involved. Our present intention, rather, is simply to bring out a few aspects which are commonly less clearly recognized, and which, therefore, may also be accounted as of special interest.[1]

It is probably possible appropriately to define this narrower theme from two aspects which, in a manner that is strange and far from self-evident, converge so as to demarcate the question. The first aspect consists in the fact that the social image of the priest of today has come to be a problem, although one that arises in different ways and in different degrees according to the differences prevailing from country to country. The priest of today is prompted by theoretical and practical considerations arising from within the Church as well as by others arising from the conditions of secular society, to ask himself afresh, and with a certain insecurity, what function he can still credit himself with in a Church in which the laity have become mature, and what role he can still regard himself as playing in a society which has become secular.

---

[1] The author has put forward similar attempts from a theological point of view in the following studies: 'The Point of Departure in Theology for Determining the Nature of the Priestly Office', *Theological Investigations* XII (London and New York, 1974), pp. 31–38; 'Theological Reflections on the Priestly Image of Today and Tomorrow', *ibid.*, pp. 39–60; from the spiritual and intellectual point of view the following of the author's works should be mentioned: 'Priestly Existence', *Theological Investigations* III (London and Baltimore, 1967), pp. 239–262, and *Knechte Christi. Meditationen zum Priestertum* (Freiburg im Breisgau, 1967); also, *Einübung priesterliche Existenz* (Freiburg im Breisgau, 1970).

The second aspect which can contribute to a precise demarcation of the theme lies in the sphere of biblical theology and the history of dogma. The findings of modern theology here – though admittedly they had not yet emerged so clearly at the Second Vatican Council – show us, namely, that down to the first few decades of the second century the official ministry of the Church had not yet acquired that clear and firm shape and place in the Church as a whole and in the individual community, nor yet that threefold articulation into diaconate, priesthood and episcopate, which we have become accustomed to in the Church from the second century onwards. Yet hitherto we have more or less taken it for granted that this goes back to the very origins of the Church. As we have said: these two viewpoints converge.

The position of the priest today within the Church and also in secular society seems to make it advisable or necessary to introduce wider possibilities of change in the outward form of the priesthood. At the same time, as we see it, the recent insights afforded by biblical theology and the history of dogma into the development of the official ministry in the Church during the apostolic age justify us, from the point of view of dogmatic theology, in allowing for a wider variation in the outward form of the priesthood without on this account calling in question its abiding nature, its genetic constitution or genotype (if we may express it so). It is from these considerations that the subject of our present brief remarks arises.

In a first section we intend briefly to indicate the findings and the scope in terms of doctrine (at least within Catholic theology) of these recent insights arising from the study of biblical theology and the history of dogma. In a second section certain consequences will be drawn from this with regard to possible variations in the concrete form of the official priesthood, consequences which admittedly we shall here be stating merely as doctrinally possible (a point which we shall have to emphasize still more strongly at a later stage). This is not *ipso facto* intended to imply any decision on the question of whether such variations are or are not opportune on ecclesiastical, pastoral or spiritual grounds, or from the point of view of secular society.

We have said that biblical theology and the history of dogma have yielded fresh insights into the history of the priestly ministry in the apostolic age. Admittedly it is important to understand aright what the 'new features' here consist in. Protestant biblical theology and history of dogma has already long been emphasizing these findings, though in a manner which makes them appear irreconcilably opposed to Catholic doctrine on the official priesthood. Probably it is partly for this very reason that it is only in the most recent times that Catholic exegesis and history of dogma for its part has come explicitly to uphold these findings and also to maintain that they are wholly reconcilable with the Catholic doctrine of the priesthood as rightly understood. Obviously we cannot here provide any proof of the assertions we are putting forward in terms of exegesis and the history of dogma. To attempt any such proof from the sources of the New Testament and of history would take too much time.

For our present considerations it is unimportant whether the theses we are putting forward are fully developed as they stand, whether they call for further precisions etc. Nevertheless for the study we propose in the second section of our considerations it is important firmly to recognize that the theses we have in mind are not inconceivable from the point of view of dogmatic theology. In other words we can take them as our starting-point for our practical considerations.

In order to understand the statements which we shall have to make explicitly and directly concerning the priesthood in the apostolic age certain preparatory investigations would be advisable. In itself a presenta-tion of the so-called *jus divinum*[2] in Catholic ecclesiology should be adduced. Here, however, we can make only a few brief statements on this point. The *jus divinum* in the Church does not necessarily have to be traced back to any explicit declaration on the part of Jesus or of an apostle as one endowed with revelation (any more than many propositions which doctrinally speaking are absolutely binding). The *jus divinum* can also be implicitly present in other realities of revelation or in propositions re-lating to these, and may emerge from such realities or propositions in the conscious awareness of the Church only by a gradual process. The reali-ties which we nowadays declare to be *juris divini* within the Church were not necessarily all present right from the origins in the primitive Church. We say that revelation closed only 'with the death of the last apostle', and by the same token not all the realities which are *juris divini* need necessarily have been present from the origins. At least within the apostolic age (and we should avoid naively identifying the end of this with the physical death of Paul or the last of the Twelve),[3] such realities could appear for the first time, could acquire firm form and then come to belong to the irreversible and eternally valid stock of realities belonging to the Church

---

[2] On this cf. the author's article, 'Reflection on the Concept of "Jus Divinum" in Catholic Thought', *Theological Investigations* V (London and Baltimore, 1966), pp. 219-243.

[3] On this cf. the author's *Inspiration in the Bible* (Edinburgh and London, 1961).

throughout all ages. They do not on this account forfeit their character as being of divine right. It cannot in fact be proved that a reality of the kind we are speaking of was present in all areas or in all the decades of the apostolic age, nor is it possible in any way to prove the contrary as a matter of more or less certain historical fact. Here we are passing over the question of whether, and in what sense, it may even be possible or conceivable to speak of a development of the *jus divinum* (and not merely of our conscious awareness of it) in the post-apostolic Church.

These then are the preliminary remarks we need to make concerning the historicity of the *jus divinum* in the Church. This in itself makes it possible to conceive of a degree of variation in the official ministry which is not inconsiderable. But following upon these preliminary remarks we may now put forward a few theses with regard to the official ministry in the Church of the apostolic age. As we have said we are doing this without presenting the arguments from biblical theology and the history of dogma supporting these theses.[4]

If we want to achieve a right understanding of the official priesthood, one that does justice to its nature and is historically credible, we should not simply assume as self-evident the position that right from the very origins of the apostolic age there were three offices in the Church, namely bishop, priest and deacon, and that these and only these were always present within her as clearly distinguished and defined. Even abstracting for the time being from the question of whether there were not yet other offices in the Church at the end of the apostolic age, such as for instance that of the *didaskolos*, abstracting too from the further question of how on this showing any place is left for the Petrine office, whether as included in or as presiding over this triad, it is in any case uncertain that this triad existed in all parts of the apostolic Church or in all decades of the apostolic age in such a way that we should regard the episcopate as an official leadership, monarchic in character and presiding over the *presbyteroi* within the Church. This, it is true, is the picture which seems to be reflected in Ignatius of Antioch, though here it applies primarily to the Syrian Church. We wish to authenticate the nature of the Church's official ministry, and especially of the priesthood as doctrinally

---

[4] In this context attention should also be drawn to the *Letter of the German Bishops on the Priestly Office – a Biblical and Doctrinal Aid*. This document was issued on the 11 November 1969, and a special printing of it was disseminated (Treves, 1969). In the following period the subject emerged at the level of the universal Church with the preparations for the Synod of Bishops of 1971 at Rome, and was brought increasingly to the fore. Here we need only to remind ourselves of this discussion.

defined, on the basis of scripture and the apostolic age. And precisely because of this we must first proceed from the single ministry found in the local Church in the concrete, for it is here that the Church as such achieves its manifestation. By comparison with this single official ministry we can regard as secondary the ways in which it is subdivided and articulated into several possible higher or lower offices regarded as subordinate functions within the single supreme official ministry in the Church or in a given local Church. At the same time, as we have already pointed out in our introductory remarks, this position does not necessarily imply that we cannot any longer regard this way of subdividing the official ministry as of *jus divinum*. This single official ministry, i.e. the single power of direction within an ecclesiastical community in all its dimensions does, it is true imply an apostolic succession to the extent that even according to the very earliest tenets to be found in the records of the Church she must have had an official leadership of this kind, and to the extent that the Church relies eternally upon the witness of the apostles and upon that which she herself was right from the origins in the apostles and through them. It is also clear that when we say that this necessary and ultimately single official ministry within the Church has authority to claim allegiance in faith and conscience from the individual, this authority is based not upon the will of the officially appointed leader, but upon the authority of the Church as one and whole which was brought into being by the Christ-event, and upon the fact of being authentically derived from her. This means that this authority must be called apostolic and deriving from Christ in the fullest sense. Scripture bears witness to the uniqueness of the apostolic office, though it is not something which constitutes merely the first stage, in a temporal sense, of the official ministry in the Church. Yet with regard to this apostolic office we should be cautious in calling the bishops the successors of the apostles in a sense which goes beyond what has just been said. After the apostles the officially appointed ministers in the Church (however they may figure, whatever names they may be called by in the New Testament itself) did not simply receive the powers of the apostles (only a few special privileges being withheld). What they received, rather, was an official ministry which was necessary and which carried the apostolic Church forwards, one which, even though deriving from the apostolate and of its nature closely similar to it, nevertheless represents a new official ministry with a line of succession of its own. The situation here is precisely parallel to that of the post-apostolic Church which is not simply the apostolic Church itself as projected into a subsequent age, even though it is permanently based upon this apostolic

Church. As a matter of principle, and precisely in its bearing upon our later considerations, it is important to recognize that the articulation of the single official leadership in the Church into several distinct offices with distinct functions of their own is secondary. In this sense it seems that in the apostolic Church as it existed in various regions and in various decades there were variations of constitution among its communities, some being more presbyteral and collegiate in character, while in others a monarchic form of episcopate was more prevalent. Here we can set aside the question of what the various national and cultural backgrounds and origins of these variations of constitutions in the different communities may have been, how far, for instance, the characteristics they display are in part Judaeo-Christian and in part Hellenistic. A further question which must remain undiscussed here is how these communities, with their sharp divergencies of structure, gave expression in historical, social and institutional ways to that unity of the Church which is, on any showing, conferred upon them by Christ himself, and which, according to the tenets of the apostolic age, must also be given concrete manifestation. As we have already said, yet a further question which must remain unexplored for our present purposes is how far and in what way this ministry was articulated and subdivided according to the special needs of a given community to cater for further functions over and above those which in a later sense are called the episcopate, presbyterate, and diaconate. In the situation as we have presented it it is also obvious that we cannot establish any firm or definable boundaries, as consciously recognized at that time, between the official ministry and ministers in the strictly juridical sense of the term on the one hand, and the free charisms which existed in the Church on the other, which were recognized as a necessary part of her life, and which under certain circumstances were not immune to a certain process of institutionalization. It is important to notice also that on any realistic view of biblical theology we are not in any position to establish that in New Testament times a special power was recognized with regard to the celebration of the Eucharist such that it was reserved only to a few and conferred by the laying on of hands. All that we can establish from this is that at the Last Supper the Lord entrusted his Church with the anamnesis of his death. This is obviously not to dispute the fact that it must have been borne in upon the Church's conscious awareness ever more clearly that the normal celebration of the supreme mystery had to take place under the direction of her officially appointed leaders, and that the recognition of this as it developed can perfectly well be conceived of as having been achieved even within the apostolic stage of the history of the *jus divinum* in the Church.[5] At the end of the apostolic age, in the Deutero-Pauline epistles, we see that the normal way of appointing an individual to the leadership of a community was through the laying on of hands. There is no difficulty in conceiving of the conferring of this official ministry by the laying on of hands and as accompanied by prayer as a sacrament and also as having been instituted by the Lord. For undoubtedly in virtue of its content and its function within the Church founded by Christ an official ministry of this kind does imply an irrevocable promise of grace by God such that, by the assistance which God causes to be imparted to the official ministry, he continuously assists his Church and guarantees her effectiveness to save and her indefectibility. Again the sacramentality of order is based upon the Church as derived from Christ and upon her special quality as the eschatologically victorious sign of God's will to save.

If therefore we seek to determine the task of the priest as official minister on the basis of the New Testament, we should not take as our starting-point the power to celebrate the Eucharist, even though since the apostolic age this has, at least in normal cases, been reserved to the priesthood. The legitimate starting-point in the New Testament for determining the nature of the official priesthood is to be found, rather in the function of official leadership of a Christian community. A further factor, corresponding to this, is that the lines of demarcation between episcopate and presbyterate in the New Testament are still very fluid and indeterminate. 'Leadership of a community' still includes both. It is obvious that leadership of a community is not to be conceived of according to the model of leadership functions in a secular society, but rather must be conceived of on the basis of the nature of the Church itself as the fruit of salvation and as mediating salvation. On this basis – and this also means on the basis of the Church as the single community of the faith and of avowed missionary commitment – the preaching of the gospel cannot be excluded from this function of leadership. The 'ministry of the word', as an official commission, is certainly to be numbered among the functions of any such official leadership in spite of what we find, for instance, in Ephesians 4. Here the relationship between the 'shepherds' and the 'teachers' is still not sufficiently clearly defined, and hence we have to allow for the possibility that in the theology of some later writings of the New Testament a certain basic autonomy is ascribed to the teachers as

[5] On this cf. in the present volume 'What is a Sacrament?' and also the earlier study, *The Church and the Sacraments*, Quaestiones Disputatae 9 (Edinburgh/London, 1963).

compared with the shepherds, the bishops. (These 'teachers' and 'shepherds' belong to the beginning of the post-apostolic age, as distinct from the apostolic age in the strict sense.) We must consider the nature of the word of preaching and of faith uttered on the basis of Christ's commission, i.e. the radical 'event' character and exhibitive character of the word of preaching in general. In the light of this the connection between the power to preach and the power to dispense the sacraments as vested in the official leaders of the Church is relatively easy to understand. The word that is effective *ex opere operato*, that which is uttered in the sacraments, is the word of preaching in general in its most intense form. It is the word which the Church utters with an absolute commitment to the individual in significant situations in the concrete circumstances of his life as emanating from the Church's own irrevocable promise of grace. A further point, arising from what has been said, bears upon that conception of the priesthood which was put forward at the Council of Trent, and which throws into relief the Eucharistic and reconciliatory power attached to it. While in its positive content this is in no sense disputed, it probably does need to be freed from that one-sidedness which is the outcome of the Counter-Reformation bias, and to be set in a broader context, one which is attested not only by the New Testament but also by tradition as a whole. Hence it is unnecessary here to provide a further special interpretation on the basis of the official teaching of the Church of these theses formulated on the basis of the New Testament concerning the doctrinally binding quality of the official priesthood. Such interpretations have already explicitly been made, chiefly at the Fourth Lateran Council, at Trent, and also in more recent papal encyclicals and at the Second Vatican Council.[6]

The precise point we are concerned with in these brief remarks, largely unsupported as they are by justifying arguments, is this: the Church has at her disposal an extremely wide scope for developing variations within her necessary and ultimately *single* official ministry, in accordance with the needs of a particular age, the variations of cultural milieu etc., and of subdividing that official ministry into various individual offices, regulating the relationships between these offices, establishing and defining the functions of the particular officials, and, without prejudice to the sacramentality of the process by which offices are conferred, defining

---

[6] Obviously the discussion contained in the preparatory documents for the Synod of Bishops at Rome, 1971, as also the debates on this compilation itself, should be noticed for a fuller treatment of this point. Nevertheless they themselves for their part could not achieve any further progress on the most essential and important aspects of the question.

the concrete conditions under which they are to be handed on. Perhaps even it is open to the Church to distinguish between a normal way of conferring its official ministry and an extraordinary way, justifiable in cases of need. Possibly too it might arrange that the selection of an official minister should be by election on the part of the members of the Church or other bodies having the right to vote. All this remains fully within the scope of what is doctrinally possible, even though the justifiable concrete forms which all these matters assume in a given age or a given situation are to be decided not merely on the basis of what is doctrinally possible, but also on the basis of the *jus humanum* of the particular age involved and in accordance with its special conditions. Even if we say that the threefold division of the official ministry into episcopate, diaconate and presbyterate is binding upon the Church, and as a prescription is irrevocable and *juris divini*, something which has been developed in the apostolic age and is already abidingly present at the outset of the post-apostolic age – even then, the following point still always remains to be borne in mind: even on this showing the precise content of these three offices is still far from clear, and is surely capable of modification by the Church. Incidentally the same thing also appears in connection with other factors in the theology of order. For instance priests can confirm, and there is nothing against the position that they have a positive, albeit restricted, power to ordain others as priests. Properly speaking, therefore, the prerogatives of the episcopate can be regarded as consisting merely in a *potestas jurisdictionis* and not in a *potestas ordinis*. But the one point that cannot seriously be disputed is that such a division of the *potestas ordinis*, introducing wide variations of form and degree into it, is possible and to a large extent at least is subject to the judgement of the Church itself.[7]

A further way in which it can be shown that this single official ministry within the Church can admit of variations in the way in which it is subdivided, despite the existence of this triad of offices, is this: it is doctrinally speaking not inconceivable to suppose that the Church might consciously act in the same way as it presumably did at the end of the Patristic age and in the Middle Ages, in devising subdivisions of sacramental order. Today too the Church could create new subordinate degrees of its official ministry such as would correspond to the needs of the age without our having to deny from the outset or perforce that these had the character of

---

[7] The prerogatives of a bishop, in virtue of which only a bishop can consecrate other bishops, is relatively unimportant the moment we realize in principle that all other episcopal powers in respect both of the *potestas ordinis* and the *potestas jurisdictionis* can also be found in the so-called simple priest.

a sacrament. In the case of the episcopate, despite its sacramental character and its derivation from Christ, the appointment of a bishop can be conceived of as taking place in the most varied ways without thereby derogating from its doctrinal nature or denying that every such appointment must take place in a spirit of harmony with the entire Church and so too with the pope. In the same way also the relationship of a bishop to the *presbyterium* is subject to wide variations, for it falls virtually completely within the sphere of the *potestas jurisdictionis*. It is true that the episcopate (taken in the sense of an official power belonging to specific individuals rather than all the bishops collectively) is *juris divini*, i.e. an episcopal power consisting of an official teaching authority, an official priesthood, and an official pastoral position must exist in the Church. But however true this may be, I still do not believe that it is unequivocally certain that this episcopal power as such necessarily has to be vested in a single individual, and could not be vested in a *collegium*. If we envisage the possibility of an episcopal power having a collegiate subject then the possibility of variations in the relationship which the episcopate bears to the presbyterate becomes still clearer. Even in the case supposed there would always be a difference between bishops and priests, and yet an 'episcopate' of the kind we are thinking of as it existed in a particular Church, would have a 'presbyteral', i.e. a collegiate, structure. Although we weigh up all these doctrinal possibilities this does not *ipso facto* mean that we are recommending that they should be put into practice. Other aspects have to be taken into consideration so that not everything that is doctrinally possible is *ipso facto* advisable. It is important to ensure the continuity of a tradition which, although it may not be doctrinally compelling, is nevertheless historical. Because of this, because of pastoral requirements, because of conditions within the Church or in secular society, certain possible courses which are doctrinally conceivable may be wholly ruled out as practical measures in the concrete. Indeed the conditions of a particular age may perhaps make them morally impermissible because of the evil consequences which would ensue if they were put into practice. Thus though we are now about to draw further consequences for the re-shaping of the priesthood in our own times from the theses put forward in the first section of these considerations of ours, still we are in no sense *ipso facto* coming to any particular decision as to whether such possible courses are opportune in the concrete. On the other hand, so it seems to me, our present-day situation within the Church and in secular society is such that it is no mere futile playing with ideas for us to raise such questions concerning these possible ways of re-shaping the priesthood as an official ministry which are doctrinally possible and yet widely different from one another in their outward aspect compared with the form the priesthood has taken up to the present. Nowadays many circles and groups of priests in the most widely contrasting lands are in fact engaging in considerations of this kind. Hence it is reasonable for us to put these theses contained in our first section to the test to see whether, they are doctrinally possible, even though we are still in no sense arriving at a decision from the pastoral point of view, and even though we must unquestionably guard against the temptation of concluding that a given course is advisable merely on the grounds that it is new. It is also obvious that changes in the concrete form of the priesthood, to the extent that this form has been established by juridical decisions which are *juris humani*, can take place only with the assent of the competent representatives of this human law. (In this connection, admittedly, the question of the formation of a legitimate *consuetudo contra legem* has to remain open.) But considerations of this kind with regard to the doctrinal possibility of new forms of the priesthood are reasonable even if they can be brought to realization only in a future epoch. Even the priest of today in his life and his official ministry has a certain scope for freedom and thereby for responsibility. Realities of the future must be prepared for, and moreover they must be prepared for 'from below' because it is in no sense the case that they can be brought to realization solely by a sheer sudden decree 'from above'. The affairs of the future call for preliminaries in the present. New 'phanotypes' are prepared for by micromutations in the present. This also applies to the priesthood. And hence the priest of today must positively assume responsibility for the priesthood of tomorrow and the forms which it will assume in the concrete. This is why we are enquiring into some of the characteristics which may perhaps be conceivable in the future, which are fully within the scope of the nature of the priesthood as doctrinally defined, because this has a far greater degree of flexibility than is commonly supposed. For we are all too ready unreflectingly to identify the nature of the priesthood with the concrete forms of it to which we ourselves are accustomed in our own lives. But this will suffice by way of introduction to this second section. In what follows we shall now proceed to mention, though not in any systematic order, some of the possible variations of this kind which seem to us at least worth considering for the future of the priesthood.

Probably it would be possible to have many more specialized priests and types of priests who were more clearly distinguished from one another. The tasks, functions and ministries within the Church which its priests have *de facto* fulfilled in the course of Church history have all along varied very greatly. The priest has figured as the pastor of a concrete local community, as an expert in theology, as a contemplative monk, as a missionary among pagans, as a travelling preacher, chiefly in the apostolic orders, as an administrative official, as a politician or a poet. These and many other concrete forms of the priestly office are already to be found throughout the course of history. Yet it has been left more or less to the Church's powers of improvisation or to chance and the random changes of history to produce them. These differentiations have not been institutionalized and it has remained to a large extent obscure whether forms of this kind as they exist in concrete life have constituted variations of the priesthood as such or merely external supplementary functions in the life of the priest such that properly speaking they have nothing to do with his priesthood even though not irreconcilable with his priestly office. Today and in the future there is a question which we may perhaps have to raise precisely in view of the abundance of functions and ministries in the Church of the New Testament which mutually condition one another and which we are still far from having been fully defined. The question is whether we should not plainly reflect upon and actually institutionalize quite specific types of functions and ways of life which, while clearly different from one another, nevertheless constitute variations of the single essence of the priesthood. This question has a wholly practical bearing. In view of the social, cultural and individual differences between the men of today we may ask ourselves whether entry into the priesthood could not be opened to younger, and especially to older Christians, even when they are incapable or unwilling to undertake in principle the whole spectrum of priestly duties which we of today still regard as belonging to or concomitant with the priesthood. Perhaps side by side with the 'all-rounder' priest as we think of him we can imagine a type of priest for the future who from the outset is deputed only to a much more narrowly defined function and who has received a correspondingly more specialized formation. Such a one would be able to perform still more as a specialist in this more narrowly defined function than the priest of today is able to since the latter still has to be able to do everything that falls within the scope of his functions (at least according to the official theory). These new and more limited types of priesthood would not need simply to coincide with the earlier specialist types already recognized and put into practice though not in any proper sense institutionalized. Possible examples of such new types of priest would be the priest as artist, as a man of secular learning, as a psychotherapist, as a journalist, as a social worker, as the leader of specific forms of Christian communities developed from below which would not be identical with the local parish communities etc. There is no need to object to all this that the powers of celebrating the Eucharist and forgiving sins are powers which cannot be eliminated from our idea of the essence of the priesthood. For obviously a priest of this kind would likewise have these powers. But even while these general priestly powers would be conferred upon him he would in normal cases be ordained by an ordination which was, in a certain sense, relative, with a view to the particular human groups which his specialized task was designed to cater for. Obviously the existence of many such specialized types of priesthood would give rise to the question of whether the special functions to which they were deputed could not just as well be exercised by laymen. But while we do not intend to discuss this question in any greater detail at this point, this much at least should be said: this problem is already present in many concrete types of the priesthood as it exists today in which the assigning of such specific functions to priests excludes laymen from the same functions. In any case the priesthood as it exists in the concrete today and tomorrow cannot be restricted exclusively to those tasks which, on a doctrinal interpretation (at least in normal cases) are ascribed to the priest alone. For otherwise we would in fact have to withdraw even the office of preaching from the realm of priestly functions.

In this context we may at least make mention of the problem of combining the priestly office with a specifically secular calling which is not integrated into the priestly function as an intrinsic element in it but is exercised rather on other grounds by an individual who is at the same time a priest. Since Paul the tent-maker such ways of combining the priesthood with a secular calling have constantly recurred for reasons of necessity, because of particularly strong and unsuppressible gifts in a specialist field, or on grounds which turn out in the end to be missionary in character. Surely we do not need to explain at any length the fact that in the concrete circumstances of human life, albeit not from the viewpoint of working skills, in such a case the priestly calling must be the truly decisive and determinative factor, the true *entelecheia* of a life of this kind despite the twofold calling. To this extent in normal cases no individual should become a priest unless he is willing to engage his whole life in this priestly function, and this remains true however many specialist forms of the priesthood there may be which are consistent with this principle. Yet in view of the ever-increasing lack of priests we should boldly raise the question of whether it would not also be possible to have one or other of the above-mentioned specialist types of priest, one who in his mature years might take over the direction of a small local Christian community which would otherwise remain without a priest, and who would be ordained priest after a theological and religious formation sufficient for this purpose. For such a one would not have any further priestly functions taking him outside this small group. In such a case it would after all be conceivable that a priest might also exercise, i.e. retain, a secular calling as well.

The functions of leader of the community and itinerant preacher-instructor appear to have been combined as the outcome of a historical development at the end of the apostolic age. (It is reflected, for instance, in the Didache.) Thus the proclaimer of the word, despite the eminently priestly function bound up with his task, was in no sense attached exclusively to a particular region or a particular community. Nowadays we are faced with a great lack of priests in general and a great need of specialist priests. And in view of all this changes may be introduced in the future into parishes as they have existed hitherto. Up to now they have often covered small areas in which all the more important ecclesiastical functions were performed and were able to be performed by one priest. In the future such parishes will no longer necessarily remain simply the basic type for the organization of pastoral care in the same way as hitherto. We might conceive of teams of priests living together, their members specializing in particular fields in the manner already described and having a wider area deputed to them as their 'Church'. In any case no objection can be raised against a pastoral strategy of this kind on the grounds of the nature of the priesthood itself.

The kind of priest we are accustomed to is in a position analogous to that of a state official. He receives an academic formation as a social functionary from the leaders of the society as a whole, and is then appointed from above to a specific position as a functionary of this kind. Yet all this has properly speaking nothing to do with the doctrinal nature of the priesthood. On the basis of the New Testament and the doctrinal nature of the priesthood we can however conceive of the priestly leader of a community in quite different terms. It is true that for the due exercise of his office he needs the approval of the leader of a wider regional Church called a bishop, who for his part must once more live in union and harmony with the universal Church and so with the pope. This basic approval granted by the individual leader of the community is granted by the sacramental laying on of hands, which certainly in its turn requires specific prior conditions in the individual to be ordained. But the more integrated an individual community was from within itself, i.e. from below, in terms of faith, communal Christian love, the energy of neighbourly love, and common responsibility for the world, the more it would in a true sense have the right to present from within itself an individual Christian known to it, living with it, integrated within it for the office of leadership, a Christian who had the necessary qualities for this position of priestly leadership and who would be recognized as such a leader by the sacramental laying on of hands on the part of the authorized bishop. Perhaps it will come about that the lack of priests which is becoming ever greater will compel us to admit the need for priests of this special kind and to allow them to be ordained, priests who come from the specific community concerned and 'from below'.

A further point must be mentioned concerning the doctrinal possibility or impossibility of a priesthood 'for a limited period', for this is a question which has been raised in very recent times. The meaning of this question might be to enquire whether someone might be ordained to the priesthood with the explicit proviso made from the outset that he would place himself at the disposal of the Church in the priestly office only for a specific period. Alternatively it might be a question as to whether an individual could of his own initiative ask to be relieved of the priestly ministry with a certain right to have this request granted on the part of the Church even though no such time limit to his ministry had been paid down beforehand. There is an inclination to answer such a question in the negative on the basis of the defined doctrine of the Council of Trent concerning the indelibility of the priestly character. Yet it appears to me that this question cannot be answered on the basis of the *character indelebilis*, for this doctrine, on a precise view, is concerned merely with the impossibility of ordination being repeated. In my opinion it does not even include for certain any statement that it would be absolutely impossible for the Church, even if she wished it, so to restrict all priestly powers on justified grounds that any exercise of them would be not only unlawful but actually invalid. Furthermore on any unprejudiced evaluation of practices of *de facto* dispensing from office by degradation, secularization etc., practices which have always been in force, we shall find it impossible to assert that the Church can undertake such a course of dispensing a priest from his official ministry only when serious moral or religious offences against the priesthood and the Church have been laid before the Church. There are no clear or apparent reasons why there should not be other grounds, and moreover not merely those connected with priestly celibacy, grounds which do not presuppose any faults, and yet morally justify the priest concerned in petitioning the Church to grant him a dispensation from the priestly ministry. Already at various points in the past history of the Church such laicizations have certainly occurred. Thus we may ask, at least without having to fear a veto from the outset from the point of view of dogma, whether such cases might not become more frequent in the future on the most varied social, cultural, and psychological grounds, and whether it would not even be possible to devise juridical forms for the granting of such dispensations which would be laid down from the outset and as of general application. All this is not of course intended to dispute the fact that it is at least doctrinally conceivable that the free decision of an individual to answer God's call to the priesthood is in itself intended to be an unreserved commitment of his whole life to God and to the priestly ministry. Yet we should bear in mind the temporary vows, by means of which, according to the mind of the Church, the individual binds himself to the evangelical counsels for a time even though this can certainly not be the ultimate meaning of the evangelical counsels. And in view of this we should exercise caution when we find ourselves inclined not to allow that something analogous may be involved in the decision to embrace the priesthood.

A further point which surely arises from the considerations we have put forward in the first section is that on doctrinal grounds it is possible to conceive of the relationship between bishop and priests as subject to a greater variability than we are nowadays normally accustomed to suppose. The Second Vatican Council has developed a theology of the episcopate, and that too quite independently of the narrower question of the significance of the universal episcopate in the direction of the universal Church, which actually goes against the medieval theology of a Thomas Aquinas when he regards the episcopate as the truest and fullest mode of realization as the *primum analogatum* of order and of the priesthood in general, so that by comparison with the episcopate the presbyterate appears almost a little one-sided, as a mere instrument for the assistance of it. I believe that this view of the relationship between episcopate and presbyterate is devoid of any possible theological justification, and is determined by a certain 'episcopal-ideological' one-sidedness. Certainly we can conceive of the priests of a diocese as a senate, and the bishop as monarch. According to the laws currently in force this presbyteral senate of a bishop has certainly a subordinate position in relation to him just as the universal episcopate has a subordinate position in relation to the pope. For this universal episcopate, working with and under the pope, constitutes the subject of the supreme and full power in the Church, something which we certainly cannot say of the *presbyterium* of a diocese according to the prevailing laws. But all this is still not enough to express any clear and absolutely unchangeable relationship of the *presbyterium* of a diocese to its bishop. In concrete terms this relationship can again be conceived of in very different forms. In the concrete attitude of bishop and priests and in conformity with a possible human law in the Church it could perfectly well be the case that the bishop acts as, and is felt to be, the head of a *presbyterium*, who holds this *collegium* together, represents it, and makes it effective. This in turn would not necessarily have to imply that even at the level of some possible *jus humanum* the bishop would merely be *primus inter pares* and the executive instrument of the presbyteral college. It is possible to conceive of a temporal limitation of the office of a bishop. We may also weigh up how many functions and tasks are *de facto* gradually transferred from individual bishops to conferences of bishops. We may also consider the increasing importance of auxiliary bishops and subordinate bishops of local areas. And a further point which should not be overlooked is how variable the individual episcopal sees are in terms of size and importance for the Church in general. Nor should we forget those other questions of doctrine which remain open between bishops and priests which have already been spoken of in the first section, and which make it difficult to establish any clear lines of demarcation between the episcopate and the presbyterate. And if all these points are borne in mind then, so I believe, we are left with a broad scope for re-shaping this relationship in a manner appropriate to the times, the more so since the election of a bishop by the clergy of the diocese concerned is not doctrinally speaking impossible even though it is not provided for in the canon law now in force. No legal formula, taken by itself alone, is sufficient to express the entire human and Christian relationship between bishop and priests in all its fulness. Not everything which is not juridically institutionalized is on this account *ipso facto* secondary or unimportant. Not everything which the law prescribes is *ipso facto* also enjoined upon us by love and genuine humanity. Much that was formerly entrusted to the Christian and human resources of the bishop alone could and should be institutionalized today as a legally enforceable right of the priests. And this does not of itself imply any assault upon the doctrinal essence of the episcopate. It is possible to envisage the *presbyterium* in two distinct roles: on the one hand as a consultative senate of a monarchic bishop and as an instrument to assist him, on the other as a collegiate *presbyterium* as the bearer of the office in the diocese in union with an episcopal 'head' having the special rights proper to himself. These are not conceptual models which in practice need necessarily exclude one another. The very fact that the relationships within the communities had already assumed very varied forms even in the apostolic age should serve to warn us against any rigidity in raising either one of these conceptual models to the status of an absolute norm.

We have put forward a whole range of hypothetical points concerning the priesthood, its history, its future, and even its nature as well. Such questions, hypotheses and differences of opinion are inevitable in an age in which the social changes everywhere also make it necessary to have a fresh appraisal of the abiding elements in the priesthood and the elements which are subject to change. But in all these questions, which seem so urgent to us and render us insecure and threatened even in our understanding of our own priesthood, we priests should not forget that ultimately speaking we do after all know what we are and what we have to do. Jesus Christ the crucified and risen Lord, his grace, the inconceivable mystery which pervades our life, imparts himself to us as our goal and as the strength of our life which we call God. It is these factors which always remain, yesterday, today and tomorrow, the living force by which we live. If we believe this with our whole hearts then we can also utter it in the name of the community and with the commitment of our whole life to our brothers and sisters with an effective word, a word that embodies the presence that we preach. Now if we do this then we are priests. There are many further questions concerning the priesthood, but the first and last of these questions is after all that concerning our faith in Jesus Christ as the Lord, in whom the infinite Mystery has uttered itself to us in forgiveness and so as to endow us with divinity.

13

THE RELATIONSHIP BETWEEN PERSONAL AND COMMUNAL SPIRITUALITY AND WORK IN THE ORDERS

OUR treatment of this subject will take the form of an enquiry into life in the religious orders as such from the standpoint of Catholicism and the Church in general.

In principle such an approach implicitly contains a generation problem. Obviously the question of the precise relationship between personal and communal spirituality[1] and work in the orders is with us in all ages and in every sphere. Nevertheless our only reason for applying ourselves to this subject here and now is the special relevance which it has for us. What I mean when I say that it involves a generation problem is that the question we are concerned with is one of special urgency and importance nowadays as between the younger and older members of the orders. A further reason, however, is that this relevance arises not merely from factors present in every age between the generations within a community, but is conditioned by the development of personal attitudes and outlooks such as have precisely not always existed as they now manifest themselves on the contemporary scene.

In other words that generation problem in the narrower and commonly accepted sense of the term – i.e. the abiding tension between old and young – is rendered *essentially* more acute because in the development of our ideas and attitudes we find ourselves in a period of transition which perhaps we may characterize with all due provisos as a transition between an epoch of nineteenth-century individualism on the one hand and one of socialism on the other. Precisely in *this* situation the two generations respectively become the representatives of these two epochs. The result

---

[1] At a different level the author has defined his position on this question in his article, 'Das Gebet des Einzelnen und die Liturgie der Kirche', *Strukturen christlicher Existenz*, H. Schlier, E. v. Severus, J. Subdrack, A. Pereira edd. (Würzburg, 1968), pp. 189–198.

is that the problem assumes the same radical proportions as are always involved in the process of transformation and transition from one major epoch to another. But all this is something which cannot be entered into in any very explicit way here. In the light of this alone, and abstracting from many other considerations, it is obvious – to put it briefly – that our present-day situation viewed as a whole is specified by conflicting tendencies: the single situation in which we all live is specified by the contrasts between young and old, between individualism and socialism (taking both in a very general sense, and no value judgements being implied). The result is that each of these two entities possesses in its turn its own interior dialectic within itself while each generation is faced with a task which it genuinely has the capacity to accomplish, yet *at the same time* at which it can fail, the task namely of responding aright to the claims which the future makes upon it by maintaining in a way that endures and yet is ever new those elements concealed within the past which validly demand to survive and to persist.

In all this I am aware that I am viewing the matter from the standpoint of one who is *old*. Obviously too one of the older generation should view a problem of this kind as objectively as possible. He should strive to do justice to the other side. Yet something that is precisely involved in this objectivity which has to be striven for in this particular case is the awareness that we are incapable of experiencing in our own intimate personal feelings the fact that we are old; that that which an old man finds himself faced with as the outcome of tradition can very easily be apprehended by him as that which is new; that the only way in which he can arrive at an understanding and due respect for that which is new is invariably by a certain process of intellectual self-denial. From this it follows that in principle the same subject-matter should also be treated of by a young man, to whom that which is traditional and old is in a certain sense alien, whereas that which is new is self-evident. Only then, by bringing the old and the young face to face in this sense, by each of them voluntarily conceding to the other that which still remains insuperably alien on grounds of ultimate freedom – only then could this theme be treated of in an objectively adequate manner.

In speaking of the young and the old in this sense I am of course aware that these two concepts are very obscure. There is a biological sense of being young or old; there is a young-ness or old-ness which is a matter of one's own personal development. There are sociological grades of 'oldness' based on the milieu from which an individual may stem. This may either belong to, and be orientated towards, the more traditional factors of the past, or *alternatively* may imply the kind of social grouping which strives for a better future. And all these possible shades of meaning which may be attached to the terms 'young' or 'old' are in their turn combined in the individual in the most varied and even paradoxical ways. When therefore we simply use the terms 'young' or 'old' we are speaking very imprecisely.

In the present context when we speak of 'the orders' the realities subsumed under this heading vary very greatly among themselves. As they exist in the concrete the orders exhibit the widest variations. Despite the tendency of modern canon law to reduce all to the same level, and despite the influence of the (economic, intellectual etc.) necessities of modern life, which affect all in common, the distinguishing features of the orders are still very different in each case so that we may ask whether anything more than a vague and analogous concept can be found capable of covering them all. Yet if we take a concept of *this* kind as our starting-point we all too easily incur the danger of failing to realize the character of the individual order as a concrete reality. This is a state of affairs which must be recognized. It bears upon the judgements which we have to arrive at in the present study. There may be individual orders to which they are far from applying in any real sense. If this is the case then it is something which must be understood and excused in the light of the state of affairs described above.

NINETEENTH-CENTURY INDIVIDUALISM AND SOCIALISM

One last preliminary point: we are proceeding from the assumption that the situation of a modern kind of individualism prevailing in the nineteenth and the first half of the twentieth centuries was *the* situation which most of all left its mark upon the orders, their spirituality and their work. This is not to dispute the fact that the degree and depths to which it did leave its mark upon the individual orders varied very greatly according to their histories, their geographical regions, their functions and tasks, and above all the social milieu from which they drew their members. Nevertheless all of them shared, each in its own way, in this common lot, even in those cases – indeed precisely in those cases – in which they sought to adopt a critical attitude towards their own times or even rejected them. Obviously I am aware that the concept of 'nineteenth-century individualism' is imprecise and obscure to a degree for the very reason that it is almost always impossible to sum up in a single term that which characterizes oneself in one's historical development and in terms of special qualities which is is impossible ever to realize consciously in their fulness. The modern individualist is a man who is convinced of the special qualities of his own individuality, who attempts to reflect upon them, feels them to be of positive value and as something which he has to culti-vate. The modern individualist, therefore, feels that the rest of society, apart from a small circle of relations and friends, is that which is extra, alienating and threatening. To him the population at large constitutes the masses which he is inclined to despise. Hence he seeks to be free, first in his thinking to the extent that he feels that his convictions are not identi-cal with the convictions of society as a whole, though obviously he cannot be excused from interpreting these for himself. They are not the intelligent reproduction of the collective convictions of society. On the contrary, they are opposed to these and constantly threatened by them. He seeks also, therefore, free scope for the exercise of his powers as the sphere for his own personal and individual decisions. He is convinced of the importance of the great personalities whom he honours for the history of society as a whole. He is élitist in outlook. He lives in a world in which unconsciously and unquestioningly the necessary conditions are already provided ensuring that he is able to live individualistically in this sense. There is a society which is ready to serve the needs of this particular individual. The modern individualist is . . . We could prolong our de-scription much further, but in doing so would always be open to the ob-jection that the individual we are constructing is one who either does not or should not exist, one who we ourselves would never wish to be, even those of us who belong in the fullest sense to this age. But I believe that despite this there is such a figure as a modern individualist. He is an historical reality and can be such precisely because despite their common nature men are not always and everywhere the same.

Now let us turn to a further assumption from which we are simul-taneously proceeding. It is this: much that is observable nowadays in society, and that is beginning to stamp social living and also, to an in-creasing extent, the spirituality and the work of the particular orders, is such that without injustice it both can and should – albeit with many provisos – be brought under the heading of the socialistic factor. Obvi-ously the modern individualistic factor can, as it were, be metaphysically purified to a point at which only that element of the personal remains which exists, or should exist, always and everywhere, where that which is human in the true sense is to some extent achieved in its undiminished fulness. Again we can metaphysically sublimate the socialist factor to a point at which only that remains which, considered as an orientation towards the social and the communal in human living, belongs precisely to the very nature of the finite personal spirit which is in man. But in this context we are using the term 'personal' in a sense belonging to modern individualism, and obviously too in a sense which is morally and meta- physically entirely neutral and involves no hostile judgement. Again we are using the term 'communal' as characterizing the coming age, and again one which does not imply any hostile judgement or any glorification either. Yet in using these terms we are assuming from the outset two points: first that the *basic* metaphysical substance inherent in these two terms has an abiding validity in *every* epoch of human history, second that at the same time within the individual epochs the historically conditioned form of these two essential structures of human living and development can vary very greatly. And if all this is true then surely we are in a position to say that from the nineteenth century onwards the presentation of the orders in terms of spirituality and work was 'individualistic' in character, whereas in the coming ages the presentation of the orders in terms of spirituality and work will rather bear a 'socialistic' stamp. This of is course not to deny that this 'socialistic' factor in the approaching epochs will assume a very different guise from that which far-seeing people and prophets envisaged for it when they began to speak of it in the nineteenth century.

REALITY IN THE ORDERS

We older members of the orders are at basis nineteenth-century individu- alists. Obviously we have maintained community life and still willingly do maintain it. Perhaps even in a sense that is yet more obvious than among the younger members of the orders we have accepted a common task, a common work of collaboration, and have carried it out uncom- plainingly and without raising many problems. Certainly too there are orders which from the very nature of their traditions have made this common task part of their lives and have carried it out in a way that is obvious to them and belongs very closely to their most intimate personal lives. And certainly, from the very nature of the Church itself, and as heirs to an ancient past, the orders have not *merely* been societies made up of nineteenth-century individualists, but also in this respect a *complexio oppositorum*. But this mixture of mutually opposed elements which is present in all human life did nevertheless have a specific form, a particular balance between the opposite qualities involved which does not remain in force for all ages or binding upon them. Hence I still believe that it is justifiable for us older members of the religious orders to say that we have all been nineteenth-century individualists. It might be asserted, albeit with a certain element of exaggeration, that we have even existed in our large communities somewhat as institutionalized hermits. In fact we have been individuals who as such have lived and worked together. Particular friendships were frowned upon. On the whole it was not usual for individuals to open their hearts to one another. Each man stood on his own feet in coping with his own life. Alone he met his own interior needs and arrived at his own decisions of conscience, or at most he discussed them with a spiritual director, and even in these cases there was a certain impression of an official advisory board. The communal 'rule' which we strictly observed in the orders was at basis not so much the social institutionalization of the *community* as such, but the rational order within which it was possible at once to maintain the due rights of many individualists and at the same time their common work. Abstracting for the moment from the human factor, something which always exists among normal men, we could say that our community was primarily functional in character but was not concerned with men as such or with their personal union as distinct from their merely functional one. Even the kinds of work which we performed in common were clear in themselves, so that they did not require much discussion, at any rate not once the basic decisions had been arrived at so that all that still remained to be carried out was already fixed and clear beforehand in the plan devised for such work.[2] Obviously in practice other factors were always present at the same time: the emotional factor, friendships possibly of a very individualistic stamp, traces of inculpable eroticism, and as a matter of practical experience a sense of belonging together which went beyond that which was prescribed on the basis of our common concerns and of a somewhat aseptic interpretation of what love of neighbour should mean. Nevertheless all this was, after all, not *in principle* catered for in religious life as stamped by the nineteenth-century individualism. It was not consciously reflected upon. In fact the conscious realization of it was rather suppressed, and in any case it was hardly institutionalized or reduced to forms and modes of conduct which as such belonged to the religious life which it sought to develop. In accordance with this the relationship which individual members of religious orders bore to their superiors likewise always contained a strong element of officialdom and remoteness even in

[2] cf. the author's articles on the situation and the viewpoints involved, 'Die Zukunft der Orden in Welt und Kirche von heute', *Geist und Leben* 43 (1970), pp. 338–354.

those orders in which the superiors were frequently changed. What has been sketched in here as the mode of life of us older men really amounts only to a quite vague approximation, and should not be taken as a condemnation of it. All that we are seeking to achieve is to sketch in a mode of living conditioned by a particular age, which is, or has been, at least as legitimate and capable of fulfilment for its own times as any other which may be lived by today or tomorrow and which is justified in its own right. It was a harder more masculine mode of living, which had its greatnesses, its limitations, and not infrequently too its tragic elements in the form of petrification and lack of real warm-heartedness (this often being wrongly interpreted as the fulfilment of duty). It has in fact the same limited scope as in fact is inherent in all that is human. We older members have a life to live in common with younger ones, who bring their own special qualities into the common life and have the right to do so. This is the context in which we live and of which we must take cognizance. Yet in this context we for our part have the right to continue to live in our former mode even though, from an objective historical point of view, this can be designated as a nineteenth-century individualistic mode. We can freely concede – always taking into account the demands which common life makes upon old and young alike – that we do not view concelebrations with the same favour as the young, that we are less inclined than the younger generation to engage in long discussions and conferences,[3] that we prefer to be by ourselves, to meditate alone, than to engage in group religious discussions; that this experience of ours of a sound old tradition that has been tried and proved is not mere illusion or something that has *merely* seized upon factors belonging exclusively to the past. We must bring this personal outlook of ours – though obviously without any reactionary or intransigent hardening of attitudes – into the life of the religious orders of today in which we are and remain unreservedly involved. We must bring to them that which we have become through our own personal history. Only so can we ensure that on the one hand the true heritage of the more recent past continues to be maintained in our orders, these too being constantly and rightly bound by their own history, while on the other hand that which is abidingly valid, which was developed in a form belonging particularly to us and conditioned by our age remains alive in the future of the orders, albeit in new and altered forms.

[3] On this cf. in general the author's article, 'Alte und neue Frommigkeit', *Theologische Akademie* IV, K. Rahner and O. Semmelroth edd., (Frankfurt, 1967), pp. 9–28, and also 'Dialogue in the Church', *Theological Investigations* X (London and New York, 1973), pp. 103–121.

TRANSITION

Nevertheless we are living in a period of transition in which the socialistic factor or, to formulate it more cautiously, the communal factor in the orders is also seeking to achieve formal expression. This statement might perhaps be regarded as paradoxical, for it is in fact religious communities that are being treated of, and this makes it difficult to understand how the communal factor in such groups can seek to achieve a new significance special to the particular epoch. Yet this is in fact the case. What is being sought for is a fraternal community formed from below and constantly undergoing fresh creative formation to a greater extent than is provided for at the individual level simply by canon law. It is obvious that a stronger sense of community cannot simply be achieved by reviving the social modes of earlier communities. Rather it seeks to introduce the greater maturity, education and individuality of the person into the new forms of community life, and to have a 'democratic' form of community at the level of its social institutionalization. This does not gainsay the assertion that there is a shift of emphasis in the life of the orders towards the communal. There is a tendency to favour small communes either as wholly, autonomous or as the sort of units into which a more large-scale community is subdivided so as to achieve a fully human way of life. In the decisions which have to be arrived at in the religious life and in the work of religious communities it is sought to aim at processes of collective counselling in which all participate, each in his own way, and in which the democratic and collegiate structures still surviving from the earlier histories of the orders are effectively brought to life once more, and moreover in a way that is meaningful for modern times. These, it is felt, must be something more than mere façades designed to conceal authoritative decisions arrived at exclusively from above.[4] Here and there groupings of members of religious orders are to be discerned which are to some extent paracanonical. In this way they seek more readily to bring home to the official authorities in the orders what their aims are. There is pressure for a greater degree of intelligibility for *all* elements in the régime of religious orders, right down to their economic workings. The younger members of the orders, who are still undergoing their formation, are nowadays unwilling any longer to be treated as mere subjects for the older generation to educate. Instead they want to contribute positively to the life and activities of the order. When and if the liturgy as such is still taken

[4] On this cf. H. J. Wallraff, 'Mitgliedschaft und Mitverantwortung in den Orden heute', *Geist und Leben* 41 (1968), pp. 47–59.

seriously it is in principle and obviously an affair of the community, not merely in theory but in its concrete forms as well. In the orders an attempt is made to achieve a community which is sustained by a *more personal* commitment of the individuals *to one another*. Where the work is being done in common it should on this account be sustained to the widest possible extent by a sense of charismatic vocation and personal inclination on the part of the individuals, it should as fully as possible spring from spontaneous creativeness and invention, and should be not so much the dutiful carrying out of a plan and a task which are already laid down as such beforehand and may not be called in question. The teamwork itself should then be sustained by a conception of creative work of this kind. It is for the team to produce the plan, and for it and only it to authorize it and put it into practice. The team should not merely consist in the sum total of those engaged in the work who merely carry out a project designed independently of the team itself. Admittedly on this showing it becomes a far more difficult question how the concept of a common function can still take into account the fact that for whole decades or still longer the same task was carried out by the same order and its members. Discussions are favoured and long communal sessions. Religious conversations with an individual stamp are nowadays more frequent and more taken for granted than solitary meditation, just as in general (at least at present among us) human fellowship is in the eyes of the young, if not the only factor then at least the one which alone renders intelligible and justifiable everything else in the religious life and in the life of the order. It is no longer the official juridical structure of an order which sustains the personal life of the community at the practical level, for the younger members view these official structures and laws with a certain coldness, and do not have the impression that such things must always remain the same. The converse is true: it is the personal community life which renders the official social forms justified and bearable if and to the extent that this community life is felt to be liberating and demanding in a human sense. These juridical and official forms of social living are not laid down beforehand without question on the basis of the Church and as valid in all cases, such that they are responded to in an attitude of loyalty, this in itself being the attitude and the decision of a religious individualist and being felt to be valid and binding even when his relationship to the rest of the members of the order has become extremely questionable. Instead we are living in a kind of community which produces certain juridical structures of its own. Where therefore the sense of community as such has been lost the juridical factor is no longer felt to be binding in any true sense. On this basis (and of course on many other grounds, as for instance a far more functional interpretation of the religious life as compared with former times) we can also explain the fact that the attitude of the younger members to their order is far more subject to conditions. It is an attitude which often shocks us older men. An individual who leaves the order is no longer regarded as having failed or fallen by the way, nor is his act felt to be the outcome of an unsuitability for this order. On the contrary, it is felt to be a failure of the order itself to meet the just claims of this individual who departs from it.

THE INTERPLAY BETWEEN THE PERSONAL AND THE COMMUNAL ASPECTS

On the basis of these assumptions we are seeking to speak of the relationship between personal and communal spirituality and work in the religious orders. In doing so we are not concerned with the approach or the findings of a metaphysical or theological anthropology in relation to these two factors. For basically speaking all that would still remain to be said is something which for any Christian anthropology is obvious: ultimately speaking the personal and the communal are not factors which are in conflict with one another or exclude one another. On the contrary they mutually condition one another and grow or diminish *in interplay with one another.* All that could then be said is that communal living in the true sense can only grow and remain vital as the outcome of a decision and a responsibility on the part of the individual which is wholly personal in each case, and that the truly personal factor consists at basis in a loving orientation of oneself to others, i.e. to one's neighbour and to God. Admittedly the physical side of human nature is such that any community among men also implies those prior conditions and further effects which are entailed in the *social* forms of communal living, and these in turn can assume the most varied forms according to the particular human grouping of which they are the expression. Of course in a metaphysical and theological anthropology many difficult questions would have to be considered with regard to the attitudes involved in the personal and social factors in the individual, and the answers to these would have to be applied to the life of the religious orders. But all this will not be discussed in the present context. Here rather we shall be considering from the point of view of an older member who is individualistic precisely *why* it should be that today even in the orders a shift of emphasis from the personal to the communal is justified in terms of the particular epoch even when we older members feel it rather as fairly inappropriate to ourselves and as a threat to us; even when in the religious orders there is a further question which still remains to a large extent unsolved, that namely of the actual forms in the *concrete* which this communal factor is to assume, so necessary and pressing as it is today, and when this new mode of living, in itself justified, also carries with it a threat to that which properly speaking must constitute the life of an order and which implicitly contains its function in the Church for mankind.

An *initial* reason for a more intense and a new kind of communal living in the orders is to be found in the essentially more complex realities in which even the orders have to live and work nowadays. Formerly we had clear principles to guide us. The concrete conceptual models which we used in expressing these principles to ourselves, and which we made our own, were likewise stable even though in our particular case this society was merely that of the Catholicism of the nineteenth century, easily falling into a defensive ghetto-like attitude and being somewhat bourgeois. In that setting it was in fact possible to maintain a mentality of this kind more or less homogeneously because this kind of Catholicism was intellectually, socially and politically screened off from the rest of the world, and even as such could still command large numbers of adherents. In such a context life in the orders was relatively simple. We knew quite precisely what we should believe and think and the positions taken up by friend or foe. We had our principles and also very concrete patterns for putting them into practice. All that we had to do was already set forth clearly and beyond all question beforehand in the principles and the concrete conceptual models for applying them in practice. Today all this is different. Even for those who preserve an unconditional loyalty to the principles of the faith, and also to genuine Christian tradition, over and above that which is binding in a strictly dogmatic sense, it is often no longer so unequivocally clear what these principles imply and what under certain circumstances they do not imply. This is the outcome of the fact that the Church, if she is not to degenerate into a minor agglomeration without significance (something quite different from the 'little flock' that the Church should be, is, and will be), must apply herself in fresh and courageous ways to the social and intellectual situation as it actually confronts her today, and must not screen herself off in an artificial world which she has thought out as right for herself.[5] Christianity and the Church must not conform to 'the world'. Under certain circumstances they must take up a radically

[5] Here cf. the author's article, 'Konziliare Lehre der Kirche und künftige Wirklichkeit christlichen Lebens', *Schriften zur Theologie* VI (Einsiedeln, 2nd ed., 1968),

critical attitude towards the tendencies and fashions and factors which are presumed to be self-evident in the current age. But this is precisely something that is possible only if we really commit ourselves to the world. The prolongation of the ways of earlier times in the life and work of the Church, together with its assumed clarity, uniformity and sureness, is simply no longer possible nowadays. Even when and where the Church has to be the sign of contradiction towards a sinful and straying world, we must proclaim her contradiction in such a way that it is really hearkened to. She must adapt her message to the perspectives and outlooks of the world of today. This does not mean any strained, artificial or pedagogic transition from the world that is proper to her into that of the others, but, at least in principle, an unreserved acceptance of the world in which we Christians and members of orders inescapably have to live from the outset. On the basis of this situation it is not so clear and obvious what we mean by our *principles* of dogma and of Christian morality even though this is not to say that we can no longer have any global understanding of them or any ultimate loyalty in faith towards them.

The concrete *models* for applying these Christian principles in practice have become still more lacking in clarity. Questions must arise as to precisely *what* inescapable compulsion and the kind of freedom that there ought to be signify in their relationship to one another in life and in society; precisely *how* personal power freely to decide one's material values is related to social theories precisely of these values, or *how* we of today can communicate to an individual who has become secularized a pristine experience of God;[6] what in a true sense constitutes Christian education; how the sacraments should be conferred today in such a way as to avoid the impression that we are practising magic or empty ceremonies of an almost folklorist kind; how we can boldly accept the factor of sexuality without falling into a shallow libertinism. To these and a thousand other questions of human and Christian living we can, it is true, still to some extent readily formulate certain answers of principle as a normative framework. But precisely *how* we should answer these questions in the *concrete*, or what form the concrete models of application should assume today in which these principles are put into practice – in a world that has become interiorly and exteriorly dynamic – these are human questions which do not really have any one clear answer even though it is questions of fact and questions of morality both at once that

pp. 479–498; 'Christian Living Formerly and Today', *Theological Investigations* VII (London and New York, 1971), pp. 3–24.

[6] cf. the author's article, 'Theological Considerations on Secularization and

we are faced with. In such a world, in which that which is signified in the principles, and still more the concrete models for applying those principles in practice have become less clear, it is impossible for the life of the orders to proceed from the assumption that the norms governing *their* lives at any rate are clear and unequivocal, that they have already been tried and tested countless times in tradition, and that we should merely loyally continue to follow them. We members of religious orders too have to accept and endure the uncertainty and fluidity of our age as it progresses into a future that has still not clearly been recognized. That is the initial postulate if we are gradually to develop and to provide for other Christians a credible model of Christian living in the future. Precisely within the religious life, however, considered as a communal form of life, such a task calls for a far more intensive collaboration, and so too a dialogue among the members of the orders, than was formerly necessary. If the religious life is to remain intact experiments must be taken in it in common. If we are to undertake such experiments in common, i.e. if new concrete models are to be tested out as a matter of practical experience in the life and apostolic work of the orders, then we must first and foremost discuss with one another and so consciously reflect upon the possibilities for the future. Some may suppose that they can confine themselves to directives from above, albeit assuming a mature consideration on the part of superiors. They may regard such a procedure as still effective even for today. They may proceed on the basis that all principles and concrete models for applying them in practice are already clearly and unequivocally present, and so need only to be carried out by those who are specifically selected for the task precisely by the command of the superior. What is called for is the most active collaboration possible on the part of as many members of the order as possible in the decisions which are necessary for life and work. This is not in the first instance a postulate emanating from some romantically thought-out democratic ideal, but rather something demanded by the very nature of the case which can be discovered only if as many individuals as possible who are to bring it to reality collaborate in this process of new discovery. Orders too must avoid becoming a mere minor agglomeration *through their own fault*, becoming societies, that is to say, which still manage to sustain themselves at a cost of being reduced to a pitiful number of individuals deriving from a socially and intellectually backward milieu, and so still ready to appropriate these ideals in their outmoded form.

Atheism', *Theological Investigations* XI (London and New York, 1974), pp. 166–184.

We must guard against taking spirituality in too ideological a sense. Rather we must understand it as the Christian element and the ultimate depths of life as it exists quite normally and in the concrete. And if we do this then what has just been said will also be accounted as spirituality. Nowadays this too stands in need of experimentation, of discussion, of the community and its collaboration more than in former times. What we are seeking to express in all these rough indications is simply this: life in the religious orders of today and tomorrow is different from what it formerly was in that it calls for a greater sense of community. This can become a living force only in the personal responsibility and active commitment of every individual. And it cannot be brought about by force solely by institutions. But this deeper sense of community is necessary because it is called for by the special qualities of our own age. Obviously it is not prescribed by the contemporary situation as something which cannot fail. The situation which calls for this deeper sense of community on the part of the orders at the same time raises threats and obstacles to this sense of community. The reason is that today, by comparison with former times, there is a far greater number of different tendencies and possibilities, and in view of this this community sense is precisely not something already given that can be taken for granted, but something rather that has to be established by conscious effort with sacrifices and renunciations.

There is a quite different second aspect from which the sense of community in religious life appears more urgent nowadays than was formerly the case. The interior world of the individual is far wider, more complex and more subject to threat. Now this manifestly calls for a greater sense of community between members of religious orders as an aid for coping with this threatened interior world. We older men in the orders do in fact experience how the younger ones draw closer to one another, open their hearts to one another and, when taking the most intimate personal decisions, seek to arrive at them in community intercourse of this kind. Yet this phenomenon is manifestly not to be explained simply as sentimentality, helplessness or lack of self-sufficiency. In earlier times we had the impression (though naturally this is to put it in a somewhat simplified form) that the individual depended in his life on the force of reason and the principles embodied in this as propositionally formulated, as well as on a formal free will which either did or did not put these principles into practice. A very clear example of this approach is to be found in the unmistakable conviction of the usual moral theology that a man who is more or less normal can certainly fulfil a duty once he has undertaken it even throughout his whole life, provided only that he *wills* to do so, the more so since the grace for fulfilling such a duty can never be lacking to him (through the prayer necessary for this).[7]

Today, however, the individual, and even the member of a religious order, has a quite different experience. The powers of reason or of freedom seem to him to be only very incomplete elements in his life. He feels himself as one exposed to conditions and forces of which he can never be aware, or at any rate of which he can never have any adequate conscious knowledge. For him his personal history is something more than merely the history of his autonomous freedom. Even abstracting from the external circumstances which he cannot control, he feels his future not as something planned and realized merely by himself of his freedom, but at least equally as the fate which rises up from the unfathomable depths within his being, and which he has to endure. He has no impression that so long as normal conditions in civic life endure it is clear that the individual can always perform what is prescribed by a duty once undertaken or by a law imposed from without. The man of today feels himself as one who is threatened by himself, not as one who has sovereign control over himself. His own reality and life strike him not as a reality fully open to his understanding and possessed by him from the outset, but rather as that which gradually unveils itself to him only in the course of an unfolding development which he can never in any full sense whatever guide and direct. He feels that he can see through us older men. For him our loyalty to principles is not due to any moral excellence or real maturity on our part, but is to a large extent the outcome of the fact that we have matured and grown old in a milieu that is intellectually and socially homogeneous. And truly not everything in this evaluation is false. We older men are also the product of a milieu which the young neither have nor desire. It cannot be our task here to interpret this experience which man has of himself in its truth or in its limitations, or to assign it its rightful place within the total scope of human life. This experience will be taken as given. Our purpose is simply to explain from a new aspect why man embarks on a new and urgent quest for community life, for community discussion even to the point of psychotherapy. He flees from his inner state of threatenedness and obscurity to his fellow man. In the encounter with his fellow he

---

[7] On the duties of the members of orders cf. the ideas put forward by the author, 'On the Evangelical Counsels', *Theological Investigations* VIII (London and New York, 1971), pp. 133–167, and also the earlier remarks in 'Laie und Ordensleben. Überlegungen zur Theologie der Säkularinstitute', *Sendung und Gnade* (Innsbruck, 4th ed., 1966), pp. 359–391.

comes a stage nearer to achieving clarity about himself. The fact that the same thing happens to his fellow gives him the courage to accept the inscrutable factors in his own life. Prescriptions for life and work seem more effective as guards against the innermost uncertainty and obscurity with regard to the future even within man's own soul when they are arrived at and approved in common as the outcome of discussion with others. The fact that it happens to others as to himself gives him the courage to accept himself.

WHAT REMAINS AND WHAT FOLLOWS

We have been considering two of the reasons (certainly two among many others) for placing the chief emphasis on the communal rather the individual and personal at this particular epoch. Before proceeding to draw certain practical consequences from this it remains to be said that the member of a religious order must always – and so today and tomorrow too – be the man who is capable of living in personal responsibility as an individual and in solitude with God. Christianity is the religion of man's personal relationship with God, and it can never be reduced to merely human relationships. Christianity is the religion of dying in solitude with Jesus into one's own radical weakness and into the mystery of God as utterly outside our control. As a religion of this kind Christianity is not an ideological supplement to a life which in itself could certainly be rounded off even without this ideology. It is this rather because this solitariness and inalienable *uniqueness* in the life of man are factors which are inescapable. They may indeed be suppressed through faults or suffering, but they can never be eliminated even though there is a constant temptation and danger of excluding this solitariness and inalienable uniqueness from human life. If the life of the religious orders is intended to be a pattern of Christian living,[8] then it cannot be dispensed from the task of enduring the inalienable uniqueness of man and the solitariness of death which pervades life. Only so can it really come to know what is meant by 'God' and how we can have a personal relationship with him. Only where a Christian attitude of this kind succeeds will something more emerge from the communion between men than the putting into practice of a herd drive and the flight of man from himself into the anonymity of mankind in the mass. This is not to say that there cannot be a genuine sense of human community even without any explicit reference to God.

[8] On this cf. 'Theological Observations on the Concept of "Witness" ', *Theological Investigations* XIII.

But to present such a thing is certainly not the sole task of the sense of community of a religious order. Even a human fellowship which is at first 'this-worldly' and 'secular' — and it is to such a community that men seek to reduce Christianity in a process of 'horizontalism' — either penetrates to the ultimate depths of its own nature and so attains to God (although, it may be, only in a very unconscious sense), or alternatively it perishes in its own tragedy, the impossibility of all human love attaining its consummation. From this it follows that that which at first seems merely to be the transitory form of religious life in the nineteenth century is nevertheless something more. For all the natural and inevitable process of change in its concrete form, in its truest essence it is something which must be introduced as redemptive and salvific into that sense of human community which is to be the sign manual belonging to the particular epoch of the religious life of the future. Even in the life and work of the orders of today and tomorrow the mentality of the older members, who have hitherto been willing to live as institutionalized hermits, has an abiding function. If Christianity has to be something more than merely the due recognition of a specific mode of life belonging to a particular age, if it is also and always to provide a critique of this and to be its redemption, if it is always true that any genuine community can be truly itself only if those belonging to it can accept themselves and endure themselves in their solitariness (with God), without which all human community would become merely a sheepfold, or would necessarily imply excessive demands of a false and worldly kind, then it follows that the old ways of religious life too in terms of life and work have an abiding importance despite their conditional and transitory character in virtue of the essence that is brought to reality in this conditional state. This function of handing on an abidingly Christian element to the future would constitute an especially urgent task for the older men of the orders. Admittedly the only way in which it can be fulfilled by these older men is on condition that the personal solitariness of the individual as he finds his self-sufficiency in God alone is not misused so as to withdraw himself from an attitude of loving openness to community with his fellow. On the contrary this solitariness and self-sufficiency of his must serve as a prior condition enabling him really to give himself selflessly to his fellows. Only if the younger members notice that the heritage which we older men are seeking to hand on serves precisely to provide a basis for that genuine community which the younger members seek will we succeed in introducing into the future of the religious orders the ancient heritage in an altered form. Only so shall we be able to apply the name 'religious order' in any Christian sense at all to the future communities historically descended from the present-day orders.

Inevitably the foregoing observations have been at a very abstract level. In conclusion, therefore, certain further consequences following from what has been said must be put forward. While these cannot rid our earlier remarks of their abstract character, they should nevertheless do something to mitigate it.

In the religious life the way is undoubtedly being paved for a shift in the relationship between the individual and personal factor in its concrete form and the communal factor. This remains true even though, it may be, precisely in the orders of the future the personal factor, unique in each case, will be, in its character as inalienable and as isolated, that which is destined to become an ever-fresh task and in a sense a mark distinguishing these orders from other secular forms of society. It is in fact not the case that history must necessarily or always constitute a continuous ascending process to the higher good or the higher beauty. It could equally well be that over what might be a long period the socialistic factor might really come to predominate over all else in the form of a humanity that is manipulated in the mass, of the higher grade of domesticated animal, leading to a destruction of human freedom in the interests of a smoothly running system. It could be the case that the Christians must precisely be numbered among those who have remained pent up in the citadels of refuge of their own personal spirit of freedom and of inalienable responsibility, those who can still sustain their individuality as freedom and a state of being brought face to face with the mystery of God.[9] But even viewed in this light the communal factor in the orders of the future remains that which gives them their special quality as compared with the orders of the past. In saying this it must be admitted that our statement is to be understood in very divers ways according to whether in any given case the communal factor too in the various orders has hitherto already had a different degree of value ascribed to it. The result of this is that there are different degrees of clarity in the way in which the individual orders of the future will be distinguished from those of the past in respect of this communal factor which they will have.

The process of discovering the concrete forms which this communal factor will assume in the life and work of the orders will necessarily be gradual. Indeed it may be presumed that in a world that is dynamic and

---

[9] The ideas put forward by the author in the following article should also be understood in this sense: 'The Function of the Church as a Critic of Society', *Theological Investigations* XII (London and New York, 1974), pp. 229–249.

will continue to be so this process of discovery cannot be understood in any sense as the discovery of a fixed form of life and work for the orders, which will then in its turn remain fixed over a long period. On the contrary, since the situation will continue to remain changeable in the extreme, we may presume that there will be a continuous process of fresh improvisation in the life and work of the orders. Viewed from without, and in a spirit of unbelief, this process of improvisation which never wholly ceases will perhaps strike some as the mere prolongation of the vegetable life of an institution which was in the past so gloriously clear, unequivocal, powerful and aware of itself, but which now can neither live nor die. Nevertheless for him who believes and hopes, and does not regard himself as the lord of history, this process of improvisation making ever-fresh advances into a future that is unknown can perfectly well be accounted a mode of life which is specifically Christian in character.

Even though we constantly regard our way of life and our activities as that which is provisional and transitory, still this is not to say that the way of life which we are at present following does not, in many areas and many respects, lag behind the way of life and work prescribed for the orders of today. This is of course too generalized a conclusion, and great variations should be allowed for before we can apply it to the individual orders. The discovery of new ways for the orders in their life and work cannot be achieved without the courage to experiment. It is true of many human affairs that it is quite impossible to achieve a sufficiently clear knowledge of them merely by theoretical consideration. An indispensable factor is concrete experiment in life itself, and that too even at the risk of failure and of recognizing only too late that we have taken a wrong path. Superiors in the orders should have the courage, if not actually to inaugurate such experiments for themselves, still at least to allow them. Only so can fresh forms of communal living and communal work be discovered in an order. Initially such new forms will obviously be para-canonical, and will exist side by side with the traditional and officially institutionalized forms of life and work of the orders. This cannot be avoided. But we should also have the courage not to delay *too* long before officially sanctioning and institutionalizing such fresh forms of community life and work. We cannot at once be convinced of the value for human life of the juridical and institutional and yet at the same time hold out for a long time before allowing the new forms of religious life to be sanctioned and institutionalised. Otherwise we cannot with any justice be shocked to find that such new forms, which the younger members inaugurate and maintain, very quickly vanish once more as mere expressions of a passing fashion and so undergo a fate which they are far from having deserved and which might have been avoided for them if they had been responded to more helpfully by the official authorities in the orders. We cannot let a little plant wither by refusing to water and care for it and then sarcastically use the fact that it has so withered as an argument to show that this plant was never worth anything. This is not to dispute the fact that such processes of fresh institutionalization, which follow more swiftly than in former times upon life and its developments, are more improvised and more swift to pass away than was formerly entertained in our thinking or way of life. A further point is admittedly that a fresh attitude towards law and institution is also necessary, one which does not treat of the institutional factor as a mere trifle on the grounds that it is more improvised and more transitory than formerly, and *at the same time* does not erect it into a petrified idol either, as though it were absolutely final and definitive.[10]

However noteworthy the reforms of the liturgy up to the present may be, I do not believe that in them we have yet discovered that form of the liturgy, able to be brought to practical reality, which will bring the liturgy to its fulness as an activity of the community and at the same time as a radically personal event. Fresh forms of the liturgy as they have been and will be prescribed, however sublime and beautiful they may be, still do not remove the radical dilemma that as a matter of general principle forms which have become firmly fixed constitute a threat to the genuineness and spontaneity both of the communal and of the personal factors, if indeed they do not actually make these impossible. On the other hand forms which are absolutely free are in danger of giving free reign to arbitrariness, capriciousness and subjectivity on the part of the individual. Nevertheless if we cannot leave the concrete shaping of the liturgy (over and above its ultimate and essential structures) to chance, to the mood of the moment, to the crudity and one-sidedness of a liturgist devising free forms, still the only way out of this dilemma would surely be an intensive theological and spiritual formation of liturgists, to whom we could confidently leave the free shaping of the concrete forms of the liturgy within the framework of its essential structures. Whether such a thing is possible, whether and how religious communities might carry out creative experiments in this field – these are all questions which must remain open. But

[10] Attention should also be drawn to the considerations put forward by the author in the present volume, 'Basic Observations on the Subject of Changeable and Unchangeable Factors in the Church'.

we should at least recognize in the liturgy the need to bring the personal and the communal factors in it to their fulness, and despite all the changes in the liturgy since the Second Vatican Council these have lagged behind. Can we not discover fresh forms of religious life apart from the liturgy? I do in fact believe that meditation, as a private activity of the individual, must at all costs remain as a factor in the religious life even though such a postulate is still far from having determined the question of *how* such private meditation and solitary prayer to God is to be achieved in the concrete, and how it should be rooted in the totality of human activity on the part of the individual religious. But over and above this there are certainly new forms of religious activity as well, which are or would be in keeping with the times, and which have not yet been sufficiently developed in the average life of the orders. The older members adopt a sceptical attitude which is fully justified on rational grounds from the point of view of Christianity towards certain phenomena in contemporary religious communities especially in the USA. These appear sometimes after the fashion of New Testament glossolalia, sometimes in the form of group dynamics which are insufficiently guided by reason. But in adopting such an attitude we should still remind ourselves that we are not doing justice to the need expressed in such phenomena merely by a rigid and conservative adherence to what is old. The only right attitude towards them is to have the courage to accept new forms which measure up to the justified demands for a religious life sustained by the spirit of community. Have we already seen the after effects (in concrete and tested form) of group dynamic experience, or of those experiences which have been achieved through psychotherapeutic discussion? Would it not be possible to have a 'religious exercise' which consists neither in liturgy nor in private meditation but is sustained by a group as such? If there were such proved and to some extent institutionalized 'religious exercises' carried on by smaller groups it might be possible to avoid a misunderstanding which according to my observations often arises in the orders. Many wrong tendencies and mistaken developments occur among the members of orders which, because they do not occur in the canon of traditional moral theology, are not resisted in the orders either, and against these the religious community is powerless. It would be possible to resist such mistaken human tendencies and wrong developments without having forthwith to condemn them as sinful on moral grounds by the reaction of a group in a communal religious exercise of this kind. It might be possible to avoid much that is 'less than human' in the orders which is now present either simply because it has come to be accepted as inevitable, or which has forthwith to be resisted by means of a moral condemnation which for the most part remains ineffective.

New forms could certainly also be devised for an order to perform its apostolic work in the outside world on a new community basis. Obviously such communal work in the apostolic field has always been carried on in the orders. Conversely there will always be types of work and tasks in the orders which the individual can take upon himself without entering into any teamwork in the true sense with his own religious brethren. We may accept two points here. Religious communities in the sense of the orders properly so called, as distinct from the secular institutes, can probably not in the long run survive and cohere without *also* having a *common* task, a common work, even though not absolutely every individual member must take part in this. Second, for many reasons nowadays community must develop fresh forms for itself. And if these two points are true then what we have said also applies to the necessary community work of the individual orders. It cannot simply be carried on absolutely in the same style as is traditionally the rule. It is for instance conceivable that within a communal grouping of an order (not simply an individual abbey but one that embraces a broader region with several houses) the individual houses will each have its own distinctive character, different from the rest, and that these differences will in some sense be institutionalized. In practice something of this kind has in fact existed all along through force of circumstances. But it should be more consciously recognized, accepted and institutionalized. A house of the order lying in a poor quarter can and should have a different character, consciously institutionalized as such, from a house of the same grouping within the order which is for instance devoted to higher studies or is a house of typical intellectuals. As we have already pointed out, the concrete modes of discovering work and devising forms for it nowadays in the light of the contemporary situation requires an essentially more organized and more institutionalized form of collaboration on the part of all the members of the order concerned, and in this sense needs to acquire a more 'democratic' form.

PART THREE

The Church in the World

14

SOME PROBLEMS IN CONTEMPORARY ECUMENISM

THE subject of this chapter is headed 'Problems in Contemporary Ecumenism'. Many times in the past we have concerned ourselves with special questions in ecumenism,[1] and it would be possible here too to seize upon questions with a theological content from the range of connected subjects, and thereby to show by means of one or several concrete examples what current ideas are on the subject of the problems of ecumenism at the present day.

Yet nowadays it seems more important to concentrate upon the nature of ecumenical theology itself, albeit in an abstract and formal manner. By this method we may perhaps remain excessively pent-up at the level of generalizations and principles, and may expose ourselves to the objection that the real difficulties begin precisely at that point at which we come down to the concrete details. And yet the other and more general way of posing the question may perhaps be neither false nor inappropriate. What I mean by this is that particular questions in ecumenism often become difficult and even insoluble precisely because we have not achieved a sufficiently deep realization of what ecumenical theology really *is*, its starting-point and its aims. Thus we shall probably be in a better position

---

[1] cf. 'On Conversions in the Church', *Theological Investigations* III (London and Baltimore, 1967), pp. 373–384; 'Questions of Controversial Theology on Justification', *Theological Investigations* IV (London and Baltimore, 1966), pp. 189–218; 'The Presence of Christ in the Sacrament of the Lord's Supper', *Theological Investigations* IV (London and Baltimore, 1966), pp. 287–311; 'Some Remarks on the Question of Conversions', *Theological Investigations* V (London and Baltimore, 1966), pp. 315–335; 'What is Heresy?', *Theological Investigations* V (London and Baltimore, 1966), pp. 468–512; 'Justified and Sinner at the Same Time', *Theological Investigations* VI (London and Baltimore, 1969), pp. 218–230; 'On the Theology of the Ecumenical Discussion', *Theological Investigations* XI (London and New York, 1974), pp. 24–67.

to solve particular questions of this kind once we theologians have clarified our ideas as to what ecumenical dialogue is truly and ultimately concerned with. I will now attempt to give my answer to this question in the form of two theses. The first thesis will be concerned with the ultimate assumption on which ecumenical theology is based; the second, by contrast, will be concerned with its future form.[2] But let us begin with a few simple remarks on the problems of ecumenical theology today in general, and at the same time by attempting to strike a personal balance in judging of the possibly critical situation in which this dialogue stands.

THE CRISIS OF ECUMENICAL THEOLOGY

One who has taken part over many years in ecumenical discussion among the specialist theologians of the various separated Churches will find it somewhat difficult to take a hopeful view with regard to the outcome of such ecumenical theology. Whereas ecumenical discussions among everyday Christians all too easily fall into the error of confessional relativism, and tend over-hastily and over-facilely to bypass the doctrinal differences between the confessions, ecumenical discussion among specialist theologians, by contrast, generally relates to the classical differences of doctrine already established by tradition. Generally speaking such discussions do not achieve any advance on the problems involved, even though nowadays the theological assumptions presupposed in formulating these doctrinal differences are concerned with modern exegesis, the historical sciences, and the differences between philosophical modes of expression and ideas which have now become almost insuperable. Certainly in the last few decades we have spoken with one another more than formerly. The separated Churches have taken an interest in one another's theology. A greater exchange of subject-matter, viewpoints, methods etc. has been and is being achieved. But when we enquire as to the end-product of this ecumenical dialogue so far as the unification of the Churches is concerned we will after all be compelled in all realism to admit: this end-product is very slight. Certainly this is not merely due to the fact that we have not yet come much closer to agreement on the traditionally controversial doctrines. The main reason for the paucity of results may well lie in this: on the one hand the orthodox Roman theology is on the whole still a long

---

[2] The author has given a still fuller account of his position on the future form of ecumenical theology in the present volume in the article entitled 'Ecumenical Theology of the Future'. Here the basic theme of the present considerations is developed further and on somewhat different lines.

way from having made the dogmas of this Church really intelligible to the average Protestant Christian. On the other hand within the Protestant Churches differences are to be found as to the most basic interpretation of Christianity, and the leaders of these Churches cannot, or perhaps merely will not overcome this state of affairs (perhaps because they regard such a course as in itself contrary to the principles of Protestant freedom of belief). And these differences are so great that on these grounds alone any unification between these Churches collectively as they now stand and the Roman Church is impossible. For the latter is compelled to reject many interpretations of Christianity as heretical on the basis of her understanding of her own faith even though the same interpretations are tolerated in the Protestant Churches, and indeed to a certain extent recognized as legitimate.[3]

Obviously there are other and more general grounds for the current crisis in ecumenical theology. There are for instance those questions which now confront the whole of Christian theology and all Christian Churches, the questions of secularization, atheism, pluralism of ideas in Church and society, the osmosis between the Church and the world, the process by which to an increasing extent the national Church is being transformed into smaller communities of believers living in a diaspora situation on the basis of their own personal faith etc.[4] It is not our purpose here to treat of these questions. Rather we seek to draw attention to a certain immobility in the internal life of the Churches, a lack of movement which represents an obstacle to any ecumenical progress, and an impasse for ecumenical theology.

What we have said in abstract terms with regard to the limits of ecumenical theology is repeatedly confirmed by our experience of ecumenical work. Indeed it is a strange phenomenon. All speak of unity, declare their will to achieve unity between the Churches and their conviction

[3] On this, however, cf. also the author's remarks concerning the lack of certainty in the Catholic Church as to what heresy is. Cf. 'What is Heresy?', *Theological Investigations* V (London and Baltimore, 1966), pp. 468–512, and in the present volume, 'Does the Church Offer Any Ultimate Certainties?' Cf. also 'Schism in the Catholic Church' and 'Heresies in the Church Today?', *Theological Investigations* XII (London and New York, 1974), pp. 98–115, 116–141.

[4] In other passages the author has fully defined his position on such questions as the diaspora situation, secularization etc. Cf. 'Theological Considerations on Secularization and Atheism', *Theological Investigations* XI (London and New York, 1974), pp. 166–184; 'Church, Churches and Religions', *Theological Investigations* X (London, 1973), pp. 30–49; 'On the Presence of Christ in the Diaspora Community according to the Teaching of the Second Vatican Council', *Theological Investigations* X (London, 1973), pp. 84–102.

of the duty to work for this unity. Nor have we any right, at least in principle, to cast doubts upon the genuineness of this attitude and this resolve to work for unification. And yet as a matter of historical fact nothing or almost nothing ever happens. For the overall organization of the World Council of Churches neither is nor seeks to be a Church in its own right, and the situation is that for all the friendly contacts and discussions between the World Council of Churches and the Roman Catholic Church these have not only failed to produce any real unification – something which in fact we could still understand – but have not even brought them discernibly closer to one another. Despite all ecumenical resolves the real frontiers still remain stiff and immovable.[5]

The two theses put forward quite simply represent an attempt to discover a deeper starting-point for ecumenical theology today, and so a way of helping to escape from the impasse with which the dialogue is threatened.

THE ULTIMATE BASIS FOR ECUMENICAL THEOLOGY

I am enquiring into the ultimate basis for ecumenical theology. My initial answer to this question takes the form of a brief thesis which I will then try to explain in greater detail. The thesis runs as follows: the ultimate basis for ecumenical theology is the unity, apprehended in hope, of a belief in justifying grace which already exists and is identical on both sides, yet which, so far as theology is concerned together with the credal formula which gives it conceptual expression, is still in process of being achieved.

What is the force of this thesis in more precise detail? First it must unreservedly be conceded that for ecumenical dialogue and ecumenical theology in their contemporary form a liberal humanism, with its defence of freedom of opinion and freedom of belief within a pluralistic society has been and continues to be the only possible occasion and setting such that without it present-day ecumenical theology as it actually exists would be quite inconceivable. When we conduct an ecumenical dialogue or pursue ecumenical theology with one another despite the fact that we are divided among many Churches, then the ultimate basis for this is after all that we mutually recognize one another as Christians. But what precisely and in genuinely theological terms does this mean? Certainly it means not

[5] cf. also, however, the author's observations concerning the difference between the official representatives of the Churches and the simple believers in the article entitled 'Ecumenical Theology of the Future' in the present volume.

only that we take into account the fact that the other partner to the dialogue regards himself as a Christian. It does not only mean that we mutually credit one another with the fact that all have been validly baptized – supposing that in this we regard baptism first and foremost in its empirical reality as an external cultic act. Nor does it merely mean that despite all credal differences we empirically establish that we agree upon certain convictions more or less in the sense of the basic formula of the World Council of Churches. What it means rather is that in hope if not in an act of recognition which can be ultimately expressed in theoretical form we are convinced of the fact that the partners to the dialogue on both sides live in the grace of God, are truly justified by the Holy Pneuma of God, and are sharers in the divine nature.[6]

This conviction has not been self-evident for Christians of every age. It is only very gradually and with great toil that it has matured in the Church's understanding of her own faith to the point – so far as the Catholic Church is concerned – of achieving clear expression in the Second Vatican Council. But this conviction is now actually present on both sides.

We must now proceed straightway to discuss the question of how on a Catholic understanding of faith the significance of the Catholic creed as conducing to and necessary for salvation can be reconciled with the simultaneous conviction that some who do not share this faith nevertheless possess salvation. All that we are asking here is what this conviction means on both sides for the possibility of ecumenical dialogue and ecumenical theology. And this is something to which the thesis formulated above supplies an answer. This dialogue is possible because despite the difference in the creed as objectified and verbally formulated – in other words despite the differences of faith in this sense – we are not merely seeking for a unity of faith but are mutually crediting one another with already having it; for each of us is aware in faith, hope and love that the other is possessed by the Spirit of God, without whom there can be no belief and with whom there can be no unbelief. This statement obviously compels us to draw a distinction within that which faith signifies in the true sense. Yet while we seek neither to overlook nor to impugn the differences in the credal formulae of the faith, nevertheless each of us

[6] Some years ago the author attempted to work out the significance of hope for faith and theology. Cf. 'On the Theology of Hope', *Theological Investigations* X (London, 1973), pp. 260–272. See also his remarks on 'Salvation optimism' in the article 'Considerations on the Problem of the "Anonymous Christian" ' in the present volume.

recognizes the presence in the other of the divine Spirit of unity with the truth of God, of enlightenment and of faith. Each of us acknowledges in the other the interior witness of the Holy Spirit. And if all this is true then it becomes inescapable to draw a distinction of this kind if we are to avoid simply entertaining two contradictory positions side by side. All sorts of different interpretations may be placed upon the reality which we Catholics call sanctifying grace and which Protestant theology calls justification and salvation. It is in any case a deed of God upon us of his grace, which truly transforms us from sinners into justified men regardless of how in more precise detail we may interpret this saving event of justification, or what forms of expression of varying provenance we may use to express it.

The postulate thus arrived at of a true and common faith underlying the differences of faith between various groups of Christians as expressed verbally in their creeds is not a factor which cannot be used as a basis for any of their ideas merely on the grounds that it must manifestly lie under and beyond any process of formulating ideas in doctrinal statements. If we Christians are to overcome the confessional boundaries to the extent of mutually crediting one another with having the Holy Spirit of grace, then manifestly we must still say that the ultimate and innermost *testimonium spiritus* is present in all or must at least be presumed to be so, that the *illustratio et inspiratio* – concepts by means of which tradition seeks to clarify the movement of grace – that the wordless weeping and uttering of Abba by the Spirit in the depths of our hearts,[7] that the Johannine anointing which instructs us,[8] is present in us all even though this innermost reality of Spirit and faith is objectified and set forth verbally and conceptually in different forms in the individual confessions. We may then go on to add to this that for any anthropology of human thought or freedom which takes a somewhat deeper view, a difference always prevails (one which can never fully be overcome or eliminated) between an ultimate and basic state of mind, i.e. an unconscious self-possession on the part of the free subject, an understanding of himself on man's part which is never fully reflected upon on the one hand, and man's objectified awareness of himself, his subjectivity and his free decisions as an object on the other.[9] And if this is true, then we can see what the postulate we have formulated on theological grounds implies, the postulate namely of a general but true faith on the part of the separated Christians through and

[7] See Rom. 8:15.

[8] See 1 Jn. 2:20, 27.

[9] On this cf. the author's article, 'Thomas Aquinas on Truth', *Theological Investigations* XIII.

beyond that objectified faith which they formulate in concepts and words. It does not signify merely something which could not provide the basis for any explicit understanding. In the Spirit of God all of us 'know' something more simple, more true and more real than we can know or express at the level of our theological concepts. Here of course we must pass over the question of why even a true faith of this kind, pre-conceptual and present in the midst of our human lives in the power of the Spirit of God, does not render the faith that is objectified in concepts meaningless. This common faith at the heart and centre of human life through the power of God's grace, which is the same in all and true beyond all distortion, constitutes the true basis and the ultimate condition for ecumenical dialogue and an ecumenical theology. Given this basis the ecumenical dialogue is not a discussion in which one or other or both of the two parties involved seeks to communicate some point of doctrine to his partner for the time purely *ab externo*, such as that partner had formerly absolutely failed or refused to recognize and had rejected as an error of faith. It is not this even in those cases in which it is conducted on one or both sides with an absolute agreement of faith on the particular propositions of faith being upheld at the time. Rather it is the attempt to render comprehensible to one's partner in the dialogue that that which is put to him in terms of concepts is merely a more correct, a fuller, and a more precisely defined expression of something which that partner has already grasped as his own faith through the power of the Spirit at the ultimate depths of his own human existence as justified, and which he has laid hold of as his own truth. Thus our consideration of ecumenical theology returns to that answer to the question which constitutes its true and ultimate theological basis. This is that faith which is prior to any kind of theological reflection or theoretical and social objectification, being already present in all Christians of good will through justifying grace. On this basis ecumenical theology can and must say this: the reason that we must arrive at unity of faith at the level of conscious reflection and social living as well is that we already possess this unity at the level of God's justifying grace. The unity of faith which exists at this level implies both the possibility and the necessity of ecumenical theology. For of course we cannot say this: Because we already possess the unity of faith in the basic state in which Christians stand through grace, we no longer need the unity of faith at the level of theological objectification and social living. On the contrary we must say this: Because we possess the former kind of unity we must also strive for the latter kind, which constitutes the incarnatorial consummation of that former and more basic unity. On this basis the Catholic will understand the Lutheran at the heart and centre of his existence as one who is already an anonymous Catholic, while the Lutheran will regard the Catholic as an anonymous Lutheran at the centre of his existence. Which of the two of us is right is a point on which we are not at one, a point which ecumenical theology considers in a genuine dialogue between the Christians. But the fact that we can so understand ourselves, that we do not seek to pass from an absolute division to unity but rather that we can and must strive, from that unity already achieved in grace and that truth of God already posssesed, for the unity of the truth within the one Church – it is this that constitutes the value and the hope of ecumenical theology.

THE FUTURE OF ECUMENICAL THEOLOGY

This brings us back to the danger which threatens the ecumenical dialogue, and the need to reflect more deeply upon that which specifies ecumenical theology and its future task or tasks. In this connection we have a second thesis to propose: that which most of all constitutes ecumenical theology is the theology of the future, which has to be worked out by all the Churches each from its own point of departure as already laid down by its past history.

In the present context what I mean by my use of the term 'theology of the future' is not a theology of the futuricity of man, the hope and the making valid of the 'apocalyptic factor' in Christian faith, of political commitment etc. By theology of the future I mean far more simply that theology which is necessary as a prior condition for any preaching of the gospel in order that the gospel may appear credible in a future characterized by science, technology, cybernetics, social unity among men or on a global scale, a future which has already begun.[10]

In the ecumenical situation of today there is after all, over and above that hope against all hope which has been offered to the Christian, only *one* real chance. Only when the theologies of the separated Churches devote themselves intensively to the task of creating the theology of the future is there any hope or prospect that the theologies in the future will achieve an encounter at one and the same point. This is not to say that direct and face-to-face discussion of controversial theology should be broken off. This is necessary and does in fact yield certain partial results in the 'public opinion' of the theologians, even though it has produced

[10] Perspectives on and conclusions from this are developed in greater detail in the present volume in 'Ecumenical Theology of the Future'.

virtually no change at all in the immobility of the Church leaders over and above eirenic words and friendly gestures. But still it seems to me that a greater chance for ecumenical theology lies in working for the Christian theology of the future. All theologies and Churches must learn, each on its own account, to bear witness to the gospel of Jesus Christ in a way that is credible and intelligible to the man of the future which has already begun. If that man is to be a believer they must avoid imposing any further unnecessary difficulties upon him or demanding more of him than the necessary *metanoia* which involves the whole man. At the same time these theologies of the future must not betray the true gospel by any fashionable accommodations. And if they do all this then, so I hope, these theologies of the future as they exist in the separated Churches will become more assimilated to one another and draw closer to one another than the traditional theologies which are immediately and decisively shaped by the controversial questions of the past. I like to think, therefore, that the most important work of ecumenical theology, so far from consisting in a theology which is conducted in the form of an explicit dialogue side by side with the rest of theology in the separated Churches, will be developed within their theology as a whole and in all the disciplines belonging to it. For after all, ultimately speaking when viewed as a whole it has no other task than to investigate the question of how the gospel can be preached in a way that awakens, and claims the allegiance of faith, and that too not merely for a traditional remnant of individuals who still continue to survive for historical reasons, but for men who are to become Christians in the future from the basis of their own future situation. Viewed in this light ecumenical theology coincides with theology in general. Ecumenical theology, therefore, is to be taken as the theology of the future. This theology of the future must be pursued in the closest possible collaboration between the theologians of all confessions. If this is done, then this will of itself become ecumenical theology.

15

ECUMENICAL THEOLOGY IN THE FUTURE

THE question of an ecumenical theology of the future is focused upon *ecumenical theology*[1] as such, and so not upon that which constitutes first and last the basic task of all ecumenical concern, namely unity between the Churches. Thus it presupposes that there will be Churches that are separated from one another at least for the foreseeable future, and that in the immediate future there will still also be ecumenical theology, i.e. the discussion which the theologies of the separated Churches pursue with one another.

In setting myself to speak of the ecumenical theology of the *future* my underlying conviction is that this ecumenical theology does not simply remain the same as that which has been pursued in the past, for otherwise it would be possible to speak of an ecumenical theology of the present and one of the future simply in the same breath. On the other hand this theme cannot be taken in a sense which implies that the ecumenical theology of today and that of tomorrow no longer have very much in common. On the contrary that which they have in common is of the utmost importance. Hence it is manifest that my purpose in undertaking this task can only be as follows: I shall take as given those essential traits of any ecumenical theology of any period which always remain the same, and shall

[1] The author has long been treating of questions of ecumenical theology. Here only a few of the more significant articles may be mentioned by way of illustration. Cf. 'Membership of the Church According to the Teaching of Pius XII's Encyclical, "Mystici Corporis" ', *Theological Investigations* II (London and Baltimore, 1963), pp. 1–88; 'On Conversions in the Church', *Theological Investigations* III (London and Baltimore, 1967), pp. 373–384; 'Questions of Controversial Theology on Justification', *Theological Investigations* IV (London and Baltimore, 1966), pp. 189–218; 'What is Heresy?', *Theological Investigations* V (London and Baltimore, 1966), pp. 468–512; 'Zur "Situationsethik" aus ökumenischer Sicht', *Schriften zur Theologie* VI (Einsiedeln, 2nd ed., 1968), pp. 537–544; 'On the Theology of the Ecumenical Discussion', *Theological Investigations* XI (London and New York, 1974), pp. 24–67.

not treat of them explicitly here. Here rather I intend to set forth some of those special characteristics which distinguish the ecumenical theology of the future from that of the present day. In real human history the border-lines marking the transitions between present and future are of course fluid, and it follows that the same also applies to the ecumenical theology of today and tomorrow.

DIALOGUE WITH A SECULARIZED WORLD

An initial distinction between ecumenical theology up to the present and that of the future will consist in the fact that the ecumenical theology of the future will proceed not so much from those themes which, on the basis of the past and of the classical credal formulae of the individual Churches, have emerged from themes of controversial theology. Rather this new theology will proceed from the common task of the separated Churches and their theologies and will be concerned with the theological study of the common substance of the Christian faith and with preaching it in such a way that it can be assimilated afresh and in more effective ways by men in the so-called Christian countries even when either explicitly or tacitly they have become remote from the gospel message despite the fact of still outwardly and publicly retaining their membership of these Churches.

This first thesis calls for some clarification. I regard it as obvious that in his work an ecumenical theologian must always proceed from two starting-points: not only ecumenism but *also* the more or less official convictions of faith of his Church; that ecumenical theology as a whole will always also be thinking out afresh the classic questions of controversial theology; in other words that in addition to the fresh ecumenical ground it breaks it must also achieve progress along the same lines as formerly. The fact remains, however, that the situation for this ecumenical theology has changed precisely as the general situation of the Churches and their theologies has changed. Formerly the churches and their theologies had only each other other as partners and 'opponents' in the discussions at least so far as Europe was concerned. Today it is different. Although the majority of Europeans still adhere in a public and official sense to the Christian Churches, nevertheless all the Churches and their theologies today, individually and collectively, find themselves in a diaspora. Society at large is to a great extent secularized. The majority of the population of Europe has divested itself of any Church influence and, so far as its 'philosophy of life' is concerned, cannot be described as Christian in any real sense. Hence the first and decisive partner to the discussion for the

Churches of today must be the 'post-Christian' pagan. If Christianity and the Churches are not forever more to be reduced to a ghetto-like form which can be viewed as a historical relic from former ages continuing to live a sort of vegetable existence in the shadows of real history and ever waning in strength,[2] the Churches must take a fresh stand towards this present age as it really is. It is an age of culture of the masses, of increasing unification of spheres of human history in the world which were formerly separated, of rationalism and enlightenment, of the technology of the mass media, and whatever terms we may choose to characterize still further along these lines this age which is our own. Theology consists in conscious reflection upon the message of the gospel in a quite specific situation in terms of the history of the human spirit, in coming to terms with a quite specific *Zeitgeist*. It must view that message in the light of perspectives, and with a view to achieving perspectives, which are prescribed by a specific age. In terms of the *history of the human spirit*, therefore, and in terms of *social life* our age is a post-Christian one; one, that is, in which Christianity no longer constitutes a decisive force in society as a whole. It follows that any Christian theology must be post-Christian precisely in the sense described, i.e. it must make this secularized world which is already confronting it its partner in discussion.

The process of forming a theology which is post-Christian in this sense has of course been continuing ever since the Enlightenment – perhaps too slowly and too timidly, perhaps with too little success, perhaps with too little courage really to commit itself to the new situation of the secularized world. Perhaps too it has met with failures and not infrequently attempts to smear it on the part of Christianity itself, though true Christianity cannot endure such attempts and the contemporary world does not at basis expect them either on any true understanding of itself. This process of developing a Christian theology that is post-Christian has however been accelerated in a way that we can understand within the last few decades, and it must also be still further increased very notably. What we mean is this: the process of intelligent reflection called theology, in which Christianity attempts to understand its own nature in relation to a world that is secular, indeed post-Christian and anti-Christian, and to address itself to this world is undoubtedly nowadays the chief task and the crucial charac-

---

[2] The author has given his opinion on these problems – admittedly under different headings – in 'Theological Reflections on the Problem of Secularization', *Theological Investigations* X (London, 1973), pp. 318–348, and 'Theological Considerations on Secularization and Atheism', *Theological Investigations* XI (London and New York, 1974), pp. 166–184.

teristic of the theology of the Christian Churches. Their primary and crucial partner in discussion is no longer the particular theology of any other Church at any particular time. The theologies of the Christian Churches have now not so much to discuss with one another as to speak together with a partner common to them all who is different from them and the same for both Catholic and Protestant. This is the world that has become worldly, which is itself actively steering its own course towards its future, the world which is no longer primarily the subject of philosophical contemplation but of active forces of change, the world whose sciences are methodically atheistic.[3] In the selfsame moment in which the theologians of the individual Churches have discovered a quite new partner, one who at times is in conflict with them, the ecumenical theology of the past has perforce obtained another and lesser status within theology as a whole. The stagnation to be observed in ecumenical theology in very recent times finds at least a partial explanation in this fact and it makes this phenomenon less grievous and easier to understand than it may seem at first sight.[4] The theologies of the various Churches must simply speak to a greater extent than formerly with the world of today, and hence have inevitably less time to discuss directly with one another. We might perhaps be able to establish in detail that those theologians of all confessions who have pressed forward with the dialogue with the contemporary world (albeit when compared with one another in varying ways and with varying degrees of success) were not ecumenical theologians in any explicit sense. Again we may probably be able to establish the converse of this as well, that those theologians who are concerned with a direct ecumenical dialogue between the Christian theologies have *in general* achieved less for an interpretation of Christianity which is really capable of assimilation by the secular world of today. But – and this is now the crucial point – if the Christian theologies in general speak boldly and far more intensively than in former times with their new partner the secularized world so as to achieve a fresh formulation of Christianity within the perspectives and viewpoints belonging to that world, if in other words they pursue a theology which appears to be not an ecumenical theology at all, then such a discussion with the secular world is precisely *the* ecumenical theology of the future. For then the

[3] On this cf. 'Christianity and the "New Man" ', *Theological Investigations* V (London and Baltimore, 1966), pp. 135–153, and also 'Kirche und Welt', *Zehn Jahre Kath. Akademie in Bayern* (Würzburg, 1967), pp. 9–27.

[4] On this see also the author's ideas in the present volume, 'Some Problems of Ecumenism Today'.

various theologies of the individual Churches will discover that when they enter into discussion with this new partner of theirs concerning the basic substance of Christianity they will be speaking to him in the same way and with the same content, the more so since the themes under discussion which are necessary here have hardly any direct points of contact with the earlier themes of controversial theology. Among themselves these theologies will view the old disputed questions in quite new lights from new standpoints, and thereby, while never ceasing to uphold their standards on the question of truth, will learn a fresh reappraisal of these themes also, the importance of which has greatly diminished by comparison with former times. Thus new theologies may emerge within the various Churches which are identical with one another or at least converge in a far clearer manner than was formerly the case.

An additional point is that the common application of contemporary scientific methods, especially of the historical sciences in exegesis, and a common terminology which is achieved as a result of coming to terms with modern philosophy, will likewise contribute to such new points of convergence. Of course this is a development which has already long since begun. Thus it is already clear that on many theological questions the frontiers themselves are no longer in any sense identical with those 'official' boundary lines which separate the confessions, but rather cut across them.[5]

What has just been said should not be misunderstood in the sense of supposing that there is a unified theology to be found in every Church, or that these unified theologies will come to be more in harmony with one another. On the contrary, in every confession the pluralism among the theologies has become greater. This applies not only to the Protestant Churches but to the Catholic Church as well. But even so these manifold theologies as they exist in every Church have even now more or less clearly found their points of agreement in the other Churches. Even among us, for instance, there are theologies which are developed on the basis of exegesis or biblical theology to a greater extent than was formerly the case in scholastic theology. And this manifestation obviously finds a theology corresponding to it within the Protestant Church. Nowadays in Germany there exists in both Churches a 'political theology'. It would be possible to find in both Churches theologians in agreement with one

---

[5] On this cf. also the author's remarks in the present volume entitled 'The Church's Commission to Bring Salvation and the Humanization of the World', but also the article, 'Possible Courses for the Theology of the Future', *Theological Investigations* XIII. Here the author treats explicitly of the ecumenical aspect.

another who, more clearly than in earlier times, have commonly found a certain partnership in developing a philosophical reappraisal of the Christian message with the help of modern philosophies since Kant. Commentaries on biblical books written in collaboration already exist, and these do not have an ecumenical purpose in any direct sense but are simply written from the feeling that the exegetical methods and assumptions are the same from the outset, so that it is possible on these grounds alone to arrive at the same results, at least to a very notable extent. Similar tendencies are to be noticed in the field of Church history writing. In this connection too we can mention at least in summary form all those efforts which are conducive to a co-ordination or at least partial identification of theological work and theological instruction in the organizational and institutional areas, efforts which in America have already achieved more far-reaching progress than among us and have already found a certain acceptance in the decisions of Rome concerning theological studies and their organization. The point I am concerned with here is simply this: the new and urgent task for a theology directed towards the secular world and based on its requirements leads in all the Churches to what might be called an indirectly ecumenical theology, and it may be presumed that this can be more effective than the former ecumenical theology even though this, as has already been emphasized at the outset, must of course continue and progress as well.

'NON-THEOLOGICAL' ASPECTS OF AN ECUMENICAL THEOLOGY

Of its very nature what we have just said concerning this new indirect ecumenical theology of the future includes a second point which must now be developed and clarified in its own right. The former kind of ecumenical theology, working in terms of controversial theology, had in view at least by and large the doctrinal differences between the confessions in their theological content and the opposition between them, the only further point which it took into consideration being at most the origin and history of these doctrinal differences as developed within theology itself. This view of ecumenical theology is of course justified and must remain as long as it continues to be a mistaken view that theology has to resolve itself into other sciences.[6] Nevertheless it might be a

---

[6] On these ideas cf. the author's article in *Theological Investigations* XIII, 'Theology as Engaged in an Interdisciplinary Dialogue With the Sciences' and also 'On the Relationship Between Theology and the Contemporary Sciences'.

useful and valuable task to view the theses of controversial theology in their difference and opposition from new and non-theological standpoints, and to consider the non-theological origins, conditions and consequences of this kind which lie behind such theses. We might call these fresh aspects under which an ecumenical theology is to consider the controversial themes among the Churches 'non-theological' aspects. But in doing so I am very conscious of the problems entailed in the term 'non-theological', for it could very well precisely be the case that at an unconscious and hidden level such aspects are in fact far more 'theological', i.e. for instance conditioned by grace or as a matter of history of specifically Christian origin, though they are now present in a Christianity which has become anonymous so that we are simply failing to discern at first sight the Christian element which has become anonymous in such aspects. When therefore we say that a new ecumenical theology has to consider the theses belonging to controversial theology between the confessions from 'non-theological' aspects the term 'non-theological' as used here is intended in a very provisional and deliberately marginal sense, and signifies everything which is not explicitly affirmed to be Christian. Probably there are many such aspects and they could be more clearly apprehended if the interdisciplinary discussion of theology with the contemporary sciences, the arts, the natural sciences and the social sciences were more energetically pursued, and also more effectively planned from an organizational point of view than is commonly the case. Here, therefore, we shall be referring simply by way of example to this or that non-theological aspect which might be significant for ecumenical theology.

Thus for instance we might investigate the secular causes, in terms of the history of thought and the *development of society*,[7] leading to the divisions between the Churches of East and West, and subsequently within the Western Church itself. Obviously such causes, belonging as they do to the history of human thought and society, have already all along been taken into account as incidental factors, especially in secular history and the history of the Church. But by and large the only ways in which they have been taken into account have been such that the recognition of them has never been accorded any special importance in

[7] The author has explained his position still more fully on the importance of the interpretation of history for his own special field in three articles under the general heading 'History of Theology' in *Theological Investigations* V (London and Baltimore, 1966). Cf. 'History of the World and Salvation History', *ibid.*, pp. 97–114, 'Christianity and the Non-Christian Religions', *ibid.*, pp. 115–134, 'Christianity and the "New Man" ', *ibid.*, pp. 135–153. Here this aspect is still further entered into.

controversial theology or ecumenical theology. Obviously all such secular causal factors belonging to the history of human thought, politics or society, and so leading first to the divisions between the Churches, and as a result continuing to take further effect within the separated theologies, would be contributing factors, prior conditions etc. such that these opinions in controversial theology could not be resolved into them by bypassing the true and essential question of theological truth. Yet we may for instance take the case of the doctrine of the First Vatican Council. The fact that it did achieve its existing formulation and that it was *de facto* decided upon presupposes a quite specific situation in terms of the history of ideas, and without this it would in real terms be totally inconceivable even though this does not of itself imply any decision whatever with regard to its claim to truth. Now if we recognize this then a point for investigation in an ecumenical theology too (by means of individual examples or in more basic terms) would be whether, in what ways, and perhaps through what further historical developments this explicit doctrinal decision might affect and claim the allegiance of those Christians who have not yet, or perhaps never in any sense, experienced that particular situation in the history of human thought in the light of which alone this doctrinal decision is really conceivable as their own particular historical situation. When we take this into account it could in fact be the case that, for instance, a doctrinal decision of the kind promulgated at the First Vatican Council need not explicitly be denied by the Churches of the East. The reason is that by such a denial, just as much as by the contrary affirmation, the Churches of the East would be entering into a situation in terms of the development of ideas, whether really or in an unrealistic theorizing, which is in truth in no sense their own, while at the same time, so far as these Churches are concerned, this doctrine would not be presented in the concrete form in which it actually appears or with the practical consequences which it rightly has for Western Catholicism.[8] There is much affecting concrete life, laws and liturgy which the Roman Church, whether willingly or reluctantly, does in fact concede to the uniate Churches of the East, and which it is ready to concede also to the other Eastern Churches. Now in considerations of the kind we are speaking of, and within an ecumenical theology working with the methods indicated, such factors as these could be interpreted in a notably deeper

[8] On the subject of doctrinal differences cf. the author's articles in the present volume, 'On the Concept of Infallibility in Catholic Theology', 'The Faith of the Christian and the Doctrine of the Church', 'The Doctrinal Authority of the Church as a Subject of Dispute' etc.

manner and also with certain practical consequences. This is of course only a single small example, and only an indication of the task for an ecumenical theology in enquiring into the theses of controversial theology as to their origins and preconditioning factors in secular and social history.

Another aspect from which the theses of controversial theology might be presented in a new ecumenical theology would be their *social relevance*.[9] Ever since Max Weber attention has been drawn – whether rightly or wrongly, we do not need to investigate here – to connections between the spirit and social structure of capitalism and Calvinism. Whatever positions we may adopt with regard to this particular example, there is an interchange of influences, which pass to and fro between religious and social movements. Attitudes which are objectified in terms of theology have also a social relevance, and under certain circumstances may be clearer and more capable of critical appraisal from the point of view of this than if they are viewed solely at the level of theology. Now this can be important for an ecumenical theology. It can come to achieve a better recognition of its own subject-matter by considering the social relevance of this. In the majority of cases such an approach will presumably not be able to lead to any decision on the question of truth, but nevertheless under certain circumstances it can lead very clearly to a recognition of the deficiencies, omissions and obscurities in a particular theological statement put forward by a particular confession. Now when confessional theses of this kind are exposed in the manner suggested, and their one-sidedness, omissions etc. are recognized and then remedied, such an approach can also demand that the confessional theologies shall be drawn together. We may take, for instance, the example of the strange and still certainly problematical union of the Catholic Church with conservative and reactionary forces since the French Revolution at the end of the eighteenth century almost down to the present day (and, moreover with theological motivations as well). Could not an investigation of all this assist in discovering the biases, dangerous shifts of emphasis, and indeed errors even within the official doctrine of the Church? Could it not be the case that the changes thereby attainable within Catholic theology might make even *this* more comprehensible and more capable of assimilation for non-Catholic theologies? Could not something similar take place with regard to the Lutheran doctrine of the two kingdoms, with regard to their social and political relevance, or in the light of this rele-

[9] With reference to the sociological relevance cf. the author's article in *Theological Investigations* XIII, 'Institution and Freedom', and also *Freiheit und Manipulation in Gesellschaft und Kirche*, Münch. Akad. Schriften 53 (Munich, 2nd ed., 1971).

vance? Thus union might emerge from this, so I believe, for ecumenical theology itself as well once we enquire into the disputed theses of controversial theology from the point of view of their social relevance. A further point to be noticed is that this approach can probably also be applied to theses and disputed treatises in controversial theology of a kind to which it might not be supposed at first sight to apply because of their 'lack of worldly relevance'. This remains true even if we leave the question open of whether every theological doctrine should have a relevance of this kind or else not be regarded as theologically serious at all.

The third 'non-theological' aspect from which the doctrines which are controversial between the confessions might be viewed is perhaps the *aspect of the languages involved*,[10] in which these confessionally distinct doctrines were originally conceived, even if the first fathers of the oppositions which grew up in the Reformation in the sixteenth century in all the Churches formulated their ideas more or less in 'two languages'. Thus for instance as a theologian Luther wrote in German and Latin, Calvin in French and Latin, and their Catholic opponents of course did not confine themselves to Latin either in their writings. While recognizing this point we may perhaps recognize also that in many cases at least the whole distinctive genius of a particular language may have a special affinity with a particular confession. On this point, it is true, we shall have to exercise great caution. We shall not be able to decide the ultimate question of truth even by an approach such as this, nor may we reduce it to a relative status any more than we can invoke the evidence of history to prove that the religion of one of the higher cultures can be the most appropriate one for a particular ethnic group. Nevertheless if for instance we say that

[10] The author has frequently treated of the importance of linguistic forms for theological and religious statements from various aspects. We may recall the articles on the development of doctrine as for instance 'The Development of Dogma', *Theological Investigations* I (London, 1961), pp. 39–76; 'Considerations on the Development of Dogma', *Theological Investigations* IV (London and Baltimore, 1966), pp. 3–35, or works such as 'The Word and the Eucharist', *Theological Investigations* IV (London and Baltimore, 1966), pp. 253–286; 'Priest and Poet', *Theological Investigations* III (London and Baltimore, 1967), pp. 294–317; also 'Poetry and the Christian', *Theological Investigations* IV (London and Baltimore, 1966), pp. 253–286. Here it is a direct theology of the word that is in question; or more technical studies may be mentioned such as 'The Hermeneutics of Eschatological Assertions', *Theological Investigations* IV (London and Baltimore, 1966), pp. 323–346. Reference may also not least be made to the manifold expositions on prayer and forms of expression of devotion. The reader will readily find further expositions for all these areas of enquiry among the articles of the present volume.

Catholic Church life in its concrete historical form has a special affinity with Latin, with the objectivity and juridical qualities inherent in that language, if the German of a Luther and his theology may perhaps have, at least in part, a mutually conditioning relationship one to the other, if a similar point can be made about the theology and the French tongue of Calvin, then the study of the theological languages with their special characteristics in the original formulations of the individual confessions could be very fruitful, at least so far as the special character of the thought is concerned, in establishing the limits and the deficiencies of the theology of any given period, and it could be helpful to each particular confession in arriving at an attitude of self-criticism towards its own historical form. This in turn could have the effect of promoting the convergence between the confessional theologies which we are striving for in ecumenical theology. Again this is merely an indication, which once more implicitly demands an interdisciplinary discussion between theology and the science of linguistics, a discussion which presumably already exists in its incipient stages, although I have no information to impart on this from my own knowledge. We are pointing, then, to a 'non-theological' aspect from which ecumenical theology might be approached. We are not concerned, therefore, with asserting that no such thing exists at all in ecumenical theology in the history of the Churches or the public utterances of the confessions. What we are concerned with, rather, here is the opinion that such a method might be developed in fuller detail in ecumenical theology and applied in greater measure than in fact is the case.

CHURCH CHRISTIANS WITHOUT ANY CONFESSIONAL AWARENESS

Yet a third question might in my opinion produce notable changes in the ecumenical theology of the future. I refer to the question of the *theological relevance* of the fact, surely indisputable, that far the greatest part of the Christians who have grown up in the various ecclesiastical groupings do not have any real knowledge of the differences constituting the confessions,[11] or if they do have such knowledge do not attach any very great importance to those differences, and furthermore that where such Christians outside the circle of ecclesiastical officials and theologians do know of the differences between the confessions and regard them as important to themselves what is in question is often those differences to which the

[11] cf. the author's study, 'On the Structure of the People of the Church Today', *Theological Investigations* XII (London and New York, 1974), pp. 218–228.

official theologies of the Churches do not ascribe any crucial importance for justifying the divisions between the Churches. I cannot enter into any greater detail in establishing a fact which is here formulated only in very abstract terms. From my own experience it seems to me that it is a fact recognized by all and would probably be easy to establish demographically. In any case in my view if, as we have said, we abstract from the ecclesiastical officials and the theologians, it does seem to apply to the vast majority of Christians belonging to different confessions. It also seems to me that the situation is not that there are Christians who, as a matter of personal decision profess themselves adherents of different confessionally formulated creeds as expressing their own personal convictions (as properly speaking might after all be expected in view of the relationship between faith and Church), but rather that there are Christians differing from one another confessionally because there are confessionally different Churches.

This fact, in itself very noteworthy and far from being self-evident, manifests itself in historical and social terms and (if we like to put it so) in terms of secular psychology in the fact that these different ecclesiastical groupings in earlier history came into being through the decisions of a few individuals, the territorial overlords, small leading groups and classes, without which at that time it would of course have been to a large extent quite impossible for the members of a given Church in their broad masses to arrive at any personal decision of their own. It is also to be explained by the fact that such decisions have had a diminishing effect right down to the present day. Even today the great mass of the members of the Churches have still been born into these Churches and do not give their adherence to any particular Church as the outcome of a specifically confessional decision of faith. Historically speaking this fact that the members of a Church are constituted as such in the sense indicated in all the Churches is intelligible in view of the force of social tradition and the fact that to a large extent it would inevitably be to demand too much of the average individual to enter into controversial theological doctrines. It is psychologically speaking not very surprising either. On no account should it be maintained that there is anything new or surprising in this fact as it has been established, but I do believe that ecumenical theology has not really concerned itself theologically with this fact, or at any rate not in sufficient measure, perhaps precisely because it is historically, socially and psychologically obvious.

Yet it is a theological question too: what are the implications for a theological, as distinct from a psychological and social-empirical, sense of creed[12] and Church with regard to their differences, if it is quite impossible to say that the majority of Christians formed in a particular Church tradition know of the doctrinal differences dividing the Churches or have made them their own? What does it mean once we recognize with regard to the different Churches to the extent that they signify not institutions but men that they are constituted by men and Christians of this kind who in a *theological* sense are in no possible sense confessionally divided from one another? Obviously I do not deny that in every confessionally divided Church there are individuals who have in fact grasped the distinctive doctrines of their own particular Church and made them their own. In fact I presume that I myself am to be numbered among them, and so that I am in a sense that is theological and not merely pertaining to the sociology of religion a Catholic. But this does not dispose of the question of what the significance of this fact is: that the vast majority of the members of all Christian Churches are, from the point of view of the sociology of religion, members each of one such Church on specifically historical and psychological grounds, but not properly on theological grounds, even though despite this fact, recognized by everyone, ecumenical theology as practised on all sides properly speaking proceeds from the opposite position, i.e. acts as though within the individual Churches it were imparting its message to a great number of men who were confessional Christians in a specifically theological sense. I believe that any ecumenical theology in any Church must take a far deeper and fuller cognizance of the simple fact we have mentioned as a subject of extremely disturbing, and properly theological, enquiry.[13]

[12] On the question of the creed or the confession of faith cf. chiefly the author's studies on a basic formula of the faith. In the nature of things the problem of confessional formulae too is touched upon in this context. Cf. 'The Need for a "Short Formula" of Christian Faith', *Theological Investigations* IX (London and New York, 1972), pp. 117–126, and also 'Reflections on the Problems Involved in Devising a Short Formula of the Faith', *Theological Investigations* XI (London and New York, 1974), pp. 230–244 (together with the further literature there adduced). But the following should also be noticed: 'Pluralism in Theology and the Unity of the Creed in the Church', *Theological Investigations* XI (London and New York, 1974), pp. 3–23. Here the problems are approached from a different standpoint. For an overall survey cf. a study by one of the author's collaborators, R. Bleistein, *Kurzformel des Glaubens, Prinzip einer modernen Religionspädagogik* (Würzburg, 2nd ed., 1972).

[13] Among the disquieting aspects we should also include a question which, though much discussed, has surely not yet been thought out aright, that namely of intercommunion with all the difficult problems it entails. A few brief remarks on this are to be found in what follows. For the present we may confine ourselves to noticing two studies together with a relevant bibliography: H. Bacht, 'Zum Problem der

How this question is to be answered, what conclusions will emerge from a theologically bold and exact attempt at answering this question, it is difficult to say. And obviously it is not possible within so brief a compass as is available to us here even to sketch out an answer to such a question. Thus for instance the question would have to be posed of what status within the faith of a given Church and for the justification of a Church a doctrine could have which on the one hand is declared to be constitutive of that particular confession, while on the other it never so much as comes to the fore in the conscious faith of the vast majority of the members of such a Church on any realistic view of the matter from the aspect of the theology of faith. In this connection these individuals as they exist in the concrete circumstances of their lives and in history can no longer be regarded as represented by a territorial overlord or a small leading group, a sociological élite as may perhaps have been possible in earlier centuries not merely at the sociological level but at the theological one as well. Theological considerations of this state of affairs which belongs primarily to the sociology and psychology of religion could lead to consequences which might contribute to finding the answer to different and more practical ecumenical questions. We might think, for instance, of the question of religious instruction in common for children of different confessions, of the question of an ecumenical form of marriage, of the question of so-called intercommunion, i.e. a fellowship at the altar going beyond that which is even now already admitted, or beginning to be admitted, in this respect in the separated Churches. Such questions will certainly not be able to be answered solely on the basis of the initiative here indicated. But abstracting from minor and marginal considerations with regard to a common viewpoint as to the nature of the Eucharist, we are in my opinion far from having devoted sufficient thought to what is implied for the questions we have mentioned by the fact that the majority of Christians in the separated Churches, while they are indeed separated from one another institutionally and at the level of religious sociology, are not so in a properly theological sense, i.e. in relation to the faith which they have *de facto* made real to themselves in their heads and hearts. This is a faith which in practice does not include confessional differences, at least in those areas in which, according to the theologies of these Churches themselves, it could justify any separation between the Churches. Yet it is clear that these questions, together with their possible implications,

Interkommunion', *Catholica* 24 (1970), pp. 270–291, and also, amongst other works, K. H. Neufeld, 'Abendmahlsgemeinschaft – für und wider', *Der grosse Entschluss* 24 (1969), pp. 421–424.

cannot be thought out any further in the present context, the questions namely touching upon the difference between the kind of separation that is the outcome of religious sociology on the one hand, and the unity at the level of faith and theology of the majority of Christians within the different Churches on the other.

IS IT POSSIBLE TO ACHIEVE A CHURCH THAT IS INSTITUTIONALLY ONE?

Only one last question must be appended to what we have said in pointing out this noteworthy difference. To put it in a somewhat simplified and over-generalized form: we have Churches which are separated from one another institutionally and in terms of religious sociology. In this respect they are wholly separated from one another, whereas in terms of faith the same Churches are at one so far as the majority of their members are concerned, and in this connection are separated only so far as minor groups within them are concerned, groups with a higher degree of theological awareness, and so constituted particularly by officials and theologians.[14] Could we not make the converse true without thereby harming the conscious faith either of the majority of Christians or of those Christians who are aware of the theological differences involved? In other words could we not form a Church which was *single* in institutional terms and in terms of religious sociology in which of course the plurality of creeds upheld by those maintaining theologically distinct doctrines would be recognized as legitimate within this institutional unity? Against this it might be objected that the conscious faith of those Christians divided on theological grounds does in fact demand precisely specific institutions within their Church or alternatively excludes such institutions on grounds of faith. This would mean that a Church that was institutionally *one* in this sense would perforce run counter to the conscious faith of such individuals divided on theological grounds. For instance some would feel obliged to demand a pope while others would reject any such authority.

[14] Even in the case of the structures of institutional leadership there is surely still a wider scope available for new forms and conceptions than we are accustomed to suppose. Consequently not every possibility is yet cut off from this aspect either. This is a point which arises from the author's article in the present volume, 'Aspects of the Episcopal Office'. The proposal put forward here, therefore, is to be taken as a conceptual model. No definitive value judgement is necessarily intended either in a positive or in a negative sense. What the author was primarily concerned with was to point out lines of development and possibilities which should not simply be overlooked or forgotten.

But in response to this a counter-question might be put: would it not be possible, while according a place to such Church institutions (e.g. pope and bishops, a multiplicity of sacramental rites etc.) within the unity of this Church at the level of religious sociology still so to apply them in concrete practice that they would not do violence to the conscious faith of those who formally rejected such institutions while for the rest who formally demanded them they could be provided and so be interpreted by these according to their conscious faith with regard to the concrete application of such institutions that they were also in accordance with their tenets.

All this is intended merely as a *question* which we might go on precisely to point to in fuller detail. Yet a question still remains which has not been sufficiently clearly raised so far in ecumenical theology: the question of what conclusions arise from the fact that all Christian Churches must ascribe the fact of being separated, as distinct from any conscious faith at the theoretical level, to circumstances in the past, circumstances to which, according to their own doctrines, they should not accord any influence bearing upon the question of unity or separation, and that the separation that is truly based on faith, which should correspond to the institutional separation, is in no sense present in the great majority of the members of all these Churches. The reasons for these members still belonging to *either* this *or* that Church even today are, it is true, the outcome of a long historical line of succession. But properly speaking these reasons are not covered by those decisions of faith which could justify a separation between the Churches. Clearly this third path of renewal in ecumenical theology has been indicated in a very over-simplified and unguarded form.

The ecumenical theology of the future will be different and more comprehensive if it consists not merely in discussion between the two theologies, but actually draws new partners into the discussion: the world of today, the secular sciences, the fact that the ecumenical dialogue, from a theological point of view, is far from being such that it can *ipso facto* be conducted by the theologians in the name of the rest of Christians.

16

THE UNREADINESS OF THE CHURCH'S MEMBERS TO ACCEPT POVERTY

EVER since the Second Vatican Council we have been talking freely and at length about the 'poor Church' or the 'Church of the poor', a Church, that is, which by its poverty must show the world that its message is worthy of belief.[1] It has a duty to range itself on the side of the poor, the oppressed, the under-developed peoples. It must bring the rich face to face with the sorrows of Jesus and so fight against the contemporary structures and the dominance of capitalism and imperialism, and in so fighting against these structures with their unjust dominance it must of course begin with itself. The religious communities in the Church, the orders, are exhorted to give a new and modern sense, and a new importance to that poverty which in fact they have vowed themselves to all along.

Obviously only very little can be said here, within the compass of a brief article, on all these questions of poverty[2] as a problem for the *Church*. Anyone who fails to discover here what he believes that he is justified in seeking should bear in mind the difficulties entailed in this question. Precisely on this account too we have no intention of developing the question 'systematically'. Only a few observations are possible. Perhaps in spite of that we shall be able to make a contribution to the evaluation which the most recent Synod of Bishops (Autumn 1971) has

[1] On this cf. Y. Congar, 'The Place of Poverty in Christian Life in an Affluent Society', *Concilium* 5/2 (1966), pp. 28–39, with extensive bibliography for the French-speaking sphere, for which this subject has a special prominence. A series of significant passages in this discussion is to be found in P. Henrici ed., *Die christliche Armut* (Frankfurt, 1966).

[2] On the theme of poverty cf. the following articles by the author: 'Reflections on the Theology of Renunciation', *Theological Investigations* III (London and Baltimore, 1967), pp. 47–57, and also 'On the Theology of Poverty', *Theological Investigations* VIII (London and New York, 1971), pp. 168–124. A further work which should be mentioned here is J. B. Metz, *Armut im Geiste* (Munich, 1962).

undertaken, or at any rate has sought to undertake.[3] For the general theme of how the Church can contribute to bringing justice in the world to reality must surely include a consideration of what chances there are for actually carrying out this task of the Church.

Even in the New Testament itself we can discover a strange dualism: poverty is that which men seek to strive against in their fellows with the help of love of neighbour, a love which must not be taken as confined to one's private circle. At the same time it is that living context, voluntarily created, which is intended to make it possible for one's own life to be truly Christian. Of course it may be said that the two senses of 'poverty' are far from having the same meaning. But is that altogether true? And are the social conditions presupposed in this biblical message concerning poverty still present today as well? Whatever answers we feel we must give to these difficult questions, the situation today is at least such that a connection does exist between these two kinds of 'poverty', the 'voluntary' poverty regarded as a moral or ascetic ideal for Christians is intended to contribute to helping our fellows in their poverty. The 'coat' which one man forgoes is intended to warm his fellow.

There are poor even today who should not be such. There are under-developed peoples among whom poor of this kind are to be counted in millions, and because – at least first and foremost in principle – something *can* be altered in this, it follows that something *must* be altered in it. The Lazarus before the gates of the rich reveller is nowadays represented first and foremost by the under-developed peoples. The boundary line between Lazarus and the reveller is the north–south line encircling the entire world. In addition there are of course poor people enough even in the highly industrialized and privileged nations, people who sheerly and simply have not enough to eat, people who have been squeezed out of the work force against their will after forty years, victims of racial discrimination or unjust political persecution, people prevented from achieving a reasonable and possible rise in living standards, people living on small fixed incomes and scraping a wretched living throughout their lives, sick people who might be helped if the will to help them was there, people who cannot help themselves in life because right from the outset they have never been given the possibility of a start in human or economic terms, and so on – people who are genuinely poor. And even if we dislike criticisms of society in the form of lyrical laments, still we, who cannot

[3] On the problems involved in the theme of 'social justice' as treated of at the Synod of Bishops at Rome see the reports in *Herder Korrespondenz* 25 (1971), pp. 457–460; 472–478.

number ourselves among these poor, are rich (by some standards, however varied these may be), and rich, *moreover because* (notice the 'moreover' and the 'because' here!) those poor people are poor. As for 'alms' in the biblical sense, which should still be being given today and should conduce to greater justice as producing changes either of an evolutionary or revolutionary kind in the social structures, we either fail to give them or do not give them in sufficient measure. And here the Church quite certainly should have – indeed has – the task of preaching justice for the poor to herself, her members and the world, of recognizing and searching out these contemporary poor everywhere where the conditions and structures of wealth and power make some wretched and pitiful while according unjust privileges to others, regardless of whether this wretchedness is the direct outcome of withdrawing economic benefits or consists in other injuries. What is primarily in question nowadays, therefore, is the will to *eliminate* this poverty as rightly understood, and not directly the will to be poor. This latter kind of will is relevant – at least primarily and under existing conditions – only to the extent that the will to eliminate the poverty of *others* implies the renunciation of goods for oneself, and to that extent one's own 'poverty'. (It might be asked whether if there were no poor in any true sense the will to accept personal poverty, consumer ascesis, voluntary restraint in the fact of an uncontrolled emphasis on the enjoyment of goods, would not still always be reasonable and necessary for men and Christians. But this is a question which does not need to be raised for our present purposes.)

It is here that we begin to encounter the problem which in the following study will be restricted to the conflict between north and south. In our treatment of it we shall be assuming, without actually producing an array of statistics, that the 'world' is *de facto* failing to do what should be done to overcome this conflict; that the 'aids to development' (whatever the form they should take or whatever name should be given them) are totally inadequate. Now precisely *how* should the *Church* be a credible witness to this message that is necessary to will the struggle against poverty as understood here? The actual situation is this: a form of preaching which remains more or less socially ineffectual over a long period loses its credibility. For when the demand that something should be believed in remains on the whole ineffectual, men refuse to believe in its credibility. This may or may not be justified, but in any case we do not need here to investigate when it is right to adopt such an attitude and when not. In any case it *actually is so*. And this leads to a vicious circle. The Church preaches that it is necessary actively to will the elimination of poverty in the world, but its message is more or less ineffectual for reasons which we are just about to consider. And the ineffectualness of the Church's preaching renders her message unworthy of belief and so in its turn still more ineffectual.

Why is the exhortation to this resolve by and large ineffectual? The reasons most often adduced for this are generally speaking very superficial and emotional ones. The Church, it is alleged, does not herself practise what she preaches. She is rich. Those within her who set the standards, the pope, bishops and priests, themselves have standards of living which are too high in the advanced countries. They fail to achieve any really firm social awareness. They prefer to adhere to the rich, to the establishment in the capitalist and imperialist countries, and so on. And, so the accusation continues, even if much that we might demand or expect of these people would not make any very great difference so far as real poverty is concerned throughout the whole world, still it should be demanded as a sign and protest, as a manifestation of good will. It should not be dismissed as trivial on the grounds that after all it would not be of any use. Abstracting from *those particular* grounds which we shall straightway be showing to be valid in relation to the members of the Church in general, and which to that extent obviously also apply to the clergy of the Church, the arguments customarily adduced for the ineffectualness of the Church's preaching of poverty do not seem to be very convincing. Despite all the outcry against them the riches of the Vatican are not very great, granted the legitimate aims which it has to strive to achieve. If the pope were to sell his art treasures a fresh outcry would be raised against papal philistinism, just as it is now raised against papal riches. The clergy in our countries, priests and bishops alike (at least among us Germans, though in other countries, France for instance, it straightway becomes a different matter), certainly share far too much in the standards of the modern consumer society. They live too expensively. The story of the German bishop who either used to drive or still drives a large car, yet sought to have his episcopal standard mounted on a more modest one is perhaps after all not wholly untypical. But in all this the clergy are, after all, merely sharing in *that* deafness to the preaching of poverty which is universal. It might of course be said that the clergy should precisely take the lead in setting a good example. They may perhaps be exercising consumer restraint but they should be somewhat readier to let their light shine before men in this respect as a sign of what our attitude in the Church really ought to be. The situation is, however, that nowadays it is taken as a sign of the maturity of the laity that they are constantly seeking to enlarge upon the unimportance of the example set them by the clergy. And finally in the present context what is in question is precisely not a sign, but the far more real question of how we can bring effective help to the 'poor'. And on this showing it must after all be said that if anyone is to help it is not the Church as represented by the clergy, but the Church of all Christians, the Church of the laity that should provide this help. This brings us to a simple question: will it be possible for the Church (in the sense of the clergy) really to mobilize the Church of the laity in this resolve and this struggle against the poverty of the world?

If we are to find an answer to this true and practical question one point must be made from the outset. The actual *attempt* to achieve this mobilization, this change of awareness and attitude in the Church, must be made by individuals in the Church (clergy and laymen alike) who are aware of the situation and of this objective duty on the Church's part. This remains true even if it has to be said that the question as posed will have to be answered (by and large) in the negative. There are precisely human and Christian situations in which a course of action is demanded of one even though, on any realistic view, it is condemned to failure. (Otherwise Jesus too would not have died on the Cross.)

This is a point to which we shall be returning at a later stage. But assuming it as correct for the present, we must say this: the prospects are that the Church will not succeed in leading the struggle against poverty by means of her own 'poverty', even though in itself she has a duty to do this. The Church will not, in any adequate sense, succeed in mobilizing the Church. There is an unreadiness to accept poverty.

The first point to be made on this thesis is one that is intended to explain how in general terms it is possible to arrive at such a judgement. If we take Church history into consideration, and take serious cognizance of the teaching that the Church is a Church of *sinners*, then we cannot say that it is impossible from the outset for the Church to be capable of failing in major historical situations, or *alternatively* that such a thing is unforeseeable under certain circumstances.[4] A failure of this kind is not im-

---

[4] It may seem that some will seek to use this as ammunition against the Church in an anti-apologetic sense. To these it may simply be pointed out that according to this thesis of a possibility in principle the Church is merely sharing in the common lot of mankind and of the rest of society. In any case she is no worse in this respect than the rest of individuals or societies. Thus from a theological standpoint the question can be at most whether we can establish how far the Church should be better than the 'rest'. When we speak of failure and the possibility of this two questions still remain quite open: the question of how it is judged in God's sight and

possible because on any human estimation it has *de facto* taken place often enough in the past. Or are we to say that, for instance in the case of her confrontation with the cultures of Eastern Asia, in the dispute on rites, the Church really emerged successfully (to consider merely the more recent history of the Church)? Has she really 'coped' adequately in any positive sense with the Enlightenment? Has she reacted against modern nationalistic movements in the manner really demanded of her? Has she managed to reject the movement towards the Church state *at the right time*? Is it not through her own fault (her historical fault!) that she has in large measure lost the 'proletariat' in many countries? And so on. The case with the Church as with other societies is *mutatis mutandis* the same as with the individual man. He fails to meet the demands of a particular situation, even though it cannot and should not be said (in order to create an alibi from the outset for this failure) that he did not already have 'within himself' and from the outset the possibility of meeting this demand which his situation made upon him. Thus the Church too, as a great mass of average individuals, finds herself again and again in situations in which the requirements of the gospel, in their concrete application as determined by the particular situation, simply 'can' not be recognized with sufficient clarity and force. (The theologians would perhaps have to use the term *necessitas consequens* at this point, but it remains a 'must' pertaining to the opposite of saving history really to take that course of action which properly speaking should be taken.) We recognize an obligation and at the same time fail to recognize it. We respond to a demand, but in such a way that our response is so weak as to have no result at all, or at any rate very little. The borderline between the duty which in itself does exist and its opposite are so fluid and obscure that we can hardly ever see the situation in which the individual stands so clearly that we can say to him, 'For a Christian that is absolutely ruled out.' Again and again we find ideological justifications to give the Christian a good conscience for doing the opposite of his duty (in a given situation). (We may recall the theological justifications adduced for the apartheid policy.) The obligation is divided up among everyone in such a way that no one can be held responsible for discharging it. The preaching of high ideals is made an alibi for real deeds. Those individuals who do fulfil radical demands of the situation of this kind, at least in so far as they recognize them or are able to fulfil them, are held up as an excuse for the rest. (We may think of a Peter Claver or a Martin Luther King and similar

---

the further question of its bearing on the decision for salvation. What we are treating of here is that which is customarily called 'historic guilt'.

figures in Church history.) Even today we are still setting up monuments to the prophets in order to avoid having to obey what they preached. There is a tendency to feel that we have established that something is impossible even with the best will in the world *before* we have really tried every possible course. The doctrine of original sin is invoked, or that of the inescapable dialectic of all human realities, or the statement that the poor are always with us, the doctrine of the sublime meaning of suffering and misfortune (even when, at basis, it is solely the outcome of our own fault), or the doctrine of eternal life, the recognition that absolute social equality is neither beneficial nor possible, these and a thousand other reasons are adduced merely to avoid having to take the course of action which a given situation really prescribes. We are exhorted to advance very slowly and cautiously. The praises of evolution in preference to revolution are sung. We are reluctant to make mortgage payments which will only benefit the next generation. We say we cannot when what we really mean is we will not. Our way of formulating this may seem too 'moralizing' in tone, though this is no part of our intention, although those who describe the historical guilt of the Church in earlier ages and condemn it are all too eager to step forward with aggressive accusations and moral condemnations. Yet the fact remains: even in the Church and despite the Church's existence historical faults of the greatest magnitude are possible. Why should not the same situations apply in the case of epochs and peoples as apply in the history of individuals, situations, that is, which can only rightly be responded to by an act of 'heroic virtue'? And on this showing why should not epochs, peoples, and societies too be such that for the most part they fail to rise above these situations? After all these too are made up of very average individuals. Should we not then expect such failure from them still more than from individuals, though admittedly this fact is far from being any firm reason for excusing such failure in situations of the kind we are speaking of? (Any more than the Church in times of persecution can simply permit an average Christian to apostatize in order to preserve his life or his wellbeing.) The great mass of mankind is in fact seldom or never ready for heroic deeds (even when such are necessary, and even men who are not Christian are still subject to the impulses of the Holy Spirit). And if this is true how can we expect any such thing within the Church at all times, seeing that she is made up precisely of these individuals, who also constitute secular societies? There have always been heroic individuals in the Church. But does this *ipso facto* mean that there has been a heroic Church? The ecclesiologists should see how they can solve this dilemma. The fact we are pointing to is still far from having been adequately thought out at the theological level even though there are people enough nowadays who regard the Church as discredited by it to such an extent that for them it has become totally unworthy of belief in its claim to have been founded by God.

A case of the kind we are speaking of now seems to be in prospect, a failure, namely, of the Church with regard to the will to personal poverty undertaken to eliminate the poverty of the under-developed world. We have to say that all the prospects are that the will that is really required of the Church in this respect will not be brought to bear any more than that of secular society in the same field. The Church will act more or less in exactly the same way as secular society, perhaps very slightly better but by and large just the same. We see and yet we do not see, we will and yet we do not will, we do something and it is too little. Our unreadiness to accept poverty remains. The necessary process of changing our basic attitudes is simply too slow to meet the necessities or to ensure that what is really required will be achieved in the foreseeable future so long as it is not forced by the sheer physical facts, so long as it is subjected merely to moral appeals. The creative imagination is not there. The utopian ideal has (still) no strength behind it. The influence which the Church can bring to bear on such changes of attitude is dependent not merely upon the intrinsic power of the gospel, but also upon the general historical and social milieu. Certainly this influence of the Church – as a *partial* cause which takes effect at what may be a very invisible level – constantly works within history to change the intellectual and social situation of the secular world. But the converse is equally true. It is only when *this* situation has come to coincide with what the Church demands, and that too through a whole range of causes not under the control of explicit Christianity or the Church, are Christians in a position really to recognize precisely and effectively what course of action they should truly adopt and should long since have been adopting. Now for the most part changes of this kind in secular attitudes take place slowly, all too slowly. And because of this we cannot seriously expect that this process will be accelerated in the Church. It is much in itself if the Church does not simply form the rearguard in this action, a role which, after all, it has in many respects adopted since the Enlightenment and the French Revolution. For during this period it recognized the signs of the times only when these had already become more than signs, hard simple facts which no one in the Church could any longer evade, moreover no longer wished to evade, and which made it obvious that there was no longer any necessity to evade them. The present day is still a time in which the Church is unready to accept poverty.

The only way in which the Church's members could be induced to be poor and to embrace poverty would be for them to recognize this 'poverty' as a condition for eliminating poverty in the under-developed world. Now in practice, though in itself this inducement to personal poverty does exist it is not recognized in the Church regarded as the great mass of believers to the extent that would be necessary in order to eliminate poverty in the under-developed world. We do not see, we will not see, we cannot see. How precisely the position should be defined may remain an open question. The end result remains the same. Despite all the discussion, all the heroic efforts on the part of individuals both within and without the Church we remain indifferent towards the poverty of the world, unready to accept personal poverty. The prospects are that we will stick fast at the level of small instalment payments, the executing of half-hearted manoeuvres which serve to evade the problem, not to overcome it in any genuine sense. This will be the line of action in the Church and in secular society, each depending upon the other in this question too. Nothing more can be expected in practice even from those forced to accept what is, by our standards, a more modest way of life, any more than it is from the rich and prosperous. For no one among us likes to pay enough for a banana to ensure that the banana picker can be given a really just reward for his labour. The student who campaigns against capitalism and imperialism still enjoys his holiday trip to Tunis. The theology professor sees nothing wrong in having a house of his own (or in some circumstances two) for the pursuit of his profound studies. And so on. And it is also very difficult to say how the individual could seriously rise above the economic and social forces which are impregnated by sin – forces which can rarely actually be said simply to be sinful in themselves and of their very nature, even though they belong intrinsically to the 'acquisitive' constitution of the world, impel us to sin, are born of sin, and are there to put us to the test (*ad agonem*) in a struggle in which all of us are only too prone to succumb, falling into personal sin or making our personal contribution to the 'sins of the world' in other ways. For man is precisely a sinner both in his private and in his public life, both within and without the Church. How far this objective state of sinfulness in God's sight can be brought home to him personally or in an ultimate sense – this is in turn another question. In any case he is a being in process of becoming. He is meant to be something more than he in fact is. He recognizes this deficiency and must accept (in order to advance at all) that it is greater than can really be justified even on 'moral' grounds. And this precise point also applies to the question of the rich and the poor in the world. This is why in practice there is, even within the Church, an un-readiness to accept poverty so as to make others rich. Anyone seeking to analyse this state of affairs with greater theological precision needs only to recall the traditional theological teaching that it is impossible to avoid all sins, an impossibility that is dialectically coexistent in man with the possibility of avoiding them. Such a one needs only to transpose this teaching onto the social plane and to apply it to our special problem.

Let no one say that these terrible conclusions of ours are such as to ennervate or to kill all will to embrace poverty so as to eliminate poverty. For when we stand before the judgement-seat of God no one of us will be able to offer as a sure defence of his conduct that he was simply going along with the herd. Everyone must struggle even when he foresees that he will be defeated. And it can even be the case that God may perhaps spare this present-day world of ours taken as a whole (obviously we can, if we like, put this in secular terms) so long as he can find among its inhabitants the few just men whom he failed to find among the inhabitants of Sodom and Gomorrah. Thus the question is thrown back from the Church to the individual of whether he too – and perhaps through a real fault in God's sight – is too rich really to help the poor.

17

OBSERVATIONS ON THE PROBLEM OF THE 'ANONYMOUS CHRISTIAN'

THE central theme of the remarks which follow will be that summed up in the key phrase 'anonymous Christian'. It is recognized that the subject being treated of here is first and foremost a controversy internal to Catholic theology. I myself have given my opinions on this theme several times.[1] A. Röper has made this phrase the title of a book which has appeared in German, English, Italian and Spanish.[2] Klaus Riesenhuber has presented a comprehensive survey on this question.[3] In Japan Hans Waldenfels reacted favourably to my thesis,[4] whereas other European missionaries in the same area took up an emphatically hostile attitude to this thesis of the 'anonymous Christian".[5] Hans Urs von Balthasar[6] and Henri de Lubac[7] likewise expressed their opposition to it,

[1] On this subject cf. the earlier publications by the author: 'Anonymous Christians', *Theological Investigations* VI (London and Baltimore, 1969), pp. 390–398, and also 'Anonymous Christianity and the Missionary Task of the Church', *Theological Investigations* XII (London and New York, 1974), pp. 161–178.

[2] A. Röper, *Die anonymen Christen* (Mainz, 1963); but see also on this the critical review by H. Vorgrimler, 'Über die "anonymen Christen" ', *Hochland* 56 (1963/64), pp. 363–364.

[3] K. Riesenhuber, 'Der anonyme Christ, nach K. Rahner', *Zeitschr. f. Kath. Theol.* 86 (1964), pp. 276–303. Riesenhuber attempts to give a comprehensive and co-ordinated presentation of all the various statements by Rahner on the question.

[4] H. Waldenfels, ' ". . . omnes homines vult salvos fieri . . ." (1 Tim. 2:4). De sententia P. Caroli Rahner S.J. circa voluntatem salvificam Dei universalem', *Shingaku Kenkyu* (Tokio, 1962), no. 12. Cf. also *idem*, 'Theologische Akkomodation', *Hochland* 58 (1965/66), pp. 189–204.

[5] cf. e.g. L. Elders, 'Die Taufe der Weltreligionen. Bemerkungen zu einer Theorie Karl Rahners', *Theol. u. Glaube* 55 (1965), pp. 124–131, and also H. Kruse, 'Die "anonymen Christen" exegetisch gesehen', *Münch. Theol. Zeitschrift* 18 (1967), pp. 2–29.

[6] See H. U. von Balthasar's observations in *Cordula oder der Ernstfall* (Einsiedeln, 1966).

[7] cf. H. de Lubac, *Paradoxe et Mystère de l'Eglise* (Paris, 1967), pp. 153–156.

while E. Schillebeeckx too expressed certain objections to it.[8] These references are intended not to provide any exhaustive bibliography on the controversy, but rather to make it clear that it will perhaps be worth while to present a few further observations on the theme. Admittedly in doing so we cannot have any intention of repeating in precise or explicit terms everything which has already been said on the subject. A somewhat random selection from among the various possible aspects must be permitted.

By way of preliminary it may be pointed out that a distinction should be drawn between the question of what constitutes the best possible terminology from every point of view, and the further question of the actual reality signified by the phrases 'anonymous Christian' or 'anonymous Christianity'. So far as the terminology is concerned I do not deny that this too has a certain importance, and that not every opinion to the effect that the terminology 'anonymous Christian' or 'anonymous Christianity' are to be rejected on the grounds that many find it misleading *ipso facto* or necessarily implies a rejection of the actual reality signified thereby. But anyone who holds that the reality signified by the above phrases, or the material content they point to are of such great importance that they must be condensed within a precisely formulated terminology of this kind in order to be used in other theological considerations must, if he merely rejects the above terminology, suggest some other terminology which according to his opinion is less misleading. Now this will probably prove very difficult. I know of no convincing suggestions which have been put forward in this respect. We may concede to de Lubac that with regard to the justification of the terms which have been called in question there is a certain distinction to be drawn between 'anonymous Christian' and 'anonymous Christianity'; that the term 'anonymous Christian' may more readily be admitted than that of 'anonymous Christianity'. Some therefore may prefer to avoid the term 'anonymous Christianity', while being ready to use the term 'anonymous Christian' etc. They can count on my agreement on this point. All I would draw their attention to in this respect is that 'Christianity' can have two meanings: not merely that of 'Christendom', i.e. the sum total of Christians, and so for practical purposes the Church, but also the meaning of the 'being Christian' of an individual Christian. In this sense, then, we can speak of 'anonymous Christianity' so long as we are willing to speak of an anonymous Christian. But this is as far as we shall go in concerning ourselves with the purely terminological problem.

[8] cf. E. Schillebeeckx, *Glaubensinterpretation* (Mainz, 1971), pp. 108f.

THE REALITY OF THE 'ANONYMOUS CHRISTIAN'

The actual subject-matter with which we are properly and ultimately speaking concerned here is such that, as I believe, it neither can nor should be contested by any Catholic Christian or theologian. But two points are involved in this subject-matter:

There are men who stand outside the social unity of the Church or of the Christian Churches, who have not been reached by the explicitly Christian message, or at any rate not in such a way that their failure to embrace Christianity in any explicit sense signifies any serious personal fault in God's sight so far as they are concerned. At the same time, however, these same individuals stand in a positive and salvific relationship to God. In other words to put it in the usual theological terminology and in a somewhat abbreviated form, they are justified. They are living in the state of grace. Even those who at the level of their conscious thought interpret themselves as atheist may be numbered among such individuals, although the concept of the 'anonymous theist' who regards himself as an atheist and the concept of the 'anonymous Christian' are not identical.[9]

But the thesis of the 'anonymous Christian' includes a second point as well, and it is this that primarily and properly speaking gives it its importance and at the same time its difficulty. This individual who is justified even though he is a non-Christian is justified through the grace of Christ and through a faith, hope and love for God and mankind which are to be qualified as specifically Christian in a special sense, even though this triad, constituting the single way to salvation and possession of salvation, is something of which they are not objectively aware in the sense of having consciously explicitated their specifically Christian dimension to themselves. Merely in passing it may be remarked that we might actually apply the term 'anonymous Christian' to every individual who, in virtue of God's universal will to save, and thereby in virtue of the 'supernatural existential',[10] is inescapably confronted with the offering of God's self-bestowal and is totally unable to escape from this situation. In other words according to this terminology absolutely every man is also an 'anonymous

[9] cf. also the author's article, 'Atheism and Implicit Christianity', *Theological Investigations* IX (London and New York, 1972), pp. 145–164.

[10] On these earlier ideas of the author's see 'Concerning the Relationship Between Nature and Grace', *Theological Investigations* I (London, 1961), pp. 297–317, and also 'The Dignity and Freedom of Man', *Theological Investigations* II (London and Baltimore, 1963), pp. 235–263.

Christian'. But we prefer the terminology according to which that man is called an 'anonymous Christian' who on the one hand has *de facto* accepted of his freedom this gracious self-offering on God's part through faith, hope, and love, while on the other he is absolutely not yet a Christian at the social level (through baptism and membership of the Church) or in the sense of having consciously objectified his Christianity to himself in his own mind (by explicit Christian faith resulting from having hearkened to the explicit Christian message). We might therefore put it as follows: the 'anonymous Christian' in our sense of the term is the pagan after the beginning of the Christian mission, who lives in the state of Christ's grace through faith, hope and love, yet who has no explicit knowledge of the fact that his life is orientated in grace-given salvation to Jesus Christ.

THE THEOLOGICAL MEANING OF THE REALITY SIGNIFIED BY THE TERM 'ANONYMOUS CHRISTIAN'

So far as the first element is concerned I believe that there should be no room for doubt among Catholic theologians or Christians. There can be, and actually are, individuals who are justified in the grace of God, who attain to supernatural salvation in God's sight (and, moreover, to Christ as well), yet who do not belong to the Church or to Christendom as a visible historical reality as a result of having been touched by the preaching of the gospel in any concrete 'this worldly' sense at any point in their lives. No truly theological demonstration of this thesis can be supplied here from scripture or tradition. Such a demonstration would not be easy to make, because the optimism of universal salvation entailed in this thesis has only gradually become clear and asserted itself in the conscious faith of the Church. We can trace a course of development from the optimism concerning salvation for unbaptized catechumens in Ambrose, through the doctrine of the *baptismus flaminis* and the *votum ecclesiae* in the Middle Ages and at the Council of Trent, down to the explicit teaching in the writings of Pius XII to the effect that even a merely implicit *votum* for the Church and baptism can suffice. From this we can trace a further and more arduous course of development of the emergence of conscious faith in this regard which was even more difficult than the development of the conviction that there can be heretics and schismatics who are in good faith even outside the Church, and whose salvation cannot be doubted. Whatever may be the course of this development, whatever theological grounds there may be for justifying it, it can at all events be said that at least since the Second Vatican Council there can no longer be any room for doubt that the Catholic Church, as a matter of her conscious faith, regards it as established that it is possible even for such men of good will to be justified and to attain to supernatural salvation even though at the level of their concrete 'this worldly' circumstances, and at the level of personal history and of the kerygmatic and institutional Church, they are not Christians at all. In this connection it should be noticed that this possibility is positively asserted by the Second Vatican Council. It is not merely that in presenting a theology of the necessity of the gospel and of baptism for salvation it has been added on as a negative point that in emphasizing this necessity of the gospel and of baptism we are never-theless imposing no limits to the sovereign freedom of God's grace. The Second Vatican Council positively asserts that it is possible for the non-Christian to attain salvation, though at the same time it declares that such salvation is achieved in ways that are known to God alone. In a tacit but noteworthy correction to the officially received theology which had hitherto been more or less unanimous on this point, it was declared at the Second Vatican Council that atheists too are not excluded from this possi-bility of salvation, though here the distinctions between positive and negative atheism, between atheism of greater or lesser duration, usually accepted up to that point were not applied at the Second Vatican Council. The only necessary condition which is recognized here is the necessity of faithfulness and obedience to the individual's own personal conscience. This optimism concerning salvation appears to me one of the most note-worthy results of the Second Vatican Council. For when we consider the officially received theology concerning all these questions, which was more or less traditional right down to the Second Vatican Council, we can only wonder how few controversies arose during the Council with regard to these assertions of optimism concerning salvation, and wonder too at how little opposition the conservative wing of the Council brought to bear on this point, how all this took place without any setting of the stage or any great stir even though this doctrine marked a far more de-cisive phase in the development of the Church's conscious awareness of her faith than, for instance, the doctrine of collegiality in the Church, the relationship between scripture and tradition, the acceptance of the new exegesis etc.[11]

We now come to the second element which we have previously pointed

[11] On the whole cf. Conc. Vat. II, 'Nostra aetate' (Declaration on the Relation-ship of the Church to Non-Christian Religions); 'Gaudium et spes' (Pastoral Con-stitution) (above all the first main section: The Church and Man's Calling), and also 'Ad gentes' (The Decree on the Missions).

out in the doctrine of the anonymous Christian. This salvation of the non-Christian is achieved through an act of faith in the true sense. The doctrine of the anonymous Christian as it is nowadays presented precisely does not involve the belief that anyone can attain to justification and final salvation even without faith in a strictly theological sense merely because he does not act against his own moral conscience. It is true that the theory of a 'faith', a *fides late dicta*, which at basis amounted merely to a recognition of God at the philosophical level was sufficient for justification was rejected by Innocent XI.[12] But this has certainly no very great theological importance for our present consideration, especially since the theory of A. Straub at the beginning of the present century concerning the justifying power of a readiness to believe in principle, a *fides virtualis*,[13] never incurred the official censure of the Church. But both in Pius XII's declaration against the rigorism of Feeney[14] and in the doctrine of the Second Vatican Council it is after all clearly assumed that even in these cases of a justified pagan a *fides supernaturalis* is necessary. What is not stated in these official doctrinal declarations is how a truly supernatural faith of this kind in the strictly theological sense can come to be in the cases which concern us here. In the document of the Second Vatican Council, 'Ad gentes' No. 7, it is stated (albeit merely in an aside) that God can bring men who are ignorant of the gospel through no fault of their own to faith by ways which he knows, and that without this faith it is impossible to be pleasing to him. And in this formula what we chiefly sense is a scepticism as to whether it is possible at all, even in the most formal way, to find an answer to the question of how such a faith could ever be present in a man when this man has no contact whatever with the gospel. This sense of scepticism also finds expression in a further document of the Second Vatican Council, 'Gaudium et Spes', and moreover in almost the same words (No. 22). This then is concerned with finding the answer to the question of *how* it is possible apart from the preaching of the gospel for a true and supernatural faith to be present in a 'pagan' of this kind, i.e. an assent to God as he imparts himself in freedom and in a way which transcends any certainty which the world can offer. But the fact that we cannot find the answer to this question should not prevent the theologian from pondering it more deeply. For if he simply renounces any attempt to find an answer at all however formal, then

[12] cf. DS[34] 2123.

[13] See A. Straub, *De analysi fidei* (Innsbruck, 1922). Some of the studies here published go very far back in time.

[14] DS[34] 3872.

either the universality of God's will to save towards non-Christian humanity or the necessity of personal faith for this becomes incredible. Yet we cannot invoke either a natural knowledge of God or a primitive and ultimate kind of revelation to answer this question, for such answers will fail to solve it. The first course has already been rejected by Innocent XI and Pius XII as well as by the declarations of the Second Vatican Council. With regard to the second course, i.e. the invoking of a primitive and ultimate revelation, the way in which this has customarily been presented hitherto is in the form of a handing down of an original revelation of this kind from paradisal sources. Nowadays this is impossible both because of the findings of modern palaeontology and anthropology and also because of the findings of modern exegesis, which regards the narrative of Genesis neither as an eye-witness account of God himself as having participated in the events concerned nor simply as a record that has been transmitted through the centuries of human history. But the converse can be stated. The more we can make intelligible the possibility of a personal faith even in a 'pagan', and moreover on the basis of the normal data of theology as self-evident in other contexts, and so without any supplementary arguments constructed arbitrarily, such as have not infrequently been adduced in the past (special enlightenment at death etc.), the better can the doctrine of the possibility of justification and salvation for a 'pagan' be fitted into the totality of the Christian faith, and the clearer and more intelligible too will the doctrine become of a real, effective, and infralapsarian universal will to save on God's part. Admittedly any such theology of the possibility of a true and saving faith even in the 'pagan' must be so formulated as to avoid obscuring the importance of an explicit Christianity, with its concomitants of gospel and Church, and the necessity of the missionary preaching of this Christianity to all nations and all men. Even when all this is successfully achieved one fact remains, so I believe, concerning the breakthrough of this optimism concerning salvation for all men which (so far as our present question goes) can be prevented only by the grave personal guilt of the individual, and which at the same time regards all salvation, wherever it is present, as specifically Christian. This optimism with regard to salvation remains one of the most astonishing phenomena in the development of the Church's conscious awareness of her faith in this development as it applies to the secular and non-Christian world, the awareness of the difference between saving history as a whole and the history of explicit Christianity and of the Church. For it is true that we must not say that the Old or the New Testament simply rule out any such optimistic interpretation of universal salvation, which in the power of the Holy Spirit can hope to find a near brother even in one who is apparently most far removed. But we shall not be able to say either that this development of the conscious awareness of faith is already very clearly set forth in the New Testament or that it does not have to overcome very great obstacles which are inherent in the New Testament statements concerning the necessity of salvation coming through the gospel which is preached in its power.

HOW COULD IT BE POSSIBLE FOR THERE TO BE AN 'ANONYMOUS CHRISTIAN'?

Now how can we conceive of this possibility of faith in the 'pagan'? In attempting – nothing more than an attempt is intended – to answer this question some anthropological insights may surely be taken as given which should be explained and established more fully elsewhere: the difference and the unity between objective knowledge and that which is known on the one hand, and a non-objective, non-thematic awareness and the reality thus known on the other – in other words between 'this worldly' knowledge and transcendental knowledge, between that which is expressed in conceptual form and the further levels of significance not consciously adverted to of a given statement, between the material object and an *a priori* formal object concomitantly present with the capacity to know, between the object of knowledge and the further perspectives of knowledge – or whatever name we may choose to apply to the distinction we are seeking to draw, though in this it remains unimportant for our present purposes whether the concepts we have adduced historically speaking, and in the application of them here intended, mean precisely the same, or whether further and more precise distinctions should be introduced into them in their turn.[15] For our present purposes what we are chiefly concerned with is of course the distinction between the pairs of concepts we have mentioned. Yet it is not disputed that between them there always remains also a certain unity (not identity!). That which is capable of being expressed in 'this worldly' categories mediates the transcendental and *e converso*, although this mutually conditioning relationship is itself to be thought of not as a fixed entity, but rather as having a history of its own so that this relationship and its history are quite incapable of being expressed thematically in any full sense. If we take these

---

[15] On these observations by the author cf. 'Thomas Aquinas on Truth', *Theological Investigations* XIII, and the basic studies: *Geist in Welt* (Munich, 3rd ed., 1964) and *Hörer des Wortes* (Munich, 2nd ed., 1963).

concepts of formal anthropology as read the theory of the possibility of personal faith in a 'pagan' makes two assumptions: (1) The supernatural grace of faith and justification offered by God to men does not need to be conceived of as an isolated intervention on God's part at a particular point in a world which is itself profane. On the contrary it can perfectly well be interpreted on the basis of God's universal will to save as a grace which, as offered (!), is a constantly present existential of the creature endowed with spiritual faculties and of the world in general, which orientates these to the immediacy of God as their final end, though of course in saying this the question still remains wholly open of whether an individual freely gives himself to, or alternatively rejects, this existential which constitutes the innermost dynamism of his being and its history, an existential which is and remains continually present.[16] God's universal will to save objectifies itself in that communication of himself which we call grace. It does this effectively at all times and in all places in the form of the offering and the enabling power of acting in a way that leads to salvation. And even though it is unmerited and 'supernatural' in character, it constitutes the innermost *entelecheia* and dynamism of the world considered as the historical dimension of the creature endowed with spiritual faculties. It does not need to be consciously and objectively known as a dynamism of this kind, and even without such knowledge it is still present. (2) This grace constantly implanted in the nature of the creature and the historical dimension belonging to it as the dynamism and finalization of the history of man is, however, something of which man is *aware* in the manner in which such a reality does impinge upon human awareness. This awareness does not *ipso facto* or necessarily imply an objective awareness; it is present in the *a priori* formal objects, in the further levels of significance in the spiritual and intentional capacities of knowledge and freedom. Whether man explicitly recognizes it or not, whether he can or cannot reflect upon it in itself and in isolation, man is, in virtue of the grace offered him and implanted in him as his freedom in the mode of a formal object and of a spiritual perspective of an *a priori* kind, orientated towards the immediacy of God as his final end.[17] He brings his spiritual life to its fulness in knowledge and freedom in such a way that God in himself constitutes the ultimate point of orientation of his whole historical development in knowledge and freedom, and that too not as the God of metaphysical knowledge, as the God of infinite remoteness, but as the

[16] cf. n. 10.

[17] On this cf. the author's article, 'Concerning the Relationship Between Nature and Grace, *Theological Investigations* I (London, 1961), pp. 297–317.

God who in himself and of himself, in his own unique reality and sovereignty, constitutes the goal, as the God of eternal life. This orientation of the spiritual dynamism of man towards the immediacy of God, which is both known and unknown, is, it is true, in order to be known at all (which does not mean reflected upon as an object or capable of being adequately reflected upon by the individual) mediated through the realities of his world assignable to 'this worldly' categories. But this mediation does not necessarily need to be an explicit object of revelation. All those forms of mediation belonging to the dimension of 'this worldly' categories are sufficient for this which confront the individual in himself as a subject endowed with intellect and freedom. We are suggesting that grace brings about a change of awareness through a new *a priori* formal object, even though this change of awareness cannot be reflected upon directly or certainly by the individual as such. Now this is not a thesis discovered *ad hoc*, but a view which has always been upheld in Thomist theology even though hitherto it has probably hardly been applied to our present question – simply because we have regarded the prevenient and elevating grace too much as an isolated event taking place at a particular point, and only under specific circumstances. But if we regard the self-communication of God (considered as that which is offered to man in his freedom) as an abiding existential of the creature endowed with spiritual faculties, and thereby as the innermost dynamism of the world in general, then, assuming the validity of the above-mentioned Thomist thesis, it is clear from the outset that the total process by which man brings his intellectual nature to its fulness, in which he comes to be in act as spiritual and in his totality, is orientated by grace towards the immediacy of God in a dimension of *a priori* awareness. On any right understanding of the relationship between the dimension of transcendental *a priori*ty and that of categorial historicity in man it is clear that this supernaturally elevated transcendentality of man, of which he is aware but which is not *ipso facto* known in itself as an object, does not have a special history apart, or does not persist in any sense in a non-historical state of fixity, but rather has a history of its own within the concrete history of the individual as its innermost form and dynamism in a manner similar to that of logic, which has its initial history not in the history of the logic that is the subject of conscious philosophical reflection, but in the history of the active spirit of man himself as he shapes his world.

In the light of this we can then go on to say that the total history of mankind is nothing else than the historical mediation, in terms of historical and 'this-worldly' categories, of the supernaturally elevated spirituality of man to man himself. And at that stage at which this history comes explicitly to exhibit this supernatural dynamism, so that its presence is consciously recognized within the history – at that stage it is revelation history and the history of faith. But this is a point which cannot be entered into in any more precise detail here. What can on any showing be said, however, is this: this grace-given elevation of the transcendentality of man, i.e. the orientation of this to the immediacy of God as its final end, gives reality to the concept of revelation already at the stage of an *a priori* awareness. And it does this even though this awareness (the supernatural formal object, as the Thomist would say) has not yet been objectively apprehended at the level of conscious thought or expressed in words. And when man of his freedom accepts himself together with this *a priori* awareness which is already revelation, then that is present which can in the true and proper sense be called faith, even though this faith has not yet been objectively explicitated or conceptualized as the absolute openness of man to the immediacy of God in his act of self-imparting. Yet this *a priori* awareness of man (called revelation) is always accepted in faith wherever and whenever an individual in unreserved faithfulness to his own moral conscience accepts himself in freedom as he is, and so too in the as yet unrecognizable implications of the dynamism underlying the movement of his own spirit. It is only in the light of this that we can achieve a full theological understanding of what the Second Vatican Council says in 'Lumen Gentium' No. 16: 'Those also can attain to everlasting salvation who, through no fault of their own, do not know the gospel of Christ or his Church, yet sincerely seek God and, moved by grace, strive by their deeds to do his will as it is known to them through the dictates of conscience.' A point expressly to be noticed here is that in the following sentence this doctrine is declared to apply also to those who are inculpable atheists. And the same point is likewise made in 'Gaudium et Spes'.

On a first simple reading of this declaration we might receive the impression that what the 'pagan' is being promised here in the statement concerning the fulfilment of the dictates of conscience is a salvation which comes to be even without faith. Moreover, the emphasis on divine grace, by means of which alone obedience to the dictates of conscience can be achieved, still does nothing of itself to alter this impression. Yet salvation of this kind without true faith is ruled out by the declaration of Pius XII and the Missionary Decree of the Second Vatican Council, as we have already mentioned above.

This grace, therefore, must produce faith, and that too even in cases where no knowledge of the gospel exists. It follows that theology has an obligation to explain how such a faith is conceivable in the conditions described. We have attempted to give such an explanation and the theological data we have adduced for this purpose are only such as are already recognized in other contexts: the universal will of God to save, the supernatural specification of man entailed in this and constantly present in him, in virtue of which God's act of self-communication implanted in the innermost being of man (as offered to his freedom), that *a priori* transcendental change of awareness which is concomitantly given with this grace, and which is present even when it is not yet or not at all consciously adverted to. Anyone who rejects this theory of a possible faith in God as revealing himself and communicating himself, on whatever grounds, then incurs the task as a Catholic theologian of explaining in other ways how true supernatural faith in revelation can be present in an individual without any contact with the explicit preaching of the gospel. For the fact that such a thing is possible is explicitly declared in the official doctrinal statements of the Church cited above, even though they themselves refrain from making any theological declaration on this fact.

FURTHER IMPLICATIONS OF A THESIS

The theory of the 'anonymous Christian', therefore, states (though we do not insist upon the term 'anonymous Christian') that even outside the Christian body there are individuals – and they are to be found even in the ranks of atheists – who are justified by God's grace and possess the Holy Spirit. The theory further states that the difference between this state of salvation and that of those who are Christians in an explicit sense is not such that these 'pagans' are acceptable in God's sight even without any true faith (together with hope and love) as it were in virtue of a merely natural morality which they possess, whereas the Christians and only they achieve their justification through a faith in salvation. On the contrary the theory ascribes to these justified pagans also a real, albeit inexplicitated or, if we like to put it so, rudimentary faith. This is of course not to deny that this faith as it exists in the pagan is properly speaking designed to follow its own inherent dynamism in such a way as to develop into that faith which is objectified and articulated through the gospel, that faith which we simply call the Christian faith. The seed has no right to seek not to grow into a plant. But the fact that it is not yet developed into a plant is no reason for refusing to give the name which we give to the plant destined to grow from it to the seed as well.

It is possible, then, to envisage a man who is in possession of that self-imparting of God called grace as the innermost heart and centre of his existence, one who has accepted this in unreserved faithfulness to his own conscience, one who is thereby constituted as a believer in a form which, while it is not objectified in words, is nonetheless real, a man, in other words, who even as a 'pagan' already possesses the blessing of salvation, that blessing which ultimately speaking is the sole point of concern for Christianity together with the gospel belonging to it and all its institutions, and in relation to which everything else is merely a means, a historical objectification, a sacramental sign, a social manifestation. Now if this is true, then I cannot see why we should not call such a man an anonymous Christian, seeing that as Catholic theologians we may not doubt that such men both can and actually do exist. For after all he does possess, even though in a way hidden to himself and to others, that which constitutes the essence of what it is to be a Christian: the grace of God which is laid hold of in faith. If we are unwilling to go on from this, and to speak of an anonymous *Christianity* then I will raise no protest against this refusal. All that is involved here is simply a question of what constitutes the terminology that best suits the purpose and so a question of judgement on which I have no fixed opinion whatever. Admittedly I do regard the term 'anonymous Christian' as inescapable so long as no one suggests a better term to me.

PERSPECTIVES

Obviously many further questions would still remain to be treated which cannot be resolved here. We should have to enquire how all those new perspectives of saving history and the history of faith entailed in the theory we have put forward are to be reconciled with the viewpoint from which the New Testament regards the process by which salvation is gained and also saving history itself, albeit with very notable variations. A further point which should be discussed is the question already mentioned above as to the meaning and necessity of the mission of Christianity, a question in the light of which it is very often believed that this theory should be rejected. Admittedly in this connection there is actually a particular example to be mentioned: a Japanese who is a student chaplain in Japan has told me that the theory put forward here constitutes the indispensable condition for him such that it is only on this condition that he can perform his missionary work, precisely because he can then appeal to the anonymous Christian in the pagan and not simply seek to indoctrinate him with a teaching *ab externo*. A further question which would have to be resolved is what aspects (on the basis of the theory we have put forward) are brought to light for the appraisal of the non-Christian religions, even though this question cannot be answered *solely* on the basis of the theory of the anonymous Christian. This theory, therefore, remains ultimately speaking neutral in relation even to such controversies as have, for instance, very recently arisen between Schlette and Seckler.[18]

The question might be raised of whether a new conception of the primordial revelation cannot be developed precisely in the light of the theory put forward here, a conception which avoids those elements which are either improbable or impossible from an anthropological and historical point of view, yet which are entailed in the usual conception of the primordial revelation. It is obvious that the assumptions, in terms of existential ontology which this theory works with call for further clarification and explanation. A distinction is drawn between two factors: an original event of revelation consisting in the self-communication of God as addressed to all in virtue of his universal will to save and taking place at a preconceptual level in the roots of man's spiritual faculties on the one hand, and the objectification at the historical and conceptual level of this revelatory self-communication of God in that which we call revelation and the history of revelation in a more normal sense on the other. This distinction, which it has been necessary to draw here, could be the occasion of fruitful considerations for many other problems of theology. But, as has been said, these and many other points cannot be discussed any further in the present context. The man of today is first and foremost a man who feels himself at one (at that point at which he truly achieves the fulness of self-realization) with mankind as a whole. For all his harsh experiences of what it is to be a historical being and of history itself, whenever it is the ultimate in man, man as a whole and as final and definitive that is in

---

[18] Both authors have stated their respective positions on the problems involved several times. Cf. H. R. Schlette, *Die Religionen als Thema der Theologie*, Quaestiones Disputatae 22 (Freiburg im Breisgau, 1964) and the review of this work: M. Seckler, 'Eine Theologie der Religionen', *Hochland* 57 (1964/65), pp. 588–590. But see also H. R. Schlette, 'Einige Theses zum Selbstverständnis der Theologie angesichts der Religionen', *Gott in Welt* II (Freiburg im Breisgau, 1964), pp. 306–316 and *Colloquium Salutis – Christen und Nichtchristen heute* (Cologne, 1965). On the other hand cf. M. Seckler, 'Das Heil der Nicht-evangelisierten in thomistischer Sicht', *Theol. Quart. Schrift.* 140 (1960), pp. 38–69, and also 'Nichtchristen III. Systematisch', *HThG* II (Munich, 1963), pp. 239–242 and 'Sind Religionen Heilswege?', *StdZ* 186 (1970), pp. 187–194. A. Darlap has presented a general survey on the whole area of 'the Theology of Religions' in *Sacramentum Mundi* V (London and New York, 1970), pp. 284–287.

question, he feels himself at one with all. He does not seek any heaven from which some other man is excluded from the outset. If at the same time he still seeks to uphold nowadays the claims of Christianity to be absolute, its universal significance for each and for all, if he wills to recognize, and as a Christian must recognize a *single* meaning and a *single* dynamism running through the whole history of mankind, then he must simply have a single answer as to how and in what way he can recognize in every one of his fellows a brother in the sense in which Christianity recognizes every individual as a brother, a sense, that is, which is not merely humanist but truly Christian. There must be a Christian theory to account for the fact that every individual who does not in any absolute or ultimate sense act against his own conscience can say and does say in faith, hope, and love, Abba within his own spirit, and is on these grounds in all truth a brother to Christians in God's sight. This is what the theory of the anonymous Christian seeks to say, and, in so far as it is valid, what it implies.

18

THE CHURCH'S COMMISSION TO BRING SALVATION AND THE HUMANIZATION OF THE WORLD

'HORIZONTALISM' IN CHRISTIANITY AND IN THE CONTEMPORARY CHURCH

There have always been heresies which threaten Christianity, the Christian life, and a right understanding of the Church's task. They constitute a danger which has always accompanied the earthly life of faith and of the Church. In earlier times such heresies emerged, as the word 'heresy' = 'division' implies, within the Church herself, and were chiefly related to specific and particular points of Christian doctrine and Christian life with the result that even at the conceptual level it was customary to distinguish heresy from apostasy, meaning a falling away from Christianity as a whole. Today Christianity and the Church are threatened by a form of teaching and a way of life which, while they have indeed emerged from the Church, are far from being explicitly presented as a rejection of Christianity or as seeking to draw men out of the Church, and yet which in reality already imply in a true sense something far more than heresy. For in reality they take a course which leads to an elimination of Christianity. In other words they constitute that which, in the traditional terminology, should be called apostasy. In this connection one question which does of course remain quite open is that of the subjective dispositions of those who uphold such tendencies in the doctrine and life of the Church. We mean here the view that that which constitutes the true essence of Christianity, the true heart and centre which alone is signified in all its doctrines, the true task of the Church, consists in something which can simply be called 'love of neighbour' or (because this term has perhaps too individualistic or pietistic a ring for the upholders of this movement) 'commitment at the level of social politics and criticism of society', 'responsibility for the world'. This tendency has already been designated by the term pure 'horizontalism'.

It makes no difference for our immediate purposes where or in how many individuals or individual Churches within the totality of the Church this movement finds its support, or whether it is really supported in all its radical one-sidedness or more as a matter of emphasizing one tendency without excluding more orthodox ones. This question of the current position in Church history and Church politics is one with which we shall not be concerned in the present study. What we are referring to here is a radical horizontalism. In other words that doctrine and that interpretation of life which regards Christianity, its doctrines and in truth the task of the Church as properly speaking consisting in one thing alone: a responsibility for mankind, for the human society. 'God' is reduced to a mere cipher (old-fashioned and replaceable or for various reasons not indispensable). It stands for mankind itself, its unassailable dignity, the future which it still has to strive to achieve for itself. What we are referring to here is that doctrine and that way of life in terms of which all theological concepts, all cult and all prayer are merely things which have gradually to be replaced or perhaps things which may even have an abiding usefulness, key terms and practices which precisely bring this active responsibility to reality, a responsibility which each individual accepts for his fellows. In terms of a movement of this kind, then, Jesus is simply the most fruitful and perhaps (whatever the reasons which may be adduced, for these are not altogether clear) indispensable example of this commitment on behalf of one's neighbour and of a better society in what may even amount to a life-and-death struggle against the ruling forces in religion and politics. For this movement prayer is nothing else than a self-critical examination in which we remind ourselves of our neighbour and of our duty towards him. The Eucharist is the celebration of the true spirit of community in the light of Jesus as its most fruitful example and in its ultimate essence nothing beyond this. Correspondingly the other propositions of faith belonging to Christianity have also to be reinterpreted in the same sense, though this is something which cannot be set forth in detail here.

Obviously the activity of the *Church as such*, so long as she is not acting against her own true nature in belonging or seeking to belong, to those forces which defend their own position, which are established and oppressive, consists in a progressive education of men leading to an individual and collective commitment of this kind on behalf of their fellows, and in the concrete taking over of such social commitments on behalf of the poor, the oppressed, the exploited, the suffering within particular nations and on the international plane. The function of the Church which does justice to this interpretation of Christianity can only consist in the humanization of the world, otherwise it will, at least today, come perforce to stand for a turning away of men from their true task to a defence of oppressive forces in society, to being an opium of the people which is no longer necessary because nowadays it is really possible to deliver man from the multiplicity of his enslavements and factors leading to self-alienation so that there is no longer any need for any algesic against the pain of that self-alienation which existed in former times, and which could not be overcome in any other way.

For our immediate purposes it makes no difference whether, or to what extent, a horizontalism of this kind in doctrine or life manifests itself in its true chemical purity and absolute radicality, or whether in this respect the conditions within the individual Christian Churches are exactly the same, or whether the upholders of a horizontalism of this kind regard it rather, and perhaps with a happy illogicality, as a mere shifting of emphasis within Christianity as a whole which is demanded by the conditions of the present times, they themselves being still always ready to accept Christianity as a whole in this sense. Even if we were here prepared to assume that a horizontalism of this kind was justified, a horizontalism which, in the radicality intended, is far from being frequent in any consciously recognizable form within the Church, a consideration of this kind still has its importance. For it cannot be doubted that among Catholic and Protestant Christians alike, i.e. among those who belong to the Church right from the outset and are unwilling to withdraw from it, this radical horizontalism does exist, so that to pronounce a decided 'no' to it is not to campaign against an opponent who does not exist at all. Furthermore it is useful to make clear the further consequences which lie latent and hidden at an unconscious level in attitudes and customs of life which still bear too much of the imprint of the Church's doctrine of earlier times for them straightway or explicitly to be able to agree to a radical horizontalism of this kind.

In order to prevent any misunderstandings arising from this it must be explicitly emphasized that the serious upholders of a so-called 'political theology' have nothing to do with this radical horizontalism, and are therefore in no sense being pointed to in our present remarks. In our present thesis, as its heading explicitly suggests, we are concerned with the function of the *Church as such* of bringing salvation to men. The question we are asking, therefore, is whether this task of the Church as such is concerned merely with the humanization of the world and nothing beyond this. But in order to cope with this theme in a way that really goes to the roots of the matter this radical horizontalism itself has to be considered precisely in its very roots, and it has to be asked what a Christianity that is genuinely and totally understood really has to say to it. For only then does the question arise of the content and the ultimate and true orientation of the task of the *Church as such*, which belongs to her of her very nature.

WHAT ARE THE REASONS FOR THE SUDDEN APPEARANCE OF 'HORIZONTALISM'?

We shall first be enquiring into the reasons for the sudden appearance of this radical horizontalism in the Church. We might in fact immediately consider that what is in question here is simply that non-religious love of neighbour, that secular humanism, that ethically based socialism that has already long been in existence outside Christianity and the Church, and this might lead us to wonder why and how such a thing should suddenly become the teaching which now manifests itself within the Church herself and as the most recent and the only true interpretation of Christianity and of the task of the Christian and of the Church. To explain the fact that a secularized interpretation of human existence of this kind should now suddenly be presented as true Christianity in itself there must be reasons to be found such as did not exist in earlier times, and, moreover, as a force that is effective upon the Church herself. I believe that three such reasons might be pointed to, which in their interaction upon one another, and of course not as taken in isolation, can be held to account for this secularized horizontalism.

1. The Tendency Towards Demythologizing

The first of these reasons to be pointed to is that which might be called the tendency to *'demythologizing'*.[1] Obviously this is not the place to set forth the causes, meaning, limits, overstepping of the limits or historical development of this demythologizing movement within Christian theology, in exegesis, or in the Church. The only point that needs to be made here is quite a simple one. In this movement all historical realities are consciously regarded as subject to historical change and conditional. In other words this is a kind of historicism. And a further factor has been that process, which lasted, of course, over several centuries, by which an ancient image of the world which still dominated the Middle Ages has

[1] The term 'demythologizing' was first used in 1941 by R. Bultmann in the context of exegesis. But it quickly won general recognition as a theological category. Cf. R. Marlé, 'Demythologization', *Sacramentum Mundi* II (London and New York, 1968), pp. 65–69.

gradually been changed into the modern image of the world, the outcome of a rational approach to the natural sciences, of a modern psychology and of the modern social sciences. And in the light of all these factors in their bearing on the totality of the Christian faith it must be asked what the special content of each of them really means within the overall perspectives of modern ideas and outlooks, where and how the boundary lines must be drawn between that which is really intended and permanently binding in faith on the one hand, and conceptual models on the other, which obviously have been helpful for understanding the faith but are no longer valid now. Again it has to be asked where these conceptual models should still be retained, or where they merely make it more difficult or even impossible for us to understand what is really meant as binding in faith. To that extent, of course, some kind of 'demythologizing' is necessary and urgent today, and will be recognized as necessary by the Church's theologians, although at the same time it must be said that all theology throughout all the centuries has always been concerned with what is the essential point of such demythologizing to the extent that by it we understand nothing else than an encounter which it is necessary to achieve ever anew: an encounter between the faith which inevitably has to express itself in concepts subject to the conditions of the particular age concerned on the one hand, and the secular interpretation of existence which is constantly subject to change on the other. Yet it must be recognized that this task of demythologizing as thus understood has become more all-embracing, more urgent and more swiftly developing nowadays. And because of this a temptation and a danger has increased too, that namely of coming into opposition to those truths of Christianity which must not be surrendered by maintaining that they do not belong to what is true and essential to the meaning and the life of Christianity at all, but are merely old and now outworn modes in which an earlier age of Christianity sought to bring home to itself what the true meaning and purpose of Christianity really is. In the light of this a first cause of the movement towards a radical horizontalism becomes apparent. For this movement God too is to be numbered among those old and outworn terms by means of which Christianity objectifies to itself its innermost essence, precisely a loving responsibility for one's neighbour, finding it possible in this way to achieve a more intelligible mode of presenting it. God, therefore, is one of the ideas which must be demythologized, just as in principle the critique of religion of a Feuerbach or a Marx[2] had already demanded. Once

[2] L. Feuerbach presented his programme, 'Auflösung der Theologie' in *Das Wesen des Christentums* and *Das Wesen der Religion* (1845). On the programme of

we demythologize the idea of God only man remains. Because it was believed impossible in former times really to take man in this sense seriously in his infinite claims he came to be made a mythologem himself and called God, though admittedly only at the cost of thereby alienating man from himself also and in his claims upon us.

2. The Experience of God in a World Coloured by the Natural Sciences

A second cause of this radical horizontalism in the Church of our times, and no longer merely as it exists outside Christianity as embodied in the Church, is to be found in the fact that a man of today can no longer experience God so easily or so directly as a man of former ages believed to be possible. The man of today is a man who is above all influenced by the rationalism of the natural sciences, by approaches to experience and to knowledge in which every phenomenon which can be experienced is reduced to some other one in the closest possible functional interconnection. To the scientific learning of the modern age, but also so far as the direct feelings of the rational man are concerned, it is clear that in such a world God is not to be met with as one particular phenomenon among others. When within the context of our various experiences we fail to find an explanation for a particular phenomenon, i.e. when we cannot so account for it as to co-ordinate it with other phenomena already known to us, then we put a question-mark against it. We hope that in time some possible way of explaining it by the exact sciences may yet emerge. But what we do not say is this: 'Here God is at work in a special way.' We do not say: 'Here we find a special intervention of his in the world's course.' Nowadays we no longer want in any sense to have a God who has to be invoked as a stopper of the gaps so as to illumine to ourselves some point which still remains obscure, and to show its connection with the particular phenomena of our experience. The modern natural sciences work – and, moreover, entirely justifiably – with a methodological a-theism, and while this does not assert that God does not exist, it does make it impossible for the exact sciences to invoke God as an explanation of that which is still unexplained, or of 'this worldly' phenomena which are capable of explanation. But then it is all too easy to go on from this mental attitude, which primarily belongs to the exact sciences, and to regard it as the only legitimate mental attitude for modern man in any sense. From this it can readily be understood how an individual comes to receive the impression that while he cannot positively assert that God does not exist – since we

K. Marx cf. *Thesen über Feuerbach* (1845) and *Die Deutsche Ideologie* (1846) (written in collaboration with Fr. Engels).

must be very cautious in making such assertions on a purely negative point – still such a thing as God does not figure in his own personal life; it is an idea which cannot be verified. He feels that life still goes on as before even without it, as the example of the atheists shows, and theists are in no sense different from them when we come to examine their lives apart from this difference of opinion which remains at the level of pure theory.

Now here it is neither possible nor any part of our intention to demonstrate in positive terms how a genuine, and even inescapable experience of God can be made even today, although one which we can, and very often do, suppress. The only point to be recognized here is how this basic outlook, which is at least apparently a-theistic, on man's part leads to that radical horizontalism which is so much a force today. The Christians who uphold this horizontalism have the impression that they cannot overcome the experience in themselves, and even more in others, that God is not there so far as they are concerned. Yet for the most divers reasons, which cannot be analysed here, they still want to remain Christians and members of the Church. From this it is natural to lay hold of the theory of demythologizing, to make a virtue of necessity, and to explain that the true essence of Christianity, so far from being the true and full relationship of man to God which has been bestowed upon him by God himself in Jesus Christ in forgiveness and in raising him to a divine level, is simply the dignity and the task and goal of man himself which we, hopeless in the face of the experience of man's suffering, have projected onto an unknown 'X' in the hope that from that we shall actually return to man himself once he has put himself in a position to realize his own future and to win back for himself that glory which he has ascribed to a God. We then say not only that God is now dead, but that precisely this 'death-of-God' theology is the true secret doctrine of Christianity itself, which is only now coming to light in our present-day situation at the intellectual and social level, and which must now boldly be proclaimed. Obviously on this showing, and for a Christianity thus interpreted, Jesus becomes the first a-theist. It is only that he was not yet in a position to say precisely what he really thought and achieved in his own life.[3]

3. The New Responsibility for the World as the Meaning of Human Life

The third cause, which, together with the two already mentioned, contributes to the shaping of this radical horizontalism and exercises an influence precisely on those who view an a-theistic position with no very great

[3] This interpretation is put forward e.g. in F. Jeanson, *Vom wahren Unglauben* (Munich, 1966).

enthusiasm, and are at most regretful a-theists, those who fear that the 'death of God' will shortly be followed by the death of man as well, consists in the fact that the active self-responsibility of man and of humanity today has increased to an extent which could never really have been dreamt of even a hundred years ago, in other words prior to the new stage which has been ushered in within the totality of human history. Nowadays mankind is no longer living in an environment already predetermined for it such that it can change only the smallest details within that environment. It has begun to plan its own environment and to determine its goals, to subject it wholly to the human genius. It has made the world in which formerly it simply lived into a quarry for building a world which man is prepared to recognize only as his own world. Furthermore man has begun to alter, to plan and to reshape his own nature genetically, psychologically and socially. This new phenomenon may yet stick fast in its incipient stages. We may have to fear catastrophes in this Promethean undertaking. But this active alteration of man and of his environment by man himself has already been initiated, and in principle it can no longer be halted. This obviously lays an immense burden of responsibility upon man, such as formerly he never had to recognize or to assume. For manifestly something we are already noticing today is that this development does not simply imply an unhindered triumphal progress into a glorious future of freedom and carefree happiness. This development can just as easily become a gateway to fresh tyrannies, absurdities or ruin. The new burden of responsibility now laid upon man, which he partly lays claim to and is partly forced upon him so that the unity between these two aspects is impossible to analyse, now so preoccupies the public awareness and the attention of the individual that society and the individual receive the impression that with the best will in the world we can no longer concern ourselves with anything else except this task which man constitutes for man himself, and with the almost overpowering responsibility which it entails. Prayer, worship, and in general the intercourse with realities such as God, grace, the forgiveness of sins, salvation in the next world etc. are foreign to this view as so many childish preoccupations which carry us into a dream world and must be rejected by *that* man who faces up to the reality of his world as it really is. Thus we receive the impression that the old attitude to religion, if it still survives, is at most a matter for old people who are already excluded from this responsibility for the world and need some consolation in their old age. From this it is a natural step to yield to the temptation of making a virtue even of this necessity, re-interpreting Christianity (for the most divers reasons, connected either

with its intrinsic message or with tactical considerations, there is a reluct-
ance explicitly to pronounce it defunct) and declaring that Christianity
consists in nothing else than this responsibility which man has for the
world, which has come to be recognized only in these present times and
which must now be his sole remaining concern.

THE RESPONSE OF FAITH TO THE CHALLENGE OF 'HORIZONTALISM'

In so brief a study as this we have surely devoted enough consideration
now to the meaning and origins of that radical horizontalism which seeks
to reinterpret the salvific task of the Church, and even to assign it new
practical functions, by reducing it to a mere responsibility for the world.
The question we have now to ask ourselves is what response is to be made
to a radical horizontalism of this kind in the name of Christianity and of
the Church. In the answer we give to this question we must not content
ourselves with any cheap 'not only but also'. We must not simply set
horizontalism and verticalism side by side as the two dimensions of
Christian living. It would also be too cheap and over-facile to regard love
of neighbour simply as a moral duty and nothing more, arising from man's
religious attitude to God as the simple consequence of this and as something imposed upon man by God as the Lord of all men and of the world,
and as the guardian of the world order created by him. We must not
think of it as a duty in this sense which has to be discharged if man seeks
to live in peace with God and to attain to him as his goal. In the very
nature of the case, and in the light of a deeper understanding of Christian
tradition, and finally too in view of the necessity really to do justice to
the elements of truth in a modern radical horizontalism, it must be said
that a far greater unity exists between man's relationship to God and that
which he bears to his fellow men. Jesus himself conceives of love of God and
love of neighbour as a unity[4] into which the whole nature of man and his
task is concentrated. And in the teaching of I John this unity is given a
radically theological dimension and depth. And these in themselves are
enough to demonstrate the fact that Christian tradition knows far too
much about love of neighbour for it to be a mere moral demand upon man
which God has made as a condition of his favour towards man. The
doctrinal tradition of Christianity has always emphasized that there is no

---

[4] On this cf. the author's article, 'Reflections on the Unity of the Love of Neighbour and the Love of God', *Theological Investigations* VI (London and Baltimore,
1969), pp. 231–249.

experience of God for pilgrim man on this earth which has not been mediated through an experience of the world. Even the immediacy of man to God as constituted by God's self-bestowal in grace, in which man becomes a child of God and can truly call upon him by the name of Father, and truly has to do with him as such in prayer and worship and in the hidden sphere of his own personal love, is always mediated through the experience of the world which man finds already about him, and in which, right from the outset he has to act and be acted upon when he assumes his personal reference to God and necessarily brings his relationship to the world into this.

Now this relationship to the world, which acts as a medium in this sense, as Christian philosophy and theology consciously recognize with increasing clarity, does not consist primarily or originally in a relationship to a material environment in which, among many other factors, *men* are to be found also. Rather it is primarily a relationship to a society, the human Thou which constitutes not merely *any kind of* object in the experiential world of man, but is rather an original and constitutive element for his self-understanding as subject and for his relationship to the world. It is only in terms of this personal, social environment that man can be brought to a realization of himself as subject, and it is only in terms of this that those transcendental experiences of freedom, responsibility, absolute truth, love and personal trust are borne in upon man in which alone it can be made intelligible to him what is meant by God. For this God is not any kind of particular object side by side with many others (albeit of a peculiar excellence) which impinge upon him, but rather is present to him as the ground, the horizon, and the ultimate goal of man's own personal movement outwards towards his social environment in all its complexity. It is true that this God, in the movement of his gracious self-bestowal upon man and in verbal revelation, has assumed a relationship to man in which he functions on man's behalf not merely indirectly as an ultimate ambience of his encounter with the world, remaining forever outside his conscious awareness, but a relationship in which he himself, in a verbal revelation that is personal, in a covenant that belongs to saving history, in the implanting of his divine Spirit in the innermost heart and centre of man, becomes a direct partner of man himself. But this in no sense alters the basic fact that man can be a partner of God in this sense in a relationship that is immediate only as he who, in his relationship to his *social environment*, is always basically and inalienably orientated to God. Once this is recognized it is obvious that the relationship to God which is basically and inalienably mediated through man's relationship to his social environment can be achieved aright, and can accept and sustain the grace-given elevation precisely of this relationship by God himself only if the relationship of man to his social environment is such as it must be, i.e. if it is a relationship of ultimately unreserved trust towards his fellow man, a relationship of self-commitment to him, a relationship of responsibility for him, a relationship of love. Only on this condition can man truly realize what is meant by God to whom he is really committing himself when he begins to love God. We must go a step further. Man's total relationship in knowledge and freedom to his environment is sustained by the achievement of his transcendence over any given particular factor within this experience, and it is in this transcendence that his orientation to God is already concomitantly given and concomitantly achieved. The free achievement of a right understanding of man to his social environment, to the Thou who is his fellow, is right from the first a right understanding of God, albeit one that he may not consciously have explicitated to himself, a relationship which, as sustained by grace, also has a salvific import even when the man concerned does not explicitly or consciously recognize this and does not specifically or consciously objectify to himself in a form that can be put into words that he has already entered into relationship with God in a form that has not been expressed. In other words: where someone, by recognizing the absolute claims of his conscience in real and selfless love, is able really to rise above himself in reaching out to his neighbour, a movement towards God is already in process and has been accepted in very truth, albeit unconsciously, a movement which is initiated and elevated by grace. And this signifies a salvific event in the strictest sense of the term, and moreover even in those cases in which the man concerned, through no fault of his own, has not yet arrived at any explicit recognition of the first ground and ultimate goal of this movement which proceeds horizontally and vertically *at the same time*. This remains true even if, so far as his conscious awareness is concerned, he still believes that he is an a-theist. Of course all this does not mean that once a man has arrived at conscious knowledge of the ultimate implications of his positive and loving relationship to his social environment through revelation and grace, and therefore knows that in it he is inescapably in contact with God, he can justifiably allow this relationship to God, already implicit and inescapably present in his relationship with the world, to fall back into the level of the unconscious and unobserved. To take such a course really, seriously, and in full freedom would be to deny, if not actually to break off, even the implicit and subconscious relationship to God in freedom, and would thereby also be to break off the loving relationship to the Thou of one's fellow men by using one's freedom to deny the ultimate ground and goal of this relationship. For all this, however, the fact remains: there is a mutually conditioning relationship between our relationship to our neighbour and our relationship to that which we call God. Either of these two relationships can be more or less explicitly reflected upon and objectified in words. In the connection between the two the most manifold combinations and variations can be conceived of or actually exist. But both relationships mutually condition one another. It is true that horizontalism and verticalism can be present in man in the form of a free acceptance of love or in the form of a rejection, of hatred. But whichever form they assume both are mutually and inescapably dependent upon one another. Hence it can even be the case that the presence of God as explicitated in words and upheld by the consensus of public opinion can appear so obvious that love of neighbour appears merely as a secondary moral consequence following from this presence of God. And the converse can also be the case, that because of the absence of any theism in public opinion the individual arrives at an experience of God only or seemingly as a secondary factor when he rises above himself in committing himself to the Thou of his fellow men, in assuming a responsibility in which ultimately he stands alone without reward and as it were without any withdrawal to his own egoistical 'I'. Whatever historical changes the relationship may undergo between the vertical and the horizontal element in the self-transcendence of man, the basic relationship between horizontalism and verticalism remains the same.

Here, then, we have an ultimate, original, and indissoluble interpenetration in the reference to God and to his neighbour inherent in man's nature. And it is only within this that we can understand what God really is and also what one's neighbour really is. And it is this that constitutes Christianity's basic understanding of man. This means that Christianity does not add on the vertical dimension in man as something new and supplementary to the horizontal dimension. It does not impose *two separate* duties upon him so as to divide him. Rather it lays bare the ultimate radicality, the ultimate dignity, and the ultimate hiddenness of the relationship which man bears to the Thou of his fellow men only when speaking of God in that which, in a very imprecise and misleading image, we may call the vertical dimension, verticalism. A point that must be explicitly emphasized is that God is not thereby reduced to a cipher standing for the dignity and the future of man, so that basically speaking after all all that remains is man alone and the horizontalism of his nature. Man is, once and for all, that being which only possesses, discovers and consummates itself when it transcends itself in reaching out to that without which this being would stick fast in finitude, that being which is itself infinitely more than man. We can or could of course say with Pascal that even man himself *is* infinitely more than mere man, and on this basis we could also say that in the term horizontalism everything in man is expressed that is to be expressed about him, provided only that we really take this saying of Pascal's concerning man who is infinitely more than man with all due seriousness. And the seriousness with which we take this remains clear and is realized only if man precisely recognizes that he has discovered himself and accepted himself in his ultimate truth only if, in a spirit of adoration, thankfulness, and indeed blessed joyfulness, he surrenders himself to that which is infinitely more than man, and precisely as such has willed to become in grace the innermost and definitive life of man himself.

Finally then, after all, if we are to avoid misunderstandings and radical and fatal distortions in man's understanding of himself, we must stand by the unity and the mutually conditioning relationship of horizontalism and verticalism. And in the unity which we recognize here it is obvious that the verticalism which orientates us towards God, in so far as it can and must be distinguished from the horizontalism that orientates us towards man, has a higher dignity and of itself implies a more radical duty on man's part. Now if we say this we must straightway add once more that both dimensions are absolutely mutually conditioning, and that we cannot discover God except in our neighbour, that there cannot be any true love for God — especially in virtue of the fact that God has become man — which has not shared its utter radicality in love by extending it to man. He therefore who seeks to emphasize the higher dignity and the more radical duty of love of God, and in principle is right in doing this, should not thereby suppose that he has two entities which are in competition with one another in such a way that he can only give everything to one of the two by taking something from the other. Christianity, on any true understanding, upholds verticalism because it recognizes that without it horizontalism cannot in the long run endure, or at most will survive in a blessed illogicality in which God is explicitly denied or neglected by it in order once more implicitly to assent to him precisely in the absoluteness of love of neighbour. He who seeks to uphold a logical horizontalism must ask himself, and render account of his findings on this point to others, how much remains of man if he is not the man of God. Such a man would, after all, precisely be the mere shortlived product of a blind nature, a being brought face to face with its own misfortune, with an awareness of its own finitude, ultimately condemned in itself and in its works to ruin. Yet it is possible for one to take this man, caught as he is in an attitude of heroism for which no grounds can be adduced, with absolute seriousness. Yet the question can be put to him of why he really does this, why he does not simply regard his fellow man as a particular individual to whom he is ultimately indifferent, one particular example of a transitory human species caught up in a state of conflict which is far from being avoidable in all cases. Such a man must also allow the question to be put to him of why he strives so obstinately and despairingly against the implications which basically and ultimately speaking he has after all assented to in his absolute love of neighbour, implications in which God is included, why he does not have the still greater courage in hoping against all hope that his radical love of neighbour will issue into blessedness and, in the midst of the absurdity of existence, to believe.

THE NEW RELATIONSHIP BETWEEN 'HORIZONTALISM' AND 'VERTICALISM' WHICH HAS EMERGED IN OUR PARTICULAR EPOCH

On the basis, then, of Christianity's abiding understanding of its own nature as this has existed right from the origins it holds firm to the indissoluble unity in the midst of distinction between love of God and love of neighbour. But this is not to deny that in our own times a new relationship has emerged between horizontalism and verticalism, one that is proper to this particular epoch. Many times already in the course of our earlier considerations we have delineated this new relationship between the two abiding and mutually conditioning dimensions in man. This is an age in which, so far as society and public opinion are concerned, the existence of God and a right understanding of what is meant by this term at all are no longer self-evident factors. In such an age the mystery of that love for a Thou, in reaching out to which man irrevocably transcends himself in a certain measure, constitutes the ever new and indispensable generative spark at which the faith of the individual in God is kindled, a faith that is now lonely, no longer sustained and protected by public opinion, a faith that must emerge ever anew. For this love of neighbour, then, an eternal validity is claimed. It is in this love of neighbour that the outward movement of man from himself is achieved most radically in knowledge and freedom. And it is only in the love of neighbour as thus conceived that it becomes clear for the man of today what is meant by God and the existence of God – clear in a sense in which it never needed to be made clear at all in earlier ages. Now it follows than an experience of God that has emerged in this way has a clarity and radical depths in the life of man such as it did not have in earlier times, when, after all, there was a constant temptation to make a mere external indoctrination concerning the existence of God a substitute for this authentic experience of God. In this sense horizontalism nowadays takes a certain priority over verticalism. But this must not be allowed to contradict the basic truths of Christianity's understanding of its own nature. Nowadays in its preaching to man the Church should cry out to him 'Love thy neighbour! Love him with a love that transcends the immediate circumstances of your own private life which are constantly suspected of being tainted by egoism! Love him even when this love, in its ultimate consequences, appears to you to amount to a fatal surrender of yourself! Only then will you keep peace with the times in learning deeply what is meant by God and love for God! For this you have to surrender yourself in an act of unreserved trust to this single movement of your existence.' And if the Church were to cry this message out to modern man, then she would simply be preaching that ultimate and essential truth which she has all along been attempting to bring home to man.

A factor which we have already pointed out in connection with the third cause for the threat which horizontalism represents for us nowadays is that there is a need for a shift of emphasis of this kind in the preaching of the Church of today such as did not exist in former times. Nowadays man acquires a quite new responsibility in a world that has become dynamic. This responsibility has not yet come to be self-evident and is not yet being acted upon to a sufficient extent. And in these circumstances it must be especially emphasized and brought into the foreground even though other factors are thereby thrust into the background for a long period in view of the finitude of human awareness at the individual and collective levels. The situation in the light of the Church, therefore, is no different from that prevailing in the life of the individual. That which is most urgent and most of all demanded in the immediate circumstances of any given time, that which has to be preferred before all else and has to be acted upon even at the cost of neglecting other factors for the time being, does not always or necessarily have to be that which is objectively speaking the most important and the most valuable. If a Christian finds his house ablaze on a Sunday then he can quench the fire in his house precisely on Sunday even at the cost of neglecting his duty to worship God in the Eucharist on that day. When faced with the danger of a general conflagration of our world the Church too can, under certain circumstances, emphasize the duty of love of neighbour more radically than she has done in earlier ages, because the Christian's responsibility for the world now includes quite fresh tasks and duties such as simply did not exist in former times. If a horizontalism were to seek nothing else than to awaken and disseminate the conviction that Christians must recognize and put into effect their responsibility for the world in a far more radical manner than formerly, taking this at last as the task for the hour, then a horizontalism of this kind can only be praised as a characteristic of this particular epoch, this particular age of the Church. Obviously, however, even while putting into practice a new horizontalism of this kind, the one Church with all her complexity cannot simply lay up her cult, her theology, the cultivation of an interior religious orientation to God, as some naively idealistic souls suppose. Even in wartime the function of society is not simply to produce cannon fodder to be shot down. Even the most radical protagonists of a secularized form of responsibility for the world, for the under-developed peoples, even the most radical campaigners who take up arms against the injustice in the world sometimes go for walks, take recreation, enjoy life etc. Even a Christianity that is radically aware of its responsibility for the world should still pray, still pursue theology, still rejoice in God and his peace, thank God and praise him. And on a closer examination of all these matters it can be noticed that in the long run they are very necessary precisely for those who seek with all due seriousness their radical responsibility for the world.

WHAT HAS THE CHURCH TO CONTRIBUTE TO THE HUMANIZATION OF THE WORLD?

At this point we can apply ourselves directly to the subject of our considerations as formulated at the outset. What is the position with regard to the salvific task of the Church *precisely as such* in its attitude to the humanization of the world? We have to observe all due brevity and to be aware of the fact that any exhaustive answer to this question would have to be far more complex and include far more distinctions than is possible within the scope of this present study of ours. But before attempting to find an answer to this question one further preliminary observation must first be made.

Love of neighbour means not merely an attitude but concrete action in which the individual comes to the help of his fellow in a way that is selfless and involves personal sacrifice, and moreover is realistic as well. The giving of realistic help, in which love of neighbour must be made real, is to a large extent a matter which calls for human experience, one in which collaboration between individuals who interpret human life in the most divers ways is both possible and necessary. In other words it is a matter which, in the concrete forms it assumes, is by no means subject to, or capable of being subject to the guiding power of the Church as vested in her officials. This remains true however much this task may be and may remain a matter for the Christians of the Church. Even to this extent the humanization of the world, the concrete forms in which responsibility for the world is put into practice and organized, are far from being directly or even exclusively a matter for the official Church or for social organizations. There is a good sense in which the world is secular, the world as it exists with its possibilities and its self-elected goals, with its institutions and organizations, with its pluralism and the antagonism which this inevitably entails. This is a world which is not (either in fact or in principle) subject to the direct guidance of the official Church. It is a world which, on the contrary, is autonomous. And all this is explicitly recognized as a fact by the Church herself. This in itself *ipso facto* implies that that in which the humanization of the world is immediately subjected, in other words the process in which the horizontal task of man is in a direct and immediate sense undertaken, put into concrete practice and carried through is far from being identified with or capable of being identified with the Church. In other words to identify this subject with the Church in the sense supposed would basically speaking amount to a marked clericalism and sacralism. We cannot seriously demand of the Church, therefore, that she should feel herself to be the subject most directly responsible for the task of modern humanity in relation to the world. The Church can and must bring home to modern man, to the extent that this is possible at all, his responsibility for the world, the ultimate depths of this responsibility, with its implications of eternal salvation or perdition for man. She has the function of laying bare and disclosing these to the man of today. The Church can repeatedly stir up groups from among the Christians belonging to her and organize them in the service of this humanization of the world, and in this she can allow herself to be inspired by ultimately Christian motivations. In this process she can invoke these Christian motivations still more powerfully when her right to take this course is disputed by other Christians or Christian groups. In her official life the Church can even go on to give help to secular institutions in their efforts when this seems desirable or profitable, and when the immediate goals of these are unequivocally designed to serve the dignity and freedom of man, and can on these grounds be recognized as Christian too. The Church *as an official Church,* however, is not the immediate or proper subject for realizing in the concrete the humanization of the world. She must be ready to declare that she is not qualified in this respect, yet at the same time she must live by and represent respect for the freedom and dignity of man in an exemplary manner in her own life in ways that are appropriate to our own times. And precisely if she does this she can act as a body empowered to criticize, partly through her officials, partly through her other members in relation to the social conditions which prevail, together with all that needs to be changed in these either in an evolutionary or a revolutionary way.

Only if the Church recognizes the world's right in this sense to enter upon its own responsibility, which the Church in no sense seeks to deprive the world of, will she herself be free to undertake what is her own true saving function which she alone can fulfil. It is true that salvation itself is achieved by man in the whole scope of his life as pervaded throughout by the moving power of God's spirit. It is true that there is in this sense no sphere marked off as sacral, such that this is the only area in which man has to do with God. But it must be recognized that the whole of human existence, and so the entire world in all its dimensions, ultimately reaches out to the life of God; that there is no horizontal dimension which is *entirely whole and complete* in itself without a vertical one; that it is only through God's grace that we are set free in such a way as to be able to use and enjoy the world, and open ourselves unreservedly to our neighbour without becoming enslaved by this social and material environment of ours, without having to idolize it in order to be able to endure it. All this is a message which must be preached to the world ever anew. All this must itself be offered and communicated to the world ceaselessly in the physical sign of God also, in the power of his grace as the innermost *entelecheia* of the world itself. And over and above all this God himself must be adored in spirit and in truth. The historical embodiment of his self-utterance in the death and resurrection of Jesus Christ must be accepted and celebrated ever anew precisely because this self-utterance of God takes place in the *world* as such. All this is included in the salvific function of the Church.

Let it not be said that this is merely to set up an impotent and ineffectual ideology which does nothing to alter the real course of the world in its horizontal dimension. Even a realistic Marxism recognizes that the ideological superstructure has effects which redound upon that which constitutes its real basis. Any realistic estimate of the meaning of human life which is based on a really broad view in terms of space and time recognizes that the so-called ideological factor is itself a part of reality such that without it even the other factors in man could not exist. Because even in his so-called natural state he is incapable of existing without culture. Ideology is not a luxury which man can actually dispense with. Thus the salvific function of the Church, even in its vertical orientation to God, has a direct significance for the task of man in his own sphere. If the sun of God were ever really to set, if man ever really exhausted the resources of his past history in terms of 'ideology' to a point at which nothing was left of it, if the Church were no longer to exercise her salvific function, which seems so useless and *precisely in virtue* of so doing is indispensable – only then would it appear that man had actually lost himself, that that which he was formerly tempted sceptically to reject as illusion is absolutely necessary to life itself, that he possesses and is able to endure himself only if he reaches out beyond himself in faith, hope and love to that mystery which we call God. It is that mystery which constitutes the supra-human mystery of man himself, and it is that mystery that it is the function of the Church to serve. The better she fulfils this salvific function of hers the more uncalculating she is, the more she seems to forget man in his needs, the more she protects and preserves man even in his worldly task, the humanization of his own world.

19

ON THE THEOLOGY OF REVOLUTION

W E cannot initiate a theology of revolution in response to a transitory fashion of the modern world or of contemporary theology with the aim of making theology modern, making contact with those who otherwise have no interest in theology, nor can we attempt to develop a theology of revolution on the grounds that today theology is rightly or wrongly producing a feeling of frustration, and it is supposed that its ineffectualness in present-day society can be compensated for by transforming it into a theology of revolution or interpreting it along these lines.[1] For if we took as our basis this factor of a modern demand, then nothing more would emerge than a supplement to moral theology in a particular sphere, and the whole problem could basically speaking be reduced merely to the question of whether or not it is permissible to use physical force, possibly amounting even to bloodshed, in order to bring about social changes. It would be reduced to the question of the 'killing of a tyrant' or something similar. An additional danger which would arise if we took this as our basis would be to suppose that revolution is at most a question that concerns Africa, Latin America, or central Asia, but not one for Europe or North America.

Nor should a theology of revolution proceed from the assumption that there must in all circumstances be such a thing as a theology of revolution. For if we assume this as self-evident from the outset it will lead to an overhasty identification of religion with so-called 'positive theology' ('God's action in history'), and so too to a false identification of religion with a kind of 'orthodoxy of the left'.

Nor again should we suppose that the necessity for a revolution, or even for a revolution that is permanent, can be deduced directly or solely

---

[1] On this subject cf. E. Feil and R. Weth edd., *Diskussion ʒur 'Theologie der Revolution'* (Munich/Mainz, 1969) and the bibliography there assembled by W. Darschin, 'Bibliographische Hinweise zur "Theologie der Revolution"', pp. 365–373.

from the data of Christian revelation. On the contrary it must be shown in later arguments that a theology of revolution, to the extent that such a discipline exists at all, must proceed from the concrete experience of the situation with which we Christians and the Church as a whole are simply confronted nowadays, and which must produce its effects nowadays everywhere throughout the whole of theology, so that it should not be regarded as a supplement to a special department of moral theology.

At the same time, however, it must be emphasized that the concept of revolution is precisely *not* to be regarded as, for instance, the sole key concept of theology, or the *fons et origo* of it all, as not a few appear to suppose nowadays. We say that God's action upon man is the most effective and the most radical act of all, and that on the one hand it belongs totally to God, while on the other it is nevertheless brought to its fulness in and through the activity of man himself. But this does not mean that we can call this action of God 'revolution', for this would be a misuse of the term, and would merely have the effect of obscuring or even distorting the true nature of revolution properly so called. Again we should not call Jesus a revolutionary on the grounds that he was unmistakably opposed to the religious and political strivings of the Pharisees and Zealots. Precisely because, and to the extent that, Jesus distinguished his own mission from any directly political involvement, the work of Jesus acquires and retains a supreme social effectiveness of its own, and that too even in its effects upon secular society. What we have in mind here is a theology which includes within its purview the social and political implications of the whole of revelation in all its parts, and in this sense is intended to be a 'political theology'. Now precisely a theology of this kind must, ultimately speaking, resist any attempt to identify it with a theology of revolution. In no circumstances can a theology of revolution be regarded as the true heart and centre or the supreme point within theology as a whole. Any true and genuine theology must always be, in all its parts, a theology of eschatological hope, and it is only indirectly, and through the medium of political ethics, that a theology of this kind can determine and provide the basis for norms of human action at the secular level. To expand the concept of 'revolution' so as to cover this would merely be to render it ineffective, and could contribute nothing to the true inspiration and guidance of human activities. Obviously much that might provide a basis for a theology of revolution must be passed over here, as for instance a more detailed investigation of the relationship between the speculative and the practical reason, of the mutually conditioning relationship between reason and freedom, of the relationship between society and the individual, of the relationship which various societies of different degrees of development bear to one another, of the theology of power in general and that of the kind of power to be found in the social order as it exists in the concrete and as influenced by original sin, and so a society which, among other characteristics, always bears the stamp of sinfulness.

CONCEPTS

I would like to begin by indicating a few factors bearing on a function to which the Church is committed in general, that namely of *acting as a critic of society*. I am assuming that any radical horizontalism is not and cannot be a true interpretation of Christianity. Christianity has of its very nature something to do with the living God as such, and the name God is once and for all not an old-fashioned cipher standing for man, his dignity, and the task which man has in relation to his fellows and the society in which he lives.[2] Obviously I cannot here enter into the mutually conditioning relationship between horizontalism and verticalism, nor can I set forth the reasons for holding that these two terms in themselves, representing as they do an attempt to interpret the different dimensions in man, are capable of misunderstanding and do not rightly express the true nature both of the unity and of the distinction between God and man or of the relationship between God and man. There is on the one hand a relationship to the world, a responsibility for the world, a love of neighbour, an orientation towards one's neighbour, which constitutes the absolutely necessary and ever-abiding condition and medium for the relationship which man bears to God. On the other hand this relationship to God, even as expressed in the cult or in prayer, is not simply an old-fashioned term which, once demythologized and re-interpreted, would at basis express nothing more than 'man' and 'the relationship of man to man'.

There is a further point. Given that man has a responsibility for the world of this kind, such as in earlier times was called – perhaps quite naively – 'love of neighbour', and which must be understood as the absolutely indispensable medium for our relationship to God,[3] then there

---

[2] On this cf. the author's article in the present volume, 'The Church's Commission to Bring Salvation and the Humanization of the World'.

[3] On this cf. the author's article, 'Reflections on the Unity Between the Love of Neighbour and the Love of God', *Theological Investigations* VI (London and Baltimore, 1969), pp. 231–249.

is nowadays a love of neighbour that is socially orientated. It is not enough to say that man is a social being. On the contrary society itself is in a true sense always something more than the mere sum total of its individual members. And this also applies in the dimension of salvation and of the communicating of salvation. It also applies in the dimension of the Church. To that extent love of neighbour, regarded as the indispensable medium and condition enabling us to have a relationship to God, must not be misinterpreted as a mere personal, or perhaps even sentimental, reference of the individual to the individual. Rather in the fluid society of a world that has become dynamic love of neighbour as applied to the Christian and as the medium of his relationship to God necessarily implies a responsibility for, and a commitment to society as such. And in the light of this it becomes possible to formulate or to envisage such a thing as – if we like to call it so – a 'theology of revolution'. This can be admitted if and to the extent that revolution means nothing else whatever than a specific way (one which still awaits more precise definition) of changing social conditions, structures and institutions to man's advantage – in other words a factor which manifestly must of its very nature be present in any social commitment, which must be undertaken first and foremost by the man of Christian hope, the man committed to striving for a future that is absolute, the man inspired by love of neighbour in the true sense.

We now have something to say concerning *the concept of revolution*[4] itself. In saying it I would like once more to emphasize a point which I have already made at the outset: a study of this kind can offer nothing else whatever than a few modest considerations presented with all due provisos, and aimed at some degree of further clarification of the concept so as to achieve an understanding of all that is expressed in it. This means two things: first, we are not concerned with any revolutionary enthusiasm; second, I cannot, in order to avoid raising a middle-class bogey, disguise the fact that there may also be a legitimate possibility – indeed a duty – to undertake such a thing as a revolution in life, in society and in the world, and even for Christians, and that it is possible for this to be covered over by the narrow-minded or the bourgeois. I shall have something further to say on this latter point at a later stage.

Before we come to the concept of revolution itself I would like to emphasize one further point: in treating of the concept it would be wrong

---

[4] For a comprehensive survey on this see K. Hecker, 'Revolution', *Sacramentum Mundi* V (London and New York, 1970), pp. 359–365, and the literature there adduced.

for us to proceed from the outset from the concept or the reality of *force*.[5] Obviously the history of revolution as it *de facto* exists has always had something to do with force. But the concept of revolution should not in the first instance *ipso facto* be interpreted on the basis of the concept of force or even of violence as that through which, under certain conditions, social or political change will be, or should be introduced into a society. Unless we make this proviso we should have right from the outset an exact knowledge of what 'force' in the theological sense truly signifies, and this is by no means all that easy to define. To adopt this approach would also obscure the fact that at least today and in the future a revolution can take many forms such as cannot be brought into line with any of the usual senses in which force was used in former times. Now the difference between social and political 'evolution' and revolution is that revolution arises in those cases in which change is brought about in a political, social and cultural system by means of forces which exist outside this system as such and so proceed according to principles which are not recognized in this society itself as such either in the sense of being embodied in laws or catered for by means of other social institutions. Obviously any revolution invariably draws upon evolutive means as well such as are present in a society on the basis of the industrial and technical tendencies and forces present within it, and which are actually recognized as belonging to the very nature of the society concerned. But this does not alter the fact that the decisive forces which a revolution brings to bear are such as are not immanent within the system.

In describing the concept of revolution in these terms one point has been abstracted from: *the precise goal aimed at*, in view of which this changing of a society through means which are not immanent within its system takes place. But if we are to adopt a terminology nowadays accepted by the average man we may call such a process of changing a society revolutionary only provided that subjectively and objectively it is aimed at a greater scope for freedom and an increase in justice and harmony among all.

Even then it is obvious that the term 'revolution' cannot be applied if the forces and the protagonists involved in a social change are not merely such as are not immanent within the system but such as belong to a foreign power – in other words if what they bring to bear is not revolution but invasion.

The revolutionary process has a negative aspect: a critique or an attempt

[5] On this cf. the author's article, 'The Theology of Power', *Theological Investigations* IV (London and Baltimore, 1966), pp. 391–409.

to eliminate conditions which are socially unjust or repressive; and it has a positive aspect: the introduction of social relationships and conditions of a kind in which men can be given the widest possible scope for freedom in which to be able to live out their social relationships. A critique and an attempt to eliminate earlier social conditions without any new and effective alternatives for the setting up of a more just and more free society cannot be called revolution either. On the contrary it often implies danger and injury for any true revolutionary struggle.

We now come to the potentialities for social change present within a society yet not immanent within its system. They are sustained by a group of individuals within the society concerned which is numerically not wholly in a minority. Such a group will have two characteristics: first it will not be integrated into this society in such a way that it can exercise a real and recognizable influence upon the society as a whole so as to achieve its purpose or to be able to achieve its own aims within the society concerned as such; second, the group will be of such a kind that despite its usefulness for society as a whole in terms of economic benefits, freedom for the society, other cultural benefits etc., it will not have an adequate share in the shaping of the society. Unless the group concerned is of this kind the changes it brings about can only be such as are immanent within the system itself. The human group we are envisaging here is then compelled, in order really to be able to survive, to struggle for the elimination of the conditions of life actually prevailing, and in this sense becomes the subject in which the revolution is vested. Hence we can and must arrive at a concept of revolution such that physical or even violent force does not enter into this concept of its very nature. And despite this fact we can still distinguish revolution as conceived of here from any kind of social evolution.

In any revolution we can surely distinguish three dimensions:

The dimension of original motivation: the revolution is raised against injustice that is laid upon the oppressed until their frustration is such as to stir up a revolutionary movement.

The dimension of the recognition of certain norms: the original motivation becomes an occasion for recognizing the possibility of changing the social conditions within a given society. A new structure comes to be conceived of, capable of producing a better society, and in the light of this and in its 'feedback' effects the original motivation becomes clearer and more concrete.

The dimension of the general and particular revolutionary strategy:

various methods are conceived of through which the new society can be brought to reality. These various methods are examined as to their effectiveness in the actual situation prevailing, and the selected methods are brought to a stage at which they are capable of being applied in practice. Finally the new structures of society are given concrete reality by the specifically revolutionary procedures.

In this connection something more should be said concerning the concept of the so-called *'permanent revolution'*. This has been put forward in the most varied forms, e.g. by Herbert Marcuse and by the Maoists of China. But simply in the light of the points we have made above it follows that the concept of a permanent revolution cannot be accepted. For if and to the extent that the *actual principle* of a social change that is *continuous* within a society were to become institutionalized as such, and to the extent that any such thing is possible at all, what is actually involved in an institution of this kind, a dynamic factor of this kind becoming embodied as an effective force in society so that it belongs to society itself, constitutes in our terms something that is from the outset precisely not a revolution but an evolution. For in fact the principle of change comes to be conceived of as immanent within the system of the society thus affected.[6] And there is a further point. For the most varied reasons, sociological, futurological and even theological, it is impossible for the principle of change within a concrete society as such to become fully institutionalized so as to affect all its aspects and to become recognized as an absolute principle of this society. The concept of an absolutely totalitarian state such as integrates everything within itself is ultimately absurd and cannot be carried out in practice. Yet only a state of this kind, which would imply the diametrical opposite of freedom, could bring such a thing as a permanent revolution to reality. Yet precisely because, for reasons which I will not mention here, there cannot be any such thing as a truly *absolute* totalitarian system,[7] there cannot be such a thing as a permanent revolution in the true sense either, for precisely the principle of a continuous social change and transformation cannot ultimately speaking in any full or adequate sense be immanent within the system. Even Trotsky recognized that there would be periods of calm within a permanent revolution of this kind, periods in which develop-

---

[6] In this connection the function of a 'political theology' should be noticed. Cf. J. B. Metz, 'Political Theology', *Sacramentum Mundi* V (London and New York, 1970), pp. 34–38.

[7] On this cf. the author's observations in *Freiheit und Manipulation in Gesellschaft und Kirche*, Münch. Akad.-Schriften 53 (Munich, 2nd ed., 1971).

ment would take evolutionary forms. Even according to him, therefore, there is no really permanent revolution in any true sense.

This is not to deny that by accelerating the development of sciences and technology social changes too will develop more swiftly in the present and future than in former times, but these are still evolutionary in character even though the forms in which they manifest themselves are almost such as were formerly achieved only in revolutions. But the converse of this must also be insisted upon here: we are assuming two things: first that no society can integrate within itself all the forces of progress and change by institutionalizing them as such. Hence too authentic revolutions become necessary again and again, proceeding from forces which transcend the system itself. Secondly, we can regard the alternating evolutionary and revolutionary phases in the history of a society taken together as so many *unified* major social processes. Assuming the validity of these two points, and on this approach, it is also possible under certain circumstances to speak of a permanent revolution.

What is presupposed is the position, regarded as a tenet of faith, that in the course of the phases of her history the Church preserves an essential identity, and hence it would be possible to describe the permanent revolution as a sociological analogate in which the history of the Church might find a certain model in terms of which to interpret her own nature. For a Church can never always remain, or seek to remain, at the same level within society. This remains valid so long as she constitutes the people of God on pilgrimage and so long as she is not merely the institution which, as remaining always the same, fixed or frozen, as it were, confines herself to delivering that which is produced by souls who have already been saved and are in heaven. The Church, then, is always on the way, and tending towards a kingdom of God, an absolute future, which can never wholly be established within history, and which despite this constitutes the goal of this people of God so that the Church as always in need or reform has phases within her history which can be compared to evolutions.[8] The evidence of history shows that revolutionary phases in the past history of the Church coincided with revolutionary phases in the past history of secular society – indeed that they even emerge from these. And to that extent a comparison between a secular permanent revolution in the sense which I have just set forth as conceivable and that permanent revolution which the Church herself is is something more than simply an

---

[8] On this cf. the author's article, 'Immanent and Transcendent Consummation of the World', *Theological Investigations* X (London and New York, 1973), pp. 273–289.

artificial comparison. It actually makes clear to some extent the close mutual relationship which exists between the fate of the Church and that of the world. Precisely as the outcome of the experience which the Church has in the midst of secular revolutions, she conceives, in forms which are new and relevant, of that which in itself has all along been known to her as the outcome of divine revelation, and yet which at the same time she has to learn ever anew. And to the extent that the Church hearkens to divine revelation and to the call of the particular age both at the same time, she can through her doctrine and through her life supply the world and its societies ever afresh with that motivation which these need for the attainment of their goal and for the changes which are necessary for this.[9] This is admittedly true only provided that the Church does not think of herself as one called to be a merely conservative force. For ultimately and basically speaking she least of all is this. She must really believe that God himself constitutes her absolute future and at the same time she must recognize that she can only effectively make real this faith of hers and this hope in the absolute future – and moreover at the level of society also – provided that this absolute hope is mediated through the daring, the readiness, under certain circumstances, to undergo change herself within the course of 'this worldly' history to the extent that the summons to undergo change of this kind reaches her from the times through which she is passing. How are we as Christians credibly to demonstrate and to live out what it means to say that the Church is advancing towards a goal which transcends all these earthly realities if we seek merely to cling onto the current state of society? To do so would be to render the eschatological hope of the Church in a true sense unworthy of belief. He alone is truly a Christian who so bears witness to his hope that under certain conditions he can let go the sparrow in his hand in favour of the dove on the roof, even though for the most part worldly prudence seems to prescribe the opposite course.[10]

I must now say something about the concept of the *revolutionary situation*. A revolutionary situation exists when firstly a sufficiently large group within a society exists which, nevertheless, is not integrated into it; secondly when a revolutionary potential exists; thirdly if this group has become sufficiently aware of its situation; fourthly if it has a sufficient

[9] On this cf. the author's ideas in 'The Function of the Church as Critic of Society', *Theological Investigations* XII (London and New York, 1974), pp. 229–249, and the literature there adduced.

[10] On this cf. the author's article, 'On the Theology of Hope', *Theological Investigations* X (London and New York, 1973), pp. 260–272.

social organization. To express it in other terms: a revolutionary situation of this kind – though not one that necessarily signifies revolution itself – can exist either in a specific individual society taken in isolation or in a multiplicity of societies which are in a certain sense dependent upon one another, or even in the world as a whole, to the extent that these societies are so mutually interdependent in their existence and their prosperity that the revolutionary situation of one of these societies inevitably affects all the other societies as well. When we say in this sense that a revolutionary situation can become *global*, this obviously does not mean that such a situation is homogeneously present in all parts of the world. Despite the universality of a global revolutionary situation, such a situation can be absent in a particular society taken purely in isolation. Hence a revolutionary situation, to the extent that it exists so far as one particular society is concerned purely as an external factor, i.e. in other societies throughout the world, is not simply the same as when it is present in those societies affected by this global situation.

On any just and unprejudiced view of the present-day state of the world we must say that a global revolutionary situation does exist. In asserting this I must of course emphasize once more that this statement is valid only if we assume the concept of revolution I have just described, and only if we assume the concept of the revolutionary situation as global, which can nevertheless arise in this world as the outcome of societies in which a particular revolutionary situation is present such as does not exist in some other society taken in and for itself.

The thesis that a global revolutionary situation does exist is put forward on the assumption of the ideas developed above based on an evaluation of the economic and social situation prevailing in the southern hemisphere, i.e. in the under-developed nations. This thesis is put forward independently of and prior to the question of whether a revolution of this kind – as distinct from the revolutionary situation – already exists or is shortly to break out everywhere or in many countries of the world, and it is totally independent of the question of what means or methods will be used or should be used in order to carry out a revolution of this kind in itself. However, this global revolutionary situation does exist today because in the first place there is so close an interdependence between all the countries of the world that it is no longer possible for one part of the world to exist as a social entity without the other, and second because in many areas, and precisely in the under-developed countries, at least as applied to the country concerned itself, a revolutionary situation, or even an actual revolution already exists, and third because in this world there is an extremely explosive tension between the northern hemisphere and the southern, in other words, therefore, between the part containing the developed nations and that containing the under-developed ones, so that this contradiction really should be called global.

By way of summary, therefore, the following must be laid down: if a revolutionary situation does objectively exist in one part of the world, and if all of us in the world of today are necessarily and inevitably in the same boat (even though we egoistic Europeans of the western industrialized countries are not really willing to recognize it), and the fact that we are in one boat in this sense is becoming still more plainly manifested, then a global revolutionary situation does exist in the world of today even though this revolutionary situation may perhaps not derive from the internal structure of our particular society.

CHURCH AND REVOLUTION

We now come to the question of Church and Revolution. From the nature and the vocation of the Church, and from the means at her disposal, in view of her relative smallness measured by the world as a whole, it may be concluded that the Church cannot be the proper protagonist of the revolution which can legitimately emerge from the global revolutionary situation as universal revolution, though this is not to say anything on the question of what form such a revolution must take in itself precisely so as to supply an appropriate response to this revolutionary situation of the world.

The Church as such is not the primary or proper subject of that revolution which in itself could and should provide the answer to this global revolutionary situation in the world. Nevertheless the Church can and must act as follows: first she must recognize the justification for a revolution of this kind at least in general terms, for this revolution, the point of departure for which we have said already exists, is necessary if the under-developed world is really to obtain a share in the benefits they justifiably demand. The process of arriving at a just balance of this kind between the northern and the southern hemispheres cannot properly be called evolution, for the attainment of this just balance is at least in practice, i.e. in view of the outlook actually prevailing in society, a process which cannot be described as immanent within the system. How those forces which transcend the system can and should conduce to the striking of such a balance, what means can be used in order to arrive at it – this is another question. Because and to the extent that in the developed industrial countries of America and Europe those who seek to achieve this just balance and the resources for carrying it through are *de facto* not really immanent within the system, we must according to our terms call the process of arriving at a just and necessary balance of this kind a revolution.

One possible position is that a global change of this kind in the world should be carried out without force, and those who hold this opinion may feel themselves obliged, as a matter of duty, to use peaceful methods of revolution of this kind. But even so they cannot deny that what is in question here is a revolution. And it seems that even a peaceful revolutionary of this kind should boldly give the name of revolution to the position he is advocating, for if he appeals *merely* to good will and to principles which in practice are already recognized in this society, then he will achieve nothing.

Under Pius XI the Church has explicitly recognized that a social situation, at least within a particular country, can be so unjust and so contrary to the basic rights of man that it is possible for it to be right to use physical force against it.[11] According to Paul VI's encyclical, 'Populorum Progressio' a right to revolution exists, and moreover for Christians also, in the case of grave corruption in a state. It is true that in any theological ethics we have to examine what principles should be invoked in order to answer the question of when and under what conditions we may in practice claim the right to initiate a revolution. It may be true that the utmost prudence is called for here. Yet the fact remains that the concrete application of these principles to a revolution which may possibly be morally justified is no longer the task of theology or of the teaching authorities of the Church proper, and at the theoretical level, but is rather a matter for secular sociology, a matter of the practical reason, which admittedly is enlightened by faith and even guided by charismatic inspiration. In other words ultimately speaking it is a matter for free decision such as can no longer be theoretically reflected upon in any full sense, even though this is not to give free reign to any and every kind of frenzied primitive aggressivity on the part of the individual, without reason, without plan, without responsibility, without reflection. But a further point following from this is that a retrospective ideological justification for a concrete revolution of this kind once it has been carried through is not the task of theology either, for thereby it would be reduced to a mere cringing lickspittle fawning upon a revolution once it had succeeded. It has no need of any such theological justification and it is not the function of theology for its part to give its approval in this sense.

[11] The encyclical, 'Firmissimam constantiam' v. 28. III, 1937; cf. DS³⁴ 3775–3776.

If and to the extent that physical force in the proper sense can legitimately be used in order to safeguard or to restore fundamental human rights, if and to the extent that the use of such force on the part of groups transcending the system in order to achieve fundamental rights is likewise justified, the use of such force can also justifiably be called revolution. And conversely if the use of force is morally justified, then it also follows that the revolution carried through by means of it can be pronounced morally justified, and indeed under certain circumstances obligatory to the extent or in the degree that this use of force is morally justified or obligatory for one who avails himself of this use of force with sufficient prospect of success for the achievement, the defence or the restoration of fundamental human rights of freedom. A point which must always clearly be recognized in this connection is that the concrete forms which such fundamental rights to freedom assume are obviously influenced by temporal and historical factors and the conditions prevailing in a particular age. Hence under certain circumstances nowadays man's basic rights and his right to freedom can include factors which they did not include in the immediate or more distant past. The Church must exhort and arouse Christians to take part in this global revolution in a way appropriate to their position in society and the possibilities open to them as a duty of Christian conscience, for this is not restricted in its function to catering for the salvation of the individual. This is not to say that participation of this kind by the Christian in the global revolution as thus defined is merely a matter of his own *private* conscience or his own individual ethics. Precisely because this is not the case a theology of revolution or a theological theory of revolution must in fact be developed such as does not yet exist as manifestly or clearly as is necessary. If the Church too in her official authorities does not constitute the direct subject for carrying out a revolution, still she can nevertheless as a subordinate society be the upholder of a certain Christian motivation for such a revolutionary movement, and moreover in such a way that through her way of acting in the sphere *interior* to herself she manifests herself as a fruitful example in which the effectiveness of such motivations can be recognized, while conversely she can arrive at such ever-fresh courses of action *as a result of* her contact with the contemporary social situation.

In order to achieve a still better understanding of the theological connection which exists between the Church and the contemporary global revolutionary situation the following point must also be considered: a *mutually* conditioning relationship exists between the recognition of the situation in which Christian life has to be led in the concrete and those principles and motives deriving from revelation which determine this Christian life and give it its motive force. It is not merely that the Church applies revelation to a specific historical situation in which she is living at any given time. It is also true that from the situation itself the Church develops a new theoretical and above all practical recognition for this life as shaped and motivated by Christian revelation. Otherwise a group history would, for instance, be totally inconceivable and the life of the Church would be reduced to a mere uniform application of Christian principles to human courses of action as a material which properly speaking would remain permanently external to this life. From her own nature and for the sake of her own goal the Church seeks, therefore, to achieve a close contact with her worldly situation. I say from her own nature as most proper to her. She does this in order to realize her own self in the manner demanded of her in a specific situation. The Church must learn ever afresh from her situation as constantly subject to history in this sense and never static how the word of God must be preached and the sacraments administered in the concrete, how she herself has to strive for that kingdom of God which constitutes the eschatological salvation of mankind as such and as a whole, and how she must do this as a society and not merely as an agglomeration of individuals in a purely material sense. There is a mutual interdependence a mutually conditioning relationship between love of God and love of neighbour. These two factors are neither wholly identical one with the other nor capable of being living forces independently of one another. Neither in theory nor in practice can Christianity and the Church be understood solely in terms of a sociological horizontalism or a spiritualistic verticalism. This applies not merely to the individual Christians but also to the Church as such.[12] The Church herself cannot serve God without this worship of God in adoration and love being mediated through her service of man.

This function of the Church as serving man, through which the true and genuine cult of God is mediated and made real, demands ever-fresh experiments in concrete social living because only through the experience of these can the Church be made aware of the ever-fresh forms in which this service of man can and must be fulfilled, the more so since it is a service of society as such that is in question, and, moreover, nowadays of a society which is changing very quickly. Through her gospel the Church deputes the Christian to a worldly task which both in terms of its material content and also in its *immediate* motivation remains worldly, and so in

[12] On this cf. the author's article in the present volume, 'The Church's Commission to Bring Salvation and the Humanization of the World'.

terms both of this material content in itself and of the *immediate* motivation is common to Christian and non-Christian alike, or at least could and should be common to them both. This worldliness becomes apparent from two factors taken together: first the distinction between the natural and supernatural orders and second the impossibility of working out a *concrete* normative world order for a Christian motivation as such in a world that is never totally freed from every consequence of sin.[13] Correspondingly the task of the Christian as such for the world is not subject to the immediate jurisdiction of the Church's official authorities nor even to the immediate or direct guidance of these. Nevertheless this task for the world does have something specifically and properly Christian in it, and it should not be concluded from what has been said that the Church herself does not have any task for the world of this kind. Work undertaken for the world in this sense, and giving practical expression to responsibility for the world, can be attributed to the Church herself from the most varied points of view: first in as much as this task for the world is engaged in by individuals belonging to the Church whose ultimate and deepest motivations are expressly Christian because and to the extent that these Christians are instructed by the official teaching of the Church in the general norms and principles of social behaviour, principles which, despite their universality, do have or can have in the fullest sense a social effectiveness; further to the extent that the Christians of the Church can form groups which together take upon themselves a task for the world of this kind as something demanded by their Christian conscience, and, in so far as they are still able to do this – as is explicitly stated in 'Gaudium et spes' – even if the Christian dimension in their work is disputed by other groups of Christians. A Christian motivation, a declaration of the Christian element in a concrete social task is not dependent upon the recognition or approbation of this Christian element by all Christians or all authorities in the Church (cf. 'Gaudium et spes', Nos. 41, 43, 75), finally to the extent that the official authorities of the Church can also be under certain circumstances the ones who involve themselves in interventions of a Christian, charismatic and practical kind which cannot be deduced in any compelling sense from the Christian principles at the level of official doctrine, and yet are responses to the demands of the time and the situation to the extent that this situation is interpreted by a practical and creative intelligence.

[13] Here we should notice the author's observations in his article, 'Theological Considerations on Secularization and Atheism', *Theological Investigations* XI (London and New York, 1974), pp. 166–184.

This experience of the world, then, is one through which the Church interprets ever afresh her own insights into revelation in the Spirit which, precisely in this way, introduces them in all truth. Through them the Church must learn and must reform the activities required of her in her own sphere ever afresh in order in this way to provide an effective motivation for the world in its development and in its revolution. Thus the Church learns that she has to help the poor in their present-day social situation in a way which must be quite different from that which formerly prevailed and was followed in the Church. She learns that the poor must be set free from their self-alienation, and so not have merely to be given alms. If the Church understands this today she is recognizing that she has to manifest herself as the Church of the poor in a different way from that which was formerly the case.[14] If she presents herself in this way she is offering a fresh motivation for, and fresh examples of the attitudes and policies which secular society should adopt in relation to the poor today. In similar ways the Church learns afresh from contemporary history what concrete consequences follow for men from the so-called human rights in their general formulation. The Church must make real these human rights within her own sphere in a way which corresponds to our *contemporary* age. When she does this genuinely and honestly she is offering an example of how such rights are to be safeguarded and put into practice in the world as well. Without this process of a mutual interinfluence between world and Church, in which the Church too changes herself in fulfilling her task in and for the contemporary world, without this congruence between the task of the Church within her own sphere and that which is directed outwards to the world, her credibility would suffer and she would be reduced to a sect surviving in the backwaters of history and no longer playing her part in shaping the course of the secular world.

Finally – and in order to bring this study to an end – I would like to add the following point: it is true that the Church has no need to set up any great lament over her past. At the same time, however, she should not be silent about her historical guilt which she has incurred in the course of time by an unjust defence of social conditions under which men in the most divers social groups have had to suffer the most divers forms of injustice and severe hardship. Only through this attitude of self-criticism towards her own past and present on the Church's part can she hope to achieve credibility in any adequate sense, when she ranges herself, as is her right and duty, among those who criticize and condemn the social conditions

[14] On this see the author's article in the present volume, 'The Unreadiness of the Church's Members to Accept Poverty'.

through which a revolutionary situation has been provoked in the most varied regions of the world. The Church as a whole must also be bold and unequivocal in loosing all those ties of mutual protection and defence which still exist even today between the Church's authority and structures on the one hand and rulers and oligarchical and feudalistic social structures on the other. Such ties are to be surrendered not from considerations of sheer expediency or on the grounds that the Church sees advantages for herself in such a course, namely when the oligarchic social structures are finally overthrown by a revolution. On the contrary the Church must do this because she is obliged to do so of her very nature and in terms of her divine vocation to bring salvation to men.[15] And finally: everything which still in any sense is subject to the Church's authority must be performed in such a way that murder and torture on political grounds is eliminated from the world even though the perpetration of such terrors has hitherto not infrequently been at least tolerated by the Church or, shall we say, individuals within the Church.

Obviously all that I have said so far contains little that has any bearing upon a theology of revolution. I have sought neither to set up a revolutionary programme nor to condemn a revolution which, under certain conditions and in specific situations may be necessary on Christian principles. I have sought to present only a few considerations which, after all, must be put forward if ever any really clear and well thought out theology of revolution is to be developed, a theology which, by and large, and despite all the contributions from South America, still does not exist today, and for which, obviously, any revolutionary mood or revolutionary enthusiasm can never be a substitute.

[15] cf. also the author's article, 'Institution and Freedom', *Theological Investigations* XIII.

LIST OF SOURCES

BASIC OBSERVATIONS ON THE SUBJECT OF CHANGEABLE AND
UNCHANGEABLE FACTORS IN THE CHURCH
Lecture given at the Conference of the Rupert Mayer/Deutschland
Cartel on 8 May 1971 at Bremen. Likewise delivered on 17 November
1970 at Krefeld, on 9 December 1970 at Düsseldorf. Published in F.
Groner ed., *Kirche im Wandel, Festschrift für J. Kard. Höffner* (Cologne,
1972), pp. 23–36.

THE FAITH OF THE CHRISTIAN AND THE DOCTRINE OF THE
CHURCH
Delivered as a farewell lecture on 7 July 1971 at the Kath. Studen-
tengemeinde, Munster; published in *StdZ* 190 (1972), pp. 3–19.

DOES THE CHURCH OFFER ANY ULTIMATE CERTAINTIES?
A Lecture given at the Garmisch-Partenkirche on 9 December 1971,
at Beuron Abbey on 15 December 1971, at the Theological Academy at
Essen (21 February 1972), at Frankfurt (22 February 1972), at Kassel
(23 February 1972), Cologne (24 February 1972), Berlin (25 February
1972), and at the Caritas-Pirkheimer House at Nurenberg on 11 April
1972: hitherto unpublished.

ON THE CONCEPT OF INFALLIBILITY IN CATHOLIC THEOLOGY
This study was composed for the symposium, 'L'Infaillibilité, Son
Aspect philosophique et théologique' held at Rome (5–10 January 1971).
It was included in the Conference Report (edited by E. Castelli) entitled
L'Infaillibilité (Paris, 1970), pp. 57–72. The German version was pub-
lished in *StdZ* 186 (1970), pp. 18–31, and in K. Rahner ed., *Zum Problem
Unfehlbarkeit. Antworten auf die Anfrage von Hans Küng* (Freiburg, 2nd
ed. 1971), pp. 9–26.

THE DISPUTE CONCERNING THE CHURCH'S TEACHING
OFFICE
First published in *StdZ* 185 (1970), pp. 73–81.

THE CONGREGATION OF THE FAITH AND THE COMMISSION
OF THEOLOGIANS
A lecture delivered in Latin at the First Session of the International
Papal Commission of Theologians on 6 October 1969 at Rome. German
version in *StdZ* 185 (1970), pp. 217–230; French translation: *Informa-
tions Catholiques Internationales* 350 of 15 December 1969, pp. 33–35;
Italian translation: *IDOC* 1 (Brescia, 1970), Vol. 1, pp. 24–30.

ON THE THEOLOGY OF A 'PASTORAL SYNOD'
A lecture delivered during the Round Table Conference of the Catholic
Faculty of the University of Munster in the winter semester of 1969–70
on 21 October 1969; published in J. Schreiner ed., *Die Kirche im Wandel
der Gesellschaft* (Würzburg, 1970), pp. 1–14.

WHAT IS A SACRAMENT?
The text of a Guest Lecture delivered at the Faculty of Catholic
Theology of the University of Mainz on 21 January 1971; published in
StdZ 188 (1971), pp. 16–25, and in E. Jüngel and K. Rahner, *Was ist ein
Sakrament? Vorstösse zur Verständigung*, Kleine ökumenische Schriften 6
(Freiburg im Breisgau, 1971), pp. 65–85.

INTRODUCTORY OBSERVATIONS ON THOMAS AQUINAS'
THEOLOGY OF THE SACRAMENTS IN GENERAL
This article is based on a commentary written in 1970 as an 'Introduc-
tio' to Thomas Aquinas' 'Tractatus de Sacramentis' (edited by the Centro
Italiano Studi Editoriali); hitherto unpublished in German.

CONSIDERATIONS ON THE ACTIVE ROLE OF THE PERSON IN
THE SACRAMENTAL EVENT
Published in *Geist und Leben* 43 (1970), pp. 282–301, likewise in *Frau
und Mutter* (Düsseldorf, 1970), pp. 262–264, 303–305, 361–362.

ASPECTA OF THE EPISCOPAL OFFICE
A lecture at the General Assembly and Study Conference of German-Speaking Pastoral Theologians on 2–5 January 1972 at Innsbruck; hitherto unpublished.

HOW THE PRIEST SHOULD VIEW HIS OFFICIAL MINISTRY
A lecture to the priests of the Archdiocese of Venice on 13 November 1969; hitherto unpublished.

THE RELATIONSHIP BETWEEN PERSONAL AND COMMUNAL
    SPIRITUALITY AND WORK IN THE ORDERS
A lecture delivered at the Conference of the Union of German Religious Superiors on 22 June 1971 at Würzburg. An expanded version of this formed the basis of a lecture given at the Provincial Conference of the Jesuit Province of Lower Germany on 30 September 1971 at Frankfurt/St Georgen; published in *Ordenskorrespondenz* 12 (1971), pp. 393–408.

SOME PROBLEMS IN CONTEMPORARY ECUMENISM
Hitherto unpublished.

ECUMENICAL THEOLOGY IN THE FUTURE
A lecture at the University Extension at Bocholt on 5 February 1971; published in J. Brosseder ed., *Begegnung, Festschrift für H. Fries* (Graz, 1972).

THE UNREADINESS OF THE CHURCH'S MEMBERS TO ACCEPT
    POVERTY
First published in *Neues Hochland* 1 (1972), pp. 52–59.

OBSERVATIONS ON THE PROBLEM OF THE 'ANONYMOUS
    CHRISTIAN'
An Invitation Lecture at the Department of History of Religions of the Institute for European History (Professor Dr J. Lortz) on 22 January 1971 at Mainz; hitherto unpublished.

THE CHURCH'S COMMISSION TO BRING SALVATION AND THE
　　HUMANIZATION OF THE WORLD

Delivered as a lecture in the context of the Theological Academy at Frankfurt (13 October 1970), Berlin (16 October 1970), Cologne (23 October 1970), Essen (26 October 1970), Kassel (30 October 1970) and Büttgen on 7 February 1971; first published in *Geist und Leben* 44 (1971), pp. 32–48, likewise in K. Rahner and O. Semmelroth edd., *Theologische Akademie* VIII (Frankfurt, 1971), pp. 9–29.

ON THE THEOLOGY OF REVOLUTION

Composed in Latin and delivered at the Session of the International Commission of Theologians held at Rome on 10 October 1970. Delivered as a lecture in German at Innsbruck on 28 November 1970; hitherto unpublished.

INDEX OF PERSONS

335

INDEX OF SUBJECTS

337